MANUAL COMMUNICATION

FINGERSPELLING AND THE LANGUAGE OF SIGNS

BARBARA E. BABBINI

A Course of Study Outline for Instructors

UNIVERSITY OF ILLINOIS PRESS

Urbana   Chicago   London

FOREWORD

Many books have been published which were designed to help those who wish to learn manual communication (fingerspelling and the language of signs), and the number of such publications is increasing along with the proliferation of manual communication classes as more and more people become interested in or discover a need for learning manual methods of communicating with deaf people. From the student viewpoint, each such addition to the body of works on manual communication is helpful in its particular approach to the learning task, and in most cases these books can be utilized by the instructor. However, except for Mrs. Babbini's previous publication, An Introductory Course in Manual Communication, which is no longer available, no attempt has been made to write an instructor-oriented course of study for manual communication.

Mrs. Babbini's new manual, which is an outgrowth of her earlier publication, is unique in two respects. First, it is the only such manual designed specifically for instructors of manual communication, and it includes such helpful teaching aids as well-organized, sequentially arranged, and balanced lesson plans; teaching and remediation techniques; tests and drills; suggestions for use of various visual aids such as instant-replay, closed-circuit television; and homework assignments and games to facilitate drill and practice work.

Second, along with the instructor's manual, Mrs. Babbini has also prepared a separate companion manual for use by students, thus providing both instructor and students with coordinated materials aimed at their respective needs. To the best of my knowledge, this makes them the only such materials for instruction in manual communication.

Both experienced instructors of manual communication, and those approaching the task of teaching it for the first time, should find these manuals very helpful. Mrs. Babbini is an experienced, highly skilled teacher of manual communication and a recognized authority on the subject. She has drawn heavily upon her own experience and that of other veteran instructors in the writing of this book. The novice instructor should find her detailed lesson plans and descriptions of techniques extremely helpful and effective in developing his own particular style of teaching. The experienced instructor should find many new ideas described herein which can be added to his own repertoire of teaching skills. Of particular value to instructors will be the chapter on videotaping techniques, for this is not only an effective teaching tool, gaining in popularity, but also one which is highly suitable to the teaching and learning of visual skills such as manual communication.

Mrs. Babbini is to be commended for a valuable and worthwhile contribution to the twin tasks of teaching and learning how to communicate with deaf people in the manual modality most of them call their own, for her book fills a need many have recognized but few have attempted to fill.

Stephen P. Quigley
University of Illinois

PREFACE

The course of study outline presented in this manual represents an adapted and updated revision of the author's original publication, "An Introductory Course in Manual Communication (Fingerspelling and the Language of Signs)," which was distributed through the Leadership Training Program in the Area of the Deaf at San Fernando Valley State College in Northridge, California, in 1964. The present manual includes new and expanded teaching techniques developed by the author in the course of her classroom teaching subsequent to the release of the original manual seven years ago, as well as modifications suggested by manual communications instructors who used the original manual in their teaching.

Included among the additional techniques described herein which were not in the original edition is that of utilizing videotaping equipment in classroom teaching of manual communication, an important new development in the area of teaching the language of signs and fingerspelling, which the author deems worthy of a separate chapter by itself.

Another area in which a separate chapter has been included is that of teaching fingerspelling. It is in this specific area that most of the failures to achieve mastery of manual communications occur--primarily in the development of comprehension, or receptive ability--and such failures can be attributed primarily to the lack of adequate training in the receptive and discriminative skill of reading fingerspelling. This inadequate training is all too often the result of the instructors' lack of information about newly developed techniques of teaching fingerspelling which are specifically designed to reduce or overcome the difficulties most students experience in learning to read fingerspelling, and for this reason, heavy emphasis is placed on techniques designed to foster the development of receptive fingerspelling ability.

Among the modifications are: reorganization of the order in which the signs are taught to permit more continuity and cohesiveness to the material; inclusion of general instruction sections preceding each of the first several lessons, which give information pertinent to the material to be covered in the lesson at hand as well as any specific techniques required by the lesson; and the separation of the lessons into three distinct categories: (1) two preliminary lessons devoted exclusively to the rapid development of the expressive and receptive skills in fingerspelling; (2) eleven lesson plans in which the development of fundamental manual communication skills and rapid expansion of vocabularies of signs are emphasized; and (3) an intermediate section comprising fourteen lesson plans in which the emphasis shifts from vocabulary expansion to use of the language of signs, with increasing attention being paid to colloquial or "idiomatic" usage along with expressiveness and mood.

It must be emphasized that the present manual is designed for use by instructors in manual communication courses, not by students. While material has been included which can be duplicated and distributed to students in classes being taught with the help of this manual, the bulk of the material in this manual is for use by the instructor only, and students should not be permitted access to the tests and other instructional information which comprise most of the manual.

It is hoped that the manual will be of help to both the novice instructor and the veteran. The novice instructor will find described herein many basic techniques for teaching classes in manual communication, the underlying philosophy or rationale which led to the development of the techniques in question, and some of the human factors which influence learning favorably--and unfavorably. It was with the novice instructor in mind that the present manual was written, rather than the veteran of many semesters of such teaching. However, the veteran instructor may find herein some specific techniques he can add to his own repertoire of teaching skills, and it is hoped that he will find the systematic, step-by-step lesson plans of help in organizing his own approach to the teaching of a course in manual communication.

The efforts and encouragement of many people have gone into preparing this manual for instructors of manual communication courses. One must go back several years, to the time when the original course of study outline was born, to begin expressing one's appreciation for the help and advice that led to this revision of the original, and recognize the contributions of Dr. Ray L. Jones of the Leadership Training Program in the Area of the Deaf at San Fernando Valley State College, and Miss Virginia Vail of the Los Angeles City Schools Adult Education System without whose encouragement and determined prodding the original--and from that the present edition--might never have come into existence.

One must also acknowledge the contributions of the scores of students passing through the author's classes over the years, upon whom the techniques described here were first tried, modified, and then refined to their final form; and the instructors whose suggestions, based on their use of the original manual, led to some of the more important revisions contained in the present manual.

Special appreciation, also, is due Mr. Kenneth E. Brasel, who not only edited the manuscript in its entirety, but cooperated with the author in checking out some theories about the value of certain techniques of training over others by making his own classes in manual communication available for certain team-teaching experiments which he and the author collaborated in conducting.

The author's thanks go also to Mr. Jon Rawleigh, formerly of the National Technical Institute for the Deaf in Rochester, New York, who, in the summer of 1968, cooperated with the author in testing the feasibility of using videotaping equipment as an instructional tool in manual communication classes.

To Mr. Zoltan Ujhelyi, television engineer, and his assistants, a special word of appreciation is due and hereby tendered for the peerless assistance provided in developing the techniques described here for using videotaping and replay equipment in teaching manual communication.

To Dr. Stephen P. Quigley, also, a special word of thanks for his help and encouragement during the difficult period of writing the manual, getting the material organized, and into print.

Last, but not least, a heartfelt "thank you" to the office staff of the Institute for Research on Exceptional Children for their peerless typing help, which often went beyond mere typing into the realm of editing when errors were discovered which had escaped the combined editing of Mr. Brasel, Dr. Quigley, and the author; Mrs. Irene Lamkin, Miss Marilyn Brasel, and Miss Carla Donaldson, upon whom the heaviest burden fell--that of getting the manuscript into printable form.

CONTENTS

*Corresponding pages in Student Manual (SM)
are indicated in parentheses*

INTRODUCTION

There are many excellent books on manual communication on the market which
are designed to help those persons wishing to learn the language of signs and
fingerspelling in order to communicate with deaf people. There are also many
classes in manual communication being offered throughout the country which
are designed for the same purpose as the published books--to help those who
need or wish to learn manual methods of communicating with deaf people. There
has been a rapid increase in the number of such courses being offered in recent
years, and significant in this increase is the growing number of courses being
offered _for credit_ in colleges and universities having training programs in
the area of deafness and related fields. In many cases, these courses are required for students in such training programs, and this carries with it the
concommitant requirement for a comprehensive course of study which can meet
college and/or university requirements for use in courses offered for credit
as part of a special training program.

Along with the proliferation of courses in manual communication has come an
increasing need for professionally qualified instructors for such courses. Unfortunately, the demand has far exceeded the supply of experienced, qualified
instructors, and except for a few short-term training institutes, there have
been no systematic attempts to meet the demand for instructors for manual communication classes through training in _teaching the subject matter_. The result
has been the recruitment of many individuals who, while fluent in manual communication, have no experience or training in classroom teaching of the language
of signs and fingerspelling. Such an individual, unless he has recourse to the
advice of a veteran manual communication instructor, must develop his own course
of study in the process of his teaching, and by trial and error, build his own
techniques and procedures. The effectiveness of this trial-and-error process
depends largely upon the individual instructor's inventiveness, his prior experience in teaching per se, and/or his natural aptitude or affinity for the
profession of teaching. As might be expected, this has led to considerable
variability in teaching methodology, for, with few exceptions, none of the existing books on manual communication have been written with the _instructor_ in
mind. Those books which are organized in lesson units, while helpful to the
student in manual communication classes, offer little in the way of guidelines
to the _instructor_ using the book in his teaching. Therefore, the burden of developing supplemental teaching aids and techniques based upon the material provided in the book rests upon the shoulders of the instructor--who may or may not
have the time or the ability to rise to the occasion.

It was in response to scores of letters containing requests for methods and
material received by the author from instructors or prospective instructors of
manual communication classes that the original instructor's manual was developed
in 1964. Initially, the author attempted to answer each request personally,
outlining her teaching methods and procedures, and enclosing dittoed copies of
her lesson materials, but this soon became prohibitive in terms of time and expense. More or less in self-defense, the author compiled her lesson plans,

teaching techniques, and practice materials into a hastily assembled manual which could then be sent to those soliciting help without the need for individual responses to each request for assistance. The original manual, therefore, was written in response to an immediate need, and suffered from many inadequacies in content and organization which the author recognized--or which were called to her attention by subsequent users. Despite the limitations of the original publication, there was an immediate and unexpectedly heavy demand for copies which exhausted the limited supply within two months of issuance, a demand which has since kept pace with the proliferation in manual communication classes throughout the country. The development of the revised and updated course of study contained in the present manual was the result of the continued demand, although seven years were to pass before the task was completed, the reason being primarily lack of time, but second, the constant revisions made necessary as the author herself expanded, revised, and refined her own teaching techniques in the course of her classroom work.

Organization of the Material

The present manual is divided into two main parts. The first part includes several chapters dealing with the various aspects of manual communication; the basic procedures and techniques of teaching; drills and remediation treatments; use of videotaping equipment; and teaching fingerspelling.

The second part of the manual is the course of study outline itself, which is divided into two sections, a beginning-level section and an intermediate-level section.

The beginning section, for which fourteen separate lesson plans are provided along with individual general instruction subsections, includes two lesson plans for the teaching of fingerspelling alone; one lesson plan in which the concentration is upon teaching numbers; and ten lesson plans for teaching the language of signs and fingerspelling.

The intermediate section, for which eleven additional lesson plans have been provided (without individual general instruction subsections), includes nine lessons in the language of signs and fingerspelling which are coordinated with (and based upon) the material covered in the beginning course.

The material in each lesson is designed to be covered in a class session lasting two to three hours (preferably the latter) and includes drill and practice material, lists and word-descriptions of the signs to be taught in each lesson, and other helpful or pertinent information, as well as a step-by-step lesson plan in outline form. Also included are tests to be administered (comprehension and performance both), the words of songs which will be taught, and lists of materials the instructor will need to have on hand for each lesson.

The author assumed in writing the course of study section that the instructor planning to employ this manual in his teaching has a fluent command of the language of signs both formal and idiomatic, and that he has thoroughly familiarized himself with the methods and materials described in the first part of this manual, either through using them in previous teaching or through study of the manual itself. If such is not the case, then it is advisable that the instructor thoroughly familiarize himself with the material in Part 1 as well as the techniques and methodology, before he attempts to use the course of study section.

The appendix contains a selected annotated bibliography of books and visual teaching media the author has found helpful in preparing this manual, some of which the instructor may wish to recommend to his students for purchase as home reference books or study materials, as well as order for himself for teaching and reference purposes. In addition, the appendix contains examples of how scores on a test may be analyzed so that the instructor can identify areas of strength and weakness in his students for drills and remediation; sample evaluation sheets; and a master vocabulary list which will let him know at a glance which signs have been taught at a given time.

In conclusion, it is hoped that the manual will prove helpful to both veteran instructors and to those who are teaching manual communication for the first time.

PART I

GENERAL INFORMATION

AND

TECHNIQUES

CHAPTER 1

GENERAL PRINCIPLES

A. The Instructor

The instructor in a basic, or beginning, course in manual communication
may have had experience in teaching such courses in the past or may be approaching the task for the first time. However, veteran or novice, the instructor should be fluent in the language of signs and fingerspelling (manual
communication)--able to converse easily and fluently with any type of deaf
person from the semi-illiterate to the elite professional. While the veteran
may find this manual helpful in many ways, it was with the novice in mind--
the inexperienced instructor--that the following sections on instructional
techniques were written. The author has, therefore, gone into considerable
detail in describing techniques, tricks, and other procedural aspects of
teaching the language of signs and fingerspelling, not with the intent of
imposing her own personal style of teaching on veteran instructors whose
styles may differ, but to assist the novice instructor in acquiring the basic
skills in teaching manual communication so he may begin developing his own
teaching style sooner than would be possible if he were left to his own devices.

B. The Students

Most classes in fingerspelling and the language of signs, or manual communication, are composed of students of postsecondary school age and older. The
present manual is intended for use with this type of class, and considerable
modification would be required before it would be suitable for use in teaching
a class composed of deaf children--or any children younger than those of late
high school or college age. The teaching techniques described herein, therefore, are designed for the instructor teaching a class composed of adults,
whether young or old.

C. The Program

There are several interrelated factors involved in teaching a class in manual
communication which will have a bearing upon the approach the instructor uses
in his classroom teaching. One will be the type of program in which he teaches,
whether it is part of a larger training program devoted to preparing professional
people for working with deaf persons, an adult education program which offers
such classes for both professionals and laymen who wish or need to learn manual
communication skills, or an informal class such as those held in churches having
deaf congregations. Another will be whether the class is offered for credit at
the high school or college/university level, or is offered as a service to the
community. Still another factor will be why his students are taking the course,
whether it is required as part of their training, an immediate need to communicate

with deaf clients or relatives, simple curiosity engendered by casual contacts with deaf people, or a combination of all of these or any other reasons.

D. Teaching Adults

While these factors will influence the instructor's approach to his teaching task, the common denominator underlying all of these factors is that his class will normally be composed of adults, with adult reasons for taking the course and adult requirements of their instructor. In other words, they will be taking the course because they choose to do so, or have specific reasons for wanting to acquire manual communication skills, and not because they are "captives" of an educational system which forces them to do so until they reach a certain minimum age.

Whereas the elementary or high school teacher may get away with sloppy teaching techniques, boring his students, with giving failing grades to students he fails to motivate sufficiently toward achieving mastery of the subject matter, the instructor who teaches adults can seldom get away with such tactics without suffering retribution in some form or another.

In the adult education program, where his job may well depend upon his ability to maintain a large enough average daily attendance(ADA), the retaliation will take the form of student drop-outs from the class due to lack of interest and motivation--and when his ADA falls below the required minimum for several class sessions in a row, he will find himself out of a job.

While the instructor who is teaching in a college or university setting may fare a little better--especially if his course is required as part of the larger training program in the area of deafness--he, too, will suffer the consequences of student boredom and dissatisfaction when word gets back to the administrators of the program that his students are not progressing as well as they should. In an informal class setting, he will soon find himself teaching a dwindling class as one after another of his students find themselves "too busy" to attend classes. As adults, his students will be free to do this, to seek other ways of satisfying the need that impelled them to enroll in the class in the first place, and to express in one way or another the dissatisfaction they feel with the instructor who fails to satisfy their needs--not only their need to learn manual communication, but other needs as well--for students in manual communication classes share certain basic human needs with adult students in any course, regardless of the subject.

E. Needs of Adult Students

Apart from the need to learn manual communication, there are certain basic needs all adult students share which the instructor should keep in mind in conducting his classroom teaching. These are:

1. Need to be interested, stimulated, and motivated.

2. Need to feel they are respected as responsible adults and equals by the instructor.

3. Need to feel confidence in the instructor as a person who knows the subject matter and how to help them achieve mastery of it.

4. Need to participate actively in the classroom learning, and to be responsible for mastery of units of learning by themselves as well as with the assistance of the instructor.

5. Need to feel that the instructor is interested in them personally, as individuals as well as students, and wants to help them acquire the skills and knowledge he himself possesses.

6. Need to feel that they are progressing steadily.

7. Need to excel, to be noticed and praised for outstanding work, and to be given constructive criticism which will help them achieve excellence.

8. Need to be encouraged and to develop faith in their own ability to master the subject matter.

9. Need to feel a sense of accomplishment in mastering something they did not know before.

10. Need to know that their skills can be put to practical use.

One might add still another need to the list, for the instructor of adult students will find that, in common with children, adult students need to know "why." Unlike children, however, they require responsible answers and cannot be sidetracked or bought off with stock answers. The instructor in a manual communication course, therefore, is well advised to be prepared to answer such questions as: "Why is the sign made that way?"; "Why do deaf people have such atrocious grammar?"; "Which is better, manual or oral methods of teaching?"; "Why do deaf people often have such high voices?"; "Why do deaf people ask such personal questions?"; "Does sign language really damage the language of deaf people or is the damage done earlier--and reflected in the grammatical structure of the language of signs?"; "Which should be introduced first, finger-spelling or sign language, if you agree with the theory that holds that a deaf child should be given manual methods of communication as early as possible?"; "Will my deaf child be able to learn to speak and read lips as well as Mr. ___ or Mrs. ___ (naming deaf person who lost their hearing after they had acquired language)?" and so forth.

It is suggested that a general rule instructors should follow is to answer each question as honestly and as completely as possible, and to admit ignorance if he does not know the answer. In addition, he should attempt to be fair in his answers, to give both his own opinions and the opinions of those who are known to hold contrary viewpoints--and to specify which is which. Helpful to the novice instructor is the tactic of referring his questioners to books, journals, and articles which deal with the topic in question and asking them to read these and bring a summary to class for class discussion. This can provide him with a helpful instructional tool--as well as get him off the hook temporarily if he does not know the answer. At any rate, the instructor should strive to acquire an extensive store of background information about the various aspects of deafness and their consequences, knowledge he can pass on to his students.

F. General Principles for Teaching Adults

The teaching of adults, while incorporating many similar principles to those applied in teaching children, does require a different approach from that employed in teaching children. Adults have different requirements and require different techniques of teaching, and have to have certain basic psychological needs satisfied if the instructor is to be successful in his attempts to help them master the subject matter of the course. The manual communication instructor can meet these needs by:

1. Organizing his lessons in such a way that:

    a. Each lesson is a unit of learning the students can master with a little effort, thus providing them with regular opportunity to feel a sense of accomplishment as well as to recognize their own progress.

    b. Each lesson includes both review of previously learned material and practice in new material being taught.

    c. Each lesson includes, whenever possible or pertinent, brief side-excursions into various aspects of deafness and illustrations of the psychological, socioeconomic, and educational implications of deafness, as well as practice and new learning in the language of signs.

    d. Each lesson is relevant to what has gone before, and to the final goals of the course.

    e. It is clearly recognizable to the students that the instructor knows what he is doing, what he hopes to accomplish in the lesson, and what he expects from them in the way of assistance in achieving the immediate goals of the lesson.

2. Maintaining eye-contact with each of his students so that each will feel he is personally known to the instructor and is interesting to him.

3. Being genuinely interested in each of his students, beginning with learning their names as quickly as possible, and obtaining some background information on each.

4. Treating all of his students with respect as adults and equals.

5. Encouraging his students to ask questions and answering even the most asinine with courtesy, honesty, and completeness insofar as is possible; and by prefacing any answers which reflect his own biases with the statement that the answer is, indeed, biased--and giving the contrary point of view if one exists.

6. Encouraging participation by all students in classroom activities, drawing out those who are quiet, and seeing to it that class sessions are not repeatedly dominated by a few outspoken ones.

7. Encouraging students when they run into difficulties, helping them to overcome the difficulties, and being quick to praise when praise is deserved.

8. Encouraging students to help each other with constructive criticism as well as with praise.

9. Giving his students outside assignments which they are responsible for completing on their own time, preferably those which require contact with adult deaf members of the community, in which they will not only obtain practice in their newly acquired skills but also acquire some personal knowledge of what deaf adults actually are like--as opposed to theories, opinions, and lectures on what they are like. (This is beneficial in that it reduces the nervousness, or even fear, that many people experience when encountering a real, live deaf person for the first time, and helps them gain self-confidence.)

10. Calling his students' attention to pertinent articles in books, journals, reports, and the like, which they may be interested in reading to further their knowledge in the field.

11. Constantly striving to improve his own teaching, and to this effect, having his students evaluate the course at the end of the semester with a view toward obtaining their criticisms as well as their suggestions for improvement.

If these rules are followed--and they are rules which apply to teaching any class composed of adults regardless of the subject matter--the instructor in a class in manual communication will keep his students interested, motivated, and progressing. They will, therefore, leave the course with a sense of personal accomplishment--and many may be motivated to continue their training by enrolling in more advanced courses in the same subject.

CHAPTER 2

GENERAL PROCEDURES

A. Development of Expressive and Receptive Skills

The course of study outlined in this manual differs from the norm in two main respects. First, it gives the signs for very few nouns in the first several lessons. It was reasoned that the beginning student can always finger-spell nouns, while, if he knows the signs for the more frequently used connective words, auxiliaries, and pronouns, his delivery will be speeded up considerably more than would otherwise be the case. Therefore, the signs for pronouns, auxiliary verbs, and connective words form the bulk of the vocabulary of signs taught for the first several lessons in the language of signs.

Second, with rare exceptions, the author has separated words for which the signs are very similar, giving them in separate lessons wherever possible. The reasoning behind this decision is simple--there is less likelihood of a student confusing two morphologically similar signs if he is permitted time in which to fix the first sign in his memory before the second, similar sign is introduced.

1. Expressive Skills

In the course of study contained in the present manual, expressive (or performance) skills in fingerspelling are developed chiefly through employment of synchronized drills, as will be detailed in the section dealing with the teaching of fingerspelling.

Transmissive skills in the language of signs, while also developed by means of classroom drills and "recitals" by students, are refined and perfected through the medium of teaching the students to "sing" in the language of signs. This develops rhythm, expressiveness, and phrasing, as well as smoothness and fluidity. Along with fluency and smoothness of signs, the student also becomes aware of the different shadings of meaning lent by emphasis, size of the signs, facial expressions, and other "tonal" qualities of the language of signs; and, at the same time, acquires insight into the frequent necessity of substituting synonymns for words for which there are no signs, words which are fingerspelled in normal conversation, but which must somehow be conveyed in signs when they appear in a song. This introduces the student to word-concept analysis, a vital step in his attempt to master the language of signs with all its idiomatic and dialectical nuances, described and illustrated in more detail in Lesson 11.

Note: It is recognized, however, that not all instructors will be equally talented in manual singing, and those who do not feel adequate to the task of teaching their students to "sing" in the language of signs may want to bring in for specific lessons a "guest lecturer" who is talented in this art, and who can teach the lesson song to the class. If such an expert is not available, then the instructor should compensate by placing extra emphasis on drills and training in use of appropriate facial expressions in his classroom work with the students. The songs in the present manual have been presented in the word-descriptions in such a way as to give the conversational version rather than the true platform version of the sign, and can be taught as such if the instructor wishes, or is not able to show his students how to execute the large, flowing, platform versions actually required in manual singing.

It has been the author's experience that students seldom forget a sign they learned in a song--whether the sign was taught in the conversational version or the platform version--so it is strongly recommended that the instructor teach songs if at all possible. In any event, he should make his students aware of the differences between conventional signs and platform signs; in the shadings of meanings imparted by facial expressions and body movements, by emphasis or lack of it; and the importance of rhythm, pacing, pausing, and the like, and how all these factors affect the transmission of mood, emotion, and meaning when communicating with deaf persons in the language of signs and fingerspelling.

2. Receptive Skills

As will be seen in the individual lesson plans, heavy emphasis is placed upon the development of receptive skills, for it is a well-known fact that receptive skills are far harder to develop than are expressive skills.

As will be detailed in the chapter on teaching fingerspelling, the development of receptive skills in fingerspelling is effected primarily through use of rapid drills. These drills are designed to prevent sequential associations from forming between adjacent letters of the alphabet; to train students to recognize groups of letters rather than individual letters and to train students in synchronizing the movements of their lips as they silently speak a word with their fingerspelling of the same word. Also employed are tests and analyses of test errors to identify areas of weakness; remediation of such areas of weakness through additional specialized drills, both in the classroom and by use of filmed drills in fingerspelling; and various in-class techniques of enforced practice in reading fingerspelling in the form of roll-calls, Password-type games, and so on.

Receptive skills in the language of signs are developed primarily through means of regular comprehension tests administered in each class: drills; games; recitals by fellow classmates of sentences unknown to the rest of the class; and by constant review and reinforcement of previous learning in the form of review drill sentences including previously learned signs; teaching/learning drill sentences of the same type; and other techniques which force students to read a wide variety of sentences, statements, and the like which are delivered via manual communication.

B. General Teaching Techniques

1. Student Participation

An active student is a student who is learning. One of the most effective teaching techniques a manual communication instructor can employ is that of encouraging student participation in classroom evaluation of their own and their fellow students' performances. If videotaping equipment is used, this is most effectively accomplished by taping each student's recital, then replaying the tape so that the class and the student himself can evaluate his performance.

Rather than take upon himself the task of correcting all flaws in technique, the instructor should, at the end of the replay, ask members of the class to comment upon the performance. He should be careful, however, to elicit the favorable comments first by structuring his initial question in some such form as, "Now, what were the best features of that performance?" He can then ask the class what they have to offer the student in the way of constructive criticism--beginning all questioning by asking the performer himself what he thought of his performance.

After all comments from the students have been exhausted, the instructor should then summarize the comments (and add his own), beginning with the criticism and ending with the praise. He can then have the student repeat his recital, incorporating the suggested changes and/or correcting any errors committed in the first recital. The two performances can then be replayed one after the other, to drive home the improvement the collective suggestions made in the performance.

An ancilliary benefit to be obtained by use of this participation-inducing technique is the constant exposure the students get to reading fingerspelling and/or the language of signs, for, in order to evaluate their fellow students' performances, they must first be able to understand what the student is saying before they can decide whether or not he fingerspelled and/or signed the passage the way it should have been.

In the event videotaping equipment is not available, the same technique can be used with minor modifications. The performing student, naturally, will have to be left out of the evaluation of his own performance, but the other students' opinions can and should be solicited in the same fashion as has been described.

2. Use of Rewards and Reinforcement

The instructor is strongly urged to use a considerable amount of positive reinforcement in his teaching. This can take the form of verbal rewards such as "perfect!" or "very good," or "that is a beautifully made letter (or sign)," or nonverbal rewards such as nods and winks, or the hand held up in an F for the commonly used "just right" sign, and so on.

This is especially helpful in the case of a student who must repeatedly be corrected and helped in overcoming technical flaws, for immediate positive reinforcement when he finally executes the letter, word, or sign correctly not only tends to fix the correct movement or handshape in his habit pattern, but also bolsters his self-confidence--which may have been somewhat shaken by the series of corrections, corrections he cannot help but notice his fellow students may not have been getting.

At the beginning of the course, a well-timed word of praise can do far more to encourage and motivate a student than any number of flowery compliments later in the course. The instructor, therefore, should be generous with his praise during the first several sessions, for it is then that students will commit most of their errors and require praise to counterbalance the necessary corrections. The instructor can be more sparing with his praise as the course advances, but should never fail to reward good performance, and should also encourage his students to reward each other as well.

C. Specific Teaching Techniques

1. Roll Call

Along with drills and tests to be described shortly, an excellent means of providing practice in receptive fingerspelling is roll calling at the beginning of each class. While attendance may not be compulsory in a manual communication class, it is obviously necessary. A student who misses several classes in succession misses big chunks of the course--and often poses a problem for the instructor when he returns to class. Unless the instructor is insensitive, he is going to be touched by the plight of this absentee student when he returns to class and finds himself forty to sixty words behind his fellows, missing large parts of test sentences, and, in general, floundering around while trying to catch up. Therefore, the instructor will probably have to spend extra time trying to bring the returnee up to date, while the other students mark time or watch casually while the instructor backtracks over ground they have already covered. This often throws the instructor off schedule and prevents the employment of certain types of learning experiences which would be more valuable to the class than a rehash of material they already know.

Roll call, therefore, is stressed, both to remind the students each time how important attendance is and to provide the instructor with information which may help him pinpoint why some of his students are having trouble. For example, if he knows which lesson he gave on a particular date, a mistake on a test by a student absent on that date becomes understandable when the instructor finds that the mistake was on a sign taught in the session the student in question missed. It also affords him the opportunity to watch the rate of absences of individual students--and caution those who have missed more than two or three classes over a period of time.

Roll call can be fun for both the instructor and the class, for it eventually turns into a contest of wits (and receptive fingerspelling ability) between the instructor and the students. The instructor can try to trip the students up by

varying the way in which he calls the roll so as to upset any pattern of
responses the students may have learned to make which involves their watching for their own name only without actually trying to read and understand
the other names being called. The students, naturally, will be trying to
outwit the instructor and get their names tallied on the attendance roster
without too much effort on their part and to avoid the additional effort involved in attending to each name the instructor calls if at all possible.

Types of roll call: The basic technique for roll calling is a simple one.
Each student's name (preferably his full name) is fingerspelled at full speed
and repeated until he recognizes it and responds. The variations the instructor can use to prevent wool-gathering on the part of his class while he is
calling the roll are listed below, roughly in order of increasing "tricki-
ness." (It is presumed that when fingerspelled roll call is introduced to
the classroom routine, the students will have had at least two or three lessons in fingerspelling, including extensive fingerspelling drills of various
types.)

a. Basic roll call: The instructor goes down the list of students in
alphabetical order, to acquaint them with what their names look like
when fingerspelled, calling out the name simultaneously, then repeating it a couple of times while requesting the named student to watch
his hand carefully. Then, on subsequent roll calls, he omits the
vocal part.

b. Scrambled roster roll call: To break up patterns of expectancies (a
student with a name beginning with B, for instance, will "sleep" through
all the other names after his own has been called, if permitted to do
so), the instructor should call the roll at random.

c. Inverted name roll call: In addition to scrambling the names on the
roster, the instructor reverses the order in which he has been calling
the first and last names of the students. A variation of this is to
invert some names, but not others.

d. Repeating roll call: To break up the complacency of students whose
names have already been called, the instructor occasionally repeats a
name he has already called, thus insuring attention even by those who
have been called.

e. Misspelling roll call: The instructor deliberately misspells the names
of some of the students--making gross errors at first (e.g., Goldfein
becomes Goldfish), and more subtle errors as the students develop in
proficiency (e.g., Goldfein becomes Goldfin, or Goldfeen).

f. Cross-validation roll call: Instead of the student being called answering to his own name, the instructor selects another student at random
to tell him whether or not the called student is present. (This is
used after the students become acquainted with each other, but it can
also be used to acquaint students with each other.)

g. Scrambled-name roll call: The instructor pairs the last name of one student with the first name of another. (Useful when the class appears to be in a quiet or unresponsive mood. It usually creates laughter when neither student responds, or when both hesitantly raise their hands, looking puzzled. Also good for shaking up individual students who, after their names have been called earlier, have allowed their attention to wander.)

h. Insertion roll call: The instructor inserts names of strangers in the roll call.

As can be seen, the last two variations of the roll call can be used in the middle of another variation, primarily as attention getters, but also as tests of student alertness and receptive fingerspelling ability. There are other variations, but the individual instructor probably will want to develop his own techniques of insuring student attention during roll call in addition to those outlined above. By employing such variations, the instructor transforms a sometimes tedious chore into a learning experience which is fun for all concerned.

As the students become proficient, the instructor can inject a measure of humorous "risk" by "threatening" to mark absent any student who does not recognize his name on the first or second try.

2. Drills

The techniques described in the following section for drilling students in both fingerspelling and the language of signs are those developed by the author in the course of her classroom teaching during which she had recourse to video-taping equipment. The individual instructor may wish to modify these techniques to fit his own requirements, but it is recommended that he keep in mind the necessity of constant repetition and review if the students are to be able to retain an ever expanding vocabulary of signs and to develop the ability to use these signs in communicating with deaf people.

Use of drills: Drills, by their very nature, are repetitive and demand considerable concentration on the part of the students. It would be well for the instructor to keep several factors in mind while drilling his students: attention; physical and mental fatigue; relevancy of the drill material; and the necessity to identify faulty techniques and correct them before they have a chance to become fixed habits.

He should strive to maintain a balance between intensive programmed drills and other more entertaining or interesting forms of practice. He should also be alert to signs of flagging attention or physical distress in his students during drills, and provide breaks before the saturation point is reached. Irrelevant, nonsensical drill material should not be used except as a tension-breaking change of pace to test student attention as well as their ability to catch nonsense interspersed among meaningful material. Use of nonsense words or syllables does not provide training in receptive fingerspelling, for they require the reading of individual letters instead of complete words (although some particular nonsense syllables are helpful in training the fingers to move from one difficult letter to another in _expressive_ fingerspelling practice).

Last, but far from least, the instructor should at all times maintain _eye-contact_ with his students. Only in this way will he be able to spot errors and nip them in the bud. He will also be able to note which of his students are not paying attention, and by calling upon these students, insure that they pay attention in the future. He will also give each student the feeling that he is personally interested in helping the student—a motivating influence that pays dividends in increased receptiveness on the part of the students to the content of the lesson the instructor is attempting to help them learn.

Types of drills: There are several different types of drills in both fingerspelling and signs described in the next section of this chapter. Briefly, they can be categorized into six general classes of drills, all of which should be employed at one time or another by the instructor:

    a. _Teaching drills_: in which letters or signs are introduced for the first time.

    b. _Intensive drills_ (based upon the principles of programmed learning): in which repetition and reinforcement of units of learning are employed to rapidly increase the students' receptive and expressive skills in fingerspelling.

    c. _Discrimination drills_: in which the student is trained to recognize subtle differences between similarly appearing fingerspelled words.

    d. _Vocalization drills_: in which the student is trained to say the _complete word_, not individual letters, simultaneously with his fingerspelling (or signing) of the word, which are designed to prevent the common habit of "alphabetizing" from developing.

    e. _Review-type drills_ (conducted by the instructor): in which previously covered material is reviewed; and

    f. _Student-conducted reviews_: in which individual students conduct review drills of their fellow students on individual lessons.

    g. _Fun and game-type drills_: in which games such as Password and Bingo are employed to drill in fingerspelling, signs, and numbers.

    h. _Tests_: which are designed not only to check student progress but also to train students in receptive skills.

3. Description of Drill Techniques

    a. _Definition of "varying and verifying"_: One of the expressions which will be encountered frequently in both the general instructions preceding each lesson and in the lesson plans themselves will be the phrase "vary and verify." This refers primarily to the technique of randomly varying from signing to fingerspelling a drill word during drills, and then verifying the response given by one student by calling upon another student to tell whether or not the first student gave the correct response. The instructor either signs the word, or fingerspells it, and requests a selected student to first repeat the sign or fingerspelled word exactly as given by the instructor, then give the reverse (the fingerspelled translation of the sign--or the sign for the fingerspelled word). Assuming the other students have been watching (as they should have), the instructor then calls upon another student (selected at random) to say "right" or "wrong" about the first student's repetition/translation of the instructor's drill word. (Note: The instructor should encourage students to watch for small errors in performance even if the original student translated the drill word correctly.)

Varying and verifying is an excellent way to insure student attention to the instructor and to their fellow students, for if the instructor notices a student is not paying attention to the response of his fellow student, he can call upon the wool-gathering student to verify the first student's answer. The resultant embarrassment of admitting he was not watching is usually sufficient to insure complete attention from that time on--thereby exposing him to more training in developing his receptive ability. In addition, when it happens (as it frequently will) that the student giving the response and the student verifying his response disagree on whether the response was right or wrong, the instructor can then call upon the class to arbitrate the disagreement--thus providing extra training in discriminating between fingerspelled words or signs.

b. Teaching drills: Essentially, teaching drills are those in which new letters or signs are introduced for the first time. Since the instructor wants his students to be able to remember the newly presented letters or signs, but not necessarily in the order of presentation, he should endeavor to scramble up the order of repetition in such a way that each letter or sign is repeated (and thereby reinforced) a sufficient number of times to insure its being imprinted in the students' memories, without permitting sequential associative links to form between a given letter or sign and the ones immediately preceding and following it in the original order of presentation.

Since the technique for the introduction of the students to the manual alphabet is outlined in detail in the section on teaching fingerspelling, the general procedures outlined here will be those suggested for use in teaching all new signs. It must be remembered, however, that the general procedure of repetition and reinforcement apply to both the teaching of fingerspelling and to the teaching of signs.

(1) "Backtracking"-type teaching drills: When the instructor first introduces signs to his students, there will be limits to which he can utilize these first signs in sentences. Therefore, he must employ a "backtracking" technique to insure that the signs are repeated and reinforced a sufficient number of times for them to be learned. In essence, this "backtracking" means that the instructor will, after he has given the first two or three signs, backtrack and repeat the signs in reverse and/or random order. To illustrate, using the vocabulary of signs given in Lesson 1, the order of

presentation and backtracking could be something like this. (Underlined words are fingerspelled. Words in quotation marks are spoken aloud.)

I   "I"

I, ME   "I, Me"

I, ME, MINE (MY)   "I, Me, Mine, or My"

ME, MY (MINE), I   "Me, or _?_ (wait for student response), Mine, _?_ (wait), I"

MY, ME, I   (Wait for response after each) "Yes, My ___ Me ___ I" (etc.)

MINE   "What did I say?" (Wait for student response.)

ME   "What did I say?" (Wait for student response.)

I AM MR. _____.   "What did I say?" (Wait for student response, repeating if necessary.)

I, ME, MINE, MYSELF, MYSELF, MYSELF   "I, Me, Mine, Myself, Myself, Myself"

ME, MINE, MYSELF   "Me, Mine, _?_ (wait), Myself"

I, MINE, MYSELF   "I, Mine, Myself"

I LOVE MYSELF.   "What did I say?" (Sign the latter while saying it aloud.)

MY NAME IS _____.   "What did I say?" (Signed and spoken aloud.)

I, ME, MINE, MYSELF, WHAT, WHAT, WHAT   "I, Me, etc. (wait after each)"

MINE, WHAT, ME, I, MINE, MYSELF   "(etc.)"

WHAT IS MY NAME?   "What did I say?"

It can be seen that there is constant repetition of each sign as it is learned, and as each new sign is taught, it is immediately incorporated into a sentence the moment it becomes possible.

As the students' vocabularies of signs expand, the sentences which can be constructed become increasingly more complex and varied, and are limited only by the instructor's ingenuity at inventing sentences on the spot which combine the signs already taught.

At first, the novice instructor may find it helpful to study the master vocabulary list provided in the appendix prior to each lesson, and make up a list of short sentences which incorporate the vocabulary to be presented in the lesson, and have this list at hand when he begins the teaching drill. The veteran instructor will usually not experience too much difficulty in composing sentences on the spur of the moment, and, at any rate, is not likely to lose his composure if he does have to pause momentarily during the drill while he thinks up a sentence to use for a certain sign.

(2) "Cloze" teaching drills: The instructor will have to employ backtracking-type teaching drills for the first couple of lessons in the language of signs, but once his students have acquired a vocabulary of 40 to 50 signs, a new type of teaching drill can be employed to teach new signs. Essentially this involves teaching a new sign embedded in a sentence containing signs the students already know, without telling the students what the sign means, and asking them to guess what the sign might mean from the context of the sentence. In other words, the instructor is employing a modified form of "Cloze" procedure both to teach the new sign and to train his students to attend to the content of a signed and fingerspelled message.

This training will stand the student in good stead when he ventures out to converse with deaf people before he is completely fluent in the language of signs. Since it is likely that on many occasions deaf people will use signs unfamiliar to the student, such training in attending to the content of what the deaf person is saying will help the student learn to fill in the gaps which the unfamiliar sign(s) leave. It will, in addition, train the student to distinguish between the familiar and the unfamiliar--so that he can ask the deaf person what the unfamiliar sign means by repeating the unknown sign (if he cannot guess from the context of the rest of the deaf persons' statement). He will thus rapidly expand his vocabulary of signs by learning many signs in addition to those taught in the classroom.

To illustrate, the sentence below could be used to teach the sign for the word ABOUT, which is given in Lesson 2. The words which must be fingerspelled are underlined. The other words in the sentence are those for which the signs have already been taught (either in Lesson 1 or earlier in Lesson 2).

Did you tell him ABOUT the phone call?

It will be noted that the context of the sentence makes it very easy for the student to figure out what the unknown sign is, for the sentence "Did you tell him _____ the phone call?" is such that ABOUT is almost automatically elicited, for it is the most logical word a person could use to complete the sentence.

The instructor can increase the effectiveness of training in discrimination which Cloze-drills provide by explaining to the students what he is going to do--sign and fingerspell a sentence in which they know all but one of the signs used, and their task is to spot the unknown sign and try to figure out what it means from the context of the rest of the sentence.

After he has given them the sentence, he should then ask the students which sign was the unknown one, and try to elicit a reproduction of the sign they did not know. After several students have reproduced the sign (and shown their fellows how to make it), the instructor should repeat the sentence --this time asking the students what they thought the sign meant.

Normally, someone will come up with the right answer--or a close approximation of it. If not, the instructor can provide clues such as, "If a person can do, can do, can do a lot of things--or can do a certain thing without error a lot of times, he is said to have a lot of ____ (ability)."

While the Cloze-type drills are remarkably efficient in teaching a new vocabulary of signs, they take longer than backtracking-type drills, so the amount of time the instructor has for vocabulary drills will probably determine which of the two types of teaching drills he will employ in a given class session. If time is short, he will probably resort to backtracking-type teaching drills. If he has plenty of time, he should use Cloze drills.

To assist the instructor in becoming accustomed to the Cloze technique in drilling his students, sentences have been provided for the first four lessons in signs. However, no more Cloze sentences are provided after Lesson 4, so it is recommended that the instructor enlist the help of his students in constructing Cloze sentences (see general instructions, Lesson 4).

c. _Intensive drills_: Intensive drills, which are high-speed fingerspelling drills designed to force students to recognize rapidly fingerspelled _groups_ of letters of increasing letter-group size, are described in detail in the section on teaching fingerspelling.

Note: It is inadvisable to attempt to conduct intensive drills in _signs_, for it takes a while for a student to train his eyes to follow the spatially larger signs than it does to train them to follow rapidly changing handshapes of the fingerspelling hand (which stays in the same position). A rapidly executed sign would serve only to confuse the new student who is trying to learn the exact sequence of motions which go into the execution of the sign, and, therefore, would divide his attention between trying to remember what the sign means and trying to memorize exactly how it is made.

d. _Discrimination drills_: Another difficult task for the beginner in manual communication is acquiring the ability to distinguish between similarly appearing letters of the manual alphabet such as D, F, and K; A, E, O, M, and S; P and Q; G and H, and so on. Also confusing are similarly appearing signs such as SHORT, NAME, TRAIN, and EGG; LOOK and FACE; PEOPLE and VISIT; and other morphologically similar signs.

In the course of his teaching, the instructor will find many instances where students mistake PEAT for PET, MAN for MEAN or MEN, and so on. This usually occurs early in the course and should be the signal for the instructor to introduce discrimination drills designed to afford the student practice in distinguishing between the letters in question when they appear in words.

In addition, when comprehension tests are begun and test scores analyzed, it will be found that many of the students show weakness in comprehending fingerspelled words in the tests which include such letter groups as EA, and mistake

words such as MEAT for MET, and so on. This, also, indicates the need for
discrimination drills, which are simple but effective in training the students
to recognize the small but perceptible differences between letters, between a
three-letter word and a four-letter word, between words where the S begins the
word (such as SCAT) and where it ends the word (CATS), etc. (For the technique
used in discrimination drilling, see the section on discrimination drills in
Chapter 4, Teaching Fingerspelling.)

Discrimination drills can also be used to provide discrimination training in
signs. Either individual signs can be used for the drills or short sentences can
be composed in which only the drill signs are changed. For example, PEOPLE ARE
FUNNY and VISIT ARE FUNNY; I LIKE PEOPLE and I LIKE VISIT(S); YOU LOOK LIKE YOUR
MOTHER and YOU WHO LIKE YOUR MOTHER, all can be used in drills if the students
are clued in on what to look for. In the case of sentences which become nonsense
if the wrong sign is used, the students can be instructed to give the instructor
the sign for WRONG to show that they caught the error and RIGHT if the correct
sign was used.

   e. Vocalization drills: See section on teaching fingerspelling.

   f. Review-type drills: Essentially, reviews are a re-covering of the signs
learned prior to the lesson at hand and can be conducted by either the instructor
himself or by students selected by the instructor. In the event the instructor
administers the drills, he can employ the Vary/Verify technique described earlier,
as well as the practice sentences provided in most lessons. He can also employ
the techniques described in teaching drills and combine the previously learned
signs into sentences composed on the spot, or prepared in advance. (The master
vocabulary list provided in the appendix will help in this.)

Included in review-type drills are student recitations, and it is helpful if
the instructor requires his students to compose their own sentences and bring
them to class after practicing them. At the same time, the instructor should
have available a variety of sentences, preferably printed or written on strips of
cardboard (for durability), which he can arbitrarily assign the students from time
to time for impromptu demonstrations of their ability.

Another technique which combines review with student recitation is to select a
student to drill his fellows in the vocabulary for a given lesson. This enables
the instructor not only to assess the student's performance during his conduct of
the drill (and to take a break from conducting the sometimes tedious drilling himself), but also may afford him a measure of amusement as the class individually
and/or collectively pounces on the temporary "assistant instructor" and vigorously
corrects any errors he might be so incautious as to make.

   g. Fun and game-type drills: Early in the course, the instructor can employ
spelling games such as the popular Password game of television fame to encourage
his students in practicing their fingerspelling. Since students must both send
and receive fingerspelled word-clues to the game word, it affords practice in both
receptive and expressive fingerspelling. Bingo is another game which can be utilized effectively in helping the students to learn to recognize and use numbers.
These drills are useful learning devices--ones which both students and instructors
generally enjoy. It is unlikely, however, that they can be used as frequently as
the students would like, for any game described in this manual will usually require

at least 30 minutes to an hour of class time. The amount of new learning which can take place in a class session in which a game is played is reduced accordingly. However, the instructor can, as an inducement, promise the students a game session upon the attainment of a selected goal--for example, when all students have learned to manually sign a song without error. (See other visual aids for a complete description of how Password and Bingo can be adapted for use as drills.)

4. Tests

a. Test administration[1]: Beginning with Lesson 4 in this manual, suggested comprehension tests in both fingerspelling and sign language are provided. In addition, two written performance tests are included, the purpose of which is not so much to find out whether the students know the signs required by the test as to focus their attention upon the need to know exactly what they are doing when they execute a sign. If their signing is sloppy, it will show up in their tests, with, for instance, "Cupped hands" given when "Right-angle hands" are required. The negative feedback they get from the instructor's comments on their papers will alert them to the fact that they are not quite accurate in their renditions of some signs-- and draw their attention to the need to be crisp and clear in their signing.

The comprehension tests are designed to provide practice in receptive fingerspelling and the language of signs as well as a regular check on student progress in the development of receptive skills, individually and collectively. Although the students may suffer from the usual "test trauma" for the first few sessions, they generally become accustomed to the regular tests, and this will be reflected in their scores. Also, they soon begin to appreciate the fact that the tests are of benefit to them when their performance brings them instructor-instituted practice in troublesome letter groups, or directions from the instructor to practice with fingerspelling films which present training in these groups. The student will quickly recognize this as helpful, and the tests will become a routine part of his expectations of his instructor.

b. Grading of tests: All tests in this manual include information which will help the instructor in grading his students' papers. In brief, the number of words in each test have been counted, the percentage scores computed, and the amount to be deducted for each error is provided at the end of each test. The instructor should count the number of words the individual student missed in a test, and multiply the number missed by the amount to be deducted for each error. The result is the student's score in percentage of 100. A general rule in scoring comprehension test papers is to give full credit to the student for each correct word written if the student obviously recognized the sign or the fingerspelled word, regardless of which interpretation he chose from among the various meanings the sign may have had (e.g.,

---

[1]Students should always be allowed a brief warm-up period--such as review drills--before any receptive (comprehension) test is administered.

in the case of a student who wrote "but" when "different" was required),
and regardless of the order in which he wrote the words (e.g., a student
who writes, "My husband . . . me . . . yells . . . when I spend money," for
the sentence, "My husband yells at me when I spend money," is credited with
having 8 out of 9 words right even though "me" and "yells" were transposed).

In grading the performance tests, it is hoped that the instructor will
emphasize that the students are to limit themselves to the beginning hand-
position only. If he does not, his chore of grading the performance test
is going to be vastly more complicated than he would expect. Some students
will follow the instructions which appear on the first page of the test and
limit themselves to giving the initial hand-position for each sign. Others,
and they are regrettably numerous, will try to write complete word-descriptions
of each sign in the test--and the instructor will find himself having to deci-
pher each and every one of these word-descriptions in order to find out whether
or not the student knows the sign. In addition, since the space provided for
answers is sufficient only for a one- or two-word answer, the writing of these
eager-beaver students is apt to be somewhat microscopic in size as they attempt
to cram 25- to 50-word descriptions of the signs in a space intended for only
one or two words, which compounds the task of deciphering.

Whether the instructor has or has not emphasized the need to limit the
student responses on the performance tests to one or two words, he should
grade the papers according to whether the student obviously knows the sign or
not. Since there is space provided for two-hand answers whether the sign is
made with one or two hands or either, each fully correct answer is given full
credit. In borderline cases, where, for instance, a cupped hand is required
and an open hand is described by the student, it is best to grant the student
full credit but to make a notation to the effect that a "cupped hand" is better. Less acceptable errors, such as using "O hand" for "S hand," can be
penalized by the deduction of one point if the sign is otherwise accurate,
and a notation should be made on the student's paper to the effect that the
penalty was imposed because of sloppiness. Also, when a student indicates
only one hand when two hands are generally used (such as in NONE, where two
O hands are normally used, but one hand can be used), he can be granted full
credit, but should be cautioned against such usage unless he has one hand full.
It is well to remember that these comments, cautions, and admonitions should
be made on the student's paper, preferably in ink of a different color than
that used by the student. In addition, all incorrect responses (or items left
blank) should be corrected or filled in with the proper hand-position.

It is suggested that the instructor strive to maintain a class average of
80 to 85 percent on all tests. A higher average does not necessarily mean that
the instructor is doing an excellent job of teaching, nor that his students are
remarkably adept; it may indicate only that the instructor is delivering the
test sentences at too slow a speed. A lower class average may mean that the
instructor is pushing the class too hard, or not devoting sufficient time to
comprehension drills, or merely that he is signing and fingerspelling the test
sentences too fast. A general rule of thumb is: If the class mean rises above
85, the instructor should increase the pace of his delivery of test sentences;
if it falls below 80, he should analyze the test scores to find out where the
students' difficulty lies, and institute remediation in the form of extra drills
in that area.

c. Analysis of test results: Examples of how to analyze test papers will
be found in the appendix which will help the instructor identify areas of
weakness. In these examples, it is shown how to record the number of students
missing particular fingerspelled test words or signs, and how to decide whether
a significant number of students (usually more than 5 percent of the class)
missed a given word or sign. The need for extra intensive drills in a particular letter grouping (if the word was fingerspelled), or more review drills
including the sign (or signs) missed, is indicated when errors on a given word
or sign are frequent. In addition, if the Graphic Films Corporation fingerspelling drill films (appendix) are available, students consistently missing
certain words which include specific letter groups can be directed to practice
with the reels which provide drill in these particular groups.

CHAPTER 3

USE OF VIDEOTAPING EQUIPMENT AND VISUAL AIDS
IN TEACHING MANUAL COMMUNICATION CLASSES

A. Introduction

One of the newest developments in teaching classes in manual communication
has been the introduction of instant-replay videotaping equipment as a classroom teaching aid. In a visual course, such as manual communication, the
advantages of having videotaping equipment available as a teaching aid cannot
be overemphasized. Those instructors who have used this type of visual aid
in their classroom teaching of manual communication, and/or interpreting for
deaf people, report that they will never willingly do without it again.

While such equipment is still a comparative rarity in manual communication
classes, it is becoming increasingly available as colleges and universities--
and even some of the larger metropolitan high schools--install studio-type
videotaping equipment, or purchase portable videotaping cameras and monitors
for general use. It would be well, therefore, for an instructor planning to
conduct his classes in a college or university setting, or in adult education
programs located in large metropolitan high schools, to investigate and find
out whether or not the institution has this equipment. If it is available,
the institution authorities generally are cooperative in granting permission
for its use in manual communication classes when schedules permit, for the
rationale for its use in such classes is hard to deny once the instructor presents his case.

There are two main problems likely to be encountered by the instructor in
arranging for videotaping equipment. One is the scheduling of the equipment,
and the other is the availability of a technician to operate the equipment.
If the manual communication classes are held in the evenings, as they frequently
are, scheduling is usually not too much of a problem--but obtaining technical
help in operating the equipment is likely to be a major obstacle unless the instructor is willing to learn how to operate portable equipment himself. Schools
are somewhat reluctant to let amateurs operate their expensive portable videotaping equipment, and in any event, never permit them to operate the studio-
type equipment. Therefore, unless funds are available to pay a professional
technician overtime wages for evening work, the instructor himself will have
to be "checked out" on portable equipment and operate it himself. This is far
from a satisfactory arrangement, for reasons which will be detailed later, but
it is still better than doing without any kind of videotaping equipment at all.

In the event classes are held in the daytime, technical help for either
studio or portable TV equipment is usually available on campus. However, scheduling the studio and/or equipment, as well as the technical help can be quite a
problem, particularly if the instructor aspires to hold the classes in a TV

studio-type classroom, if one is available on campus. While some colleges and universities have special classrooms with closed-circuit TV cameras and monitors, and technicians in separate control rooms who operate the equipment by remote control, the competition for the use of such rooms is likely to be fierce. However, by requesting the use of such rooms well in advance of the beginning of the semester, the instructor can sometimes insure that he will be able to teach all or most of his classes in one of these TV classrooms, and, in most cases, will have a trained technician to operate the cameras for him.

The advantages of having instant-replay videotaping equipment available in manual communication classrooms are enormous. The most important of these advantages is the instant feedback it provides the individual student on his performance in fingerspelling and signing: his use of facial expression, emphasis, body movements, pauses, positioning of his hands, size of the "box" in which he executes his signs, the errors of commission or omission he makes, and, in general, every facet of his performance which is visible to others but not normally available to him. In other words, it permits him to see himself as others see him, to compare himself with a correct model--and to take immediate steps to improve that performing image. Whereas <u>without</u> instant-replay videotaping equipment, the instructor attempting to correct faulty techniques in his students has to rely upon his own talents in mimicry in order to show his students what they are doing wrong; <u>with</u> such equipment, he has at his command the ability to show the students <u>exactly</u> what needs correcting, and further, the ability to immediately demonstrate the difference the corrections make in student performance when he retapes the students performing the corrected versions of the same material.

At the same time, the instructor gains extra teaching time, and the students additional benefits in that <u>all</u> members of the class can see what it was that one of their fellows was doing wrong--and even help with the corrections--thereby avoiding making similar mistakes themselves; whereas only the erring student's immediate neighbors may be able to observe specific mistakes in the process being corrected by the instructor.

As a means of combatting the formation of faulty techniques of fingerspelling and signing, videotaping equipment cannot be surpassed. It is far harder to eliminate faulty techniques once they become habitual than it is to prevent their formation in the first place, and with videotaping equipment, the instructor is enabled to stop such developments before they become fixed.

A student who has watched himself pumping his arm like a piston while fingerspelling individual letters; or fingerspelling in front of his face; or making his signs so large that his hands disappear off the edge of the TV monitor screen, or so small that they are hard to understand; or delivering an emotionally loaded sentence with a deadpan expression on his face; or "singing" a song in sign language as if he were reciting the multiplication table, generally needs little in the way of criticism from his instructor or fellow classmates in seeing the error of his ways. He can observe it for himself--and usually spots his own faults far quicker than anyone else (save perhaps the instructor). He can therefore take immediate corrective steps to eliminate the objectional features of his performance--and see the improvement at once when the corrected version is replayed along with the original for comparison purposes.

Ancillary benefits, less apparent but no less real, can be provided the students through use of videotaping equipment. In order to encourage student participation in classroom activities, the professor should ask the students themselves to help evaluate their fellows' performance. To comply with this request, the students must first of all be able to see the performing student --and to understand what the performer has said--before they are able to judge whether or not he said it right. The monitor screen is visible to all, even when the student himself is not, and this means that they can concentrate on understanding the message. This exposes them to constant training in receptive skills. Since they must also be alert to possible errors, they must know how the signs should be executed; where the hands should be positioned for maximum clarity; what the appropriate facial expression should be; and all of the other "rules" governing the use of signs and fingerspelling in manual methods of communicating--all of which the continuous replays on the TV monitor reinforces.

In addition, the vocabularies of signs for each lesson as well as other practice material can be recorded on a permanent tape and the tapes made available to students for review between class sessions--another important reinforcement technique.

Not only is videotaping equipment an excellent training and practice aid, but it can also be utilized for reward purposes by the instructor. As each student "recites" his lines, and is taped, the instructor should replay each performance without comment--then ask the class (as well as the performing student himself) what the best points of that particular performance were. A single beautifully executed sign in an otherwise mediocre or faulty performance can therefore garner a student praise from his fellows (or from the instructor if his fellows did not notice it), thus rewarding the student (and reinforcing the movements resulting in the well-made sign)--and bolstering his self-confidence before his fellows begin dissecting his performance for errors.

Last, but not least, videotaping equipment can be used for the purpose of evaluating the students (especially in intermediate or advanced classes), the course, and the instructor himself. A permanent record can be made of the end-of-course performance of the students, and this can be employed in one of several ways. It can be used to check the amount of forgetting that occurs over a period of time by retaping the students after the lapse of several weeks or months; it can be used as "baseline" performance when students move on to more advanced courses in manual communication in the same institution--and compared with their performance at the end of the second, more advanced course. Or it can be used to compare the progress of students in different manual communication courses at the same level. In any of these, end-performance tapes provide information about the effectiveness of the course, and improvements can then be put into effect where indicated. At the same time, teacher effectiveness can be evaluated by having random class sessions taped in their entirety, and the tapes submitted to veteran manual communication instructors for evaluation of the instructor's techniques. Self-evaluation is also made possible in this way, for the instructor can study the tapes of his teaching and identify areas which need improvement.

It can be seen from the foregoing that the use of videotaping equipment has much to offer both the instructor and the students in manual communication classes. If it is available, it should be requested, and every effort made to insure that permission is forthcoming for its use.

B. Use of Videotape in the Classroom

1. Facilities, Types of Equipment, and Their Uses in Teaching

a. TV studio-classrooms: The ideal location for manual communication classes is a classroom in which studio-type TV cameras, monitors, lighting, and microphone pickups are installed as a permanent part of the classroom equipment. These are sometimes to be found in the education or psychology departments of institutions of higher learning, where they are employed to train students who plan to become teachers, psychologists, or counselors. If the institution also offers a major in the field of television engineering, it will generally not only have such studios but also a supply of experienced television engineers--as well as technicians in the form of upper-class or graduate students who can be available to operate the equipment during manual communication classes as part of their training.

Normally, the engineer or the technician operates studio-type videotaping equipment by remote control from a separate control room, and, depending upon the number of cameras in the classroom, can assist the instructor in a variety of ways by framing on the monitor screen whatever the instructor requests, in any way the instructor may wish it done--including split-screen presentations if more than one camera is available. He can, if the instructor requests, zoom in for medium close-up shots of the student from the waist up; "squeeze" the student by making the framed picture smaller (for correcting tendencies to one-sided signing); raise the framed picture (to force a student signing too low to raise his hands); lower the framed picture (to force a student sign-ing too high to lower his signs); zoom in close so that only the fingerspelling hand of a student is shown (to illustrate errors or tiny superfluous movements of the fingers during fingerspelling); and, in general, tape any activity taking place in the classroom, all by remote control via verbal instructions from the instructor speaking into a microphone hanging from a cord around his neck.

The author has taught in a TV studio-classroom for three years at the Uni-versity of Illinois and wears a lavalier-type microphone on a long cord which leaves her free to move around the classroom and to use her arms. Figure 1 illustrates the arrangement of the TV cameras and equipment, and the seating arrangements in the classroom in which the author has taught. It can be seen from the figure that there are three cameras, and that these cameras were placed so that they could cover every area of the classroom. The main camera, situated in the back of the room, focused on the author-instructor at all times, following her as she moved about the room. Unless the technician was otherwise instructed, the picture from the main camera was always the one shown on the large TV monitor screen, and was visible to all of the students in the room. This meant that even when the instructor moved to the far corners of the room to help individual students correct technical flaws in their fingerspelling

Figure 1

Arrangement of TV cameras and equipment in a classroom-type TV studio used by author in teaching manual communication at the University of Illinois.

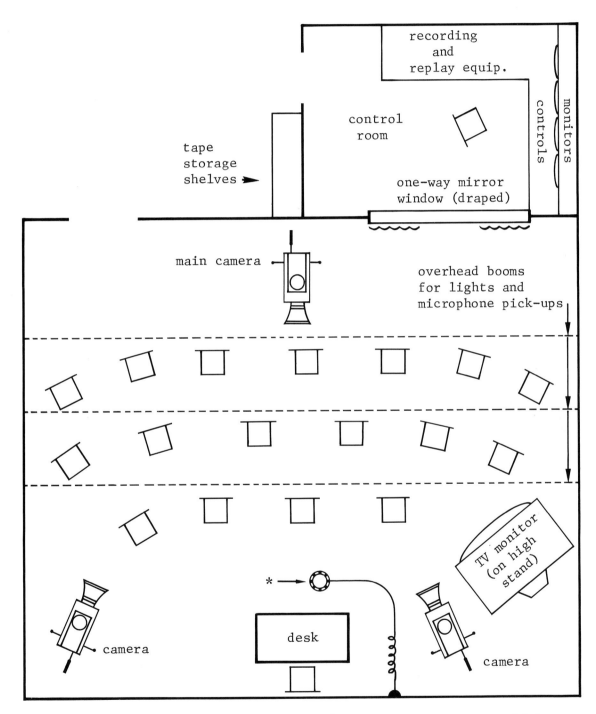

*Necklace (lavalier) microphone with 50' cord for instructor, which permitted instructor to walk around freely, and to have both hands free for use in teaching.

or signing, those students whose direct observation of the remedial instruction was blocked by other students (or by the fact that the instructor had her back to them) could still observe the activity on the TV monitor.

The same TV camera was also employed to record individual student "recitals" when the instructor summoned a student to the front of the room to practice delivering esentences, or to conduct review-type drills of his classmates. The two side cameras in each corner of the front of the room were used to tape individual student performances while they remained in their seats. By means of zoom lenses, individual students could thus be singled out and framed in the monitor so that all members of the class could observe the performance of any given student regardless of where he was sitting in relation to the observers.

Since everything the instructor and students said in the course of a class session was clearly audible to the technician in the control room through a battery of microphones on booms (as well as through the instructor's lavalier microphone), she delivered her instructions to the technician simply by prefacing her instructions with the technician's name, then requesting him to focus upon whatever it was or whomever she had in mind. To assist him in locating the student in question, the instructor would move close to the student and point at him with her finger while, at the same time, requesting that the student raise his hand to help the technician locate him. While the cameras were zooming in on the student, the instructor would give the student brief instructions on what she wished him to do, then, checking to see that the picture framed in the monitor screen was clear and free from blockage by other student heads or bodies, and that the hands and face of the student in question were clearly visible, whe would give him the signal to go ahead.

On occasion, she would give further instructions to the technician over the microphone, such as: "Back up a little bit, please"; or "Can you squeeze this student a little bit--his signs are too large"; or "The picture is a little blurry, can you adjust the focus (or the contrast, etc.)"; or "Give this one a full length frame--she will be moving around a bit in singing a song"; or "Will you come in on the hand alone, please?"; or "I will be asking this student (pointing) to say something to this student over here (pointing), and would like you to be ready to record both what the first student says and the second student's answer immediately afterward. Will you train separate cameras on these two so as to be ready?"; or "Will you split the screen and frame this student in one half, and that student in the other?"

In all cases, the instructor would wait until the picture shown on the monitor was what she requested--a matter of a few seconds--before giving the student(s) the go-ahead signal. This insured that the full performance was captured in detail exactly the way she wished it, and the few moments' delay while the cameras were being panned and focused on the student were nearly always filled with instructions to the student on what he was to do. On occasion, the instructor would find that her instructions had not been understood, and the technician had erred--upon which the instructor would apologize and correct her instructions so as to obtain the desired angle, shot, or picture. All of this was accomplished by means of verbal instructions given in a normal tone of voice, but preceded by the technician's name.

Immediately after the student finished his initial performance, but before making any comments, the instructor would request a replay by saying "Mr. _____, would you replay that please?" She would then ask the class (as well as the performer himself) what they had noted about that particular performance (taking pains to structure her question in such a way as to elicit favorable comments first, and then opening the discussion to constructive criticisms). Whenever possible, the instructor endeavored to see that all criticisms of the performance came from the students themselves, and from their classmates--requesting still another replay of the taped performance if errors were committed which she noted but which the class did not.

In addition, any student noting an error and commenting upon it was required to show the performing student how to do it correctly if he could, with the instructor serving as arbitrator if more than one student attempted to correct the performer--and their versions did not happen to coincide.

The instructor would summarize all criticisms, including her own, and then recall what had been good about it by restating the praise. In the event the student's performance had been so bad that little or nothing was found to praise, the student himself usually knew it before anyone else. In such cases, the author generally resorted to comforting quips such as "Well, you had a nice twinkle in your eye anyway," or a teasing "Wha' hoppen?" "Did you have a fight with your roommate/boyfriend/girlfriend/mother/coach/etc. and are still in a battling mood the way you fought your way through that sentence?"

In using videotape, the instructor will find himself frequently being cast in the role of comforter, for the little ego-boosting deceptions practiced by instructors not having access to videotape equipment--such as lavish praise of mediocre performance in hopes of encouraging a slow student--are simply not available to the instructor employing videotapes. The student can see for himself how atrocious (or how good) his performance was and no amount of insincere flattery is going to soften the impact.

To offset this sometimes traumatic knowledge is the instructor's ability to work with him immediately to improve his performance to the point where even he can see that praise is justified. This can usually be accomplished in a short time by the instructor's judicious application of the balm of humor to jolly him out of his funk; then patiently working with him through several repeat performances until he comes up with one which is worthy of honest praise before the instructor goes on to the next student. It has been the author's experience that this approach has resulted in some of the most unpromising of students developing remarkably good ability in manual methods of communication in a far shorter time than one would expect from observing their performances early in the course.

After criticisms and comments on any particular performance have been summarized, the instructor would require that the student repeat the sentence or passage, incorporate any suggested corrections or modifications, and have him taped during this second performance. The instructor would then request that the technician replay both performances consecutively so that the student and his fellow classmates could all see the improvement resulting from the corrections.

It must be remembered, however, that such versatility in the employment of videotaping equipment depends in a large measure upon the facilities, the type and amount of equipment, and the availability of experienced technicians to operate such equipment.

b. Portable TV equipment: While not as versatile as TV studio-classroom equipment, portable videotaping equipment can be employed in much the same way in classroom teaching of manual communication as studio equipment. The primary difference lies in the fact that the operator of the equipment usually must be inside the classroom--and often happens to be the instructor himself.

Unless the instructor has an assistant who is able to operate both the camera and the replay equipment (see Figure 2), teaching generally must come to a halt while the instructor tends to the camera and replay mechanism. In this case, it is usually more efficient to set the camera up in a fixed spot in the classroom, such as that illustrated in Figure 3, and have each performing student come up to a selected spot in the front of the room to "recite" rather than attempt to tape the student in his seat. This spot can be marked by a chalked X on the floor of the classroom (to avoid having to readjust the camera angles before each student performance), or by the simple device of putting a book, a blackboard eraser, a ruler, or something heavy enough to stay in place and serve as a marker for student position during taping. The instructor then need only to make minor adjustments in the focus and the vertical angle of the camera (to adjust for student height) before proceeding with the taping.

Once the instructor has become familiar with the operation of the camera, he can employ it in much the same way as was described for studio equipment. He can zoom in for close-ups, "squeeze" students into smaller frames, compensate to the right or left (and, by having two students stand close together and filming both of them at once, imitate the split-screen technique the author used to teach conversational manual communication), and so on, the only difference being that the instructor himself, or his assistant, is operating the equipment instead of its being operated by remote control from another room. Some delays are inevitable, to be sure, but the benefits in increased teaching efficiency more than offset the delays.

Other time-saving techniques employed by instructors using portable videotaping equipment include having the students line up for their performances and then taping them one after the other. The location of each taped performance is marked by noting the footage before and after the performance, leaving blank spaces of a few minutes in length on the tapes between each performance by advancing the tape without recording anything on it. (A second, corrected performance can thus be added to the tapes later after each performance has been analyzed and evaluated by the instructor and the class.)

When the initial performances of all students have been taped, the instructor can rewind the tape to the first performance of the first student, replay only that performance, and then stop the camera while the class discusses the performance. After the student has received the feedback on his initial performance, the blank section left on the tape between his performance and that

Figure 2

Arrangement of TV equipment when using portable equipment in a regular classroom <u>with</u> the assistance of a technician.

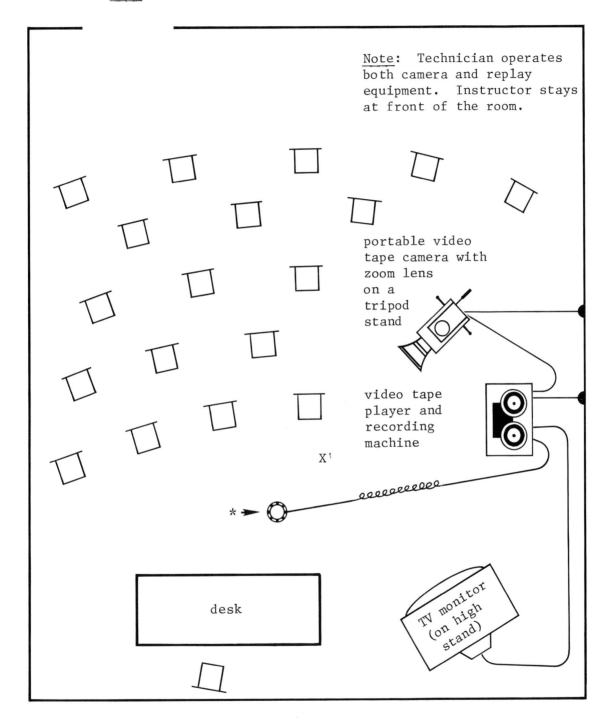

<u>Note</u>: Technician operates both camera and replay equipment. Instructor stays at front of the room.

portable video tape camera with zoom lens on a tripod stand

video tape player and recording machine

desk

TV monitor (on high stand)

*Lavalier microphone with 50' cord.
X marked on floor for positioning of students during performances.

Figure 3

Arrangement of TV equipment when using portable equipment in a regular classroom <u>without</u> the assistance of a technician.

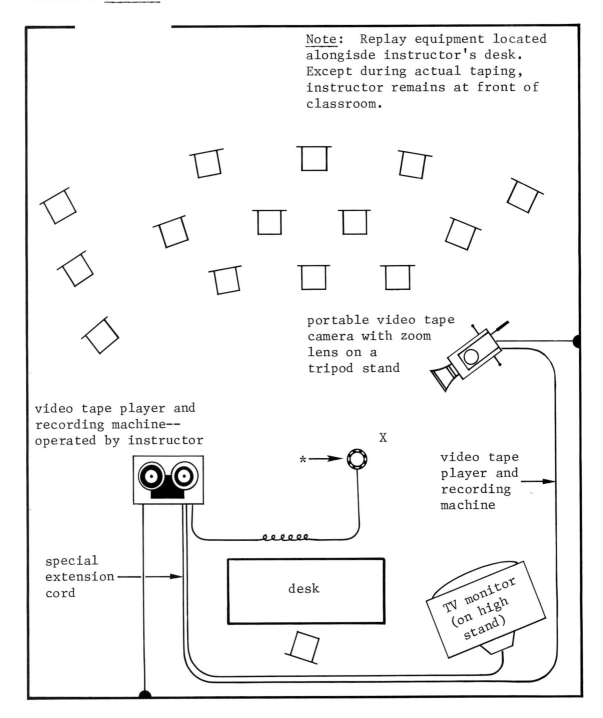

*Lavalier microphone with 50' cord.
X marked position for student performances.

of the next student can be used to tape him while he is performing the amended version.

It is well to allow students time in which to practice the amended version before taping them if this technique is used, for the practice increases the students' chances of a successful second performance.

The instructor can then rewind the tape to the beginning of the student's initial performance, and show both performances consecutively (to illustrate the improvement made by the changes) before going on to the initial performance of the next student.

If at all possible, the instructor should try to obtain a technician who can operate the camera and replay equipment so that the instructor is free to concentrate upon his teaching. (Once in a while, a student will be found in the class who has experience in operating the type of equipment the instructor is using--in which case the student can sometimes be used to assist. However, the instructor still must know how to operate the equipment, for the student himself must be taped on occasion.) Sometimes, also, the instructor is provided with a teaching assistant, particularly if the class is large, and this assistant can often be trained to operate the equipment, thus relieving the instructor of the responsibility.

2. Materials

In planning for the use of videotaping equipment, the instructor should figure on about one hour of taping time per reel of videotape. If he must purchase his own tapes, or must recommend the purchase of tapes to the administrators of the program in which he is teaching, he should plan on a minimum of three reels, at a cost of from $30.00 to $60.00 per reel, depending upon the size of the tape. Half-inch tape is the cheapest, but suffers from the handicap of limited utility, since instructors generally purchase portable videotaping equipment which takes tape of one inch or larger. Half-inch tapes, therefore, can be used and shown only on the comparatively rare half-inch equipment. The most expensive tape is that used on the studio-type videotaping equipment, and is usually one and one-quarter to two inches in width. However, tapes are reusable, so it is only the initial purchase that is likely to be costly. Subsequent purchases are needed only to replace badly damaged or worn-out tapes, a situation which is not likely to arise frequently if reasonable care is exercised in handling.

Three reels are recommended, for the following purposes:

1st reel: Working tape--the tape the instructor uses in his classroom work. Since previously taped material is automatically erased when new material is recorded on the same section of the tape, the instructor can use and reuse the same tape over and over.

2nd reel: Permanent record tape--on this tape, the instructor will want to permanently record either the essentials of each lesson for reviewing purposes by the students (as in beginning classes in manual communication), or, in the case of the intermediate/advanced/interpreting class, the baseline level of performance of his students at the beginning of the semester, which can then be compared with the performance recorded at the end of the semester if blank sections are left on the tape between student performances.

3rd reel: This tape can either be reserved as a spare, or used for permanent recording purposes if it is desired that permanent records be made of both the lesson essentials (for review) and student performances at the beginning and end of the course.

A word of caution, however: Tapes should be rotated between semesters to equalize the wear and tear, for the working tape will be subject to far more handling and usage than the other two. Unless the instructor wishes to re-tape the lesson essentials each semester, or changes the content of his lessons radically, it is recommended that the tapes containing the lesson essentials (vocabulary of signs, and so on) be reserved while the other two tapes are rotated each semester.

3. Techniques for Using Videotaping Equipment
    in Remediation of Errors

There are numerous errors in fingerspelling and signing that students can make which, if not corrected immediately, can become habitual. The section that follows deals with the more common of these, and offers techniques for the use of videotaping equipment in combating these errors and preventing their becoming habitual stylistic aberrations.

a. Use of videotaping equipment in remediation of faulty fingerspelling: Clear, smooth fingerspelling, with no noticeable extraneous movements of the fingers, hand, or arms should be the goal. In addition, the hand should be positioned comfortably in front of the shoulder for maximum visibility--and the words being fingerspelled should be pronounced as words (not as individual letters).[1] The eye should be able to concentrate upon the lips, with the peripheral vision catching the fingerspelling on the hand--which should be close enough to the lips for this to be accomplished without undue strain.

(1) Errors in hand-position: The instructor should develop an automatic habit of checking the hand-positions of his students both during his classroom teaching and when they are reciting on videotape. This is especially important if his class is at all sizable, for, in their efforts to make their hands visible to the instructor in the front of the room, some students may automatically raise their hands higher than normal, or shift them from one side to the other from the correct position in order that the instructor can see their hands--and, without realizing it, develop the habit of doing all of their fingerspelling from this deviant position. In addition, the instructor may unconsciously contribute to faulty hand-positioning in his students his own efforts to make his hand visible to students in

_____

[1] See section on fingerspelling (vocalization drills) for remediation of the "alphabetizing" habit, as well as later in this chapter.

the back of the room if he raises his hand above the normal position. A raised platform is recommended when the class is large. (The instructor should make sure, by holding his hand up in the proper position and asking, that all students can see his hand without his having to raise it, and instruct those who cannot to shift their chairs until they can. He should also make sure that all students are positioned in such a way that he can see their hands without their having to shift them out of the proper position in relation to their bodies.)

If despite instructions and corrections during classroom work faulty hand-positions in height or distance from the body are shown by individual students, the students should be taped fingerspelling a short sentence, full-face to the camera if the error is in the vertical-horizontal plane positioning, or profile (or 3/4 angle) if the error is in the front-to-rear plane (such as the hand held awkwardly high and back alongside the ear, or too low and too far forward).

The first taping should be made without the student watching himself in the monitor (the instructor can stand near the camera for full-face shots, so that the student will have someone to whom he can direct his spelling). He should then be shown how he appears, and the class encouraged to help with the criticism. He should repeat the performance--this time watching himself in the monitor and making corrections. To help fixate this corrected hand-position, the instructor can have the student lower his hand, then raise it to the proper position and spell a word or two several times until he can raise his hand to the proper position without any hesitation.

(2) Errors in palm direction or hand angle: By videotaping student performance in spelling a few words, little is needed in correcting faulty palm direction or angle of the hand from the wrist. The student can see for himself that unless his palm faces forward, his fingerspelling is hard to read. A profile shot of the student's hand during fingerspelling is usually sufficient to correct excessive angling of the hand from the wrist, especially if the instructor stands alongside the monitor and demonstrates with his own hand in profile the correct angle (or straight line) formed by hand and wrist.

(3) Fingerspelling in front of the face: Most easily corrected of all is the error of fingerspelling in front of the face. If this is captured on videotape, the fingerspelling generally can barely be made out against the background of the face--and the student himself will instantly correct the faulty position if allowed to watch himself during his performance.

It would be well to note at this point that the instructor should watch for background problems created by students' clothing--and point out to them how important a good background is to clear reading of fingerspelling and signs. Black and white videotape lends added emphasis to this, for the hands are hard to see against figured or "busy" backgrounds in the form of prints, stripes, or plaids worn by the students. The same applies to heavy beards and moustaches on male students which make lipreading difficult (as the instructor can easily demonstrate by having the student taped while silently mouthing a few words), or long hair on female students, which must constantly be brushed back from the face or the head tossed frequently, both of which can and <u>will</u> be mistaken for part of what the student is saying.

(4) <u>"Pumping" errors</u>: One of the most common errors noted among beginning students (and among some fairly advanced students as well) is the error of "pumping," or pushing the hand forward with each fingerspelled letter. It is also one of the most difficult to eradicate if allowed to continue beyond the learning of the first few letters of the manual alphabet.

The instructor, therefore, should be extremely quick to note this tendency developing in any of his students and move to correct it immediately. The correction entails instructing the student to use his <u>other</u> hand to hold his fingerspelling hand steady if he cannot do it otherwise (or even to have a neighboring student hold the wrist of the fingerspelling student's hand); and using videotape to show the student how peculiar the pumping of his hand appears, and how it hampers the understanding of his fingerspelling.

It has been the experience of the author that this tendency to "pumping" is likely to recur in any student showing such a tendency at the beginning of the course, and remediation is a recurring need for those students throughout the first several weeks of the course, and perhaps even later.

(5) <u>Superfluous movements of the fingers during fingerspelling</u>: Most commonly seen superfluous movements of the fingers during fingerspelling are those when the student transits from A to T, A to N, and A to M. There will be an excessive raising of the fingers from the A to the next letter, which results in the AT looking something like ALT, the AN looking like AUN, and the AM looking like AWM. This is easily perceptible by students when the fingerspelling of the erring student is taped and replayed. The instructor can then show him how to practice to help correct these particular errors by holding a flat sheet of paper, cardboard, or a book on top of his knuckles (but extending forward a few inches), and spelling AT, AN, AM, and AS. If his fingers move too far upward between A and the next letter, the paper, cardboard, or book will jump upward noticeably--whereas if he does it correctly, there is little perceptible upward movement of whatever he is holding on top of his hand.

There are other superfluous movements the students can make, but these are usually amenable to correction once the student has been shown, via videotape, what the unnecessary movements are that he is inserting into his fingerspelling and is shown by the instructor how to correct them.

(6) <u>Mouthing the individual letters being fingerspelled instead of the complete word ("alphabetizing")</u>: Another common habit among beginners as well as among some veterans who should know better, is that of "alphabetizing," or, pronouncing each individual letter being fingerspelled instead of saying the complete word, usually when the lip movements are <u>not</u> accompanied by voice. It is also one of the most exasperating habits from the standpoint of lipreading deaf people, particularly if the deaf people

are typical in that they focus their eyes on the lips and depend upon
peripheral vision to capture the signs and fingerspelling. For example,
"P..s..y..c..h..o..l..o..g..y," when all letters are individually pronounced, is vastly more difficult to understand than the word "psychology,"
when one is attempting to use lipreading to reinforce one's comprehension
of what is being fingerspelled.

Remediation of the alphabetizing habit consists of preventing its development by teaching and drilling the students from the very beginning
to synchronize their fingerspelling with the vocalization of the very first
words they learn to fingerspell. Drills incorporating such synchronization
of fingerspelling and vocal pronunciation should be part and parcel of every
fingerspelling drill conducted by the instructor.

An effective way for the instructor to utilize videotape in combating
alphabetizing (apart from showing the students who make this type of mistake how they appear on TV) is for the instructor to have himself taped
while fingerspelling a short, simple word such as WIDE several times, during which he mouths each individual letter. He then can have the tape replayed in class, and, covering his hand on the monitor with a sheet of paper,
promise an A for the course to any student in the class who can figure out
what he is saying. (The author has employed this several times, and has yet
to give an A for this particular task.) None will understand, so he can then
remove the covering paper and, having the tape replayed again, instruct his
students to focus their eyes on his lips and try and catch what is said on
his fingers without looking at his hand. An occasional student may catch it
then, but normally most of them will still not be able to understand the word
(unless they cheat and look at his hand). The instructor can then fingerspell
the word for the class, this time mouthing the word "wide" silently. At this
point a large part of the class will finally catch the word. Further admonitions are usually unnecessary (although the error will likely come up from
time to time as students forget while concentrating on spelling difficult
words later in the course). When this happens, the instructor should wait
for someone in the class to notice and call it to the performing student's
attention during the dissection of the student's performance afterward. If
no one notices, the instructor can prod them.

(7) Failing to mouth words silently while fingerspelling (or signing):
This, also, is a common error, and many old-time interpreters are as guilty
of this as are beginners. It is remedied easily by the instructor's holding
a sheet of paper over the performing student's hands on the monitor during
the replay, and then asking the class what the student said. Naturally, no
one will know, and the students are thereby alerted to watch for this error
in both their own and their fellows' performances.

(8) Lack of facial expression while fingerspelling: Although more likely
to be a problem in teaching the language of signs than in fingerspelling, the
current increase in the acceptability of fingerspelling in teaching deaf children makes it important that facial expressiveness be taught in fingerspelling
as well as in the language of signs. Deadpan deliveries of emotionally loaded
fingerspelled sentences are easily seen when such deliveries are recorded on
tape.

Remediation consists of calling it to the student's attention (or seeing to it that the class does), and helping the student toward using facial expressions as an assist to understanding. The former can be accomplished by either covering the fingerspelling hand on the monitor during replay and asking the class what kind of a mood the student appeared to be in; or by letting the other students (if they have had previous experience with the correction of deadpan expressions) catch the error and call it to the performer's attention. Helping the student develop appropriate facial expressiveness can be accomplished in many ways. He can be directed to say the sentence aloud (without fingerspelling), lending as much emotion as is called for by the sentence, then instructed to repeat it exactly the same way--while coordinating it with his fingerspelling. If the student still has trouble, he can be instructed to talk to another student as if he were feeling the emotions implied in the sentence --and the other student instructed to respond in kind--with both performances being taped.

The instructor himself can compose a sentence on the spot which would normally elicit as a response the sentence the student is attempting to execute--and force a reaction from the student by delivering his own sentence in a forceful, expressive manner so that the student will respond in kind.

Still another technique is to have a student attempt to silently convey an emotionally loaded message at first without using his hands or speech, but using facial expression and body movements; then, in consecutive steps, adding silent speech, then fingerspelling the "body English" of the message.

b. _Use of videotaping equipment in correcting errors in signing_: Many of the techniques described for correcting errors in fingerspelling are basically the same as those used in correcting errors in delivery in the language of signs. The basic approach is identical--that of taping the student during his performance, replaying the tape so that the performing student and his fellows can analyze the performance for its strengths and weaknesses, retaping him during performance of a corrected version of the same passage, then showing both performances consecutively so that the differences can be observed. (If time is limited, only the corrected version can be replayed--but both performances should be shown occasionally, for valuable learning is to be obtained by this demonstration of immediate improvement resulting from corrections.) While the basic technique of using videotape to assist learning is the same for both fingerspelling and signing, there are certain common errors peculiar to the language of signs for which the instructor should be alert. These are listed below, along with suggested remedial treatment utilizing videotape equipment. Before listing the errors, however, it would be well to list the criteria against which the instructor and the students should measure any student's performance.

First, the signs should, if the passage is conversational in tone, stay within a signing "box" which is roughly delineated by the top of the head, the waist, and the span marked by the breadth of the shoulders. For clarity, the signs should fill this box--i.e., be large enough so that a sign which moves in any direction should either begin or end near the outer limits of the box, or both.

If the passage is a poem or a song, or "platform" in nature, the outer limits of the box should be increased in size from six to eight inches on each of the four dimensions, and the signs should be enlarged proportionately.

Second, there should be no hesitation between signs. The delivery should be smooth, with transition from one sign to another accomplished without jerkiness or pauses of undue length (except as required by the sentence context), with the hands generally neither too high nor too low.

Third, the signs should be executed crisply and definitely, with no slurriness or indefiniteness unless the passage in question calls for a "drawling" delivery.

Fourth, the facial expression should be appropriate to the mood implicit in the passage being signed; and the amount of emphasis or force, speed, and vigor with which the signed passage is delivered should be appropriate to the context of the passage.

Fifth, the words being signed and fingerspelled should, whenever possible, be mouthed silently and simultaneously with the signing and fingerspelling of the same words on the hands.

Finally, if fingerspelled words are intermixed with signed words, the fingerspelling hand should be correctly positioned and the fingerspelling crisply executed as was described earlier.

4. Areas in which to Watch for Errors in the Language of Signs,
    and Use of Videotape in Correcting such Errors

   (1) Errors in positioning the hands relative to the body: There are four errors in hand-position relative to the trunk that students commonly make. These are: (1) signs executed too high relative to the body; (2) signs executed too low relative to the body; (3) signs executed too far from the body; and (4) signs executed too close to the body. They may occur by themselves, or in combination--usually too high and too far from the body, or too low and too close to the body. Normally, the student signing too high or too low will be able to see this immediately when his performance is replayed on videotape (or have it called to his attention by his fellow students and/or the instructor). He may then be able to correct the error without further ado, but if he has difficulty in accomplishing this, or shows a tendency to slip back into this habit despite verbal corrections, the instructor can employ a variety of technical tricks to combat this tendency.

   (a) Too high[1]: In the student who executes his signs too high--that is, one who makes almost all of his signs above a line running through

---

[1]Note: These flaws can be corrected in the way described even when TV equipment is not used.

the middle of the chest--there is usually a companion tendency to hold the elbows _away_ from the body a good three inches or more. This is most easily and simply combated by requiring the student to hold a folded sheet of stiff paper in each of his armpits by arm pressure alone, and by requesting that the framed picture on the TV monitor be lowered until the student's head is at the top edge of the screen and his waist at the bottom, then requiring him to _center_ his signing in the middle. He is thus forced to hold his elbows closer to his body, and his signs are thereby lowered. At the same time, since his elbows are restricted in their movement due to the necessity of keeping the papers in his armpits in place, this prevents his executing his signs too far from his body as well.

Repeated practice in this manner will usually counteract the tendency toward too high signing, but care should be taken to discontinue it when the need is past, in case the opposite habit be developed of keeping the elbows rigidly at the sides at all times, resulting in a cramped-appearing delivery.

(b) _Too low_[1]: Probably the most effective way of counteracting a tendency toward signing too low--i.e., executing most of the signs below a line running through the middle of the chest--is to place the student behind a podium (or holding a sheet of paper in front of the lower half of his torso), thereby forcing him to raise his hands in order for his signs to be seen, and raising the TV monitor picture so that the lower edge of the picture is about three inches _above_ the student's waist.

If the tendency toward too-low signing is accompanied by the hands being too close to the body, additional refinements can be employed to force the hands forward and away from the body. One is to have a supply of spring-type clothespins on hand, several of which can be pinned down the front of the chest so that they stick out and interfere with the signing unless the hands are held far enough away from the body to clear them (or pinned under the arms at the waistline if the problem lies in the elbows being held too close to the body--or pinned _both_ along the chest and under the arms at the waist). Another is to borrow a small shoulderstrap purse from one of the female students, and hand it by its strap around the performing student's neck so that the purse itself interferes with the signs unless they are made far enough in front of the body to clear it. Other objects can be employed in much the same way, with the criterion being that it be about two or three inches in thickness, and capable of being attached in some way to the student at chest level and/or at the waistline under the arms.

(c) _Too far from the body, or too close to the body_: The remediation for these errors is different from that described for too-high or too-low signing only in that when showing the student what he is doing wrong,

---

[1]_Note:_ These flaws can be corrected in the way described even when TV equipment is not used.

it is best that the instructor arrange for the student to be taped in profile during his performance. Other than this, the remediation is the same as for too-high or too-low signing, since errors in distance from the body generally are accompanied by errors in vertical positioning.

(2) Errors in size of signs: There are two errors students can make relative to the size of the signs: too large and too small. In the case of too large signing, the signs are inappropriately oversized, giving a windmill effect to the performance, and, since the hands have a longer distance to travel in returning from the end position of one sign to the beginning position of the next, the speed of the return journey of the hand tends to make the hand overtravel, resulting in a "bounce" at the beginning of each sign.

In the small signing the signs are confined within a "box" far too small, resulting in a cramped, hard-to-read delivery--or giving the impression that the signer is a very timid person. In some cases, a companion habit will be noted where the head will be ducked down slightly to meet the hand coming up for signs made up and around the head or forehead. Remediation of both of these faults involved using the videotaping equipment to "squeeze" the subjects by framing them (on the monitor screen) in such a way that the top of the picture is level with the tops of their heads, and the bottom of the picture is level with their waistlines, or even smaller, depending upon the amount of correction needed. (The normal picture would frame the student from about two inches above his head to about two inches below his waistline, and be slightly skewed to the student's right in the case of a right-handed student, and slightly to the left in the case of a left-handed student--to allow for signs which flow from center front out to the right or left as the case may be.) Remediation specific to the two faults is:

(a) Too large signs: After "squeezing" the student, direct the student to watch himself on the monitor (he should be facing the camera with the monitor slightly to one side of the camera) and to keep his hands within the picture. If the beginning "bounce" is still noticeable despite this squeezing, direct the student to hold the end position of each sign until he is certain he knows the next sign, then go directly from the end position of the first sign to the beginning position of the next. This usually results in the elimination of both overlarge signs and bounciness.

(b) Too small signs: After "squeezing" as for overlarge signing, direct the student to watch himself on the monitor, and make sure that his hands "hit" the edges of the screen on signs that go away from center front, and that his signs nearly fill the screen. If this is unsuccessful, enlarge the picture framed by an inch or two, and repeat the instructions to "hit" the edge of the picture. It may take considerable repetition, to the point of forcing the student to make his signs overlarge for a while, before this tendency can be corrected. Also helpful are the techniques described for remediation of too low and too close signing.

In both too large and too small signing, however, the instructor should be aware of the need for the student to develop <u>tactile and kinesthetic cues</u> as well as visual cues, which tell him automatically that his signing is of appropriate size. This is best accomplished by a three-stage remediation treatment:

1. To reduce the multiplicity of factors engaging the student's attention, have him work on <u>each</u> sign in his sentence while watching himself on the monitor until each is appropriately sized, before requiring him to combine the signs in a sentence.

2. Then have him monitor himself on TV while delivering the sentence in total (repeating if necessary until he gets it right).

3. Finally, with student instructed <u>not</u> to watch himself on the monitor, have him repeat the sentence again as a check on whether or not his perception of the size of his signing "box" has changed.

If necessary, stages 2 and 3 should be repeated until it is evident that he has internalized the tactile, kinesthetic, and visual cues associated with the correct signing size.

(3) <u>Errors in rhythm of delivery</u>: Most common error in rhythm, especially in beginning students, is staccato signing. Caused in part by the student's inability to rapidly recall each of the signs required for a given sentence or passage, it can become habitual if not corrected early.

(a) <u>Staccato signing</u>: Videotaping usually makes it fairly easy to correct this habit, for once the student sees for himself how choppy his delivery is, he knows the importance of correcting this error and will work toward achieving smoothness. Helpful to him are instructions to hold the end position of each sign until he is sure of the next sign, then to move his hands directly into the beginning position of the next sign. (A variation of staccato signing is <u>arhythmic</u> signing--where some signs are executed smoothly and consecutively, while other signs in the same performance are delivered jerkily or out of position. This is generally attributable only to inexperience--some signs will be remembered more readily than others--and will usually disappear as the student gains in skill. Such deviations, however, are good for training the other students in catching small errors in performance or style, and should be duly noted during discussions of the performances.)

(b) <u>"Metronome" signing</u>: A different type of error in rhythm, usually correctable during training of students in using expression and emphasis, is that of "metronome" signing. In this, the student may execute each sign clearly, crisply, and smoothly, but execute each sign so evenly spaced in time as to give one the impression he is signing in time to the clicking of a metronome. As a result, there is no expressiveness to the delivery--words, clauses, phrases, and sentences all run together in a sing-song monotony. While this is to be preferred to staccato or arhythmic signing, it limits the student's ability to get meaning and mood across. Since this is usually a companion habit to expressionless signing, the remediation will be discussed when the latter is described.

(c) <u>Dropping the hands between signs</u>: Another common error made by students is that of dropping the hands slightly between each sign, which also gives a sing-song or staccato effect. Like staccato signing, this is correctable by instructing the student to hold the end position of each sign until the next one is clearly visualized, then moving the hands directly into the beginning position of the next sign.

(4) <u>Facial expressions</u>: Three general categories of errors in use of facial expression (and body movements) can be identified: (1) expression-less deliveries (deadpan signing); (2) inappropriate facial expressions; and (3) overexaggerated facial expressions (often accompanied by exaggerated mouthing of the words being signed and/or fingerspelled as well). It is these flaws that lend themselves most readily to correction by using videotaping equipment, for not only can the student himself see the discrepancy between what he is saying on his hands and what he seems to be saying with his face, but also it is the one fault most likely to be picked up by his fellow students as they attempt to understand what he is saying. If they have to strain (as they usually do at the beginning) to understand what he is saying on his hands, they will automatically search for additional clues in his face and lips. Not finding the clues they are seeking, they jump on their hapless fellow student for not providing same, or for misleading them into thinking he is saying something else--or for assaulting their sense of decorum with his grotesque grimaces. Once the students are aware of the fact that part of the understanding of what is said in the language of signs lies in the reading of facial expressions, body movements, and lip movements, and have it driven home to them in the difficulties they, personally, encounter in understanding someone who does not employ such aids to comprehension, they are quick to give the offending student negative feedback whenever they spot this particular type of error.

Remediation consists of helping the student toward development of appropriate facial expressions, use of emphasis, pauses, bodily gestures and movements, and this can be accomplished by requiring students to practice the <u>oral</u> rendition of a variety of emotionally loaded sentences, using the tone and inflection which normally is required in speech, and then synchronizing this with their signing. An additional technique for training in expressiveness is to have students attempt to convey ideas, concepts, and moods by facial expression alone; then by facial expression and lip movements together; and then by facial expression, lip movements, <u>and</u> signing-- with pauses inserted in the signed and fingerspelled sentences where they would naturally occur if the sentences had been spoken aloud. All of these should be videotaped and played back for the performing student so that he may assess his own performance while his fellow students are doing so.

Also effective is the tactic of, during replay of the performance on the TV monitor, covering up the signing hands of the student and having the class concentrate upon watching the performer's face. This is particularly effective in the case of exaggerated facial expressions or lip movements, for the grimacing to be seen then is seldom comforting to the ego of the student guilty of this habit--who may have performed admirably otherwise.

In conclusion, videotaping equipment can be used in an extremely effective manner as both a teaching aid and as a remediation device. It must be remembered, however, that many of the techniques described in the foregoing sections can be applied to teaching manual communication <u>without</u> videotaping equipment. However, it is not possible to employ such versatile and helpful learning aids as immediate feedback for the student himself, nor the more involved techniques of "framing" to correct flaws in hand-positions, size and direction of signs, and so on. Regardless, it is hoped that the foregoing will be of help to those who have access to videotaping equipment as well as those who do not.

C. <u>Other Visual Aids</u>

Other visual aids which can be employed in classroom teaching of manual communication include overhead projectors and transparencies, films, word and number games which can be adapted for use as visual aids, and the instructor himself.

1. Overhead Projectors and Transparencies

Overhead projectors and transparencies are excellent visual aids in several ways to the instructor in a class in manual communication. The instructor can prepare ahead of time such transparencies as:

a. Practice sentences, which can be uncovered one at a time, and students selected to "recite" the sentence for his fellows' evaluation of his performance of the projected sentence.

b. Examples of the language used by deaf persons, to illustrate the grammatical peculiarities which are reflected in the language of signs.

c. Words or sentences which were in a test, which can be shown after the test for class discussion of mistakes, and so on.

d. Pictures illustrating some facet of daily living, which can be used to teach the signs for all the items in the picture.

The instructor can also keep on hand some blank transparencies and a grease pencil for on-the-spot illustrations of, for instance, the difference between how a sentence is written or spoken, and how it is signed and fingerspelled; or for pertinent instructions to the class which otherwise would have to be written on the blackboard; or for writing down as they occur to the students and the instructor different sentences illustrating the different concepts of a word which, depending upon sentence content, influence the signs to be used for that word (e.g., "run" in "Run to catch a bus" is signed differently than the same word in "a run in your stocking"); and, in general, to use the overhead projector and transparencies as a substitute for a blackboard. The instructor can face the class at all times; he will not have to tire his arm writing on the blackboard, and will not have to pass around a single copy of material which would otherwise have to be duplicated in some way or another. The time thus saved in eliminating essential-but-time-consuming physical activity not connected with actual teaching can be used to better advantage, while, at the same time, conserving materials as well as enabling the instructor to spend more time in direct observation of his students, their reactions, and their performance.

2. Films

Films, particularly those giving instruction in fingerspelling, can be of great help to the instructor. Students can practice receptive fingerspelling between classes if such films and projectors are available--either in a fixed location available to all students, or available on a home-loan basis. In addition, if the films are those which include drills in letter groups, the instructor can refer his students to particular reels providing practice in specific letter groups when test scores show that individual students persistently miss words containing these letter groups. Also helpful are short documentary films dealing with various aspects of deafness which will be of general interest to students.

3. Games

a. _Password_: A game popular for a number of years on television, and generally available in kit form in toy shops and department stores, Password involves attempting to guess a certain _key word_ from one-word clues provided by a partner-player before opposing players can guess it. Points are awarded to the team whose receiver-player successfully guesses the key word, with the number of points determined by the number of trials (or clue words) it was necessary to provide before the key word was successfully guessed.

Adapting Password for use in manual communication classes: It can be seen that a word game such as Password is admirably suited for use in fingerspelling practice. Not only are the students forced to practice fingerspelling by word clues and responses, but they are also forced to read fingerspelled word clues on the hands of all of the other players if, as receivers, they are to have a chance at guessing the key words. In addition, the students will soon find that spelling slowly to help their own partner will _also_ help the opposing teams--so they quickly learn to spell faster, at least to the upper limits of their partners' ability to read fingerspelling in an effort to join the ability of the opposition to read their word clues. If their fingerspelling is unclear, they hear about it instantly from the other players, who cannot understand the clue word they are trying to give their partners.

More important, in their concentration on winning the _game_, the players begin to forget the fact that they are _using their hands_ to do something they would normally use their _voices_ to do. In short, their attention and concentration shifts from what they are doing with their hands and fingers--i.e., the method they are using--to the _message_ they are trying to send or to receive. (As a result, they tend to be impatient with anything that gets in the way of comprehension, such as faulty fingerspelling techniques or errors, and their corrections/criticisms of their fellows are often far more effective and lasting than those of the instructor of the class.) This shift is an important factor in the ability to develop fluency in manual communications.

In view of the fact that the hands of all players must be clearly visible to all other players if each player is to know what has been used in the game in the way of clue words and responses, it is recommended that Password games be conducted with just two teams to a game. (The number of games going on at the same time would be a function of the number of students in the class.)

The instructor who wishes to employ Password as a learning device to help his students has two choices available to him in the way of materials for the game. He can purchase sufficient numbers of Password game kits to provide one kit to every four students in his class--or he can construct his own game kits. If he uses the ready-made kits, which sell for approximately $3.00 each (1971), a large class where four or more kits would be needed will make this an expensive alternative. On the other hand, the words in the commercial kits provide a wide variety of words for which clue words must be found and fingerspelled--and this helps the process whereby the student ceases to concentrate upon the mechanics of fingerspelling per se and shifts his attention to the concepts and meanings of the words being transmitted. The importance of this shift in attention cannot be overemphasized, for the sooner a student begins to concentrate upon what he is saying and forgets how he is saying it, the sooner he will begin to feel natural in using manual methods of communicating, and the sooner he will begin to develop fluency in this method. In any event, the instructor should purchase one Password game kit so he can familiarize himself with the rules of the game.

If the instructor constructs his own Password game kits, he can utilize the master vocabulary, letter grouping, and practice word lists, and thereby insure that the words used in the games will be those with which the students have become familiar. Construction of the game kits is simple. Six words can be typed or printed by hand on each of a deck of 3 x 5 cards, and six different words can be printed on another deck of 3 x 5 cards. The two decks together constitute sufficient material for a single class session in which Password is played. One deck (all with identical words on the cards) would be distributed among the senders, and the other deck (in which the words, while identical among cards within the deck, are different from those printed on the other deck) distributed among the receivers (for when they, in turn, become senders).

The instructor can prepare several such two-deck game kits, and number them so that when one kit has been used, it can be retired for the next semester's classes and a new one used.

Since the players concentrate upon only one key word at a time, six-word cards are usually sufficient for one game. However, some players will be extraordinarily fast and others will be slower, so it is a good idea for the instructor to keep a few extra cards on hand on which different words than those in the original decks are printed. These extra cards can be given those players who finish their game well in advance of the scheduled time, and would otherwise have to sit around waiting for the other teams to finish. As an alternative, the instructor can, if he wishes, pit the groups of players in all of the separate games against each other--and stop the play when one group of players gets through their twelve words before any other group does so. The latter alternative often encourages faster play (and thereby faster fingerspelling) as the groups compete to see who can get through their list first.

The procedure involved in playing Password in manual communication classes is identical to that described for regular Password, the only difference being that fingerspelling is substituted for verbal communication.

Note: The decks of instructor-prepared Password cards can also be used as drill cards for single signs in a fast "spelling bee" game in which players are divided into two equal numbered teams, and the word on the card fingerspelled (or signed) rapidly by "captains" (chosen one from each side), with each player on each captain's team having a chance to sign (or fingerspell) the word back, a different word given to each player in turn. Each unsuccessful try causes a player to be "out" (the instructor being referee), with the winning team being the one which gets through their deck first with the least number of dropouts due to errors. (The odd player can substitute for the instructor as referee if an odd number of students is present.)

b. Bingo: Bingo is a game which can be played by any number of people. Essentially, it involves random drawing (from a drum or basket) of a ball, a disc, or a block upon which a number is printed. This number is announced to the players, who have in front of them a card (or two) upon which randomly selected numbers have been printed in squares. If the number which was drawn appears on the card of a player, he covers that number with a circlet of cardboard, a bean, or whatever he has been provided with in the way of covering markers. The objective is to cover with the markers all of the numbers in a given row or column, or the diagonal across the center of the card, before any other player does so. When this has been accomplished, the player yells "Bingo!," and the game ends.

Some versions of Bingo have pictures instead of numbers on the cards, and on the balls/discs/blocks in the drum or basket as well. These are usually sold in specialty shops which cater to people wishing unusual games for baby showers, bridal showers, and the like. If they can be located, they are very effective in providing practice once students have been taught the signs for the objects pictured on the cards.

The most widely available version of Bingo, however, is the game in which twenty-five numbers are divided into squares on the Bingo cards, with five rows, five columns. Each column is headed by a single letter, which in combination with the others, spells B I N G O. Normally, also, there are no numbers larger than two digits, with 99 being the highest number in the game.

Adapting Bingo for use in manual communication classes: As a means of drilling students in recognizing and using numbers, a Bingo game cannot be surpassed. After numbers have been taught, they can be firmly fixed in the repertoire of the class by the introduction of Bingo. Since there is a little bit of a gambler in everyone, Bingo is usually very popular with students, who try very hard to learn the numbers in order to be able to compete.

The instructor should be aware that he, personally, may encounter some raised eyebrows and/or startled looks from his colleagues as he carries his

Bingo game to and from the classroom, particularly if his classes are held in an educational institution. Bingo has long been associated with gambling, which is illegal in most states, and school administrators tend to become understandably nervous if one of their instructors appears to be flouting the law--especially when the instructor is being paid to teach, not conduct gambling games on school time. In addition, if he leaves his classroom door open during sessions when the Bingo game is being played, the instructor had best be prepared for suddenly galvanized attention as casual passers-by glance into the room and recognize the Bingo game. He will have a fascinated audience standing outside his doorway until the observers have satisfied their curiosity about what is going on in his silent classroom. It would therefore be best to carry the game to class in a paper bag or briefcase, and keep the classroom door closed during the game.

To conduct the game, the instructor simply selects one student to act as "caller" of the numbers (or the signs if the picture version of the game is employed), with a different student calling each game. (Only the caller gets practice in performing the numbers, so the instructor should attempt to see that each student in the class gets a chance to call a game.) He then should, depending upon the level of proficiency his class has achieved in numbers, instruct the caller to preface each number with a B, I, N, G, or O (usually given on the disc or ball drawn from the hopper), hold the letter for a few moments, and then give the number to be called. He should then repeat it until all students have recognized the number (the number of repetitions necessary will decline steadily during the game itself, as well as over the weeks of the course). However, the student should not, at any time, repeat the number verbally, even if after several repetitions a few of his classmates still have not recognized the number. Nor should the instructor permit any of the other students to help each other verbally.

At first, the Bingo game can be played exactly as instructed in the printed rules accompanying each game kit. In other words, all of the numbers would be under 100. This, of course, means that the students will not receive practice in numbers above 100, so, after the students have become adept at numbers under 100, the instructor can introduce modifications to the game to afford practice in the 100s, 1,000s, and higher. Table 1 illustrates the levels of complexity the instructor can add to the game by imposing additional requirements.

It can be seen, therefore, that the instructor can employ regular Bingo games to provide practice not only in the numbers included in the game kits, but also in numbers not provided. Once the basic numbers have been learned and practiced, the instructor can then teach how to use the numbers in dates, in giving the time of the day, in giving house numbers of street addresses, and so forth.

D. Summary

In conclusion, manual communication is a visual method of communication. Learning to communicate with deaf people on one's hands is a task which can be successfully accomplished only through visual learning--which, in turn,

Table 1

Adapting Basic Bingo Game to Provide
Practice in Numbers over 100

	B	I	N	G	O
Hypothetical number drawn	7	36	55	78	93

Student will call:

	B	I	N	G	O
Level I (no change)	B-7	I-36	N-55	G-78	O-93
Level II (add a single constant to all numbers)	B-107	I-136	N-155	G-178	O-193
	.	.	.	.	.
	.	.	.	.	.
	.	.	.	.	.
	B-907	I-936	N-955	G-978	O-993
Level III (add a sequentially changing number to all numbers)	B-107	I-236	N-355	G-478	O-593
Level IV (add two numbers, one of which remains constant, and the other of which changes in sequence)	B-1,107	I-1,236	N-1,355	G-1,478	O-1,593
	.	.	.	.	.
	.	.	.	.	.
	.	.	.	.	.
Level V (add two or more numbers, all of which change in sequence, and/or one changes and others remain constant)	B-1,107	I-1,136	N-1,155	G-1,178	O-1,193
	.	.	.	.	.
	.	.	.	.	.
	.	.	.	.	.
	B-1,907	I-1,936	N-1,955	G-1,978	O-1,993
	.	.	.	.	.
	.	.	.	.	.
	.	.	.	.	.
	B-9,107	I-9,236	N-9,355	G-9,478	O-9,593

Note: Multiples of 10,000--or even millions--may be substituted for the hundreds and thousands illustrated above.

requires <u>visual</u> instruction. A student learning manual communication must be able to <u>see</u> what he is to learn if he is to be able to imitate on his own hands what he sees his instructor doing with his hands. While he is receiving visual stimuli from the instructor's movements, and attempting to imitate those movements, he is also developing a complex schema of visual, haptic (kinesthetic), and cognitive cues which, with repetition and reinforcement, become imprinted upon his memory as he works his way through a series of <u>successive approximations</u> of the desired performance until he can successfully execute the criterion performance.

It stands to reason, therefore, that whatever facilitates the process of establishing the correct movements; prevents the fixation of one or another of the approximations of the correct movements; and provides reinforcement of the visual, haptic, and cognitive stimulus patterns associated with the criterion performance, will also expedite the learning process.

In addition, it is a well-established fact that immediate feedback in the form of knowledge of results has a considerable influence upon the rate at which a task is learned. Insofar as a student in manual communication is concerned, the best and most efficient way of providing him with knowledge of the results of his attempts to approximate the criterion of performance (set by the instructor's demonstration) is to show him exactly how he appears while doing so--and to do this immediately after said performance so that the fixation of the visual, haptic, and cognitive cues associated with the <u>approximation</u> of the desired performance can be prevented.

In this way, the student can see for himself where his approximation differs from the criterion, and immediately substitute a closer approximation-- or the criterion performance itself--thereby providing himself with a newer schema of stimulus cues, which replace or extinguish the faulty schemata.

To this effect, use of videotaping equipment has no peer in providing instant feedback to the student in manual communication classes, thus enabling the instructor to both teach the correct performance and to remedy any developing errors in technique before they have a chance to become a fixed pattern of behavior. Other visual aids such as overhead projectors, films, and games can--and should--be employed to facilitate learning of the language of signs and fingerspelling, and every effort should be made to obtain these helpful aids if at all possible.

CHAPTER 4

TEACHING FINGERSPELLING

It is a truism that learning to read fingerspelling is the most difficult task facing the student in his attempts to learn to communicate manually with deaf people. For this reason, heavy emphasis is placed upon the development of receptive fingerspelling ability throughout the course: drills are designed primarily to develop the ability to read full-speed fingerspelling, and secondarily to develop fluency in expressing one's self in fingerspelling; suggested techniques for drilling in the language of signs include hidden practice in reading fingerspelling; tricks and games the instructor can play on and with his students incorporate still more extra practice in reading fingerspelling; and, in general, no opportunity is lost to provide the student with practice in reading fingerspelled words whether the lesson deals with fingerspelling per se, or with the language of signs.

In addition, by means of the test analysis examples in the appendix, the instructor is shown how to analyze the errors in comprehension made by his students on tests of both fingerspelling and the language of signs so that he may quickly perceive which letters or letter groups are giving his class trouble and intensify his drills on these particular letters/letter groups. If he has access to instructional fingerspelling films (see recommended teaching aids in bibliography), he can also direct his students to specific reels which provide practice in the letters or letter groups the students are experiencing difficulty in reading.

A. Rules for Teaching Fingerspelling

It is recommended that the instructor plan to devote all of the first two class sessions to teaching his students to fingerspell and to read fingerspelling.

The importance of correcting faulty fingerspelling techniques at the very beginning cannot be overemphasized. There are two primary rules governing the teaching of fingerspelling which the instructor should follow in order to insure that his students develop both expressive and receptive fingerspelling ability as rapidly as possible, and that they learn to form the letters clearly and crisply on their hands. These rules are:

1. Prevent linking associations from forming between adjacent letters of the alphabet.

2. Force the student to attend to groups of letters, rather than individual letters, fingerspelled at full speed from the very beginning.

With respect to the first rule, the rationale behind the prevention of associative links from forming between adjacent letters of the alphabet are these: (1) Since most students in manual communication classes have been "conditioned" to expect to be taught to fingerspell in the traditional sequence of A, B, C, and so on, just as they learned their ABCs in childhood, it creates less dissonance if the instructor ostensibly follows this A, B, C pattern in teaching the letters of the alphabet. However, unless steps are taken to prevent it, sequential associative links form between A = B, and B = C, C = D, and so forth. Therefore, without realizing it, when he wishes to recall the handshape of a specific letter of the alphabet a student may fall into the habit of starting at A and mentally ticking off the handshape of each subsequent letter until he arrives at the one he wants. As might be expected, this results in an impediment to his learning to fingerspell rapidly--and may also cause him to make extraneous movements of his fingers between finger-spelled letters as he mentally goes through the alphabet in search of the second, then the third letters (and so forth) of the word he is spelling.

The same process is in operation when such a student tries to read finger-spelling--and usually results in a major obstacle to his developing receptive fingerspelling ability, because few students can perform these mental searches fast enough to keep pace with the fingerspelling of another person and still have time to mentally arrange the individual letters into a word before being presented with the second word, or sign, or whatever followed the initial fingerspelled word.

It can be seen, therefore, that the prevention of the formation of these associative links is of major importance in the development of both expres-sive and receptive fingerspelling skill. This can be accomplished with rela-tive ease by the instructor in the course of his teaching of the manual alpha-bet, regardless of the fact that he is teaching the letters of the alphabet in sequential order, if, from the very beginning of instruction, he presents the letters one at a time and immediately begins incorporating the new letter into a word or a series of words as soon as he has taught the first three letters of the alphabet.

In other words, the instructor should teach A, B, and C, then immediately break the first, weak associative links forming between A = B and B = C by rapidly spelling CAB, and asking his students what he spelled, repeating it until all students have caught the word. He should then have his students synchronize their fingerspelling with his own in spelling CAB, beginning slowly, and stopping to correct errors in handshapes as well as in the move-ments of the fingers from letter to letter, then gradually increasing the speed of his own fingerspelling until all of his students are spelling CAB smoothly and rapidly. Only then should he introduce D--and block the forma-tion of any associative links between C and D by immediately using D in words such as BAD, DAD, DAB, CAD.

As each new word is introduced, he should require his students to first recognize the word; then spell with him at a gradually increasing pace of delivery, and finally, vocalize the word simultaneously with their finger-spelling as is described below.

B. Drills

1. Vocalization Drills

When all students have mastered the smooth and rapid fingerspelling of
any drill word, the instructor should introduce vocalization drill. This
drill requires the students to say the word aloud, synchronizing their vocalization of the word with their fingerspelling--and should be part of every
intensive drill in fingerspelling. The reason behind this requirement is
that students learning fingerspelling for the first time always begin by
laboriously spelling out the individual letters of a word (and this is reflected on their lips) as they labor through the individual handshapes representing each of the letters of a given word.

What is seen on the lips, therefore, are the individual letters of, for
example, B, A, and D, instead of the word BAD. This habit is difficult to
break once it is established--but its formation is relatively easy to prevent. By requiring the students to vocalize, the auditory feedback of "B,
A, D" creates instant dissonance and discomfort (negative reinforcement) whereas the silent mouthing of the same letters does not (see Chapter 3 on videotaping for more information on this).

The instructor, therefore, should make it part of the fingerspelling drill
routine to include a few moments of "chorus" in which both the students and
the instructor fingerspell and vocalize each drill word simultaneously and in
concert. (The instructor should also explain how to "drawl" the words until
the speed of fingerspelling increases to the point where excessive drawling is
not necessary; and how to break longer words up into more easily pronounced
syllables to slow down the speech to the point where the fingerspelling can
keep up.)

2. Intensive Drills

As was explained earlier in the general procedures section, intensive drills
involve the teaching of the students to recognize increasingly larger groups
of letters. Beginning with a basic two- or three-letter group, the instructor
starts the drill by slowly leading his class through the smooth transition between successive letters comprising the letter group; synchronizing their spelling with his; requiring proper pauses at the end of each spelling of the drill
group, and vocalization; then gradually speeding up the rate at which he and
the students are spelling the group of letters.

He then tells the students to lower their hands (and rest) but to keep their
attention on his hand. Next he spells the letter group rapidly several times
as fast as he can fingerspell, being sure to pause after each spelling of the
letter group, and stressing to the class that they should try to imprint on
their visual memories the pattern of movement made by his hand each time he
spells the letter group in question.

At this point, after eight or ten repetitions of the letter group, the instructor may want to do as the author does during intensive drills, and lower his hand as a signal that a test word will follow.

Adding one or two letters to the letter group to make a word, he should then fingerspell this word once, at full speed, then ask the class what the word was. (If necessary, he can repeat the word one or more times--until every student in the class knows what the word is--but all repetitions should be at full speed--and the instructor should stop and ask the students what the word was after each repetition.)

It is suggested, however, that the instructor require fingerspelled responses to his questions--to prevent a fast student from verbally tipping off his slower classmates before they have caught the word.

Once all of the students know what the word is, he should drill them on the word--leading them through slow repetitions, adding synchronization drill, and then vocalization drill. After each student has successfully fingerspelled and vocalized the word, the instructor should repeat the intensive drill--using the test word as the new drill letter group, then, adding one or two (or three) letters to the word, give a new test word. An example of how a single two-letter letter group can be expanded is given below, along with the suggested drill procedure. (Other examples of expansion of letter groups into words of increasing complexity and length will be found at the end of this chapter.)

Basic letter group:	Instructor fingerspells:
AS	AS, AS, AS, AS, AS, AS, AS, AS (lower hand, then raise it)
	WAS (Ask, "What was that word?" Give single, full-speed repetition until all students have recognized it.)
	WAS, WAS, WAS, WAS, WAS, WAS, WAS (lower hand, etc.)
	WASH ("What was that word?," etc.)
	WASH, WASH, WASH, WASH, WASH, WASH (lower hand, etc.)
	WASHER ("What was that word?," etc.)
	WASHER, WASHER, WASHER, WASHER, WASHER, WASHER (lower hand, etc.)
	WASHING ("What was that word?," etc.)

WASHING, WASHING, WASHING, WASHING,
WASHING, WASHING
(lower hand, etc.)

WASHINGTON
("What was that word?," etc.)

WASHINGTON, WASHINGTON, WASHINGTON,
WASHINGTON . . .
(lower hand, etc.)

WASHINGTON, D.C.
("What was that?," etc.)

In the example given above, the basic letter group is AS, the basic word is WAS, and the expanded words (in order of increasing complexity) are WASH, WASHER, WASHING, WASHINGTON, and WASHINGTON, D.C. In order to make most effective use of intensive drills, there are certain procedural steps which should be followed in sequence. These steps are outlined below.

Steps to be followed in intensive drill:

Step   Activity

1.   Introduction: Instructor introduces basic letter group (AS), spelling it several times.

2.   Synchronization drill: Students follow instructor in spelling basic letter group, synchronizing their fingerspelling with his, slowly at first, and then with gradually increasing speed, matching his pacing and speed (AS---AS---AS).

3.   Vocalization drill: Students practice synchronizing their fingerspelling with pronouncing the letter group, by saying the word aloud ("as," "as," "as"), while fingerspelling the letter group (AS, AS, AS).

4.   Memorization: Students rest their hands and try to memorize the pattern of movement instructor's hand makes while instructor fingerspells letter group several times at full speed (AS, AS, AS, AS, AS).

5.   Introduction of basic word: Instructor lowers hand, asks, "What is this word?," then fingerspells basic word at full speed (WAS).

6.   Response: Instructor waits for response to his question; repeats basic word; waits for response; repeats word again if necessary, and waits for responses--until all students have responded correctly.

7.   Discrimination drill: In the event several students mistake the basic word (or an expanded word) for another, similar word, the instructor should take a few minutes for discrimination drill (see next section) to help students discriminate between the basic (or expanded) word and the one for which it was mistaken.

8.   Recycle I: Instructor repeats steps 1 through 7 using the basic
     word (WAS) in place of the basic letter group, and introducing the
     first expanded word (WASH) in place of the basic word in step 5.

9.   Recycle II: Instructor repeats steps 1 through 7, using the first
     expanded word (WASH) in place of the basic word, and introducing the
     second expanded word (WASHING)--and so on through all subsequent
     recycles.

3. Discrimination Drills

Discrimination drills are very important for the development of receptive
fingerspelling ability. Most students encounter difficulty in discriminating
between E and A, E and O, A and S, A and M, Q and P, D and L, U and R, and
other letters where the configuration made by the fingers is similar. By
exposing the students to the need to attend to tiny differences--as takes
place in discrimination drills--the instructor is providing them with practice
in recognizing small cues upon which the meaning of a fingerspelled word depends, even if they do not "see" each fingerspelled letter clearly and separately in a rapidly fingerspelled word.

To conduct discrimination drills, the instructor selects two words, similar
in appearance on the hand when fingerspelled rapidly, and fingerspells each
one of them slowly, and clearly, and points out the differences between them
which the students should watch for.

He should then spell each word rapidly in alternation, vocalizing the words
each time he spells one of them, to familiarize his students with what the
rapidly fingerspelled words look like, and the differences between the two.

Then, selecting the key letters in each word upon which the meaning depends,
he should instruct his students to hold their hands up in the key letter of the
word they think he spells. For example, if the two words are HEED and HEAD,
the key letters would be E for HEED and A for HEAD. Therefore, if a student
thinks the instructor has spelled HEED, he would hold his hand up in an E; if
he thinks he recognizes HEAD, then he would hold his hand up in an A. (This
avoids the confusion resulting from conflicting auditory responses coming
from different parts of the room simultaneously as different students think
they recognize different words--a situation which is confusing to both the
instructor and the students. By requiring fingerspelled letter responses, the
instructor can perceive, by swiftly scanning the students' hands, who has and
who has not correctly read the word he spelled.)

After instructing his students on how to respond during the discrimination
drill, the instructor should fingerspell the two words at full speed several
times, with the order in which they are spelled randomized. After each spelling of either word, the instructor should glance rapidly around to spot those
who "guessed" wrong, and repeat the same word until he sees their hands change
to the proper key letter. He will find that, with experience, he will develop
an almost automatic ability to spot those whose hands are not in the correct
key-letter position--either they do not change when they should, or they change

when they should not--and these minor deviations from the visually perceived patterns of change/no change soon become so obvious to the experienced instructor that he can identify them immediately even when they are not in his direct line of vision. At first, however, the instructor must train himself to watch for these deviations, to keep his eyes busy scanning the hands of his students lest he overlook those who are most in need of his help.

The instructor will find that his students will experience the most difficulty in discriminating between the following letters, pairs of letters, and short words containing the troublesome letters or groups of letters (or in ascertaining the presence or absence of key letters in the words):

1. A, E, and S
2. A and M
3. E and O
4. M and N
5. M and E
6. N and T
7. G and H
8. P and Q
9. L and D
10. K and D
11. D and F
12. K and P
13. R and U
14. A and EA (e.g., MEAN-MAN)
15. O and OA (e.g., CAT-COAT)
16. O and OO (e.g., SON-SOON)
17. OA and EA (e.g., MOAN-MEAN)
18. MA and NA (e.g., SMACK-SNACK)
19. -DY and -LY (e.g., COMEDY-COMELY)
20. -NY and -TY (e.g., RUNNY-RUNTY)
21. (occasionally) BA and CA or BE and CE (e.g., BAD-CAD; BENT-CENT)
22. I and Y

The instructor should always be alert for students confusing any of these letters or groups of letters when students are responding to his regular fingerspelling drills--and immediately initiate a few minutes of discrimination drill to help his students learn to differentiate between the words giving them trouble, as well as between the troublesome letters themselves. (Preliminary Lessons 1 and 2 contain lists of discrimination drill words.)

C. Remediation[1]

During all drills, whether teaching/learning, intensive, or discrimination, the instructor should strive to be alert for errors of commission or omission. He should watch in particular for students having difficulty in transition between one letter and the next; for those alphabetizing individual letters of a word instead of saying the complete word; for those holding their hands in an awkward position relative to their bodies or at a deviant angle relative to the wrist; for individual deviant letters spelled by students who form other letters correctly; for "pumping," in which each letter spelled is emphasized by a slight downward or forward push of the hand; for tiny extraneous movements of the hand or fingers as a letter is formed (such as raising the fingers too high between A and N, so that the word AN looks like AUN); for "staccato fingerspelling," where the hand is opened slightly between each letter of a word; and finally, for small errors in finger and/or thumb position in certain letters

[1] See also the section on use of videotaping equipment to correct errors in fingerspelling.

such as A, D, E, O, S, and Y. The most common errors in the last-named
grouped are as follows:

Errors made on A:

1. Made like an S (with fingernails hidden in palm), although the thumb
    is in the correct position for an A.
2. Made correctly except thumb is extended or thumb is too far forward,
    giving an almost-S appearance.
3. Tilted to one side so that thumb is almost parallel to the ceiling.

Errors made on D:

1. Index hand used as D, with thumb half-way up the second finger of the
    hand (looking like a sloppy K).
2. Tilted to one side, or backward.
3. Middle finger used instead of index finger. (A bad tendency.)

Errors made on E:

1. Second knuckles on thumb (fingernails hidden).
2. Space left between thumb and fingertips.
3. Only the first two fingers placed on the thumb (not the short-cut
    E), with the result looking like a sloppy O.

Errors made on O:

1. (Most common and hard to correct.) Ball of thumb joined to ball of
    middle finger instead of to index finger (looking like no. 3 of E
    errors above).
2. Middle knuckle of thumb extended sideways, and fingers curved too
    much, giving a cramped, foreshortened appearance to the O.
3. Balls of all four fingers jammed together on the tip of the thumb,
    forcing the knuckles of the four fingers to spread apart.

Errors made on S:

1. Made like an A (with fingernails showing), although the thumb is in
    the correct position for an S.
2. Thumb too low, resulting in the configuration described in no. 1 of
    E errors described above.
3. Thumb too high, looking like a sloppy A.

Errors made on Y:

1. (Most common.) Fingertips jammed against the palm, forcing little
    finger forward.
2. Index finger extended instead of thumb, thus making the sign for
    male cow droppings, instead of Y. (A frequent mistake.)
3. Both thumb and index finger kept close to the sides of the palm,
    making it look like the student is making a sloppy I.

There are other errors made, but those listed above are the most commonly seen in beginning classes in manual communication. The letter I is often made like a Y (described in the Y errors list); M and N are often made with the wrist angled sharply forward; K is frequently made with the middle finger pointing forward or downward (thus making it easy to confuse with D); the thumb is often held too close to the palm in L; and extended sideways in G, H, and sometimes X.

All too frequently the instructor will find that some of his students have either learned from, or are practicing with, manual alphabet cards they have obtained somewhere--and some of their fingerspelling errors are the result of such learning or practice. By the nature of the illustrations--which have to show the hands in 3/4 view for some letters if the finger positions are to be clearly visible--the students gain the impression that the hand must be held at the angle given in the illustration, and this results in position and angle errors with respect to palm direction and hand-to-wrist angle for certain letters (although other letters may be executed correctly).

To combat these types of errors (which can develop even when alphabet cards are not to blame), the instructor should repeatedly stress the rule that the palm always faces the person one is fingerspelling toward (except for G, H, J, P, and Q); and that the hand is always held vertically with respect to the floor, the ceiling, and the wrist (except, again, for the above-named letters).

In addition, the plane formed by the knuckles where the palm joins the fingers on letters where the hand is closed (or partly closed) should be kept parallel to the floor/ceiling. (To illustrate the latter point, the instructor can demonstrate, by placing a book on top of his hand while making the letter A, exactly where these knuckles should be in relation to the horizontal-vertical plane. The book, if his hand is in the correct A position, will remain balanced--whereas it will slide off if the wrist is angled incorrectly, as in a "slanted" A.)

As was mentioned in some detail in Chapter 3, videotaping equipment can be of considerable help in correcting errors in fingerspelling technique. A student's faulty technique can be recorded on tape and immediately replayed so that the student (and his fellow students) can perceive the errors being committed and correct or avoid them.

Videotaping equipment also provides the instructor with a means for reinforcing excellent performance--for he can record the performance of a student doing exceptionally well on certain letters (or in overall performance), and call the class's attention to it. In this way, students who would not otherwise be able to see the performer because of their position in the classroom will have the advantage of seeing examples of both faulty technique (which they can work to avoid) and excellence (which they can work toward). By providing positive reinforcement for good performance, the instructor encourages the performer to continue to strive for excellence in order to maintain his standing, and also encourages other students to work to earn similar praise.

D. Tests

In many lessons, beginning with Lesson 4, tests in receptive fingerspelling have been included in the lesson plans. Tests are helpful to both the instructor and his students, for they permit identification of troublesome areas in which the instructor can provide extra help. The examples of test analysis in the appendix will help the instructor learn how to tally the errors his students make on particular words and identify the letter groups giving trouble to individual students as well as to the class as a whole. He can then institute remediation treatment in the form of extra drills in the offending letter group, or direct individual students to practice with fingerspelling films affording drills in reading those particular groups.

It is generally best to begin testing early in the course by giving the students a break; that is, by slowing down the rate of delivery of finger-spelled test words to a pace the instructor feels the majority of the students will be able to read, and by employing more repetitions (up to three) than he will later in the course.

The first tests are usually somewhat traumatic for the students--so by programming the students for success instead of fright-induced failure, the instructor helps them over the initial hurdles and instills in them a measure of confidence. As they become accustomed to daily tests, the instructor should speed up the rate of his delivery of test items and reduce the number of repetitions. The instructor should strive to maintain a class average on fingerspelling tests of between 80 and 85 percent. (For more information on tests, see Chapter 2.)

E. Summary

In conclusion, fingerspelling is perhaps the most important, and certainly the most basic, part of learning to communicate with deaf people. The instructor should bend every effort to train his students in both receptive and expressive fingerspelling ability, and should make fingerspelling drills and practice an integral part of every class session--and this applies to all manual communication courses from the beginning level through the advanced course insofar as training in receptive fingerspelling is concerned.

Regardless of the level of transmissive ability a person may have achieved in the language of signs, his ability to read fingerspelling usually lags far behind his ability to transmit--unless he is a deaf person who has used it all his life. Even veteran interpreters of outstanding transmissive ability are sometimes deficient in this respect--so it pays the instructor in manual communication classes to give his students every opportunity to develop receptive fingerspelling ability. This entails constant drilling; constant exposure to fingerspelling; constant remediation; and, in general, a lot of plain hard work if his students are to have the best possible chance to master the difficult task of learning to read the flying fingers of deaf people to whom fingerspelling is second nature.

F. Letter Groups and Words for Intensive Drills in Fingerspelling

The following letter groups and words based on the groups are for use in intensive drills in fingerspelling. The groups and words are designed to rapidly expand the size of the group of letters and words a student can recognize, even when such groups or words are fingerspelled at full speed.

Students should be cautioned not to attempt to recognize each individual letter of a group or word, but to concentrate upon the pattern of movement the hand makes in transition from one letter to the next, and to try to recognize only those letters which interrupt the memorized pattern of movement—for such deviations from the memorized pattern mean that the instructor has introduced an "expanded" word. (Basic letter groups, basic words, and "expanded words" are exemplified below.)

Basic letter group	Basic word	Expanded words (in order of increasing complexity)
AS	WAS	WASH, WASHING, WASHINGTON, WASHINGTON, D.C.
AT	BAT	BATH, BATHED, BATHER, BATHING, SABBATH, SABBATICAL

AT group

ate, pate, patter, pattern, patterning

bat, bate, abate, abated, abating
    bath, bathed, bather, bathing
    Sabbath, sabbatical

cat, cater, scat, scatter, scattering

date, dates, updates, updating

fat, fate, fated

gat, gate, grate, ingrate,
    ingratitude
    gate, negate, negotiate

eat, eating, eaten, beaten, unbeaten

hat, hate, hated, hating,
    chatting, chattering

Kate, skate, skating

late, later, latter, platter

mat, mate, matter, smattering

nat, nature, natural, gnat

oat, coat, coated, coating

rat, rate, rating, grating

tat, teat, threat, threaten,
    threatening

vat, vats, cravats

watt, watts, kilowatt

AN group

any, many, Germany

ban, Cuban

can, can't, recant, canteen

Dan, Danny, Daniel

fan, profane, profanity

and, hand, handle, handling

Jan, Jane, Janet, janitor

land, landed

loan, loaned

man, mane, germane

nan, nanny, nannies

pan, pant, pants, panty, pantry

ran, rant, ranting, granting

sand, sander, sanded, sanding

tan, tanned, suntanned

van, vane, vanes, paravanes

wand, wander, wandering, squandering

want, wanted, wanting

AM group

cam, came, camel

dam, damn, damning, dame, madame

ream, cream, creamery

fame, defame, defaming

gam, game, games

ham, hamper, hampering

jam, jamb, jamboree

lam, lame, blame, blaming

loam, loamy

mam, mama, mammal

Pam, pamper, pampering

ram, ramp, tramp, tramping

Sam, same, sesame

tam, tame, tamed, untamed

vamp, vamps, vamping, vampire

exam, exams, examine, examination

AS group

base, abase, baseball

cast, casts, caster

dash, dashes

fast, faster, fastener

gas, aghast

has, haste, hasten

last, blast, blasted

mask, damask

nasty, dynasty

past, paste, plaster

quash, squash, squashed

rasp, rasps, grasps, grasping

sass, sassy, sassily, sassier

task, tasks

wasp, waspy

TH group

than, thank, thanking

that, that's

the, then, they

this, thistle

there, bothered

them, anthem

thy, worthy

those, these

throw, thrown, overthrown

throne, enthrone

thrice

thin, think, thinking

thick, thicken, thickening

than, Nathan, Jonathan
thank, thankless

thaw, thawing

their, thief, thieves

thigh, thighs

thing, nothing

thirst, thirsty

thong, dipthong

thorn, thorny

thread, thready, threading

threat, threaten, threatened

thresh, threshing

thee, three, threw

thrift, thrifty, thriftiness

throb, throbbing, throbbed

throng, throngs, thronging

thumb, thumbed, thumbing

thwart, thwarted

thyme, rhythm

thus

OA group

boat, boats

coat, coats, coating

foal, foals

loam, loamy

moat, moats

roan, groan, groaned

64

goat, goal, goalie

hoar, hoary

soak, soaked, presoaked

toad, toady

EA group

beat, beater, beaters

cease, decease, deceased

dear, dearly

dead, deadly

eat, eaten, beaten

feat, fealty

gear, geared

heat, hear, heater

heal, heals, healing

heap, heaped, heaping

Jean, jeans, Jeannie

leap, leaped, leaping

lean, clean, reclean

mean, meant

meal, mealy

near, nearly

pear, appear, appearing

pearl, pearly

ream, dream, dreamy, dreamily

seam, steam, stream, streaming

veal, reveal, revealing

weak, weakly, weekly

yearn, yearns, yearning

zeal, zealous, zealousness

IS group

disc, discrete

heist, heists

gist, druggist

hiss, hisses

whist, whistle, thistle

rise, arise

sis, sister, mister

kiss, kissed, kissing

list, listed, enlisted

miss, dismiss, dismissing

anise, anisette

vista, vistas

wish, swish, swishing

whisk, whiskey, whiskery

ER group

berry, berries, raspberries

eery, leery

inter, infer, interfere

germ, german, germane, Germany

herd, herder, herded, shepherded

weird, weirdo, weirdly

jeer, Jerry, Jerry's

butler, butlers

mere, merely, formerly

learner, learned

period, periodic, periodically

queer, queerly

career, careers

seer, sheer

cere, sincere, sincerely

tern, stern, sternly

veer, severe, severely, severing

very, every, everything

were, weren't

lawyer

vizier

OO group

boon, baboon

coon, raccoon, raccoons

food, flood

good, goods

hood, hooded

loon, loony

mood, moody

noon, noodle

pool, spool

room, groom

soon, sooner

stool, stoolie

wool, woolly

yoo, hoo, boo-hoo

zoo, zoom, zooming

EI group

being

ceiling

either

heist

receive

neither

deign

feint

conceive

weird, weirdly

IE group

bier

died, studied

fie, fiery

hie, hied, shied

lie, lied, belied

amie, amiable

client, clients

piece, pierce

quiet, quietly, quietude

sienna, Vienna

tier, tiered

vizier

OE group

aloe, aloes, buffaloes

Boer, Boers

coerce, coerced, coercion

doe, doer

foe, foehn

hoe, shoe, shoed

Joe, Joey

sloe, sloe gin

Moe

poem, poet, poetry

roe, zeroes

toe, toes, toeing

woe, woes

QU group

quad, squad

quick, quickly

quack, quake, earthquake

equal, equality

squawk, squawks, squawking

square, squared, quarrel

tequila

quill, tranquil

quantity, piquant

quarry, quarried

quart, quarter

squall, squalid

squab, squabble

quiz, quizzical

quorum

sequel, sequelae

mosque, masque

acquire, acquired

quirt, squirt, squirted

OM group

bomb, bombs

aplomb

comb, combing, recombing, recommending

dome, domes, domestic

foment

grommet

home

axiom, axioms

mom, moment, momentus

noma, nomad

boom, booms, booming

pom, pomme, pommel

pomp, pompon, pompous

romp, romper

some, handsome

tome, epitome

vomit, vomits, vomiting

woman, womanly

zoom, zooming

ON group

eons, peons

bone, bones, bonnets

cone, coney, corny

Don, done, condone

eon, neon, neons

fond, fondle, fondled, fondly

gone, begone, begonia

hone, honest, dishonest, dishonesty

lion, lions, scallions

long, belong, belonging

among, amongst

soon, sooner, spooner

wrong, wrongs, wronging

son, song, evensong

tone, atone, stone, stony

won, won't

yon, yonder, beyond

Words combining two or more letter groups

stone	anthology
another	antique
other, bother, bothered	pander
this, thistle	sander
than, thank	wander
either, neither	German
equate, equal, equality	

Note: For more drill groups, see Guillory's book (References).

PART II

COURSE OF STUDY OUTLINE

25 Lesson Plans

INSTRUCTIONS FOR USING COURSE OF STUDY
OUTLINE AND LESSON PLANS

The following section of the manual is divided into twenty-five lesson plans, each of which the instructor should be able to complete in a single class session of at least two hours in length.

The twenty-five lesson plans are divided roughly into two main parts although the division is more arbitrary than real. The first part, which includes two preliminary lessons in fingerspelling, one lesson in numbers, and ten lessons in the language of signs, comprises the beginning course of study. The second part, which begins with Lesson 11, comprises the intermediate course of study and includes nine lessons in the language of signs. Of the 586 signs described (and taught) in this manual, 374 are taught in the beginning course and 212 in the intermediate course.

The first two lessons deal exclusively with the teaching of fingerspelling, while the rest deal with both fingerspelling and the language of signs. To avoid confusion, therefore, the two lessons in fingerspelling are titled "Preliminary" lessons to differentiate them from the lessons in which signs are taught, while the latter lessons begin with "Lesson 1."

Each of the lessons, including the preliminary lessons, is organized in such a way as to make the instructor's task as easy as possible. The lessons in the beginning course are all preceded by a general instructions section.[1] It is recommended that the instructor read the general instructions section preceding each of these lessons a few days before the lesson is to be taught so that he may prepare in advance any materials he may need for instructional purposes as well as any materials to be distributed to the students during that particular class session.

Organization of each lesson is as follows:

1. A general instruction section which should be read by the instructor prior to each class session, which includes in narrative form:

    a. Pertinent information on the material to be covered in the lesson.
    b. Teaching techniques and other helpful information and tips.
    c. List of materials needed for the lesson in question.

2. A lesson plan in outline form which includes sequentially arranged teaching tasks the instructor should endeavor to accomplish in the particular class session. These tasks are arranged in the order in which they should be approached, with each unit designed to reinforce

---

[1] General instruction sections are not provided after Lesson 8 since it is assumed that the instructor will have developed considerable familiarity with these particular techniques of teaching by the time he has finished teaching the first eleven sessions of the course.

and augment what preceded it. Within each lesson plan will be found such teaching aids as:

a. Letter groups, drill words, and sentences which can be used to provide practice on previously learned material as well as new material.
b. Suggestions as to types of drills to be employed for both fingerspelling and the language of signs.
c. Tests of receptive ability in both fingerspelling and signs, and in two lessons, tests of performance ability.

3.[1] Materials which should be duplicated and distributed to the students for home practice and/or information in the event that the students have not been required to obtain the companion student's manual, "A Course of Study Outline for Students" (Babbini, 1973), or in the case where the student manuals have been ordered but have not yet been received. These materials are characterized by the notation DUP which appears in the upper right-hand corner of the page, and are of five different types, with the lesson to which they belong indicated by the number preceding the DUP notation, and the type of material indicated by a code letter following the DUP notation. The coding is explained as:

a. DUP-V: Vocabulary word descriptions.
b. DUP-P: Practice words, sentences, etc.
c. DUP-M: Miscellaneous material of an informational nature. In the event there is more than one DUP-M item in a given lesson, the different items are indicated by an additional small letter (DUP-M, a; DUP-M, b; etc.).
d. DUP-TRM: Transparency master which can either be duplicated and distributed to the students or reserved for instructor use and made into an overhead transparency for projection on a screen in class.
e. DUP-TEST: The two performance tests, which should be duplicated,

---

[1] It has been the author's experience that such coding is extremely helpful to office staff (and to the instructor) charged with the responsibility of duplicating and collating lesson materials and assorted practice materials, stapling together the separate pages of several different types of DUP materials for a single lesson without getting them mixed up, and filing them so that they are easily recognizable as belonging with a specific lesson. They are easily identified and readily accessible to the instructor.

In distributing DUP materials, the instructor should wait until the end of the class session to distribute the materials, for if he does not, he may find himself competing with the DUP materials for the student's attention.

It is also a good idea to punch holes in all DUP materials so that students can put them in three-ring binders.

but distributed to students only at the time the test is administered.

Underneath each DUP line will be seen figures in parentheses. These figures refer to the page number (first digit) out of the total number (second digit) of pages comprising the DUP unit. In the event the code (1) is seen, it means that the DUP unit consists of just a single page.

Note: It is recommended that students be required to obtain the student's manual, for this will save the instructor's having to duplicate a considerable amount of material in this manual for student's use. Included on the DUP material sheets are references to the page number in the student's manual where the same material can be found, which will be of help to the instructor in assigning homework, other practice and study, and required readings.

EQUIPMENT AND MATERIALS FOR THE COURSE

Below will be found a check list of equipment and materials which it is suggested the instructor in a basic manual communication course obtain. In addition to the suggested basic materials, a list of materials needed for the teaching of each lesson is given in the general instructions sections of the first eight lessons and in the lesson plans after the eighth lesson.

Although a companion student's workbook for this course is available and recommended, no text or reference book is required for the course outlined in the present manual, but the instructor may wish to have his students purchase one of the several books on sign language which are available through the Communication Skills Program of the National Association of the Deaf (NAD) which is located at 814 Thayer Avenue, Silver Springs, Maryland 20910, or directly from the authors (see bibliography). If the instructor has personal copies of these books, he can bring them to the first few class sessions so that students may examine them and decide which, if any, they wish to purchase. He can then order the books himself (or have his institution order them for him), and when they come, collect the money and forward it to the seller.[1] An extremely helpful booklet, however, is the one on fingerspelling by Lavera Guillory (see references), and it is recommended that the instructor obtain one to supplement the letter groups and basic word lists provided in Chapter 4 (Teaching Fingerspelling).

Suggested Materials for Course:

1. Videotaping equipment, either studio-type or portable, if at all possible. Three reels (one hour's playing time each) of videotape to fit the equipment.

2. Fingerspelling films and projectors for them. Both films and projectors are available on loan from Media Services and Captioned Films. For information, write to:

> Media Services and Captioned Films
> Division of Educational Services
> U.S. Office of Education
> Washington, D.C. 20202

Recommended:

a. The American Manual Alphabet (Graphic Films produced training film series of thirty four-minute reels of fingerspelling drills and tests).
b. Fingerspelling Films for Counselors (International Communications Foundation series of nine four-minute training films of three levels of difficulty).

----

[1] Note: Some authors prefer that payment accompany the order. Therefore, when ordering from individual authors, it would be well to inquire. The NAD will sell on consignment.

Note: Both recommended film series come in cartridge-type continuous reels which require cartridge-type projectors.

3. Overhead projector and a supply of transparencies for same.

4. Roster and grade record book.

5. Password game(s), either purchased or constructed by instructor.

6. Bingo game(s), number type. If available, the picture type also. One pound jar of dried beans to use as markers (the purchased Bingo games seldom have enough markers).

7. Mimeographed or dittoes (or otherwise duplicated) copies of the vocabulary word-descriptions, the practice materials, tests, and so on, given herein, for each of the lessons in the manual (these can be prepared ahead of time, or in advance of each lesson as the course progresses), unless the workbook, "Course of Study Outline for Students" (Babbini, 1974) is required.

8. A file cabinet (or other storage space) in which to store the duplicated paper materials for the course as they accumulate, as well as the games.

9. Patience and a sense of humor.

COURSE OF STUDY OUTLINE

PRELIMINARY LESSONS 1 AND 2:

The Manual Alphabet and Fingerspelling

A PREFATORY NOTE TO PRELIMINARY LESSONS 1 AND 2

There are several practical considerations which dictated the author's separation of Preliminary Lessons 1 and 2 (which deal exclusively with the teaching of fingerspelling) from the remainder of the lessons in the manual. First, a manual communications instructor should concentrate upon giving his students a firm foundation in expressive and receptive fingerspelling--particularly the latter--before he introduces any signs. Although some veteran manual communication instructors may disagree, it has been the author's experience that the development of fingerspelling skill is retarded if both fingerspelling and signs are introduced simultaneously at the beginning of a course in manual communication. What apparently happens is that the students find the signs far more interesting, picturesque, and easier to learn than fingerspelling. Their attention, therefore, is divided, with signs garnering more than their share of student attention, interest--and practice time.

This cannot help but have a negative effect upon the students' ability to develop expressive and receptive fingerspelling skills--and the instructor will find himself fighting an uphill battle throughout the course to see that the students master these essential skills as competition from signs increases in proportion to the increase in the number of signs the students learn as the course progresses.

If, on the other hand, signs are withheld until the students have mastered the manual alphabet, and have developed fundamental skills in both expressing themselves in fingerspelling and in reading short, fingerspelled words and sentences, the instructor will find it much easier to maintain steady progress in increasing his students' receptive and expressive skills in both fingerspelling and the language of signs. In short, he will be loading the dice in such a way that, when the more interesting signs are introduced and begin competing for student attention and practice time, the students will already have developed fundamental skills in fingerspelling which will counterbalance the competition posed by the introduction of more and more signs.

Second, if his students can fingerspell and read fingerspelled words, they have an immediately utilizable skill. They can converse with deaf persons, albeit slowly, from the very beginning; whereas without this skill, their opportunities for conversation are extremely limited until their vocabulary of signs is far more extensive than it can possibly be for the first several lessons. In addition, the instructor can employ a wider variety of drilling techniques from the very beginning of the course--all of which will provide his students with practice in fingerspelling at the same time they are learning new signs. He can fingerspell the word for which he is going to teach a sign. He can immediately use in a sentence the sign he teaches, by fingerspelling the other words in the sentence for which he has not yet taught the signs--an important consideration when one knows that the language of signs is not a collection of individually signed or fingerspelled words, but a means of communicating thoughts, ideas, opinions, and the like, all of which normally require clauses, phrases, sentences, and paragraphs rather than individual words. The introduction of sentences, therefore, should come as early in the course

as possible--and is possible <u>only</u> if the students can fill in with <u>finger-</u>
<u>spelled</u> words the gaps between the signs they have learned.

A third consideration which influenced the decision to separate the two
lessons in fingerspelling from those which include lessons in the language
of signs was that of organization of the material for ease of reference by
both instructor and students. Except for a list of words for fingerspelling
practice, and miscellaneous informative DUP materials, the first two preliminary lessons do not include formal "lessons" in the sense of vocabulary word-
descriptions such as are provided for the lessons in which signs are taught.
It would be confusing, therefore, to have the formal lessons (word-descriptions)
begin with Lesson <u>3</u>--when no Lessons 1 and 2 exist. The author, therefore, has
begun with Lesson <u>1</u> those lessons in which <u>signs</u> are taught, and for convenience's sake, has labeled the two lessons in fingerspelling "Preliminary Lesson
1" and "Preliminary Lesson 2."

PRELIMINARY LESSON 1[1]

(SM 25-32)

First Class Session

GENERAL INSTRUCTIONS

The primary goal of Preliminary Lesson 1 is to teach students the manual alphabet from A to N, although it may be possible to teach the whole alphabet if time permits. By this goal it is meant that the students will not only be able to make the letters on their own hands smoothly and correctly, and to fingerspell words without undue hesitation, but also to recognize each of the letters when the instructor fingerspells them--and to recognize fingerspelled words which use these letters.

However, before the instructor approaches the task of teaching the manual alphabet, whether A to N or the whole alphabet, there are certain administrative details common to all first class sessions of any course which must be handled, although some of this detail can be done prior to the scheduled opening session. There are, in addition to administrative detail and recording, other time-consuming tasks which further reduce teaching time in the first class session--those of acquainting the instructor and the students with each other and of orienting the students to the course with regard to requirements and expectations.

Depending upon the size of the class, the type of institution in which the class is held, the amount of administrative trivia which must be coped with for bookkeeping purposes, and the amount of previous experience the instructor has had with opening sessions as well as with the enrollment procedures of his particular institution, coping with nonteaching tasks may consume anywhere from a quarter to half of the first class session, or even most of it. For this reason, the material to be covered in Preliminary Lesson 1 has been kept to a minimum.

Preparation for the first class session: The very first thing the instructor should do prior to the opening session of his course is inspect the premises in which he is to teach. This should preferably be done a day or two in advance--or at least several hours before the time scheduled for the first class meeting. He should personally inspect the room, noting whether the lighting is adequate, the room is of sufficient size and has adequate seating capacity, and ascertain whether or not the chairs in the room are movable. (If the chairs are not movable, it is recommended that a different

---

[1]Note: The following was written on the assumption the instructor has read Chapter 4, Teaching Fingerspelling, and has thoroughly familiarized himself with the techniques and procedures outlined therein.

room be requested.) If the room is large, but the number of seats available seem to be limited, it would be a good idea to find out whether or not a supply of folding chairs is available and, if so, to arrange to have half-a-dozen or so on hand just in case the enrollment exceeds expectations (a common occurrence). He should also, if he is not familiar with the premises, ascertain the location of the nearest fire escapes, restrooms, and water fountains --and, perhaps, vending machines.

In addition to inspecting his classroom, the instructor should arrange to have the DUP materials (listed at the end of the general instructions) duplicated in advance of the class session so that they can be distributed to the students, and he should also obtain some kind of a roster and grade record book (sometimes available without charge to instructors in educational institutions, but purchasable in any stationery store if not). Also helpful, for reasons which will be explained shortly, is a supply of 5 x 7 index-type cards. The experienced instructor also brings with him to the first class session a supply of extra pencils and notebook paper--for students who come unprepared.

Enrolling the students: If the instructor is required to register or enroll his students himself (instead of its being done for him by the institution personnel), he will also have to obtain a supply of official registration forms-- and will have to familiarize himself with the procedures involved if necessary. This may also involve the collection of a registration fee (as in the case where the class is part of an adult education program) which must be turned in to the institution staff--all of which can be very confusing to the novice instructor unless he takes the time to learn the procedure and organizes his approach to minimize the confusion both he and the students are likely to experience.

In the event the actual registration and/or enrollment of the students is done for him prior to the first class session by the institution staff, the instructor will normally be provided with an advance roster of students who have registered or preregistered for the course. Unfortunately, this does not guarantee that the names on the advance roster will match the faces of those students who appear for the first class session. The author has taught for many years, during some of which preregistration was required, and not once in her experience did it happen that the names on the list of preregistered students coincided exactly with the faces of those appearing for the first class. There were inevitably a few who had heard about the course too late to preregister in time to be included in the advance enrollment roster, which was generally prepared at least a week in advance of the first class session. In addition, there were those who had been brought to the class by students who had preregistered--who wanted just to "observe" the class to possibly add it if the instructor's permission could be obtained (which was usually forthcoming unless the class was extremely large). There were also members of the administrative staff who became interested and decided to sit in on the classes without bothering to go through formal registration procedures. Finally, there were sometimes a few students who changed their minds about taking the course, or were prevented from taking the course because of schedule conflicts they had not foreseen, who did not show up although their names were still on the advance roster. It is, therefore, with a bit of skepticism that the instructor should regard any advance list of students which he may have been provided--and prepare for a larger number than the advance roster indicates he should expect.

Getting Acquainted and Orientation of the Students

Getting acquainted: One of the most effective ways of making each student in a class feel that the instructor is personally interested in him, and is going to make every effort toward helping him to master the subject matter, is for the instructor to associate the student's name with his face as quickly as possible, so as to be able to call upon individual students by name during classroom discussions.

Therefore, once the administrative and mechanical requirements of getting the course under way have been completed, the task facing the instructor should be that of associating the names of individual members of the class with their faces. A good starting point would be a calling of the roll--if an advance roster has been provided--during which he should endeavor to make some sort of associative link between the name and the face of the person who responds when the name is called. An example of this could be an extremely dark-haired young lady with a Nordic-sounding name--the mental link could be "Sure doesn't look like a Swede, but has a Swedish name." Or a young man with a heavy moustache with a Germanic or Jewish name--"Looks like Einstein--and has a name to match." Or someone who has a first name similar to someone the instructor knows personally--and even looks a bit like that person--in which case the instructor can mentally identify the student by "Like Jane Doe in name and appearance."

Hathaway Guessing Game: However, these associative links are apt to be somewhat tenuous--and sometimes difficult to make--so the author has for several years employed what she calls the "Hathaway Guessing Game" (named after Dr. William Hathaway, from whom she learned the technique). Essentially, this is a game in which the instructor attempts to guess, from student-provided information written on 5 x 7 index cards, which faces belong with the names, hobbies, and other information on each card. In the process of guessing, the instructor takes advantage of the extra information about each person in the class, associates it with the name provided on the card, and then, finally, with the face of the person who is finally identified as the writer of the capsule biography on the card. Figure 4 gives an example of the card the author requests her students to complete and turn in early in the first class session of each course she teaches. (The information required for the card can either be written on a chalkboard in the classroom or illustrated on a transparency and projected on a screen so that the students will know what is wanted in the way of information.)

It also helps if the instructor will, during the first two class sessions, make every attempt to contact each student directly at least once during the course of his instruction--and request the student's name (the response can be verbal at first, but after they have learned the alphabet, it should be fingerspelled), after which the instructor repeats the student's name both verbally and in fingerspelling, while looking at the student's face and endeavoring to fix the name with the face.

Not only does the Hathaway Guessing Game assist the instructor in quickly getting to know his students as individuals, but the information on the card is helpful in providing a summary of the students' reasons for wanting to learn

Figure 4

Hathaway Guessing Game Card

Name: Major: Year: Degree:
                               (if in school)   (in school)   (if any)

Address:

Phone:

Marital Status: Number of children if any: Ages:
                                                           Sex:

Hobbies:

Previous contacts with deaf persons:

Reasons for taking this course:

Where did you learn about this particular course?

manual communication, where they learned about the course (useful for publici-
zing future courses), and, incidentally, their addresses and phone numbers in
the event they must be contacted.

However, getting acquainted is not just getting the instructor acquainted
with his students--it also means getting the students acquainted with the instructor and with each other. It is only fair that the instructor give the
students the same amount of information about himself that he has requested
they provide him, so the instructor should briefly outline his own pedigree,
teaching experience, hobbies, and so forth, so that his students will know
something about him.

Getting the students acquainted with each other usually takes care of itself
without extra effort on the part of the instructor, but while he is attempting

to guess the faces belonging with the data on the guessing game cards, he can introduce students having common hobbies to each other if they are not already acquainted. And since he will be reading aloud the information on the cards prior to trying to guess who the writers are, each student will know something about each of his fellows, which the student can mentally catalog and use to help him remember the other person. Simple proximity in the same class will do the rest if the atmosphere is kept informal and conducive to open discussion.

Orientation: Once the instructor has completed the mechanical details of getting the course under way and made a start at getting acquainted with his students, he should begin the actual course work by orienting his students to the course itself--what they can expect in the course, and what will be expected of them. There are three main areas in which the students are likely to ask questions, particularly if the course is offered for credit in an institution of higher learning. The three areas are:

1. Requirements of the course with respect to:

    a. Attendance
    b. Outside assignments and/or homework
    c. Text or reference books or other required reading

2. Grading, particularly the instructor's policy on:

    a. Grading of tests, type of tests to expect, and weighting of tests.
    b. How performance will be evaluated.
    c. Types of things which influence the instructor's grading.

3. Course content and expectations:

    a. The goals of the course, or what students may reasonably expect to learn during the course.
    b. How the instructor plans to teach the course so that the goals can be achieved.
    c. How the students will be able to utilize the skills acquired during the course.

Requirements: With respect to attendance, the instructor should stress the fact that the students plan to attend every class session and explain why attendance is important. Students who miss a single class will immediately find themselves behind the rest of the class and those missing more than two or three sessions during the whole course will have to work extra hard to keep up with the others. The instructor should also point out that a student who misses class not only penalizes himself, but also his fellow students, for, unless his classmates provide him with out of class assistance in learning the signs which were taught in the class or classes he missed, they are going to have to have to mark time while the instructor himself tries to help the absentee catch up by retracing for the laggard one's benefit the ground the rest of the class has already covered, which, in view of the material still to be covered, wastes valuable time.

A policy the author has followed in insuring attendance and keeping absenteeism to a minimum is to call the roll each time the class is held and to inform students that a maximum of three excused absences are permitted without penalty to the student _if_ such absences are not sequential and if the student shows that he has, on his own time, made an attempt to learn the material taught in the missed lessons without the instructor's having to halt instruction to bring him up to date.

The students were also cautioned that if more than two class sessions were missed in succession, or from four to six class sessions over the course, the student could expect a lowered grade unless he had good reason for his absenteeism and, in addition, had demonstrated to the instructor's satisfaction that the absences had not kept the student from keeping up with the rest of the class.

In the event a student missed six or more class sessions, it was suggested that the student drop the class and re-enroll at a time when he could be sure of more regular attendance, for it was reasoned that a student missing six or more sessions would be too far behind to ever catch up, and it would be unfortunate for a low grade to become part of his permanent transcript.

Outside assignments and homework: These should be part of any manual communication course held under college or university auspices. Among the DUP materials at the end of Preliminary Lesson 1 is a list of assignments the instructor may wish to adapt for use with his own classes. The purpose of these assignments, which the author requires of her students, is to force the student to learn something about the social lives of adult deaf people in his community, to become acquainted with at least a few of them, and to practice his newly learned skills with them. This contact with adult deaf people is a valuable learning experience regardless of the students' reasons for taking the course, for it introduces them to the end product of all programs designed to socialize, educate, and habilitate deaf persons from childhood on.

In addition to the DUP assignments, the instructor may want to require that his students read particularly interesting books and articles dealing with deafness, with deaf people, and/or with the language of signs. He should, therefore, make up his own list of required or recommended reading and have this list duplicated and distributed to the class in addition to the DUP materials provided in the present manual. The author recommends two books in particular: IN THIS SIGN, by Joanna Greenberg (1971), and SIGN LANGUAGE STRUCTURE, AN OUTLINE OF THE VISUAL COMMUNICATION SYSTEMS OF THE AMERICAN DEAF, by W. C. Stokoe (1960). IN THIS SIGN is an excellent and amazingly accurate portrayal of the lives, thoughts, and feelings of a fictional deaf couple who can only be considered representative of thousands of deaf people actually existing today. Stokoe's book on the other hand is an interesting experiment in trying to devise a way of _writing_ sign language, and as an example or research and study of the language of signs, it is a classic. It should, therefore, be read by any serious student of the language of signs.

Other homework assignments can require students to compose sentences utilizing the signs they have been taught, to practice them until they can sign and fingerspell them without error, then bring them to class for recital purposes as well as to give their fellow students practice in _reading_ sentences delivered in the language of signs; and to write sentences including words for which the signs will be taught (Cloze sentences) in the next lesson, and so forth.

Grading: With respect to grading, each instructor will devise his own policy on grading if grades are to be assigned in his course. The author's policy has been to give each new class the choice of a "Blanket B" (in which everyone in the class receives a grade of B for the course regardless of performance) or working toward a grade of A, B, or C. (The author gives a grade lower than a C only in the event a student is obviously goofing off, has a poor attendance record, and resists suggestions that he work a bit harder OR drop the course. An interesting phenomenon has been that the author has yet to teach a class which elected the "Blanket B." All have elected to work toward grades.)

Grading, in a manual communication course, relies rather heavily on the instructor's subjective evaluation of a student's performance. Tests of their comprehension ability--or receptive ability--give but one measure of performance, and are therefore inadequate as measures of overall ability. In addition, a student may do poorly on the first several comprehension tests, then suddenly start improving in the latter part of the course to the extent that he scores among the highest. To penalize such a student for initial poor performance by averaging test grades across the semester would be tantamount to penalizing him for working hard to improve. The author's policy, therefore, is never to assign a student a comprehension grade lower than his final test score.

By the same token, the student's performance test scores (the two written performance tests) are disregarded in assigning a final performance grade, for performance too can improve markedly in the final weeks of the course. The purpose of the performance tests, therefore, is informational in nature-- to let the instructor know where areas of weakness are in his teaching and to alert the students to the need to perform signs accurately and precisely.

Performance grades should be based on the final performance of the students, which the author usually assesses during the "final exam," which requires each student to deliver a short essay (of the student's own choosing) in the language of signs during the last two class sessions while both the instructor and the other members of the class evaluate the performance on a specially prepared evaluation sheet (see appendix). The final grade assigned each student was the mean of his comprehension "final" and his evaluated performance, with his attendance record deciding his grade if it happened to be on the borderline between one grade and the next.

An instructor not teaching in a formal educational program has no need to assign official grades, but he may wish to anyway as an incentive to his students to work harder. He should remember, however, that low grades tend to discourage students and be more lenient in grading than he would if teaching in a formal program where grades are required.

In any event, once the instructor has chosen the policy he will follow in grading his students, he should inform his students what his grading criteria will be. To encourage active student participation in the classroom activities, he can also state that one of the factors which will influence his grading is the amount of participation the individual student contributes to the classroom dynamics. (Whether this factor enters into his judgment or not, merely stating that it does often suffices to transform an otherwise passive group of students into an active one--and an active student is a student who is learning.)

Course content and expectations: With respect to the content of the course, the instructor should briefly outline what he expects to accomplish during the course. He should tell the students what they can expect in the way of training: drills, recitals, games, and other learning devices; relevant extra learning in the area of deafness in the form of brief side-excursion lectures; outside assignments and the reasons why they are assigned; and exposure to his, the instructor's, biases. (Regarding that last, the instructor might employ one of the author's techniques--that of prefacing any remarks she knows to be reflective of her own biases by informing the students that a "Babbinism" is forthcoming.)

He should also tell his students what they can reasonably expect to be able to do at the end of the course with their new manual communication skills. They cannot, for instance, expect to be able to communicate with all deaf people of every level of language achievement once they have completed a beginning course-- but they should reasonably expect to be able to communicate, even if somewhat slowly, with deaf people who have fairly good language skills.

They cannot expect to be able to readily understand the rapid signing and fingerspelling of deaf persons talking among themselves, but they should be able to understand most of what is said to them directly by individual deaf persons even if they have to ask for frequent repetitions. They should also be made aware of the fact that developing their receptive skills will be the toughest part of the learning, and that the instructor intends to make every effort toward helping them acquire receptive skills even as he provides them with expressive skills.

Beginning the Instruction

At this point, the instructor should be ready to begin the actual teaching, although he may want to preface instruction with a brief history of the language of signs. (The author, however, usually dispenses with this step since the DUP material at the end of Preliminary Lesson 1 as well as the student workbook includes a synopsized history of the language of signs which the students can read for themselves.) To insure that the students actually read it, the instructor can require that they do so before the next class and come to class prepared to discuss it by asking questions. If he uses this tactic, the instructor should plan to devote a few minutes to such discussion during the class sessions to follow.

Teaching the manual alphabet, A to N: The registration of the students and/or compiling a roster, getting acquainted, and orienting the students to the course inevitably will consume a large part of the first class session. Therefore, rather than attempt to teach the whole manual alphabet from A to Z in whatever time he has remaining, the instructor should probably concentrate on teaching only half of it--from A to N--and seeing that his students thoroughly learn these letters individually as well as in combination with the other letters in words.

If he has managed to keep the preparatory procedures to a minimum and has ample time remaining, he can go as far beyond N as he has time--and perhaps complete teaching the manual alphabet--if he has sufficient time to thoroughly drill the students in all of the letters he teaches. Otherwise, it would be better to concentrate on teaching some of the letters--and teach them thoroughly--than to skimp on the last few letters in order to teach them all in one class session.

Signs to be taught: The signs for the personal pronoun I should be taught, and the sign for the word AND, but other than those two signs, the first two lessons should be devoted solely to teaching and drilling in the manual alphabet. It should be possible for the students to learn the manual alphabet thoroughly in two intensive lessons. However, if the instructor feels it necessary, a third preliminary lesson can be taught before signs are introduced-- but normally two lessons will suffice to thoroughly acquaint the students with fingerspelling--and give them the ability to read short fingerspelled words and sentences delivered at about half normal speed. (For the technique of teaching fingerspelling, see Chapter 4, Teaching Fingerspelling.)

At the end of the session the instructor should pass out any necessary DUP materials, explain each briefly, and request that the students bring to class from that time on, a notebook or three-ring binder, paper, and pencils--and all DUP material the instructor provides (or the workbook if it is required for the course).

MATERIALS NEEDED FOR PRELIMINARY LESSON 1

For instructional purposes:

1. Class roster book (and/or registration cards, etc.), pen/pencil
2. A supply of 5 x 7 index-type cards
3. Outlined lesson plan (or this manual)
4. Chalkboard, or OH projector and transparencies (for Hathaway Guessing Game information)
5. Samples of student workbook and/or reference books on the language of signs

DUP materials (to be duplicated and distributed to students if necessary):

	SM Page
1. A brief history of the language of signs (FS-1-DUP-M, a; five pages)	1
2. Assignment sheets (FS-1-DUP-M, b; three pages)	181
3. Bibliography of books on the language of signs (FS-1-DUP-M, c; four pages)	185
4. List of words for home practice in fingerspelling (FS-1-DUP-P; one page)	30
5. Illustrated manual alphabet (FS-1-DUP-M, d; two pages)	28, 29

PRELIMINARY LESSON 1

LESSON PLAN OUTLINE

The instructor should, just before scheduled class time, write his name and the course number on the chalkboard (or have it ready on an overhead projector transparency).

I.   Registering students, or compiling of roster.

II. Hathaway Guessing Game, or other get-acquainted techniques.

III. Course outline.

   A. Course requirements:

       1. Attendance
       2. Completion of outside assignments, reading assignments
       3. Participation in classroom activities, asking questions, and so on
       4. Tests

   B. Grading policy, if grades are to be assigned.

       1. Class can elect to take Blanket B, or work toward grade
       2. Final grade depends on three main factors:

           a. Final comprehension test scores. Can be based on:

               (1) Average of last five comprehension tests
               (2) Or, overall average, with student option of dropping worst five tests before comprehension grade is computed

           b. Performance, as evaluated during course (by instructor), on two performance tests and on "final exam" (by instructor and fellow students).
           c. Attendance, which will influence borderline grades.

       3. Relative weights are: comprehension, 60 percent, performance, 40 percent, with attendance weighted only in event grade is borderline, unless more than four absences, in which case lower grade will be assigned than that earned. (Student should be able to negotiate, however.)

   C. Course content.

       1. Fingerspelling, expressive and receptive skills. Heavy emphasis on latter.

2. Language of signs, expressive and receptive skills. Heavy emphasis on latter.
3. Lectures on various aspects of deafness, and problems of, opinions, biases.
4. Exposure (if possible) to guest lecturers, some of whom may be deaf persons.

D. Course expectations.

1. Acquisition of basic, fundamental skills in language of signs. Types of deaf persons with whom can (and cannot) be used.
2. Familiarity with some of the psychological implications of deafness as well as with language problems of deaf people.
3. Knowledge of socioeconomic activities of deaf people in vicinity.

E. Method of teaching course.

1. Drills, recitations, games, and so on.
2. Other equipment (such as videotape) which will be used, and how used.
3. Both teaching and remediation of faulty techniques will be used as techniques.
4. Films and other visual aids (if available for use).
5. Ground rules instructor wishes to establish:

   a. Breaks, if permitted, during classroom instruction, when, and for how long.
   b. Smoking, if permitted.
   c. Verbal communication during class (suggestion: forbid after fifth lesson in the language of signs).
   d. Questions--interrupt, or hold until after class.

IV. Rules of the institution, and other miscellaneous information (assuming students are unfamiliar with the institution).

A. Rules governing student behavior while on campus.

B. Location of nearest fire excapes, shelters, water fountains, rest rooms, coffee dispensing machines, and location of facilities in which films or tapes of language of signs or finger-spelling can be reviewed if available, as well as times when these facilities may be used.

V. Brief history of the language of signs (optional).

VI. Teach signs for I and AND.

VII. Teaching the manual alphabet, A to N.

A. Words which can be used in teaching and discrimination drills.

Student Has Learned (New letter introduced is underlined)	Teaching-Drill Words	Discrimination Drill Word-Pairs[1]
A̲B̲C̲	CAB	---
ABCD̲	DAD, BAD, DAB, CAD, CAB	CAD-BAD, DAB-DAD
ABCDE̲	BED, BEAD, BEADED, DAD, DEAD, DEED, DEEDED	BED-BEAD, DEAD-DEED BEAD-BADE
ABCDEF̲	FAD, FADE, FADED, FED, FEED, DEAF, FACE, FACED, FACADE	FED-FEED, FAD-FED FADE-FEED, FACE-FADE
ABCDEF̲G	FAG, FAGGED AGE, AGED ADAGE, EGAD GAFF, GAFFED EGG, EGGED	GAFF-FAG FAGGED-FACADE
ABCDEFG̲H	HAD, HEAD, HEED, HEADED, HEEDED, GHEE, HAG, HEDGE, HEDGED	HEAD-HEED, HADE-HEAD
ABCDEFGH̲I	HID, HIDE, BID, BIDE, GIG, FIG, DIG	HID-HAD, BID-BED BID-BAD, BIDE-BADE DIG-FIG, BID-HID
ABCDEFGHI̲J	JAG, JAGGED JIG, JIGGED JIFF, JEFF FIJI, JAB, JIB, JIBE	JIG-JAG, JIFF-JEFF JIB-JAB
ABCDEFGHIJ̲K	KID, KIDDED KICK, KICKED JACK, JACKED JAKE, CAKE, CAKED	JAKE-JACK KIDDED-KICKED CAKE-JAKE
ABCDEFGHIJK̲L	LEAK, LEAKED, BLEAK LAKE, FLAKE, FLAKED BLEED, BLED LID, LIDDED, GLIDE GLADE, BLADE, BLADED	LAKE-LEAK, BLEED-BLED BLEAK-BLEED

---

[1]See Chapter 4, Discrimination Drills.

ABCDEFGHIJKL<u>M</u>	MAD, MADE, MEAD, MAKE	MADE-MAKE, DAM-DAMN
	DAM, DAMMED, DAMN, DAMNED	BEAM-BALM, BALM-CALM
	DAME, MADAME	MACK-BACK, DAME-DEEM
	CAME, BECAME	
	CALM, BECALM, BECALMED	
	JAM, JAMMED	
ABCDEFGHIJKLM<u>N</u>	ING (repeat several times)	MAN-MEN, NECK-HECK
	MAN, MEAN, DEMEAN, DEMEANED, DEMEANING	MEAN-MANE, CLING-CLANG
	NAME, NAMED, NAMING	LEAN-LANE
	CAN, CANE, CANED, CANING	
	NECK, NECKED, NECKING	
	(and all previous verbs given which can end with -ing)	

B. Drill Sentences[1]

1. Jake had a faded face.
2. Dad liked his bed.
3. I'd like to make a cake.
4. I had a leaking head.
5. I am fagged!
6. The beading had faded and flaked.
7. He kidded Jack Lane.
8. Did he call me?
9. Macie made a cake lacking an egg.

VIII. Distribute DUP materials if necessary (if workbooks have not arrived, or are not required), explaining each.

IX. Concluding remarks, and reminders to students to bring workbooks <u>or</u> notebooks, paper, and pencil to next class.

---

[1]Optional. May be omitted if insufficient time remains. May be used as drill in Preliminary Lesson 2 if omitted in this lesson.

(SM 1)

A BRIEF HISTORY OF THE LANGUAGE OF SIGNS

The antecedents of the modern language of signs are buried in the mists of antiquity, but one thing is clear: from earliest recorded history, it is known that gestures (or signs) have been employed for communication between groups of people of dissimilar languages and cultures. Gesture language, therefore, is one of the oldest--if not the oldest--means of communication between human beings.

It stands to reason that some form of rudimentary gesture language must surely have been used by people in antiquity in communicating with deaf people, but the idea that a gesture language could be developed to the point where it could be used as a formal method of communicating does not seem to have occurred to anyone until the sixteenth century. Part of the reason for this appears to be the generally accepted theory that deaf people were uneducable. They were thought to be incapable of reasoning, of having ideas or opinions, and, in some cultures, they were considered to be possessed of the devil, or in the bad graces of the gods. They were, therefore, figures of fun, scorned, reviled, or even feared. It would have been a brave person indeed who would consider going against the prevailing public opinion of the times and putting the theory to the test.

In the sixteenth century, however, a brave person emerged in Girolamo Cardano, an Italian physician, who raised his voice to dispute the theory that deaf people were uneducable. Cardano held that the hearing of words was not necessary for the understanding of ideas; and devised a code for teaching deaf people which, unfortunately, was never put into use. However, his words fell on fertile ground, and although slow to germinate, eventually began sprouting, and paved the way for dispelling the attitude that deaf people were incapable of learning.

It was in Spain that the first successful attempts to educate deaf individuals were made. A Spanish monk, Pedro Ponce de Leon, succeeded in educating the deaf children of several noble Spanish families so that they could be declared legally qualified to inherit the estates of their families. Spanish law at that time was such that a person, in order to inherit property, had to be literate--to be able to read and write--and de Leon succeeded in providing his deaf pupils with these skills. The theory that deaf people were uneducable, therefore, was disproved.

It is interesting to note, also, that de Leon apparently was able to teach his pupils to speak in addition to teaching them to read and write. Presumably he was also able to teach them to read lips in the process of teaching them to speak, but these skills apparently were interesting ancillary benefits obtained by the deaf children after the good monk had accomplished the main task required of him by his noble employers--that of teaching their deaf heirs to read and write so that they could inherit the family estates.

Some time later, Juan Martin Pablo Bonet developed the one-handed manual alphabet, which has descended almost unchanged to that used today. Bonet also wrote a book on education of deaf people, in which both the manual alphabet and some signs were advocated as the method whereby the tutor could communicate with his pupils while providing them with an education.

While individuals like de Leon and Bonet were pioneers in proving that deaf persons could be educated, and that a formal gesture language could be employed for the purpose of communicating with deaf people in the process of educating them, their success was limited to a few select individuals to whom they acted as tutors. Education of deaf people, therefore, was restricted to the very rich, or those of royal blood, for only they could afford private tutors for their deaf children. It was in France and Germany that public education of deaf children began. It was also in those two countries that the methods controversy was born--the argument over whether deaf children should be taught with or without the employment of the language of signs--an argument which has persisted to this day.

In France, Abbe Charles de l'Epee founded the first public school for deaf children. In addition to being considered the father of public education for deaf children, Abbe de l'Epee is also regarded as the father of the modern language of signs. Abbe de l'Epee was convinced that sign language was the "natural language" of deaf people, and held that their education should be based on the use of this "natural" language. However, the language of signs as used by deaf people of that day was rudimentary, and the abbe recognized that the crude signs employed by deaf people of that time were too limited for use as tools in an educational program. He, therefore, attempted to develop and refine the existing language of signs into a full language which could be more effectively used in educating deaf people. The language of signs used today has been derived in a large part from that developed by Abbe de l'Epee, although it has undergone considerable refinement in the years since the good abbe first put it into use.

Samuel Heinicke was Germany's counterpart of France's Abbe de l'Epee. Heinicke, however, shared only two of the abbe's convictions--his belief that deaf people were educable and that they could be educated in public education programs. In contrast to de l'Epee, however, Heinicke believed that deaf people could be educated through speechreading alone. He, therefore, was the forerunner of modern-day advocates of the so-called oral method of instruction (called the German method in Heinicke's day and for some time afterward). Heinicke's philosophy still forms the basic foundation for the belief in the oral method, although his methods of teaching have also undergone many changes and refinements over the years.

Education of deaf children in the United States can be considered to have begun with the arrival upon the scene of Thomas Hopkins Gallaudet. A minister, Gallaudet was approached by Dr. Mason Cogswell, whose daughter, Alice, was deaf. Dr. Cogswell had heard that deaf children were successfully being educated in Europe, and wished Gallaudet to journey to England to learn the methods being employed there to teach deaf children such as his little girl. From this request was born the career of a man who was to become one of the most famous educators of the deaf in the world, a man who was also responsible for the introduction of the language of signs into the United States.

Gallaudet's plan on departing for England was to study the English methods of instructing deaf children, then to extend his trip into France where he would study the French methods. He planned to select the best of both methods, and combine them in a comprehensive plan for educating deaf children in America, beginning with little Alice Cogswell.

Unfortunately, when he outlined his plans to the English educators of the deaf, they reacted by refusing him permission to learn their methods unless he agreed to abandon his plan to study the French methods and combine only the best of the two. (It is ironic that this reaction is still common today in the late twentieth century, for there are pockets of blind belief in one method of instruction over all others, and proponents of such methods are apt to be adamant in insisting that their method be used in its entirety, with no contamination from other methods permitted--and prospective students who wish to study the method, but will not promise to adhere strictly to that method to the exclusion of all others, often find it difficult to obtain permission to enroll.)

After several months of frustrating negotiations with the English experts, an event occurred which caused Gallaudet to give up his plans to study in England. Abbe Sicard of France, a noted educator of deaf people in that country, arrived in England on a lecture tour with two of his most outstanding pupils, one of whom was a young man by the name of Laurent Clerc. Gallaudet attended one of the lectures given by Sicard, and was so impressed by the ability of the two deaf pupils, Clerc in particular, that he immediately abandoned his negotiations with the English and went to Paris to study with Sicard.

At the conclusion of his studies, Gallaudet returned to America, bringing with him Laurent Clerc. Clerc subsequently became the first deaf teacher of the deaf in America, and he helped Gallaudet found the first school for the deaf in this country, the American Asylum for the Deaf and Dumb in Hartford, Connecticut, which subsequently became the American School for the Deaf.

Since the French method of instruction involved the use of the language of signs, Gallaudet brought back with him a knowledge of this form of communication, a skill he and Laurent Clerc taught to others. From this beginning, the language of signs spread rapidly to all corners of the country, and soon was known by nearly every deaf person from one end of the country to the other.

In time, other methods of instructing deaf children came into the country-- those which did not employ the language of signs, and, in fact, forbade its use--but the language of signs was firmly established among deaf people themselves by then, and has remained the national language of deaf people in America. Despite over a hundred years of repeated efforts to eradicate it or to stop its steady spread to each new generation of deaf people, even to those who are supposedly isolated from such "contamination" by rigid rules designed to prevent its being learned by deaf children, only a few deaf adults today fail to acquire the ability to use sign language somewhere along the way, and to make it part and parcel of their communicative lives.

Gallaudet, in bringing the language of signs to our country, released the lid of a Pandora's box of troubles for later oral method advocates, a lid nobody has ever been able to force shut again. But for deaf people, his release of the lid opened up a means of communication with the world around them, and they, themselves, have since developed it and refined it until it is today a classical, beautiful, and picturesque language of gesture in which the great majority of deaf people communicate their thoughts and feelings to each other--and to those hearing people who have taken the trouble to learn the language of signs.

The language of signs is idiomatic, it incorporates pantomime, it is individualistic--and sometimes highly confusing to a beginner. But it is always interesting, and a student in the language of signs will find it greatly rewarding as he progresses to better and better communication with his deaf pupils, co-workers, clients, relatives, and friends. Such a student may, if he persists in learning the language of signs with all its subtleties, nuances, and idiosyncracies, eventually become so fluent that he can help his deaf compatriots in one of the most vital ways a hearing person can help deaf people, by interpreting for deaf people, and opening the door for deaf people to experience at first hand the audible events which go in the sometimes baffling world of the hearing.

Bibliography source: Quigley, S. P. Historical background, education of the deaf. In Education of the Deaf. A report to the President by the Advisory Committee on Education of the Deaf in the United States. U.S. Government Printing Office, 1965.

(SM 181-183)

OUTSIDE ASSIGNMENT SCHEDULE

Course Number
Instructor

Assignment I: Due date:

Assignment II: Due date:

Assignment III: Due date:

Completion of all the following assignments by the due date is <u>required</u> of all students in _____

(course number and title)

Assignment I:

Construct a calendar of the social, religious, education, and sporting events arranged by the people in the local "deaf community" for their own amusement or betterment, which will take place from now to the end of the semester.

Assignment II:

Attend one or more of the activities listed in the calendar constructed in Assignment I. Single out at least one deaf person (<u>not</u> the same one that your fellow students single out, <u>please</u>) at this event, and, <u>without making it obvious</u> that it is a required class assignment, engage this deaf person in conversation long enough to elicit the following information about him/her:

1. Name (and spell it correctly, for your instructor probably has a lot of friends among the members of the local deaf community).

2. Occupation.

3. Cause of deafness (don't worry about the question seeming to be a "personal" one; it is not considered personal by <u>deaf</u> people).

4. Age at onset of deafness.

5. Marital status.

6. Number of children, ages, sexes.

7. Hobbies.

Write a report of your experience including:

1. Your reactions before, during, and after the event.

2. What modes of communication you used (sign language, fingerspelling, pantomime, pen and paper, and so on), and the relative amount of each you used, both to make yourself understood and to understand the deaf person with whom you were talking.

3. The required information about the deaf person with whom you conversed. Include also such information as to how well the deaf person could understand you and you him/her, orally or otherwise. Cite examples of the way in which he constructed his language, if at all deviant.

Assignment III:

Prepare a proposal for a project you, as a student taking a course in manual communication (M/C), can initiate and carry out in order to accomplish the goals listed below. (Limit papers to not less than three nor more than ten pages.) Show how the project can be carried out (with adaptations if necessary) in your home communities as well as in the community in which the university is located. Show how the following goals can be attained through your project:

1. Help you, as a student in manual communication, practice your skills while, at the same time, acquiring some insight into what adult deaf people are like.

2. Provide some social, economic, educational, or welfare service to deaf persons in the community which will provide benefits not now provided, or improve existing services to deaf people in some way.

It would be helpful if, when writing your reports and proposals, you all follow a standardized format in writing. (Typed papers are preferred, on standard weight paper, not flimsy paper, but neatly handwritten reports will be accepted.)

For Assignment I, a graph-type calendar of events is required.

For Assignment II, in writing your report on Assignment I, please present the information required in the same order in which it is given in the description of the assignment on the preceding page. (Note: A cold-blooded, factual description of your reactions is not wanted. You will get static from your instructor if you follow such a format as "Reactions before: Scared spitless. Reactions during: Nervous. Reactions after: Relieved." For some newcomers to the field of deafness, this is one of the toughest assignments they can be called upon to perform for the first time, deliberately going up to and engaging in conversation with a deaf stranger, but one of the most rewarding in the long run. Writing about it often helps you to view the experience in the proper perspective, and, as the psychologists would say, helps you to identify any residual "trauma" still lurking about in your psyche.)

For Assignment III, the preferred style of presentation is that outlined in the APA Publications Manual. Briefly, the format should follow the pattern below.

I. Introduction. (Cite what exists in the area in which you are interested in inaugurating a project, on local, state, and/or national levels.)

II. Justification. (Justify your project: why it should be inaugurated; whether there is a need for this particular type of service; or why you feel deaf people would benefit from it or enjoy it, and so on.)

III. Procedures. (Explain in detail how you would go about inaugurating your proposal; how you think it could be funded; where you would recruit project staff members; who would help plan and/or conduct the project; how you would publicize it so that deaf people would hear about it and take advantage of it; any problems you might encounter and how you would deal with them.)

IV. Anticipated results. (Explain what you think the results of your project would be.)

V. Replication. (Explain how you would go about setting up a similar project in your home community, or how you would adapt your project to fit the needs of deaf people in your home community.)

Note: If the class elects to work toward a grade, your performance on Assignment III may spell the difference between an A and a B (or a B and a C) if there is any doubt about your performance up to that time.

(SM 185)

BIBLIOGRAPHY OF SELECTED BOOKS AND ARTICLES
(FOR STUDENT USE)

Note: Prices listed do not include postage or applicable local taxes.

1. Babbini, Barbara E. An Introductory Course in Manual Communication:
    Fingerspelling and the Language of Signs. Northridge, Calif.: San
    Fernando Valley State College, 1965. (Out of print.)

2. Babbini, Barbara E. Manual Communication. A Course of Study Outline
    for Instructors. Urbana, Ill.: Institute for Research on Exceptional
    Children, 1971. (Available only to instructors in manual communication
    classes.)

3. Becker, V. A. Underwater Sign Language. U.S. Divers Corp., Cat. No. 1919.
    (Available from author, Supervisor of Physically Handicapped, Public
    School System, San Francisco, Calif. Price, if any, unknown.)

4. Benson, Elizabeth. Sign Language. St. Paul, Minn.: St. Paul Technical
    Vocational Institute, 1969. (Price, if any, unknown.)

5. Boatner, Maxine T. A Dictionary of Idioms for the Deaf. U.S. Department
    of Health, Education, and Welfare, 1967. (Available through the NAD,
    price unknown.)

6. Bornstein, H., Hamilton, Lillian B., and Kannapell, Barbara M. Signs
    for Instructional Purposes. Washington, D.C.: Gallaudet College Press,
    1965. (Available without cost while supply lasts.)

7. Casterline, Dorothy, Croneberg, C. C., and Stokoe, W. C., Jr. A Diction-
    ary of American Sign Language on Linguistic Principles. Washington,
    D.C.: Gallaudet College Press, 1965. ($6.95)

8. Cissna, R. Basic Sign Language. Jefferson City, Mo.: Missouri Baptist
    Convention, 1963. (Out of print.)

9. Davis, Anne. The Language of Signs. New York: Executive Council of
    the Episcopal Church, 1966. ($4.95)

10. Delaney, T., and Bailey, C. Sing unto the Lord: A Hymnal for the Deaf.
    Hymns translated into the language of signs. St. Louis, Mo.: Ephphetha
    Conference of Lutheran Pastors for the Deaf, 1959. ($2.00)

11. Falberg, R. M. The Language of Silence. Wichita, Kan.: Wichita Social
    Services for the Deaf, 1963. ($2.75)

12. Fant, L. J. Say It with Hands. Washington, D.C.: Amer. Ann. of Deaf,
    Gallaudet College, 1964. ($3.50)

13. Fauth, Bette L. and W. W. A Study of the Proceedings of the Convention
     of American Instructors of the Deaf, 1850–1949, Chap. XIII: The
     Manual Alphabet. Amer. Ann. of Deaf, 96, 292–296, March, 1951. (Re-
     prints may be available without cost.)

14. Fauth, Bette L. and W. W. Sign Language. Amer. Ann. of Deaf, 100,
     253–263, March, 1955. (Reprints may be available without cost.)

15. Fellendorf, G. W., ed. Bibliography on Deafness. A selected index.
     Volta Rev., A. G. Bell Assoc., Washington, D.C., 1966. (No list price.)

16. Geylman, I. The Sign Language and Hand Alphabet of Deaf Mutes. In
     Proceedings of the Workshop on Interpreting for the Deaf. Muncie,
     Ind.: Ball State Teachers College, 1964, 62–90. (Available in limited
     supply without cost.)

*17. Greenberg, Joanne. In this Sign. Fiction. New York: Holt, Rinehart
      and Winston, 1971. ($5.95)

**18. Guillory, LaVera M. Expressive and Receptive Fingerspelling for Hearing
       Adults. Baton Rouge, La.: Claitor's Book Store, 1966. ($1.00)

19. Higgins, D., C.S.S.R. How to Talk to the Deaf. Newark, N.J.: Mt.
     Carmel Guild, Archdiocese of Newark, 1959. (No price listed.)

20. Hoeman, H. W., ed. Improved Techniques of Communication: A Training
     Manual for Use with Severely Handicapped Deaf Clients. Bowling Green,
     Ohio: Bowling Green State University, 1970. (No price listed.)

21. Kosche, M. Hymns for Singing and Signing. 116 Walnut St., Delavan,
     Wis., 53115. (Date and price unknown.)

22. Landes, R. M. Approaches: A Digest of Methods in Learning the Language
     of Signs, Virginia Baptist General Board, P.O. Box 8568, Richmond, Va.,
     23226, 1968. ($2.95)

23. Long, J. S. The Sign Language: A Manual of Signs. Reprint. Washing-
     ton, D.C.: Gallaudet College Bookstore, 1963. (No price listed.)

**24. Madsen, W. J. Conversational Sign Language: An Intermediate Manual.
       Washington, D.C.: Gallaudet College Bookstore, 1967. ($2.50)

25. Myers, L. J. The Law and the Deaf. Dept. of Health, Education, and
     Welfare, Washington, D.C., 20201, 1970. (No price listed.)

**26. O'Rourke, T. J. A Basic Course in Manual Communication. NAD Communica-
       tive Skills Program, 905 Bonifant St., Silver Springs, Md., 20910,
       1971. ($4.50)

27. Peet, Elizabeth. The Philology of the Sign Language. Reprinted pamphlet.
     Buff and Blue, Gallaudet College, 1921. (Available without cost while
     supply of reprints lasts.)

*28. Quigley, S. P., ed. Interpreting for Deaf People. Workshop report.
U.S. Dept. of Health, Education, and Welfare, Washington, D.C., 20201,
1965. (Available without cost while supply lasts.)

29. Rand, L. W. An Annotated Bibliography of the Sign Language of the Deaf.
Unpublished master's thesis. Seattle, Washington: University of
Washington, 1962. (May be available by writing the author, c/o Univ.
of Wash.)

30. Riekehof, Lottie L. Talk to the Deaf. Springfield, Mo.: Gospel Pub-
lishing House, 1963. ($4.95)

31. Roth, S. D. A Basic Book of Signs Used by the Deaf. Fulton, Mo.:
Missouri School for the Deaf, 1948. (Out of print.)

32. Sanders, J. I., ed. The ABC's of Sign Language. Tulsa, Okla.: Manca
Press, 1968. ($8.75)

33. Siger, L. C. Gestures, the Language of Signs, and Human Communication.
Amer. Ann. of Deaf, 113, 11-28, Jan., 1968. (No price listed.)

34. Smith, J. M. Workshop on Interpreting for the Deaf. Workshop report.
Muncie, Ind., Dept. of Health, Education, and Welfare, Washington,
D.C., 1964. (Available without cost while supply lasts.)

35. Springer, C. S., C.S.S.R. Talking with the Deaf. Baton Rouge, La.:
Redemptorist Fathers, 1961. ($2.50)

*36. Stokoe, W. C. Sign Language Structure: An Outline of the Visual Com-
munication Systems of the American Deaf. Research paper. Buffalo,
N.Y.: University of Buffalo, 1960. ($2.00)

37. Taylor, Lucille N., ed. Proceedings of the Registry of Interpreters for
the Deaf. Conference report. Wisconsin School for the Deaf. Delavan,
Wis., 53115, 1965. (Available without cost while supply lasts.)

**38. Watson, D. O. Talk with Your Hands. Menasha, Wis.: George Banta Pub.
Co., 1963. ($5.00)

39. Wisher, P. R. Use of the Sign Language in Underwater Communication.
Lithograph. Washington, D.C.: Gallaudet College Bookstore. (Date
and price unknown.)

---

*Recommended additional reading.

**Recommended for purchase as additional reference book or supplementary
text.

LIST OF WORDS FOR PRACTICE IN FINGERSPELLING

A to N

Cab	Clanking	Leaning
Cabbie	Jibbed	Cleaned
Bedded	Bleeding	Clacked
Faded	Necking	Blacken
Deaf	Blended	Blackening
Dean	Beamed	Ham
Abel	Backed	Heeded
Able	Named	Jill
Enable	Liking	Jibe
Faded	Biking	Kicked
Facile	Hiking	Lick
Defamed	Clinging	Knack
Indeed	Mane	Fleck
Magic	Image	Flicked
Blend	Glide	Fallen
Blending	Gadding	Needing
Bleak	Aga	Heeding
Flaked	Again	And
Kicking	Gained	Hand
Jabbed	Faced	Banded
Clammed	Flea	Manned
Calming	Deflea	Maned
Hedged	Lacking	Becalmed
Man	Macie	Babe
Meaning	Jake	Damage
Declined	Jim	If
Jamming	Jamb	Had

THE MANUAL ALPHABET, A TO L
(FRONT VIEW)

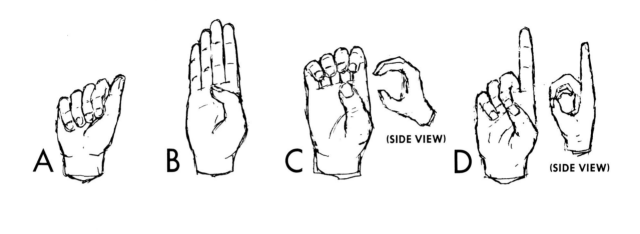

A   B   C (SIDE VIEW)   D (SIDE VIEW)

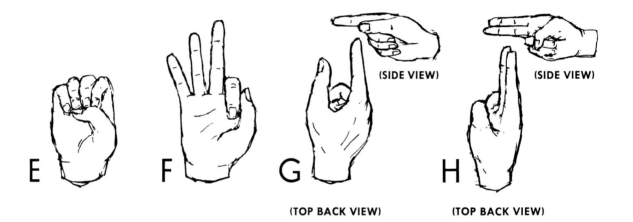

E   F   G (SIDE VIEW)   H (SIDE VIEW)

(TOP BACK VIEW)   (TOP BACK VIEW)

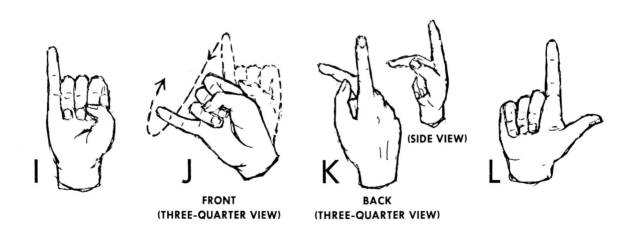

I   J   K (SIDE VIEW)   L

FRONT
(THREE-QUARTER VIEW)   BACK
(THREE-QUARTER VIEW)

THE MANUAL ALPHABET, M TO Z
(FRONT VIEW)

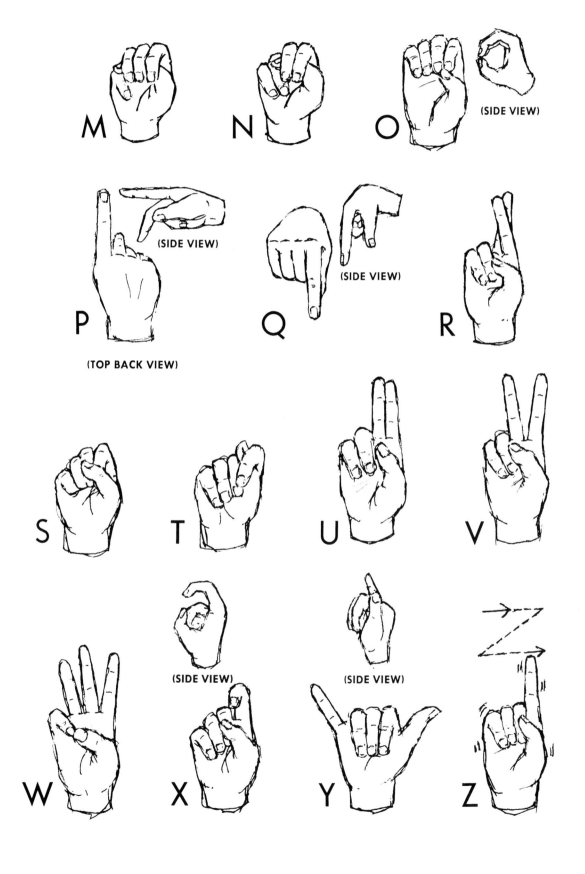

M

N

O

(SIDE VIEW)

P

(SIDE VIEW)

(TOP BACK VIEW)

Q

(SIDE VIEW)

R

S

T

U

V

W

X

(SIDE VIEW)

Y

(SIDE VIEW)

Z

PRELIMINARY LESSON 2

(SM 25-32)

Second Class Session

GENERAL INSTRUCTIONS

Unlike the first class session, a large part of which was devoted to the mechanics of getting the students properly enrolled/registered, acquainted with the instructor and each other, and oriented as to course content and requirements, the second class session can be devoted almost entirely to teaching and drilling in the manual alphabet.

The primary goal of Preliminary Lesson 2 is to teach the remaining letters of the manual alphabet, from O to Z, and, through review and drills, to bring the students to the level of _receptive_ fingerspelling ability at which they can read short words including specific letter groups at full speed; longer words including the same letter groups at a slightly reduced speed; and random words (those not including previously practiced letter groups) at about half the normal rate of fingerspelling speed. At the end of the lesson, they should also be able to fingerspell accurately, albeit slowly, with a minimum of errors in technique or finger placement any words the instructor should ask them to spell. They should also be able to synchronize their fingerspelling of drill words with the instructor's spelling of the same word--and be able to vocalize the word simultaneously with their fingerspelling of the word, although they may have to drawl the word a bit when speaking it.

The task of the instructor in Preliminary Lesson 2 is to review the letters previously taught (in Preliminary Lesson 1) by a quick run through of some of the drill words used in Preliminary Lesson 1, checking both student receptive skills and expressive skills and correcting any developing errors in technique before going on to teach and drill the remaining letters.

If he neglected to do so during Preliminary Lesson 1, the instructor should at this point introduce the vocalization drill in which the students say each word simultaneously with their fingerspelling of the word--and make it a point to require vocalization of each drill word introduced from that time onward. During vocalization drill, he should make an attempt to check each individual student several times on different words, particularly those which have more than one syllable, to make sure that the synchronization is accurate in that what the eye sees and what the ear hears is the same:

	Synchronized	Delayed	Premature
Fingerspelling:	BEATING	BEATING	BEATING
Voice:	"beating"	------ "beating"	"beating" ------

106

In addition, the instructor should keep a sharp eye out for alphabetizing
--the vocalizing of <u>individual letters</u> (by watching the students' lips as
they fingerspell a word, he can easily spot this fault by reading their lips).
In other words, instead of saying "beating" while fingerspelling BEATING, the
student would be saying "bee, ee, ay, tee, eye, en, gee." Alphabetizing is
an exasperating habit which is difficult to break if it is allowed to become
established, but is easy to prevent if the instructor constantly drills the
students in vocalizing <u>words</u>--and is quick to correct any student he sees
alphabetizing. (While concentrating on spelling a difficult word, also, some
students will alphabetize who were not previously guilty of doing so, or who
had seemingly overcome the habit, and the instructor should be able to spot
this and correct it immediately.)

At this point, also, the instructor should begin using an adapted version
of the varying and verifying drill routine (described in the drills section
of General Procedures) in which he fingerspells a word, selects a student at
random to (1) fingerspell back the same word; and (2) then tell what the fingerspelled word was; after which the instructor calls upon another randomly
selected student to judge whether the first student was right or wrong. While
doing this, the instructor should add the signs, RIGHT and WRONG, to those
taught in Preliminary Lesson 1 (I and AND), and require that the "verifying"
student give his opinion of the first student's response by signing RIGHT or
WRONG.

<u>Note</u>: The adapted version of the varying and verifying routine for use
with <u>fingerspelling alone</u> does not include a signed response to a fingerspelled word (and the reverse), since the students will only have been taught
four signs. For more information on drilling techniques, see Chapter 4,
Teaching Fingerspelling.

If sufficient time remains after the alphabet has been taught and drilled
upon, the instructor may wish to introduce Password and have the students
play this game until the end of the class session.

MATERIALS NEEDED FOR PRELIMINARY LESSON 2

<u>For instructional purposes:</u>

1. Roster book
2. Completed Hathaway Guessing Game cards
3. Lesson plan (or this manual)
4. Letter grouping word list
5. Password game (optional)

<u>DUP materials:</u> (if necessary)

<u>SM Page</u>

1. List of words for practice in fingerspelling A through Z
   (FS-2-DUP-P, one page) 30
2. Explanation of hand-positions (FS-2-DUP-M,a, one page) 37
3. Hand-positions (illustrations) (FS-2-DUP-M,b, one page) 36

LESSON PLAN OUTLINE

I.   Register or enroll any new students appearing for the first time in this session.

II. Announcements or other nonteaching information which students should have.

III. Roll call. Use Hathaway Guessing Game cards to refresh memory, setting aside cards of absentees or latecomers. (The instructor can later tally students' names in roster book if he keeps the cards of absentees separated from the rest.)

IV. Review of Preliminary Lesson 1, teaching signs for RIGHT and WRONG first, and explaining vary-verify routine.

   A. Individual letters, brief and rapid drill on each, with order of presentation randomized. (Should not consume more than five minutes of class time.)

   B. Drill words for review of Preliminary Lesson 1 (fingerspell rapidly, vary and verify, then lead class in vocalization of each drill word before going on to the next).

Cab, Cabbie	Lake, Flaked
Bad, Baddie	Bleed, Bleeding
Bead, Beaded	Leak, Bleak
Fade, Fading	Blend, Blended
Face, Faced	Make, Making
Age, Rage, Mirage	Made, Pomade
Egg, Egged, Begged	Calm, Becalm
Hid, Hidden, Hiding	Jam, Jamb
Kick, Kicked, Kicking	Jack, Jacked

   C. Use practice sentences given at end of Preliminary Lesson 1 to drill in reading sentences.

V.   Teach remainder of manual alphabet, O to Z, using teaching drill, discrimination drill, and vocalization drill (see Chapter 2, Drills, and Chapter 4, Teaching Fingerspelling).

   A. Words which can be used in teaching and discrimination drills.

Student Has Learned	Teaching-Drill Words	Discrimination Drill Word-Pairs
ABCDEFGHIJKLMNO	MOM, MOMMIE JOKE, JOKED, JOKING NONE, NOON MOON, MOONING COKE, COOK, COOKING HOME, HOMED, HOMING CONE, CONED, CONING	MOM-MAMA, MOMMA-MAMA MOAN-MEAN COKE-CAKE MOON-MEAN, GO-HO COKE-COOK, GONE-HOME
ABCDEFGHIJKLMNOP	POKE, POKED, POKING COPE, COPED, COPING PAT, PANT, PANTING MOP, MOPPED, MOPING, MOPPING	PEEK-PEAK, POKE-PACK COPE-CAPE, PAT-PANT
ABCDEFGHIJKLMNOPQ and U	QUAD QUICK, QUACK, QUACKED EQUAL, EQUALED, EQUALING	QUICK-QUACK, PICK-QUICK PACK-QUACK

ABCDEFGHIJKLMNOPQR
and U
	RAN, RAIN, GRAIN,
	  TRAINED
	BAR, BARN, BAIRN, CAIRN
	QUICK, QUICKEN, QUICKER
	HARD, HARDEN, HARDENING
	  GARDENING
	FAR, FARM, FARMER
	FUR, FURRED, FURRIER
		RAN-RAIN, HEAT-HEART
		
		PAT-PART, QUICK-QUIRK
		REAL-REEL, RATER-RATED
		HARDEN-GARDEN

ABCDEFGHIJKLMN
OPQRS and U
	AS, HAS, HASH, HASING
	SOCK, SOCKED, SOCKING
	SHOE, GUMSHOE
	SHIP, SHIPPING
	SLIP, SLIPPED, SLIPPER
	QUADS, SQUAD, SQUADRON,
	  SQUADRONS
	RAINS, STRAIN, STRAINING
	  STRAINER, UNTRAINED
	LICK, SLICK, SLICKER,
	  SLICKERS
	JOKES, JOKERS
	SUM, SUMS, SUMMER
		SACK-SOCK
		SACK-SLACK, HASH-GASH
		SLIP-LIPS
		QUADS-SQUAD
		TRAINS-STRAIN
		SHONE-SHINE
		MUSH-MASH
		SUN-SIN
		SUNG-SING

Student Has Learned	Teaching-Drill Words	Discrimination Drill Word-Pairs
ABCDEFGHIJKLMN OPQRS<u>T</u>U	MUST, SMUT, MUSTER, MUSTERING MISTER, MASTER, MASTERING RAT, RATE, GRATE, GRATING ART, PART, PARTING PORT, SPORT, SPORTED QUART, QUARTER, QUARTERING QUIRT, SQUIRT, SQUIRTING TERN, STERN, STERNER BUS, BUST, BUSTED, BUSTER	MUST-BUST, MUST-SMUT MISTER-MASTER, PORT-PART PANT-PART, PANE-PATE POET-PEAT, SATE-SANE
ABCDEFGHIJKLMN OPQRSTU<u>V</u>	VAN, VANE, PARAVANE EVE, EVEN, SEVEN, SEVENTEEN EVIL, DEVIL, DEVILED, BEDEVILED EVE, LEVEL, LEVELING DIVE, ENDIVE VERSE, VERSED, ADVERSE, DIVERSE, DIVERSIFY RIVE, RIVAL, ARRIVAL RAVE, CRAVE, CARVE, CARVING	VAN-RAN, RENT-VENT DIVE-DIRE, CRAVE-CARVE CAVE-COVE
ABCDEFGHIJKLMN OPQRSTUV<u>W</u>	AS, WAS, WASH, WASHING, WASHINGTON, WASHINGTON, D.C. WORD, WORDS, SWORD, SWORDS HOW, SHOW, SHOWER HAD, SHAD, SHADE, SHADOW DOWN, DAWN, DAWNING	WISH-WASH, WORDS-SWORD WORD-WARD FOREWORD-FORWARD HEW-HAW DOWN-DAWN HEW-HOW

Student Has Learned	Teaching-Drill Words	Discrimination Drill Word-Pairs
ABCDEFGHIJKLMN OPQRSTUVWX	OX, FOX, FOXED, OUTFOXED EXAM, EXAMINE, EXAMINATION EX, EXERT, EXERCISE FLEX, REFLEX, FLEXED, FLEXIBLE EX, EXACT, EXACTLY, EXTRACT	EXACT-EXERT, EXACT-EXTRACT EXHORT-EXERT EXHIBIT-INHIBIT OXEN-EVEN
ABCDEFGHIJKLMN OPQRSTUVWXY	YOU, YOUR, YOU'RE SLIP, SLIPPER, SLIPPERY SILL, SILLY YELL, YELLER, YELLED, YELLOW RIVE, RIVAL, RIVALRY PORT, SPORT, SPORTY BAY, BAYED, BAYOU, BAYOUS RAY, HOORAY MAY, MARY, MARRY, MARRYING MERRY, MERRILY LOW, BELOW, BELLOW, YELLOW PART, PARTY, PARTLY	YOUR-YOU'RE SILLY-SALLY, MAY-BAY MERRY-MARRY, MERRY-MERRILY PARTY-PARTLY PARTLY-PORTLY PORTLY-PERTLY
ABCDEFGHIJKLMN OPQRSTUVWXYZ	RAZZ, CRAZE, CRAZY, CRAZILY JAZZ, JAZZY, JAZZILY ZOO, ZOOM, ZOOMED, ZOOMING	COZY-CRAZY, ZIG-ZAG CRAZY-CRAZILY

B. Practice sentences for drilling.

1. The cat sat on the mat.
2. She sewed a yellow dress.
3. Better be a bit blunt.
4. Did Donna do the dishes?
5. Fat cats feed their faces.
6. The girl gave George some gum.
7. Has Hattie had any help?
8. Bill will kill the kid when he finds out.
9. Jack joked with Jake.
10. Kay will make a cake if you will ask her to.
11. Will you lend me your ladder?
12. Maybe Mary made a mistake.
13. The band planned a keen concert.
14. The room was soon too hot.
15. Pack a picnic lunch for the party.
16. They quickly went to the Quad.
17. Rich rakes ruin reputations.
18. Sarah was sad about her sister.
19. They tooted their own horns.
20. The show was very vulgar.
21. Were you washing with soap?
22. Exams require exact answers.
23. Did you yell loudly enough?
24. He is crazy about jazz.

VI. Password game, if at least twenty minutes' time remains. Otherwise, postpone.

VII. Distribute DUP material if necessary, explaining each.

VIII. Concluding remarks. Briefly summarize do's and don'ts of fingerspelling, and inform class that signs will be introduced in next class session.

LIST OF WORDS FOR PRACTICE IN FINGERSPELLING

A to Z

adz	lace	sister
fan	last	uncle
map	with	apple
law	and	black
box	bank	mine
jar	cold	grasp
sky	none	ideal
hat	purple	open
mat	queer	quill
cow	rested	glove
job	union	teach
you	velvet	learn
bat	winter	thank
aero	yearly	come
want	flirt	done
dare	jealous	quit
each	excel	sign
man	family	since
life	coax	trying
way	snow	tomorrow
red	where	experience
hear	twins	school
rock	zebra	explain
wife	were	understand
kiss	pink	maybe
green	home	stinker

Practice Sentences (Fingerspelling)

1. The quick brown fox jumps over the lazy dog.
2. Now is the time for all good men to come to the aid of their party.
3. Peter Piper picked a peck of pickled peppers.
4. Quit exaggerating, you crazy creep!
5. We will learn signs in the next lesson.

(SM 37)

EXPLANATION OF HAND-POSITIONS

1. Open-hand (fingers-closed): In this position, the hand is open, palm
    flat, and fingers and thumb all are together.

2. 5-hand: (Also called open-hand, fingers-spread.) In this, the hand is
    open, palm flat, and fingers and thumb all are separated as when one
    indicates the numeral "five."

3. Alphabet-hand: In this position, the hand forms whichever manual letter
    the "hand" calls for; i.e., an A-hand means a hand in position indica-
    ting the manual letter "A."

4. Open-and hand: This position is the one the hand assumes at the begin-
    ning of the sign AND.

5. And-hand: This position is the one the hand assumes at the end of the
    sign AND.

6. Index-hand: In this position, the hand assumes the configuration it
    does when one wants to indicate the numeral, "one" (the thumb should
    be across the fingers remaining against the palm, not alongside the
    index finger nor extended away from the palm).

7. Right-angle index-hand: Similar to index-hand, except that the index
    finger is bent at the palm to form a right angle with the palm (from
    the palm to the tip, however, the index finger remains straight, not
    bent or hooked).

8. Right-angle hand: In this position, the fingers of an open-hand bend at
    the palm to form a right angle with the palm, the fingers, themselves,
    remaining straight from the palm knuckles outward. The thumb is
    placed against the second knuckle of the index finger, not extended
    nor placed against the palm.

9. Cupped-hand: In this, the open-hand is slightly bent at the palm (fingers
    remain straight from palm outward) and the tip of the thumb is aligned
    with (and placed against) the second knuckle of the index finger, thus
    forming a little hollow in the palm of the hand.

10. Clawed-hand: In this, the fingers and thumb of the 5-hand are all curved
    and hooked to make a claw-like hand. If one pretends to grip a large
    softball, one will have the correct configuration.

11. Touch-hand: (Basic configuration for all affective, sensing, and emotion-
    conveying signs.) In this, the hand is spread in the 5-hand position,
    but, the middle finger only is dropped slightly toward the palm. The
    other fingers and thumb remain extended as in 5-hand position (not
    illustrated!).

HAND POSITIONS

1. OPEN-HAND (FINGERS-CLOSED)

2. 5-HAND

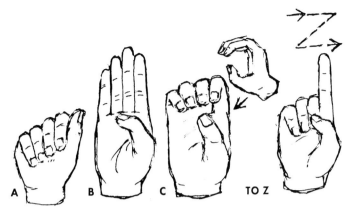

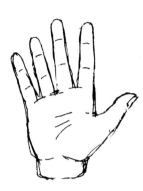

A   B   C   TO Z

3. "ALPHABET" HANDS

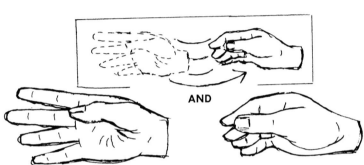

AND

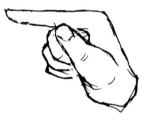

4. OPEN-HAND

5. AND-HAND

6. INDEX-HAND

7. RIGHT-ANGLE INDEX HAND

8. RIGHT-ANGLE HAND

9. CUPPED-HAND

10. CLAWED-HAND

11. TOUCH-HAND

Evaluation of Students

Student's name _____ Semester grade _____

	Class	Instructor	Above	Average	Below[1]

Errors _____

Clearness of signs _____

Clearness of fingerspelling _____

Lack of hesitation in delivery _____

Speed of delivery _____

Smoothness of delivery _____

Facial expression _____

   Total points _____

   Minus errors _____

   Total evaluation score _____

Optional scoring (if instructor is knowledgeable about statistics):

	Above	Average	Below

Error score[2] _____

Comprehension score[2] _____

Correlation score[2] _____

_____

[1]Above = above class average; Below = below class average, etc.

[2]Error score = percentage of errors spotted out of actual number committed. Comprehension score = How closely student's evaluation of fellow students' performance coincided with that of instructor. Correlation score = rho (rank order correlation) score--comparison of student's rating (ranking) of their fellows' performances with instructor's ranking of same students' performances.

[3]Note: If correlation score is below approximately .570, score shows student ranked fellow classmates according to their performance quite differently than instructor did. If above .58, ranking of classmates was pretty much the same as instructor's. If score was high (in the .70's or .80's) then student and instructor disagreed on the relative ranking of only one or two other students.

COURSE OF STUDY OUTLINE

LESSONS 1 through 19

The Language of Signs and Fingerspelling

LESSON 1

(SM 32-44)

THE LANGUAGE OF SIGNS

Third Class Session

GENERAL INSTRUCTIONS

With this lesson the instructor will begin teaching the language of signs to his students. It is assumed that by the time this lesson has been reached, the students will have learned the basic fundamentals of fingerspelling, and within limitations, can both express themselves (slowly) in fingerspelling, and read most fingerspelled words at approximately half normal speed. The present lesson and all those following are designed to increase the receptive (reading) speed in fingerspelling; increase expressive fingerspelling speed; and regularly add new signs to the vocabularies of the students along with providing them with practice in both using and reading these new signs and fingerspelling in sentences.

Another assumption the writer has made is that the instructor has thoroughly familiarized himself with the drills described in the Specific Teaching Techniques section of Chapter 2, for it is primarily through these drills that the receptive skills are developed.

The primary goal of Lesson 1 is twofold. First, the students will be introduced to the various drill routines and become acquainted with the types of responses they will be expected to make during drills; and second, they will learn thirty-eight signs--mostly personal pronouns--all of which are easily mastered.

It has been the author's experience that the signs which may give the student the most trouble are those reflexive personal pronouns which end in -self or -selves. The most common error students make is to use the possessive form of personal pronouns (i.e., YOUR, HIS, HER, THEIR) in place of the reflexives. It was for this reason that a list of "rules" governing the execution of various personal pronouns was included in the vocabulary word-descriptions of the signs. If the instructor will emphasize the importance of memorizing these rules, the students should have little trouble remembering the various pronouns.

Another error which is seen with comparative frequency is that of using YOUR for YOU, and the reverse. However, students usually correct themselves immediately--or their fellows will correct them--so the instructor should not be unduly concerned if this error should manifest itself from time to time.

It cannot be stressed too heavily that the instructor should at all times

118

be alert for developing faulty techniques in execution of both fingerspelling and signs, and move to correct them immediately lest they develop into habits which will be difficult to eradicate. It helps tremendously if the instructor develops the habit of analyzing student mistakes in technique, breaking down the movement of the fingers or hands into the component units of movement so that he can isolate exactly which of the component movements the student is doing wrong--particularly if the executed sign or fingerspelled word has some odd quirk to it that the instructor cannot identify at once, but makes the sign appear deviant even if recognizable as the sign for a given word.

If the instructor has access to videotaping equipment, remediation of faulty techniques usually is simple. If he does not, he will have to demonstrate with his own hands what the student is doing wrong--exactly what he is doing wrong. Therefore, the wise instructor develops an analytical eye for all the successive tiny movements which together constitute a correctly executed sign or smoothly fingerspelled word, so that he can quickly analyze a mistake and show the student exactly how to correct it. The instructor will find the section on the use of videotape equipment in remediation, Chapter 3, very helpful in combating and preventing the development of erroneous techniques whether he has access to videotaping equipment or not. Also helpful will be the section on errors in fingerspelling and their remediation in Chapter 4.

Occasionally when the sign for RIGHT (correct) is taught (but far more frequently when KEEP, VERY and/or MEET are taught) some students will inadvertently misposition their palms or their fingers so that a vulgar, four-letter word is signed instead. When this happens (and the instructor should be alert for such mistakes), the best policy is to immediately correct the student, and tell him what he said. (The author begins this by halting her teaching, then, with a smile and a raised eyebrow, she says to the innocently offending student, "You know, you're swearing at me!") There are various ways of informing students what the goofed-up sign turned out to mean, without departing from socially acceptable language if the instructor is too delicate to use the exact word. These are listed below, along with the words most often mis-signed in this way:

1. RIGHT, VERY, MEET, KEEP, CAREFUL: The four-letter word meaning sexual intercourse.

2. The letter Y: (Index finger instead of thumb extended.) Fertilizer from bulls.

3. ODD, MISS: The familiar twist-nose sign for fertilizer (human variety).

4. WORK: (1) (with palms-facing-each other sign for WORK.) Another four-letter word describing the same activity as in 1 above (banging). (2) (when little-finger edge of one fist is pounded on the thumb-edge of other fist.) What Mommies and Daddies get very upset about when they catch their children doing it. (Masturbation)

5. MORNING: Two ways this can be mis-signed, which mean, respectively:

   (1) (with right palm open.) What happens when a male is aroused

physically by the sight of a lovely, undraped female. (Erection)

    (2) (with right palm closed in a fist.) (a) Same as 1, above; and (b) the commonly used insult Latins give their enemies when they say, "F--- you."

6. Name signs beginning with B: (Made on the forehead or chin.)

    (1) On the chin: a female dog. (Bitch)

    (2) On the forehead: a person whose father and mother are not married to each other. (Bastard)

7. Name signs beginning with G: (With tips of index finger and thumb touching chin.) A man who prefers the company of his own sex. (Gay or homosexual)

8. PAL, LEMON: A female who prefers the company of her own sex. (Lesbian)

9. HOLY: Where a sinner is supposed to go. (Hell)

10. FRENCH: (When D and F are still being confused.) The word which sounds like those big things which hold back the waters of a river and form lakes. (Damn)

11. ABILITY: (When hands are held too high and too close to the chest.) Female mammary glands. (Knockers)

12. SCOLD: (When hand is held too low.) Male sex organ, or colloquial term for same.

The above are the most common, but there are others which will occur from time to time, and the instructor should not hesitate to caution students when he spots this type of error. He should tell them what their mistakes mean--for it is probably the best way of protecting them from committing similar errors in the future.

Not only will they be careful about not botching up a polite sign and inadvertently transforming it into a vulgar one, but they will be protected from practical jokers whose idea of fun is to deliberately teach beginners vulgar signs but tell them the signs mean something else.

In addition, parents and teachers in such classes are thereby equipped to monitor their children's language--for, in common with hearing children, deaf children pick up the naughty signs, but, unlike hearing children, they often can use these signs with impunity--because their parents and teachers all too often do not know the signs and therefore do not discipline them for using socially unacceptable language.

In teaching signs, the instructor should endeavor at all times to give the referents of each sign as he teaches it, the reasons why individual signs are made the way they are, if at all possible. It assists a student in fixing a sign in his memory if he is immediately able to associate it with the components of the object or concept it describes.

Note: The lecture, "Do's and Don'ts," in Lesson 1 also appears in the student's manual. Instead of giving this lecture in class, therefore, the instructor may elect to assign this as homework reading, after which it can be discussed in class.

In addition, the instructor should also try to teach all of the variations of a given sign which he knows--those which are not included in this manual. Due to the great number of local dialectical variations, it was not possible to include word-descriptions of all the variants, so only the most commonly used, or "classic," signs have been described herein.

The instructor should also not feel bound by the vocabulary of signs provided in each lesson, but should introduce extra signs as they occur to him in the course of teaching any given lesson, or as the need arises. This is especially important after the beginning course has been completed, for it is assumed that the instructor will use the vocabulary provided for the intermediate lessons as a guideline for expansion of students' vocabularies of signs, rather than as a fixed list of signs to be adhered to without deviation.

It goes without saying that the instructor should keep a record of all extra signs taught in class, and drill on these as well as on the signs listed in each lesson. He should also remind his students to do the same, preferably in their workbooks on the page provided for Notes. However, the instructor should keep in mind that students will have more difficulty recalling extra signs during the early part of the course since they will not have word-descriptions to refer to, and the instructor may want to provide these by writing such word-descriptions himself and distributing them to his students. As the students become more facile in manual communication, however, it will be easier for them to recall extra signs taught in class, and there will be less need for word-descriptions.

MATERIALS NEEDED FOR LESSON 1

For instructional purposes

1. Lesson plan, or this manual.
2. Lecture notes (Do's and Don'ts).

DUP materials[1]   SM Page

1. Vocabulary word-descriptions, Lesson 1 (1-DUP-V, five pages) ...   38
2. (Optional) Do's and Don'ts, and I'll Be Doggoned's of the
   Language of Signs   14

---

[1]In this and all succeeding general instructions or lesson plans, any reference to DUP materials required for a given lesson can be disregarded unless students have not been required to purchase the companion Course of Study Outline for Students (Babbini, 1974) or in the event the workbooks have been ordered, but have not yet arrived.

LESSON PLAN OUTLINE

Third Class Session

I. Roll call (roll call should be fingerspelled from this time on).

II. Announcements, if any.

III. Summarize previous two lessons on fingerspelling, with particular emphasis on rules of position, the need to vocalize complete words, and so on.

IV. Brief drill in fingerspelling. Use letter groups AT, AN, AM, and AS, Chapter 4, F.

V. Brief fingerspelling test. (Students should not be graded on this test since it is more for the instructor's information than for grades per se.) Spell out whole test once, instructing students to just watch without attempting to write down the words, then go through it word by word, spelling each word twice, stopping after the second spelling to allow students to write down what they understood. (Those who understand the whole test will be easily spotted--they will laugh.)

1.	Papa	7.	Mama	13.	And
2.	Loves	8.	Is	14.	Papa
3.	Mama	9.	In	15.	Is
4.	Mama	10.	The	16.	In
5.	Loves	11.	Grave	17.	The
6.	Men	12.	Yard	18.	Pen

(18 words, -5.6 for each error)

VI. Lecture: Do's and Don'ts and I'll Be Doggoned's of the Language of Signs (optional).

VII. Introduction of signs:

A. Explain and demonstrate hand-positions, and explain what vocabulary word-descriptions are to be used for (for recall purposes after sign has been learned, not for learning purposes).

B. Signs to be taught in this lesson:

1. I	14. Himself, herself	29. Confused
2. Me	15. It (a) & (b)	30. Not (a) & (b)
3. My	16. Its	31. Understand
4. Mine	17. They, them	32. No
5. Myself	18. Their	33. Yes
6. You (sing.)	19. Themselves	34. Hello
7. You (pl.)	20. We, us (a) & (b)	35. Goodbye
8. Your (sing.)	21. Our, ours	36. Question mark
9. Your (pl.)	22. Ourselves	sign
10. Yourself	23. What (a) & (b)	37. And
11. Yourselves	24. How	38. Right
(a) & (b)	25. Practice	39. Wrong
12. He, him; she,	26. Think	
her (a), (b)	27. Know	
& (c)	28. Don't know	
13. His, hers		

(Total signs taught after this lesson: 39)

New signs taught:

Variations of the above signs: New signs (not in the lesson
                                        plan):

VIII.   Drill for teaching Lesson 1 vocabulary.

Examples of backtracking drill sentences. (Words underlined should
be fingerspelled. Words in capital letters are the signs which have
just been demonstrated. Teach the signs first, then use them in a
sentence, and then ask class what was said.)

1. I saw MY father.
2. That book is MINE. Give it to ME.
3. I will do it MYSELF.
4. YOU are my friend.
5. YOU all are nice.
6. Is this book YOURS?
7. Tell all YOUR friends to come. (Plural YOUR)
8. You YOURSELF must do it.
9. Study your lessons YOURSELVES.
10. HE said it was OK.
11. HER sister is pretty.
12. She hurt HERSELF.
13. IT was funny.
14. Put IT on the desk. (Object IT)

15. The dog bit ITS tail.
16. THEY came to see us.
17. They sold THEIR house.
18. They got THEMSELVES in trouble.
19. WE will help you with it.
20. We cleaned OUR room with her help.
21. Our teacher made us do it OURSELVES.
22. WHAT is your name? (Specific WHAT)
23. WHAT did he say? (General WHAT)
24. HOW are you?
25. How do you KNOW he THINKS so?
26. I DON'T KNOW what he said.
27. She is very CONFUSED.
28. You must PRACTICE all the time. (Plural YOU)
29. They are NOT coming to practice today.
30. If you DO NOT practice, you will not learn.
31. She did not UNDERSTAND what they were doing.
32. He said "No!" when I asked him.
33. YES, that is what they told me.
34. HELLO, how are you?
35. GOODBYE, we will see you tonight.
36. Are they RIGHT or WRONG????
37. You AND I have a lot of work ahead of us.

IX. Summarize lesson by going through signs which have been taught.

X. Pass out DUP material, if necessary, explaining each.

XI. Concluding remarks.

(SM 38)

WORD-DESCRIPTIONS OF SIGNS IN LESSON 1 VOCABULARY

Note: The student will find it helpful to remember that there are certain
basic hand-positions and movements which are used in combination to indicate
specific personal pronouns, and whether the pronoun is singular or plural.
These are described below in summary form for quick reference purposes. For
more detailed descriptions see the word-description of the sign for each pronoun.

Key Hand-Positions (or handshapes):

Index-hand: Used for all personal pronouns used as subject or object except
    for I, WE, and US (described in detail below).

Open-hand, fingers-closed, palm flat: Used for all possessive forms of per-
    sonal pronouns except OUR (in which the palm is cupped, not flat).

A-hand: Used for all pronouns ending in -self or -selves (reflexives).

Key Hand and Arm Movements:

Hand makes single movement ending on center of own chest: All first-person-
    singular pronouns.

Hand moves straight toward person being addressed: All second-person-singular
    pronouns.

Hand describes semicircle directly in front of center of body: All second-
    person-plural pronouns.

Hand makes a single, straight movement to one side (or the other) of center
    front: All third-person-singular pronouns.

Hand describes semicircle, beginning and ending off to the left (or right)
    of center front: All third-person-plural pronouns.

Hand begins sign on one shoulder and, describing semicircle in front of chest,
    ends at other shoulder: All first-person-plural pronouns.

1. I: I-hand, palm toward left, thumb touching chest.

2. ME: Right angle index-hand, finger pointing toward and touching chest.

3. MY: Open-hand, fingers-closed, palm flat, placed on chest, palm to chest.

4. MINE: Same as MY.

5. MYSELF: <u>A-hand</u>, palm to left, knuckles to ceiling, bump thumb against chest <u>twice</u>.

6. YOU (singular): With <u>index-hand</u>, palm to floor, point at the person being addressed.

7. <u>YOU (plural)</u>: Similar to YOU, except that hand describes a semicircle from left to right (or the reverse) to point at several people instead of a single person, with the center of the semicircle being directly in front of the signer.

8. YOUR (singular): With <u>open-hand, fingers-closed</u>, palm forward, push hand a few inches toward person being addressed. Do <u>not</u> use to mean YOU'RE!!

9. YOUR (plural): Similar to YOUR (singular) except that hand describes a semicircle to encompass several people instead of just one (like in YOU (plural)). Do <u>not</u> use to mean YOU'RE!!

10. YOURSELF: With hand in <u>A-hand</u> position, palm to left and thumb on top (and slightly extended), push hand <u>twice</u>, rapidly, a few inches toward person being addressed.

11. <u>YOURSELVES</u>: (a) Similar to YOURSELF except that hand describes semicircle to encompass a group instead of pushing twice at one individual.

    (b) Similar to YOURSELVES except that hand pushes once toward each of several individuals in a group. (Used when it is desired that particular emphasis be placed on individuals within a group, rather than the group as a whole.)

12. <u>HE, HIM, SHE, HER</u>: (Usually fingerspelled when the words begin a sentence, or if there is a need to discriminate between two or more persons, or between two persons of different sexes. <u>Always</u> fingerspelled when the person being discussed is first mentioned in a sentence or conversation.)

    (a) Point at the person and then fingerspell HE or SHE as the case may be.

    (b) Point at the person being discussed, if present.

    (c) If person being discussed is not present, it ordinarily suffices to use the colloquial sign--<u>A-hand</u>, palm to self, thumb to right and extended, jerk hand to the right in a brief gesture, similar to the common gesture used by hearing people to pantomime "Get a load of him!"

13. <u>HIS, HERS</u>: Similar to YOUR (singular) except that the hand pushes toward the person being discussed if present. If person is not present, the hand pushes off to the right (or left) of center rather than toward person(s) being addressed.

14. **HIMSELF, HERSELF:** Similar to YOURSELF except that the hand is pushed twice toward the person being discussed (if present). If person is not present, the same sign as for YOURSELF is used, but the hand pushes twice to the left (or the right) of center instead of directly at the person or persons being addressed.

15. **IT:** (a) If an object, point to it.

    (b) If used as an indefinite "it," fingerspell.

16. **ITS:** Same as for HIS or HERS. (Possessive form only as in, "I sent the dog it ITS bed." Do not use for the contraction "it is.")

17. **THEY, THEM:** Similar to YOU (plural) except that the semicircle described by the hand is positioned to the left (or to the right) of center, with the semicircle beginning to the left (or right). Note: The "Get a load of him (them)" gesture can also be used, but thumb should describe small, horizontal semicircle from front to rear to encompass more than a single "He" or "She."

18. **THEIR:** Similar to YOUR (plural) except that the semicircle is off to one side as described in THEY, THEM.

19. **THEMSELVES:** Similar to YOURSELVES (a) and (b), except that the semicircle is off to one side as previously described for THEY, THEM, and THEIR.

Note: In all the following first-person-plural signs, the following movement from right shoulder to left shoulder (for a right-handed person) is the basic movement of the sign, with only hand-positions changing according to the word being signed: The right hand, palm to left, touches the thumb side of the hand to the front of the right shoulder, then describes a semicircle in front of the chest, the hand rotating so that the movement ends with the little finger edge of the hand against the front of the left shoulder.

20. **WE, US:** (a) Indicate both words with index-hand performing the shoulder-to-shoulder movement described above.

    (b) For WE, use W-hand instead of index-hand, and for US, use U-hand, in both cases, performing the movement described above.

21. **OUR, OURS:** Perform movement described above with hand in cupped-hand position. (Some people prefer to use an O-hand, but most people still use the cupped-hand.)

22. **OURSELVES:** Perform movement described above, using an A-hand, thumb edge of hand against right shoulder and slightly extended. However, do not rotate hand so that the sign ends with the little finger edge of the hand against the left shoulder—simply touch the thumb edge of the hand to both shoulders.

23. **WHAT:** (a) Natural sign. Both hands in 5-hand position, palms to ceiling, in universal gesture of helplessness.

(b) Left hand, in 5-hand position, palm to ceiling. Draw index finger of right hand across fingers of left hand from index finger to little finger, like running a stick along a picket fence

24. HOW: Both hands in A-hand position, palms to floor, index finger knuckles touching. By turning both your wrists, simultaneously, roll the second knuckles of each hand together (or rock them back and forth quickly and briefly).

25. PRACTICE: Left hand in index-hand position, palms to self, index fingertip pointing to right; right hand in A-hand position, palm to floor and knuckles pointing forward. "Polish" index finger of left hand with the flat "bottom" of the right fist by brushing back and forth from fingertip to last knuckle.

26. THINK: Bring tip of index finger of right-angle-index-hand, palm to self, up to and touch temple.

27. KNOW: Right-angle-hand, palm to self, bring fingertips up to touch temple.

28. DON'T KNOW: Sign KNOW, then, in an abrupt "flicking water off the fingertips" gesture, snap hand around to palm forward 5-hand position.

29. CONFUSED: Sign THINK, then follow by both hands in clawed-hand positions, palms toward each other, slightly separated. Twist wrists in a "mayonnaise-jar-opening" motion to indicate metal gears getting out of synchronization.

30. NOT: (a) A-hand, palm to left, ball of thumb touching under part of chin, bring forward a few inches in front of chin.

    (b) Both hands in open-hand, fingers-closed position, palms forward and flat, cross and then uncross wrists so that hands end up side by side four or five inches apart. (Usually used in place of DO NOT, whereas NOT (a) is used as indefinite NOT, ISN'T, and so on.)

31. UNDERSTAND: O-hand, thumb touching temple. Snap index finger up into the air, other fingers remaining in position.

32. NO: Fingerspell U, O quickly, snapping fingers and thumb together.

33. YES: Right hand in A-, S-, or Y-hand position (all are acceptable), palm forward and knuckles to ceiling. Nod hand from the wrist (keeping arm stationary) like a head nods on the neck.

34. HELLO: Right hand in open-hand, fingers-closed position. Bring to forehead in a "saluting" gesture, then move hand forward a few inches.

35. GOODBYE: Natural gesture--wave the fingertips of the raised right hand in the universal "bye bye" gesture.

36. QUESTION MARK SIGN: With hand in X-hand position, wiggle index finger
    up and down rapidly.

37. AND: Open-and-hand, palm to left, thumb edge of hand uppermost, move
    hand quickly to the right a few inches, closing it to and-hand.

38. RIGHT: Both hands in index-hand position, index fingertip pointing for-
    ward. Begin sign with right hand directly above left hand, index
    fingers parallel and pointing forward, with hands separated about
    three inches, then bring right hand down briskly until it makes abrupt
    contact with the left hand. (Be careful with this sign. Remember, it
    is made with INDEX-HANDS, not H- or V-hands!)

39. WRONG: With right hand in Y-hand position, palm to self, thumb to right
    and little finger to left, rap second knuckles of middle three fingers
    against chin.

<u>Note to the instructor</u>: The following is a copy of material appearing under the same title in the introductory section of the companion <u>Course of Study Outline for Students</u>, a workbook designed for use by students in classes being taught by instructors using the present manual. If students have not been required to purchase this workbook, the instructor may wish to duplicate the lecture and distribute it instead of giving the lecture himself. However, regardless of what the instructor decides to do with regard to the "rules" outlined in the lecture, he should familiarize himself with the material, particularly the exemplary sentences for the use of the sign for LOOK, so that he will be prepared to demonstrate the ways the sentences are signed.

DO'S AND DON'TS, AND I'LL BE DOGGONED'S
OF THE LANGUAGE OF SIGNS

Do's and Don'ts:

There are certain rules that one must observe in communicating with deaf persons in the language of signs. Some of them are obvious, like making sure you are facing the deaf person and he is looking <u>at</u> you before you start signing, because if you don't, you're likely to end up talking to yourself, not to him. Other rules are not so obvious. To take one example: You are aware, of course, that a deaf person <u>must</u> look directly at you when you are talking with him, whatever means of communication--oral or manual-- you are using, but are you aware that you should look at him too? Of course, if he is using the language of signs without using his voice, you will jolly well have to look at him. BUT--and here is the sticker--some deaf people use <u>both</u> signs and speech at the same time, and it is all too easy for a person who can hear and who can understand the deaf person's speech, to let his eyes wander away from the deaf person's face even if he is listening to his speech with total attention, and the deaf person thinks he's lost his audience. Common courtesy, therefore, dictates that a person keep his eyes on the deaf person until he has finished what he is saying, regardless of whether he is saying it orally, manually, or in a combination of the two methods.

Another rule has to do with your attitude. This can best be stated as, "Don't 'talk down' to deaf people." By and large, deaf people are of normal intelligence despite any language deficiencies they may have, and the quickest way to turn them off is to attempt to patronize them. Patronization is as insulting to the deaf person as it is to a person with normal hearing, but few hearing people seem to appreciate this fact. Indignities a normally courteous hearing person would not dream of inflicting upon another hearing person, he often does not hesitate to inflict upon a deaf person; and these can range from forcing unwanted help upon a deaf person who is perfectly capable of handling his own affairs--through heedless disregard for the deaf person's feelings by discussing him verbally with another hearing person as if the deaf person was not present--or were an object instead of a human being with feelings--to the insulting situation where a hearing person with whom a deaf person has been conversing allows another hearing person to interrupt the conversation without apology or explanation, and the two hearing people then proceed to exclude the deaf person by carrying on their conversation verbally. Whether the exclusion of the deaf person is unintentional or deliberate, he seldom can follow the fast verbal conversation by lipreading alone, so he is left standing, abandoned, with the egg of humiliation all over his face because his erstwhile conversational partner apparently did not consider him interesting or important enough to either pay him the courtesy of an apology or explanation, or intelligent enough to be included in the new conversation with the other hearing person.

If one were to imagine one's self in a similar situation in a foreign country, where one has only a limited command of the language of that country, one can begin to appreciate the resentment the deaf person feels at being abandoned and subsequently ignored while two natives--one or both of whom he knows could carry on their conversation in his language if they had chosen to do so--chatter away without a thought for his feelings.

In all honesty, it must be admitted that deaf people themselves are guilty of this breach in good manners, particularly those who have the ability to both speak and sign simultaneously, and exclude hearing people with limited manual communication skills from their conversations. However, the hearing person in such a situation does not normally feel insulted and usually is quick to remind the deaf person of his limited signing skill and asks for a vocal replay. On the other hand, the deaf person, sensitized by a lifetime of being made to feel like a second-class person, of being snubbed, ignored, and patronized both intentionally and unintentionally, does not call the social faux pas of his "betters" to their attention. Rather, he withdraws in hurt and resentment, and soon wanders away to seek more congenial--and dependable--conversational partners.

The situation just described is far from uncommon. Even veteran interpreters for deaf people sometimes forget deaf people are present and carry on verbal conversations with other hearing people which exclude the deaf people. Generally, however, the good interpreter will soon remember, apologize, and thereafter make an attempt to keep the deaf person informed of what is being said. Sometimes the interpreter will do this by attempting to interpret what each person is saying: other times he will just sign and fingerspell his own remarks as he is making them, and trust to the deaf person's lipreading ability to pick up the other person's remarks when aided by partial knowledge of what is being discussed. If the interpreter chooses the latter approach, the good one usually will keep a weather eye on the deaf person, and if he appears to be getting lost, the interpreter brings him up to date by interpreting the remarks he did not catch.

You may be asking at this point what you, a complete newcomer to the language of signs, can do which would help you avoid a situation in which you are interrupted by another hearing person who must talk to you in front of a deaf person with whom you have been trying to communicate. It is really simple: Observe the common courtesy of apologizing for the necessary interruption. A simple "Excuse me," which is one of the first signs you will learn in this course, will enable the deaf person to wait a reasonable length of time for your attention to return to him before he will start to feel abandoned for more interesting company. If you must accompany the other hearing person elsewhere, excuse yourself and give a brief explanation of why you must leave.

If, on the other hand, your conversation with the other hearing person is not urgent--or private (in which case you should conduct it in another room!)--and it lasts longer than just a few minutes, you should then attempt to bring the deaf person into the conversation if he is still patiently standing around waiting for you. This is not always easy to do, particularly if the deaf person is shy, or knows his speaking ability is poor, and your receptive manual communication skills are limited. However, it can be done in such a way that the deaf person, whether he participates actively in the conversation or not, at least _feels_ included--and may be enabled to follow the conversation to a degree. A few fingerspelled or signed key words can narrow the conversational topic down to the point where the deaf person's lipreading ability may enable him to catch most of what is being said.

It should be obvious that it is extremely rude for two hearing persons to carry on a verbal conversation in the presence of a deaf person if _both_ hearing persons are fluent in manual communication. The rudeness is intensified if, in addition, one such hearing person interrupts without apology or explanation a conversation between the other hearing person and the deaf person--then proceeds to engage him in verbal conversation without either hearing person using his manual communication skills, or making any attempt to include the deaf person, regardless of how urgent the discussion between them may be.

Few deaf people forgive an insult of this sort, for they know it would take but a moment for one or the other to apologize and explain (if possible) the reason for the interruption--particularly if it results in his conversational partner leaving him to go off with the newcomer. It would be well, therefore, to keep this in mind toward the time when you become fluent in manual communication, for there will be times when you will find yourselves in exactly such a situation as has been described--and the way you handle it may spell the difference between making and retaining friends among deaf people, and never getting to first base with them.

It can also determine your future effectiveness in any work you may do with deaf people; between rapport with them, and resistance from them; between acceptance of your services and any help you may be able to provide them, and complete rejection of everything you represent, personally as well as professionally. Deaf people have long memories--and, often, long tongues. An insult to one is soon known to many, via the efficient "deaf grapevine" of rumor, and the person who did the insulting soon begins to encounter inexplicable reserve among deaf people, both those with whom he has previously enjoyed a good relationship, and those he is meeting for the first time, all without knowing why. And, like all gossip, the facts fed into the "deaf grapevine" become distorted and magnified in the retelling.

Therefore, even if you are trapped in an unwilling conversation with a crashing bore who just happens to be a deaf person--and welcome the interruption like manna from heaven--_do_ observe the rules of common courtesy by apologizing for the interruption, and excuse yourself before you make your escape.

One might wonder at this point why deaf people are so sensitive about such matters as being treated with politeness and consideration by people who can hear, especially when one learns that deaf people are often apparently extremely rude to each other as well as to hearing people. A sociologist would perhaps attempt to explain this by drawing an analogy between the deaf subculture and those of other minority groups such as black people. A parallel can be drawn in some respects, but not in others. Black people know that some white bigots think they are an inferior race--but the black people themselves know they are not. Deaf people also know that some hearing people consider them to be inferior--but, differing from black people, deaf people often suspect that maybe the hearing people are right. Where black people, depending upon the degree of militancy with which they view the white race, regard manifestations of respect, courtesy, and consideration as confirmation of their knowledge of the equality of their own race to that of the whites, and only what they feel is their due, deaf people regard such manifestations as offers of friendship and indications that the hearing person can be trusted and depended upon not to kick the props out from under their fragile self-esteem.

Several research studies have shown that deaf people do suffer from very fragile egos. Their self-image is low, for they have been conditioned since childhood to feel that they are inferior to normal children. Parents and teachers chatter away among themselves without regard for the child with straining eyes who is trying to catch what they are saying by watching their lips. In addition, they frequently discuss him in his presence--a fact of which he instantly becomes aware when he sees a hand casually brought up to the mouth so that his lipreading ability is defeated, or when the lip movements become deliberately small or stiff, and thereby hard to read; or when the head is ever so casually turned away from him so that he cannot see the lips; or when any of the small subterfuges hearing adults practice are employed in a blithe assumption that the deaf child will not know he is under discussion among those who control his destiny.

Unfortunately, he often does know, for he will have learned at a very early age what it means when a hearing person in his environment attempts to interfere with his ability to see the lips, and read them, just as a hearing child learns very young that when adults resort to spelling out words, or to whispering, or even to various types of "codes," that the topic under discussion is not meant for his ears, and, egoistically perhaps, he decides that he is the topic any time this happens.

A hearing child can fight back. He can develop rabbit ears which enable him to understand a whispered conversation from another room. He can learn the "codes." He will eventually learn to understand even spelled-out words. And, eventually, he learns that such sotto voce conversations do not always concern him.

The deaf child, on the other hand, cannot fight his way to understanding. Not only is his lipreading ability all too often inadequate to the task of understanding grown-up conversation, but the subterfuges employed to further impede his ability to lipread by blocking or obscuring his sight of the lips are almost always successful. In addition, the one word he will most often recognize on the lips is his own name--and the few times he sees his own name filtering through the impediments thrown up to screen the conversation between his elders just serve to reinforce his belief that he is always the topic of conversation between hearing people any time he sees a hand move up to scratch a nose, a face turned momentarily away from his as the owner's attention is attracted by something on the other side of the room, or lip movements become different as the speaker's mood changes. So the seed is planted of later suspicion of conversations between hearing people which have often been called "paranoid" by many who deal with them as adults.

To be sure, the deaf person learns in time that he is not always the topic of conversation between two hearing people who black him out by shifting from manual to verbal communication. In time, also, he becomes somewhat philosophical about unintentional rudeness in cases where the conversational blackout occurs when two hearing people, one or both of whom lack manual communication skills, start conversing with each other and unwittingly exclude him from understanding. But, in the case of those who could keep him in the conversation but do not take the trouble to do so, a deep, underlying resentment comes to the surface and colors both his reaction to the exclusion and his perception of the situation as it pertains to him. He feels unimportant, rejected, and suspects that the exclusion may be deliberate so that they could discuss him.

A sophisticated, verbal deaf person may recognize his own reactions as immature, and, knowing that his resentment may be clouding his judgment, call the oversight to the attention of the careless ones. But the majority of deaf people will simply withdraw into themselves--and cross off the names of the erring ones from their lists of hearing people they feel they can trust.

The above rules can be summarized as:

1. Do keep your face and hands toward the deaf person with whom you are speaking.

2. Do maintain eye contact with the deaf person with whom you are conversing. He has to keep his eyes on you all of the time you are speaking--and expects you to do the same when he is talking to you, whether verbally or manually.

3. Do not cover up your lips or face with your hands, or turn away from deaf persons present when talking with other hearing people. This applies to deaf children as well as deaf adults. If you must discuss a deaf person (child or adult) with another hearing person, do so at a time when the deaf person is not present. Leave the room if necessary--just as you would if a hearing child/adult were to be discussed--or wait for a time when he can be discussed in private.

4. <u>Do not</u> allow your attention to be diverted by another hearing person and engage in a verbal conversation with that person in the presence of the deaf person with whom you may have been conversing until interrupted without at least apologizing for the interruption.

5. <u>Do</u> make every attempt to include any deaf person present in any conversation you are having with another hearing person. If you have manual skills, use them. If the other person also can use manual communication methods, the fact that <u>you</u> are using yours will often remind him to use <u>his</u>; if it does not, you can subtly increase the likelihood of his remembering by interpreting <u>his</u> remarks to the deaf person. If he cannot use manual methods of communication, ask the deaf person if he has understood the other hearing person's remarks, and if he has not, tell him what was said.

6. <u>Do not</u> treat the deaf person like a child or a cretin. His language deficiency and/or lack of sophistication may cover up an excellent mind--his I.Q. may be much higher than yours--and if you treat him like a half-wit, he will respond with subtle contempt. So grant him the dignity and respect due a normal person of the same age.

There are other more technical rules--those dealing with the mechanics of the language of signs and the nature of the handicap rather than psychological or sociological aspects:

1. To get a deaf person's attention, a gentle tap on the shoulder or arm is best. The foot can be stomped if the floor is wooden and/or carries vibrations, or the hand rapped on the table, but care should be taken not to make the stomping and/or rapping too vigorous or sudden, for many deaf people are "spooky" in the sense that an unexpected loud vibration makes them jump. Turning the lights on and off is also an effective attention-getter.

   <u>Note</u>: Drumming fingers and tapping feet can drive a deaf person up a wall, as can kicking his chair, and so on. In addition, stomping the feet or slapping a table to emphasize a conversational point is sure to net you the attention of every deaf person within vibration range; so, unless you are intent on attracting their attention (or bugging them), it is best to control any tendencies toward drumming, tapping, stomping, pounding, or any such vibration-causing nervous mannerism.

2. In fingerspelling, the palm always faces forward except for G, H, J, P, and Q.

3. Unless otherwise specified (or in the case of a left-handed person), in any sign involving movement of one hand while the other remains still or makes smaller movements, the <u>right</u> hand always does the moving or makes the larger gesture.

4. Fingerspelling is generally done by the right hand alone (or the left hand alone in the case of the left-handed person). One should avoid

fingerspelling with first one hand and then the other unless this is done to make a distinct separation between two objects, two radically different one-word concepts, and so on. (The latter technique is seldom used except by expert users of manual communication and should not be attempted by beginners.)

I'll Be Doggoned's:

There are many things about the language of signs which often inspire the reaction of "I'll be doggoned!" from the beginner. In some cases, it is a rueful exclamation, as when the beginner finds that one sign can mean anywhere from three to eight or nine different words (e.g., NEED, MUST, HAVE TO, NECESSARY, OUGHT TO, SHOULD) are all signed alike; or the reverse, where one word can be signed over a hundred different ways depending upon the context in which it is used (e.g., RUN for a bus, RUN for the presidency, etc.).

In other cases, it is an exclamation loaded with surprise and admiration when the student finds that a single sign can express far better than words a whole range of emotions, depending upon the amount and type of emphasis, the facial expression, and the speed at which it is delivered (e.g., FOR: What for?) (a child whining); What the blazes did you do that for??? (angrily); What's that for? (curiosity).

And, when one takes a single sign, such as LOOK, and shows all the various ways in which the basic, two-fingered LOOK sign can be used, the reaction is one of, "Well, I'll be utterly doggoned!" at the versatility of the language of signs.

All of the following concepts can be expressed merely by employing one or two hands, in the basic V-hand position, and moving them around to give a graphic picture of what the eyes are doing and seeing:

1. Instructor looking at individual students in the class.

2. Individual students looking back at the instructor.

3. All students collectively looking at the instructor.

4. Instructor looking around the class, at students, at the room, at something over to the left or right of himself, and so forth.

5. Instructor "looking back" at the past events of his life.

6. Instructor looking forward to future events.

7. Instructor standing on top of a hill and looking at the view.

8. A wife, whose husband is being the "life of the party," glaring at him.

9. The husband's too-casual avoidance of her glare.

10. Eyes meeting across a crowded room--a boy and a girl, strangers to each other--neither of whom wants the other to know that he/she is staring.

11. The eyes of a boy giving the once-over to a pretty, curvaceous girl.

12. A double-take, then a stare.

13. The eyes of a woman casually shopping down a store aisle, or window-shopping.

14. The eyes while hunting intently for something or someone.

15. A snub in which the eyes are deliberately averted.

16. A contemptuous up and down appraisal of someone guilty of a social faux pas.

17. The contemptuous look directed toward the speaker himself.

18. The mutual startled looks of two women who discover themselves wearing the same dress at a big social shindig, the hasty averting of their eyes, then the covert looks sneaked at each other to assess how well they look in the dress compared with the other person's appearance.

19. The raised eyeballs and "Oh my gosh" look of someone who has just discovered an exasperating error committed by someone else.

20. The examining of each other's faces, hair, eyes, lips indulged in by two people deeply in love who are cuddled together on a sofa.

21. The big-eyed stare of a little boy who meets his football hero in person.

22. The bored, patient look of a person who is forced to endure a long-winded chronicle of another person's surgery.

23. The surreptitious glances of a practical joker who is trying to keep a prospective victim from knowing he is being watched for his reaction when the trap snaps shut.

24. The quickly darting eyes of a professional thief casing a joint with a view toward thievery, and his eyes during the theft.

25. The innocent stare of a cheating husband when his wife accuses him of stepping out on her.

26. The puzzled glances students give each other when the instructor signs a test sentence they did not quite understand.

27. The commanding "Look at that!" of a mother who finds a broken vase.

LOOK is just one sign among many which can be used in this way. As you have probably begun to suspect after watching the ways in which one basic hand-position can be used to illustrate the moods and concepts inherent in any of over two dozen different situations, facial expression, body movements, and the amount of emphasis one places on a given sign, as well as the speed with which the sign is executed, all play a vital role in conveying mood.

One might say that the aforementioned factors take the place of tone and inflection in _speech_, and, like tone and inflection in speech, are vital to the conveyance of meaning as well as mood. If one were to imagine speech in which there was no tonal inflection, no voice modulation, no emphasis, no pauses--just a monotone in which all words sound the same--then one begins to understand what expression, emphasis, and speed mean to the language of signs. They give it meaning, mood, and _life_.[1]

Another "Don't" is _do not_ get upset when you find that there are regional variations in given signs which confuse you the first few (or several) times you attempt to communicate with a deaf person in the language of signs. These are more or less the "dialectical" variations you would normally hear in the language spoken in different parts of the country, and will soon cease to throw you once you learn to concentrate upon the deaf person's message (and his lips) rather than on individual signs.

Your instructor will, insofar as is possible, teach all the acceptable variations he knows for any given sign so that you can _recognize_ them when you encounter them, but he may require that you learn to use the signs _he_, himself, uses. It must be recognized at the outset that while the person doing the signing has a choice in which sign among several possible variations he will use, he has no control over the sign the _other party_ will use. Therefore, he should learn to recognize all of the acceptable variations even if he does not use them in his own signing.

The signs which are described in the word-descriptions you will be given in this course are, for the most part, those used by students at Gallaudet College in Washington, D.C., for Gallaudet has long acted as a "melting pot" in that students from all parts of the country congregate, exchange, adopt, and adapt signs among themselves, then return to their home communities and disseminate their modified sign language among deaf people in their localities. The Gallaudet signs, therefore, are more likely to be known by deaf people throughout the country than are local variations.

---

[1]There are, however, limits to the amount of facial expression, bodily movements, and emphasis one should place upon one's signing. Just as an extremely loud voice, exaggerated variations in tone and inflection, and over-dramatic vocalization in an ordinary conversation are jarring and unpleasant to the ear, over-exaggerating mugging, violent gestures, and too much emphasis are inappropriate to the language of signs unless called for by the context of the conversation or story. One should strive for the optimum--just enough expression, emphasis, and speed to suggest clearly the mood the speaker is trying to convey, and no more.

Also, do not become discouraged when you find you have trouble at first in reading what the deaf person is saying. Developing receptive skills is the roughest part of learning manual communication, and this is the reason why your instructor will be giving so many comprehension tests, drilling you so hard in receptive fingerspelling, and insisting that you use the language of signs with your fellow students as much as you can. After the first few times, you should gradually begin to be able to understand most of what your deaf friends say, even if it takes a while before you are able to read the fast-moving hands of two or more deaf people talking among themselves.

Finally, do practice at home. While your instructor can help you tremendously in developing your receptive or reading skills, in the final analysis the responsibility for developing your ability to express yourself in the language of signs (your expressive skills) will rest upon your own shoulders. Your instructor can show you the signs; teach you how to execute them correctly; remedy any errors in technique you may make; show you how to use them in various ways to express different meanings and moods; and see to it that you are exposed to them many times in the classroom. Unfortunately, he cannot help you practice each and every one of the hundreds of signs you will learn in this course enough times so that you will be able to remember them instantly and automatically whenever you need them. That part is up to you, and no one else.

Therefore, overlearn your signs--try to use each one at least ten to twenty times in a variety of sentences--and you will "own" the sign in the sense that you will not forget it. If you do this, as your vocabulary of signs increases, you will soon find yourself "thinking" in sign language--a phenomenon which marks the end of the preliminary bumbling stage of the raw beginner and the beginning of the development of fluency in the beautiful, picturesque, funny-- and always interesting--language of signs.

LESSON 2

(SM 45-50)

Fourth Class Session

GENERAL INSTRUCTIONS

The primary goal of Lesson 2 is to increase the vocabulary of signs students have learned by 31 words, to introduce them to <u>recitals</u> in which they must stand up in front of the class and sign selected sentences the instructor provides, and to begin the task of remediation in which both the instructor and his students will take part from this point onward.

The vocabulary of signs provided in Lesson 2 includes several auxiliary verbs, and the instructor should explain that these are frequently left out of the sentences signed by deaf people. However, in the event that the class includes a number of teacher trainees, deletion of the auxiliary verb should be presented as an <u>option</u>--something they should be aware often occurs with deaf children and adults, but not necessarily what they themselves would use even when talking with language deficient deaf adults--and something they should <u>avoid</u> doing when teaching deaf children.

Also included in the vocabulary are the days of the week. (The next lesson, Lesson 3, will include an expansion of the TIME concept from this beginning.)

Recitals, which are important to the student in that he is forced to use his newly acquired skills in front of people, are also helpful to the instructor in that he is thus enabled to assess how well individual students are mastering both fingerspelling and the execution of signs. It also affords him the opportunity to begin drawing other students into the classroom procedures by asking their comments and/or criticisms of the reciting student's performance. In addition, it exposes the other students to more training in their <u>receptive</u> skills and to styles of fingerspelling and signing which are different from that of the instructor. The reciting student quickly becomes aware of any sloppiness in his signing and fingerspelling when his fellows complain that they cannot understand his version of a sentence <u>because he did not sign clearly enough</u>, <u>used the wrong sign</u>, <u>or slurred his fingerspelling in some way</u>. (See Chapter 3 for information on how to utilize videotaping equipment to make this procedure even more effective.)

Although practice sentences are provided for this lesson, it is suggested that the instructor assign as regular homework the requirement that each student bring to class three sentences (these sentences should be collected at the end of each student's recital, as they can be utilized in future drills; the instructor will therefore have available to him more <u>current</u> sentences than those in this manual are likely to be after the passage of time--and the topics of the student-composed sentences are more likely to reflect things the students themselves are immediately interested in).

Among the things the instructor should begin to train his students to watch for in the recitals of their fellows, and to incorporate in their own performances, is the vital factor of expression of the mood implicit in each sentence. A student who signs the sentence, "I am confused," should be told to look confused and not to concentrate so hard on the correct execution of the signs and/or fingerspelling that his delivery is deadpan.

Students will probably be very nervous when they are first called upon to recite, so the instructor should be gentle with his criticisms during the first few sessions in which recitals are a part of the classroom procedure. He should also, if at all possible, find something to praise--and try to elicit for the reciter some praise from the other students as well--before he allows or gives criticism. (As a general rule, however, the instructor should begin at once to let his students do most of the evaluating and criticizing of their reciting fellows before he adds his own comments and/or criticism.) As time passes and the students become accustomed to regular recitals, the instructor can become stricter about individual student performance.

MATERIALS NEEDED FOR LESSON 2

For instructional purposes: Lesson plan 2.

DUP materials (if necessary):   SM Page

1. Word-descriptions of signs in Lesson 2 vocabulary
    (2-DUP-V, four pages)   45

LESSON PLAN OUTLINE

Fourth Class Session

I. Roll call.

II. Announcements, if any.

III. Fingerspelling drill. Use letter groups EA, OA, TH, and EI (or IE), Chapter 4, F.

IV. Review of signs taught in Lesson 1.

  A. Vary and verify drill, selecting signs at random. Use sentences in Lesson 1, Lesson Plan Outline.

  B. Student recitals. Call on individual students to come to front of classroom and sign one of the following sentences (keep covered with a sheet of paper all sentences not yet used, but let reciting student read the sentence he is assigned). Ask other students to tell what the reciter has said, then verify with a third student as usual.

  Reminder: Have other students help evaluate and/or correct each student's performance.

  1. I am confused.
  2. I don't know that word.
  3. I need to practice more.
  4. Will you practice with me?
  5. Did he understand you?
  6. She thinks she knows him.
  7. I would rather do it myself!
  8. This book is yours, but that one is mine.
  9. How are you today?
  10. Do you know what they said?

  Note: If class is large, and more sentences are needed, use those provided for the Learning Drill of Lesson 1.

V. Give Lesson 2 vocabulary of signs.

  A. Signs to be taught in this lesson:

1. Did you, do you, are you, were you	12. Was, were (new)
2. Will, would, future, next	13. To
3. Was, past, last, ago, back, before (a) & (b)	14. Call (summon
4. A long time ago	15. Call (phone)
5. Now	16. Name
6. Today (a)	17. Call (named)
7. Same, alike (a), (b), & (c)	18. Introduce
8. Different	19. Dumb, stupid, ignorant (a) & (b)
9. But	20. Word
10. About	21. Sign
11. Am, are, is, be (a) & (b)	22. Language
	23. Story, sentence (quote)
	24. Fingerspelling
	25. Tell, say, said
	26-32. Days of the week

(Total signs taught after this lesson: 71)

New signs taught:

Variations of the above signs:　　　　New signs (not in the lesson plan):

B. Sentences which can be used for teaching (learning) drill and practice purposes:

Note: In this and all following lessons in which such sentences are provided, the first time a new sign is used in a sentence, it is capitalized. Subsequent uses of the sign in sentences are in regular upper/lower case. Words underlined are those for which students do not yet know signs (or no sign exists for the word), and therefore must be fingerspelled; or they are words which should be fingerspelled in the context of that particular sentence despite having a sign.

1. DID you see her there? (Use ? for DID)
2. Are you coming with us? (Use ? for ARE)
3. Were they going to practice TODAY? (Use ? for WERE)
4. What are you going to do NOW?
5. Has she been in TO see you today?

6. He and his <u>brother</u> <u>look</u> ALIKE.
7. We <u>are</u> <u>all</u> <u>in</u> <u>the</u> same <u>class</u>.
8. DIFFERENT <u>people</u> don't <u>always</u> think <u>the</u> same <u>way</u>.
9. I <u>can</u> <u>go</u> <u>with</u> you BUT she <u>cannot</u>.
10. Did he <u>tell</u> you ABOUT <u>the</u> PHONE call?
11. Today IS <u>Mary's</u> birthday.
12. <u>Two</u> <u>years</u> AGO, we <u>went</u> to Europe.
13. <u>It</u> <u>was</u> <u>a</u> LONG TIME AGO, and <u>I</u> <u>have</u> <u>forgotten</u>.
14. <u>In</u> <u>the</u> <u>past</u>, <u>things</u> WERE different.
15. Don't BE so STUPID.
16. She is <u>just</u> confused, not dumb.
17. He CALLED her <u>a</u> <u>bad</u> NAME.
18. Will you INTRODUCE me to your <u>friend</u>?
19. <u>Dinner</u> <u>is</u> <u>ready</u>. <u>Please</u> CALL <u>Daddy</u>.
20. I don't know <u>that</u> WORD. What <u>does</u> <u>it</u> mean?
21. What <u>is</u> <u>the</u> SIGN <u>for</u> that word?
22. Sign LANGUAGE <u>is</u> <u>easy</u> to <u>learn</u>.
23. He <u>told</u> me <u>a</u> STORY I didn't <u>believe</u>.
24. <u>It</u> <u>is</u> <u>best</u> to practice signing and FINGERSPELLING <u>in</u> SENTENCES, not <u>just</u> words.
25. She <u>came</u> <u>on</u> MONDAY, and <u>left</u> <u>on</u> <u>Wednesday</u>.
26. Today is THURSDAY. Yesterday was WEDNESDAY.
27. Next TUESDAY, we will <u>have</u> <u>an</u> exam.
28. Last SUNDAY, we <u>all</u> <u>went</u> to <u>church</u>.
29. <u>The</u> <u>party</u> will be <u>held</u> SATURDAY <u>night</u>.
30. <u>Thank</u> <u>God</u> <u>for</u> FRIDAY.
31. Did she SAY what <u>time</u> they are <u>leaving</u>?

VI. Vary and verify drill on words in Lesson 2 vocabulary. (Omit if time is short.)

VII. Homework assignment: Ask students to compose three sentences using signs learned in Lessons 1 and 2, practice these sentences, then bring them to the next class prepared to recite them for the group.

<u>Note</u>: It is suggested that the instructor make this a standard homework assignment from this point on. He should instruct students to fingerspell words in their sentences for which they have not yet learned signs, or any time they forget the sign for a word.

VIII. Pass out DUP material, if necessary, explaining each.

IX. Concluding remarks.

(SM 45)

WORD-DESCRIPTIONS OF SIGNS IN LESSON 2 VOCABULARY

1. DID YOU, DO YOU, ARE YOU, WERE YOU: Either ? (question mark sign) YOU,
    or fingerspell DID then sign YOU (substituting DO, ARE, or WERE as
    necessary). Most commonly used is the ? sign.

2. WILL, WOULD, FUTURE, NEXT: With right hand in 5-hand position, palm to
    left and fingertips to ceiling, touch thumb to angle of jaw then draw
    whole hand upward and forward about eight or nine inches out in front
    of the cheek. For FUTURE, extend the gesture further forward in two
    motions, the second motion being a spiral extension of the first.

3. WAS, PAST, AGO, BACK, BEFORE: (Note: BEFORE is signed like this only
    when the sentence is something like "I have been there before.")
    (a) Right hand in open-hand, fingers-closed position, palm to right
    shoulder. Move hand back over right shoulder (or tap balls of fingers
    to right shoulder).

        (b) Right hand in 5-hand position, palm facing left and fingertips
    to ceiling. Circle hand upward and backward until thumb rests against
    right shoulder.

4. A LONG TIME AGO: Similar to WAS, PAST, AGO, BACK, BEFORE (b) above except
    that hand describes larger circle, moves slower, and repeats the circle
    two or three times.

5. NOW: Both hands in either right-angle or Y-hand positions, palms to self.
    Drop hands slightly until palms are facing ceiling.

6. TODAY: Sign NOW, NOW rapidly. (Note: NOW is also used to indicate THIS
    in signs indicating the present time such as THIS MORNING, THIS AFTER-
    NOON, THIS EVENING, and TO- in TONIGHT. TODAY can also be signed an-
    other way, which will be described in Lesson 4 vocabulary.)

7. SAME, ALIKE: (a) Both hands in index-hand position, palms to floor and
    fingertips pointing forward. Bring hands together so both index fingers
    are parallel and touching along their full length.

        (b) Right hand in Y-hand position, palm to floor, knuckles facing
    forward. Move hand from left to right and back again twice (keeping
    hand in same hand-position, and making the movement from the elbow,
    not the wrist).

        (c) Like (b) above, except that both hands are used, and move in
    opposition to each other (i.e., left hand moves to the right and right
    hand moves to the left, then both hands reverse direction, and so on).
    However, this sign is commonly used to mean MATCH (or MATCHING) as well
    as SIMILAR.

8. <u>DIFFERENT</u>: Both hands in <u>index-hand</u> position, palms forward, and index fingers crossed at the second knuckle. Keeping hands in <u>index-hand</u> position, separate hands (uncross fingers), ending sign with both hands about twelve inches apart and parallel. (<u>Important note</u>: Use the <u>elbow</u> as the fulcrum for the movement.)

9. <u>BUT</u>: Identical to DIFFERENT above, except that the <u>wrist</u> is used as the fulcrum or pivot joint for the movement, and the hands end up about six inches apart.

10. <u>ABOUT</u>: Left hand in <u>and-hand</u> position, palm and fingertips pointing to the right; right hand in <u>index-hand</u> position (or <u>right-angle index</u>), palm to self. Circle tip of right index finger around fingertips of left hand.

11. <u>AM, ARE, IS, BE</u>: <u>Note</u>: Auxiliary verbs, if used at all by the signer, are usually fingerspelled. However, there are two ways—one old and one new—of signing some of them:

    (a) Right hand in <u>index-hand</u> position, palm to left and fingertip to ceiling. Touch thumb side of index finger to center of chin, then bring hand straight forward two or three inches (old sign which is sometimes used to indicate any of the above words). Used primarily in platform signing.

    (b) Using the same chin-out movement of the hand, substitute the following hand-positions for the <u>index-hand</u> required for the old sign:

    AM: <u>A-hand</u>
    ARE: <u>R-hand</u>
    IS: <u>I-hand</u>
    BE: <u>B-hand</u>

12. <u>WAS, WERE (new signs)</u>: Similar to the new signs for AM, ARE, and so on, except that after the chin-out movement, the hand proceeds to sign PAST (described earlier). The hand-positions used are:

    WAS: <u>W-hand</u>
    WERE: <u>R-hand</u>

13. <u>TO</u>: Both hands in <u>index-hand</u> position; left hand palm to self, and right hand palm forward. Left hand remains stationary, about six inches in front of and to the left of right hand, while right hand moves forward until ball of right fingertip touches ball of left fingertip.

14. <u>CALL (summon)</u>: Both hands in <u>open-hand, fingers-closed</u> position, palms to floor. Tap back of left hand with fingertips of right hand, then bring right hand back and upward, ending sign with right hand in <u>A-hand</u> or <u>right-angle hand</u> position in normal fingerspelling position in front of right shoulder.

15. CALL (phone): With right hand in <u>Y-hand</u> position, bring hand to cheek
     in such a way that the thumb is in the position a telephone earpiece
     would be held, and the little finger is in the position of the tele-
     phone mouthpiece.

16. NAME: Both hands in <u>H-hand</u> position, fingertips forward and palms facing
     each other, place second knuckle of the middle finger of the right hand
     on the second knuckle of the index finger of the left hand so that the
     fingers of both hands make an X.

17. CALL (as in "What are you called?"): Sign NAME, but after fingers are
     crossed, move both hands forward about six inches (if the person being
     called/named is second or third person), or backward toward self (if
     the sentence is first person, such as "They call me Joe").

18. INTRODUCE: Similar to NAME above except that before the fingers are crossed
     in the NAME sign, they are held about twelve inches apart and then si-
     multaneously describe downward curving arcs, coming back up to end in
     the sign for NAME.

19. DUMB, STUPID, IGNORANT: (a) Right hand in <u>A-hand</u> position, palm to self.
     Knock knuckles against forehead.

     (b) Right hand in <u>V-hand</u> position, palm forward. Bring hand back-
     ward and knock the knuckles joining fingers and palm against forehead.

20. WORD: Left hand in <u>index-hand</u> position, palm to right and fingertip to
     ceiling; right hand in G-hand position, palm facing left hand. Touch
     tips of right index finger and thumb to <u>top third</u> of left index finger.
     (Referent here is to part of a slug of type printers make on linotype
     machines.)

21. SIGN: Both hands in <u>index-hand</u> position, palms forward and fingertips
     angled toward ceiling. Circle the hands around each other, making the
     circles move <u>backward</u> and <u>downward</u> before going forward and upward (or
     <u>counterclockwise</u> when signer is viewed in profile from the right).

22. LANGUAGE: Both hands in <u>L-hand</u> position, palms forward and fingertips to
     ceiling. Touch thumbs to each other, then move hands slowly apart about
     eighteen inches, while simultaneously rocking both hands from side to
     side so that the thumbs point alternately toward the ceiling then toward
     each other (fingertips remain pointed forward).

23. STORY, SENTENCE: Similar to LANGUAGE above except that <u>F-hands</u> are used.
     However, SENTENCE is often followed by QUOTE, in which the hands are
     placed about eighteen inches apart, at shoulder height, both in <u>V-hand</u>
     position. The fingers of the V are then quickly bent to look like the
     quotes at the beginning and end of a sentence being quoted.

24. FINGERSPELLING: Right hand in 4-hand or 5-hand position, but bent at
the palm (bent-4 or bent-5-hand position) so that the fingers remain
straight but the hand is bent when viewed in profile. With palm and
fingertips pointing forward, move the hand from left to right about
six or eight inches while waving each of the fingers alternately up
and down (keeping them straight) so that the fingertips describe a
sort of rippling motion. (The thumb does not move.)

25. TELL, SAY, SAID: Right hand in index-hand position, palm to self, and
fingernail of index finger against soft underside of chin. Draw hand
straight forward to about six inches in front of chin. (Note: There
are several variations of signs having to do with talking, conversing,
speech, lectures, and the like, which your instructor will demonstrate.
All are modifications of the sign described above, with slight variations in hand-position or motion, and some use two hands instead of
one, and so forth.)

26. DAYS OF THE WEEK: Signs for the days of the week from Monday through
Saturday are all made with the hand in regular fingerspelling position
in front of the shoulder, palm forward. The hand makes a small, clockwise (from the signer's viewpoint) circling motion. The hand-positions
used for each are:

MONDAY: M-hand
TUESDAY: T-hand
WEDNESDAY: W-hand
THURSDAY: H-hand
FRIDAY: F-hand
SATURDAY: S-hand

SUNDAY is made with both hands in open-hand, fingers-closed position,
palms forward and fingertips to ceiling. With hands about eighteen
inches apart and held at shoulder height, push both hands forward
simultaneously twice. (This is similar to the sign for WONDERFUL,
although there are differences in the amount of emphasis used as
well as slightly different movements. Your instructor will demonstrate these slight differences.)

NUMBERS LESSON

(SM 51-55)

Fifth Class Session

GENERAL INSTRUCTIONS

Numbers, in the language of signs, fall somewhere in between the formal manual alphabet and formal signs. They cannot be categorized as one or the other, but must be placed in a special category by themselves. For this reason, only a few pertinent word-descriptions for signs have been provided for the numbers lesson, even though the students will be learning a considerable number of new items to add to their manual communication repertoires.

This is the reason why only a few formal signs are introduced during the fifth class session--it would be expecting a bit too much of students to have to assimilate all the new hand-positions for indicating numbers, the rules governing usage, the exceptions to the rules, and so forth, in addition to thirty to forty new signs as well.

It has been the author's experience that if one attempts to introduce both numbers and new signs in the same class session, one must dispense with essential drills in order to do so, and the students suffer from oversaturation to the point where they always seem to have difficulty remembering both the numbers and the signs taught in the same lesson, regardless of the amount of later drilling they receive on those particular items.

The numbers lesson, therefore, is one in which the sole concern of the instructor will be in thoroughly drilling his students in fingerspelling, thoroughly reviewing all signs previously taught, checking student progress in expressive fingerspelling and signing, and teaching and drilling his students in numbers and the few signs pertinent to numbers.

It should be anticipated that the larger part of the class session will be consumed by this drilling, reviewing, teaching, and drilling again, but part of the drill in numbers (and in fingerspelling if at least one hour of class time remains) can be made more pleasant for the students by the employment of Bingo (and/or Password) games. It should not be felt that Bingo (or Password) is purely "fun" for the students--it provides valuable practice the students might otherwise not obtain. A few Bingo sessions can take the place of hours of tedious drilling in class, and save the students from having to resort to rote memorization procedures when practicing at home.

The instructor will find, if he examines the DUP material provided for the students as well as the practice sentences in the lesson plan, most of the different ways in which numbers are indicated, and he can teach these as he goes along. Briefly, the different ways of indicating numbers are listed below:

1. Single digit numbers.
2. Double digit numbers under 20.
3. Double digit numbers 20 and over.
4. Hundreds (less than 1,000).
5. Hundreds (1,100 and up).
6. Thousands, millions.
7. Strings of isolated digit-numbers (e.g., house numbers).
8. Combinations of single/double digit-numbers (10.1, 12.95, 101.5, etc.)
9. Time concepts (8:35 a.m., "around 5:00," etc.).
10. Dates (April 5, 1945).
11. Ranked numbers (first, second, third, etc.).
12. Money (under $1.00, to $9.00, over $10, and combinations).
13. Forties, fifties, etc.

MATERIALS NEEDED FOR NUMBERS LESSON

For instructional purposes:

1. Overhead transparency of numbers "rules" (if OH projector and screen are available; otherwise, copy the numbers rules on the chalkboard).
2. Copies of the practice material.
3. Bingo game, in case there is time for a short game before the end of the class.
4. Password game.

DUP material (if needed):	SM Page
1. Word-descriptions of signs taught in numbers lesson (Numbers-DUP-V, two pages)	51
2. Illustration of numbers on the hand (Numbers-DUP-M, one page)	52
3. Numbers for practice (Numbers-DUP-P, one page)	54
4. Directions for signing numbers (Numbers-DUP-M,b, one page)	53

NUMBERS LESSON

LESSON PLAN OUTLINE

Fifth Class Session

I. Roll call (introduce one of the variations described in Chapter 2, C, 1).

II. Announcements, if any.

III. Fingerspelling drill. Use letter groups IS, ER, OO, and QU, Chapter 4, F.

IV. Review of signs taught in Lessons 1 and 2.

   A. Vary and verify drill. Select signs at random. (Use Master Vocabulary List in Appendix if necessary.)

   B. Student recitals of homework sentences. Sentences which follow can be used if students forget homework (or bring too-simple sentences to class). Can also be used as a brief test if desired.

      1. I will phone you about it.
      2. Please practice your vocabulary words.
      3. Will you be OK now?
      4. I know I'm dumb. Don't confuse me.
      5. Did you understand what he said?
      6. Hello, how are you today?
      7. Mary called Jane to dinner.
      8. Fingerspelling is not hard if you practice a lot.
      9. I don't know what he thinks about it. Do you?
      10. Last Monday, I met a boy called Snooker.
      11. They got themselves into a lot of trouble.
      12. I, myself, don't think it will happen.

V. Teach numbers and signs associated with numbers:

   A. Signs to be taught in numbers lesson:

      1. Number
      2. Many
      3. Much, above
      4. Less
      5. Few
      6. Several
      7. How many, how much
      8. Old
      9. How old
      10. More
      11. Than

(Total signs taught after this lesson: 82)

New signs taught:

Variations of the above signs: New signs (not in the lesson plan)

B. Utilize numbers for practice list (Numbers-DUP-P) to drill students on single numbers or number groups. (List should be distributed at the _end_ of the class.)

C. Comprehension practice in numbers (vary and verify as usual).

1. It cost me about $3.50.
2. I will phone you about 8:30 tonight.
3. We practiced until 12:00 midnight last night.
4. There were about 45 people at his party Saturday night.
5. Her daughter is 16 years old--going on 21.
6. She is in her early 20s.
7. On March 23, 1948, my daughter was baptized.
8. I live at 14706 South Meany Street.
9. We had to pay $5.95 for the darn thing--then found it for $4.50 in another store.
10. There were more than eleven hundred (11C) people at the ball.
11. Today is _____, 197_ (use current date).
12. They didn't introduce the speaker until almost 9:00.
13. Several of us got over 95 on the exam.
14. How many signs do you know now? (81)

VI. Bingo and Password games (for remainder of class session) if at least one hour of class time remains. Divide class in two groups, and have half of them play Bingo, while the other half plays Password. At the end of 30 minutes, switch groups so that the students who were playing Bingo play Password, and vice versa.

    Note: If only 30 minutes remain, have whole group play Bingo (or Password, if instructor feels the class hasn't yet mastered numbers well enough to enjoy the game. In this case, schedule Bingo for next class session--at least 30 minutes of it.)

VII. Pass out DUP material, if any, and explain.

VIII. Concluding remarks.

NUMBERS

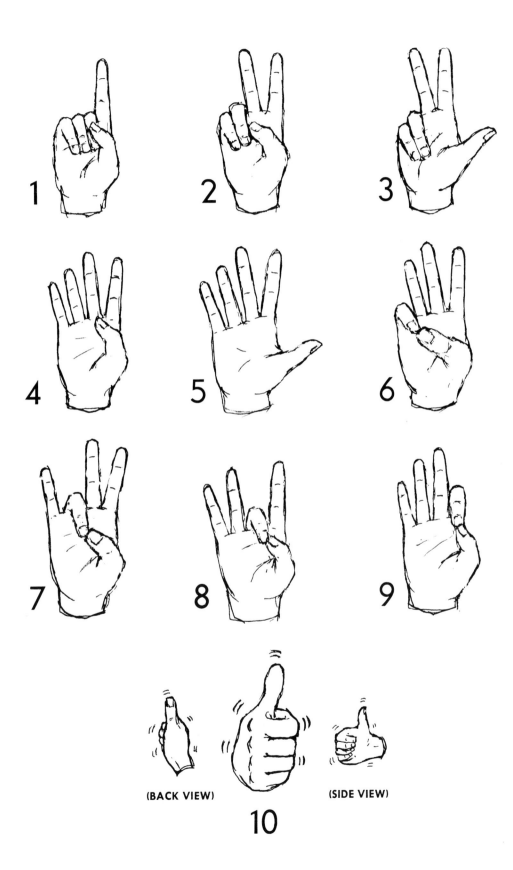

(BACK VIEW)   (SIDE VIEW)

10

(SM 53)

DIRECTIONS FOR SIGNING NUMBERS

Direction of Palm

1 . . . 5	Palm faces <u>toward yourself</u>.
6 . . . 9	Palm faces <u>forward</u>.
10	Palm faces <u>left</u>, thumb points toward ceiling.
11 . . . 15	Palm faces <u>toward self</u> again.
16 . . . 19	<u>A-hand</u>, with <u>palm to self</u>, then <u>palm forward</u> with the number.
20s	Except for 22, begin with <u>L-hand</u>, <u>palm forward</u>: 22 is the "oddball" number of the 20s.
30s, 40s, 50s, etc.	<u>Palm always forward</u>: hand always makes a slight sidewise motion while in the first number, then changes to the hand-position of the second number.
100s	<u>Palm always forward</u>: Spell 1C, 2C, etc., snapping the fingers up into the <u>C-position</u>.
1,000s	Spell 1, 2, 3 (or whatever), <u>palm forward</u>, then place right <u>M-hand</u> in center of palm of other hand: or spell 12C, 14C (for twelve hundred, fourteen hundred, etc.).
1,000,000	Spell 1, 2, 3 (etc.), <u>palm forward</u>, then place right <u>M-hand</u> in center of palm of other hand, lift it up again (a couple of inches), then replace it in palm a few inches forward of the position in which you placed it the first time.

Helpful Hints:

1. When giving a date, the name of the month is usually fingerspelled, but <u>abbreviated</u> (except for months with short names--March, April, May, June, and July) exactly as it is abbreviated in writing. February, therefore, becomes Feb., August becomes Aug., etc.

2. When stating a time, the left wrist is tapped once, then the time is given exactly as spoken. 8:30, therefore, becomes (tap wrist) 8, 30 (not 8, 3, 0).

(SM 51)

WORD-DESCRIPTIONS OF SIGNS TO BE TAUGHT IN NUMBERS LESSON

1. NUMBER: Both hands in and-hand position, palms and fingertips facing each
   other. Touch fingertips of hands together twice, rotating hands in opposite directions (i.e., left hand moves counterclockwise, and right
   hand moves clockwise when viewed from the right profile) slightly before
   touching fingertips the second time. (Also used to mean PUT TOGETHER,
   as in assembling something.)

2. MANY: (Either one or both hands can be used. Use both for emphasis.)
   Both hands in modified E-hand position (like E-hand except that the thumb
   covers the fingernails), palms to ceiling. Snap fingers of hands open to
   open-and position, then repeat quickly.

3. MUCH, ABOVE: Both hands in right-angle position, palms and fingertips facing
   each other. Place fingers of right hand on top of fingers of left hand,
   then raise right hand about four or five inches (left hand remaining stationary).

4. LESS: The reverse of MUCH, above, in that fingers of right hand are placed
   under the fingers of the left hand, then the right hand is lowered a few
   inches (left hand remaining stationary as before).

5. FEW: Right hand in A-hand position, palm to ceiling. One at a time (but
   rapidly), extend index finger, then middle finger, then third finger
   (keeping little finger in place with the thumb), using the thumb as a
   "brake" on each finger, until hand is in W-hand position.

6. SEVERAL: Like FEW above, except that little finger joins the other fingers
   in its turn, so that the hand ends up in a position in between 5-hand and
   open-and-hand.

7. HOW MANY, HOW MUCH: Sign MANY, but raise the hand sharply while the fingers
   are opening, beginning the sign at about waist height, and ending it at
   about shoulder height. (Almost like you were throwing a ball up in the air.)

8. OLD: Right hand in C-hand, place thumb-edge of hand against chin, with palm
   to left. Close hand to S-hand and lower it as if gripping a beard and
   pulling it downward.

9. HOW OLD: Sign OLD, then HOW MUCH.

10. MORE: Both hands in and-hand position, palms and fingertips facing each
    other. Touch fingertips together twice, rapidly.

11. THAN: Both hands in B-hand position, palms to floor. (Right hand's finger-
    tips point forward, left hand's fingertips point toward right front). With
    fingers of right hand a few inches above left fingertips, drop right hand
    below left hand quickly, striking fingertips of left hand with edge of right
    index finger in passing.

(SM 54)

NUMBERS FOR PRACTICE

7	1,456	April 11, 1965
9	3,430	June 13, 1962
8	4,587	August 29, 1925
3	6,902	September 30, 1943
10	1,786	December 7, 1941
5	2,345	October 31, 1901
14	1980	November 4, 1934
19	1942	January 20, 1932
24	1492	January 1, 1966
21	1964	February 14, 1962
67	1932	April 16, 1941
98	1957	March 25, 1867
37	1961	April 12, 1945
41	$.01	August 14, 1943
62	$.05	May 30, 1984
76	$.10	March 7, 1916
86	$.15	December 8, 1914
90	$.25	May 15, 1917
16	$.20	January 13, 1976
11	$.75	February 28, 1966
23	$1.00	July 4, 1965
124	$1.50	June 27, 1942
160	$.57	July 24, 1776
240	$2.89	November 27, 1964
342	$3.98	January 30, 1965
458	$4.00	February 8, 1932
679	$25.00	Today, the _____
		(use the date this
		list is distributed)

Practice Sentences Using Numbers

1. I'll see you around 8:00 tonight.
2. He is in his early fifties.
3. They live at 21453 South Main Street.
4. Our new color TV cost us $755.59.
5. You can't buy liquor if you're under 21.
6. In 1492, Columbus sailed the ocean blue.
7. In November, 1970, we had a very heavy snow.
8. There were 1,349 people at the ball.
9. About 1,300 people were killed in the quake in Iran.
10. It costs $.39 at Safeway, but $.27 at I.G.A.

LESSON 3

(SM 56-62)

Sixth Class Session

GENERAL INSTRUCTIONS

Lesson 3 introduces the first formal test, this one on <u>fingerspelling</u>. It is assumed that by the time the sixth class session is scheduled, the students should have developed enough facility in reading fingerspelling for their skill to be tested. The test provided will afford the instructor the opportunity to gauge the progress of his students in this area, particularly their ability to recognize the letters A through G, singly and in combination. If the instructor will, as he corrects the papers, tally the number of errors made by the students on each word, he will be able to identify any letters or letter groups consistently missed by the class, and can institute more drills on these particular letters or letter groups. For instance, if several students consistently misread MEAN for MAN, it indicates that more discrimination training is needed in EA versus A, and so forth. A few moments spent in tallying fingerspelling errors can pay large dividends in reducing or eliminating specific difficulties students are encountering which are slowing their progress in developing receptive ability in fingerspelling. (See Appendix for method of analyzing test errors.)

At this point, it would be well to caution the instructor about the <u>timing</u> of tests. In no case should any test be administered when the students are "cold." Tests should always be preceded by at least twenty or thirty minutes of warm-up drills and practice, and the instructor should endeavor to include in the drills those letter groups and signs which he knows will appear in the test. In addition, if the instructor should note during the drill preceding the test that the students have forgotten certain signs (which appear in the test), he should endeavor to return to those particular signs a couple of extra times during the drill. It would be unfair to expect the students to remember a sign in a test when the instructor himself has been lax about drilling on that sign.

Lesson 3 will add 29 signs to the vocabularies of the students, a large part of which deal with expressing various time concepts. In Lesson 3, as in Lessons 2 and 4, teaching (learning) drill sentences are included for the instructor's convenience. However, since the instructor will wish to insure <u>maximum partici-pation</u> by the students themselves in the learning process, beginning with Lesson 4, he should require <u>his students</u> to compose sentences which can then be used for learning drill purposes. In other words, he should require that the students bring to class sentences including the words for which signs are to be taught in that particular session—sentences which both include the signs previously taught <u>and</u> are constructed in such a way that the word for which a new sign is to be taught will be elicited by the context of the rest of the sentence. (This tech-

157

158

nique is adapted from the familiar "Cloze" procedure used in testing language development of children.) For instance, if the sign to be taught is YESTERDAY, the sentence most likely to elicit YESTERDAY would be one in which the day previous to the one in which the class is taking place is named. For example, if it happens to be Monday, March 29, the Cloze sentence most likely to elicit YESTERDAY would be:

_____ was Sunday, March 28.
(YESTERDAY)

However, it is likely that the students will have some difficulty in composing appropriate Cloze sentences the first time they try, so, although the homework assignment for Lesson 3 is for them to compose such sentences for use in learning drills, the lesson plan for Lesson 4 still includes Cloze sentences for the instructor to use in the teaching/learning drill, just in case.

Subsequent to Lesson 4, no Cloze sentences have been provided because it is assumed that the instructor will have worked with the students on their sentences, and corrected any misperceptions about the types of sentences required. He can, therefore, use the student-provided Cloze sentences from that time on. (Or he can compose his own, but this is a time-consuming chore he may eventually decide to let his students perform after all.)

Regardless of whether he requires his students to provide the sentences for the teaching/learning drill, or composes his own sentences, he should make use of the technique if at all possible. It has been the author's experience, bolstered by reports from other manual communication instructors whom she instructed in the technique, that the effort the students are forced to put into guessing from the context of a sentence what an unknown sign means appears to sharply increase their ability to recall the sign later. Many psychological studies have shown that recall is facilitated if a student has to work at learning, rather than if he sits passively and merely absorbs what is being taught. He will also recall material which poses some sort of a challenge to his problem-solving ability far better than material which places no demand upon his intellect other than simple rote memorization. That this applies to the learning of manual communication seems clearly indicated by an informal experiment the author and another manual communication instructor conducted in early 1971. A brief synopsis of this follows:

Both the author and the other instructor were teaching beginning manual communication classes in college settings, using the same material. Since the two colleges were located in cities only seventy miles apart, the author was able to assist in teaching the other instructor's class, while the other instructor was able to assist in teaching the author's class. Both classes, therefore, were exposed to identical instructing styles and taught the same material at about the same pace. The difference, however, was that the author's class was exposed to the teaching/learning drill technique involving the use of Cloze sentences in introducing new signs, while the other instructor's students were introduced to new signs by means of standard backtracking drills, with the techniques being deliberately kept different for the first five lessons in signs.

At the end of the fifth lesson in signs, comprehension tests were administered to both classes (with the other instructor administering the test each time to keep the variable of instructor-style from biasing the results). The results of the tests showed that the author's class, taught by means of Cloze sentence learning drills, scored a mean of 92 percent with only one score being under 84 percent (74 percent), and the rest clustered around 90 to 94 percent. The other instructor's class scored a mean of 82 percent, with the scores distributed all over the scale from 54 percent to 100 percent.

The findings, however, must be interpreted in light of two intervening variables: the author had access to videotaping equipment, while the other instructor did not. In addition, the author's class met twice a week, for one and a half hours each time, while the other instructor's class met once a week for two hours. The author, therefore, had one hour more time in which to drill her students, and more sophisticated equipment available for teaching purposes.

To offset these advantages, however, was the fact that the test was administered to both classes by the other instructor, which was an advantage for his own students (who were more familiar with his manual communication style since he did the bulk of the teaching while the author merely assisted), and a handicap to the students in the author's class who were less familiar with his signing and fingerspelling style (which was quite different from that of their main instructor, the author), although he had assisted her part of the time.

Regardless of the variables of time, equipment, and teaching style, the fact remains that the essential difference between the way the two classes were taught was the way in which new signs were introduced.

Subsequent testing within the other instructor's class lent support to this when, dividing the class in half, the author took half of the students and taught them new signs by using the Cloze procedure while the other instructor used standard procedures with the other half of the class. Both groups were then tested, with the tests again administered by the other instructor.

The results showed the same trend of difference in scores as was found in the earlier experiment using the two separate classes. The group learning the new vocabulary by Cloze procedures had a mean of 87 percent, while the group learning by standard backtracking procedures had a mean of 79 percent.

A repetition of the within-group experiment, a few weeks later, again showed the same difference in mean scores. After this, however, it was decided to stop the experimenting so that the other instructor could begin using the Cloze sentence teaching/learning drill procedures again, which he had refrained from using while the experiments were in progress. Needless to say, the average scores of his class began to rise almost immediately, and, while it never quite achieved the level attained by the author's class (the videotaping equipment and extra hour of instruction did make a difference), the scores were consistently higher than those attained by students in previous classes he had taught before learning about and utilizing the Cloze-type teaching drills.

The foregoing should make it clear that Cloze-type teaching drills are very effective. However, writing three different sentences for some 30 or 40 words is a considerable chore for students who may also be carrying a heavy course-load in a college or university program. Therefore, it is suggested that the instructor divide up the words among the students, and have each student write three sentences[1] for only those words he has been assigned. It must be remembered, though, that this assignment is in addition to those sentences the students are to bring to class for recital purposes. In the case of the Cloze sentences, the instructor should collect these sentences immediately before he introduces the new signs, and, selecting sentences at random, use them in teaching the new signs (the remaining sentences using a particular sign can be used for drilling). The students, therefore, will have a standard homework assignment of several Cloze sentences which must be turned in during each class session. On the other hand, the sentences the students compose for recital purposes should be collected only after the student has had the opportunity to use them, after which he must compose new sentences. Until he uses them, he can hang on to them, but the students should be cautioned to keep their recital sentences current, whether used or not, for it would be pointless to keep sentences composed for use after Lesson 4, for instance, and use them during recital in Lesson 6, when the student has learned some 60 to 70 signs in addition to those he knew after Lesson 4.

MATERIALS NEEDED FOR LESSON 3

For instructional purposes:

1. Bingo game.
2. Lesson plan.
3. Transparency of practice sentences on Do, Act, Behave, etc. (3-DUP-TRM, one page).

DUP materials (if necessary):   SM Page

1. Vocabulary word-descriptions for Lesson 3 (3-DUP-V,
   three pages)   51
2. List of words for which signs will be taught in Lesson 4
   (3-DUP-M, one page)..   61
3. List of practice sentences on Do, Act, Behave (3-DUP-TRM,
   one page)   60

---

[1]It would be best if each student is assigned a block of three consecutive words on the lists—to facilitate the instructor's being able to arrange the returned papers in consecutive order for teaching. The blocks (e.g., 1, 2, 3; 4, 5, 6, etc.) can be rotated or distributed at random among the students, or the instructor can permanently assign a certain block to each student. For a variety of reasons, rotation of blocks is recommended (not all lessons have the same number of signs to be taught).

LESSON PLAN OUTLINE

Sixth Class Session

I. Roll call (use one of the variations described in Chapter 2, C, 1).

II. Announcements, if any.

III. Fingerspelling drill. Use letter groups EN, ON, EM, and OM (Chapter 4, 2).

IV. Fingerspelling test. (Spell each word or phrase twice, then wait for students to write word down. Collect papers.)

1. Call	8. Thank	15. Goof off
2. Call me	9. Thank you	16. Excuse
3. Mean	10. Calm	17. Excuse me
4. Mean man	11. Calm down	18. Crazy
5. Bask	12. Under	19. Crazy as a loon
6. Basket	13. Understand	20. That is all
7. Basketball	14. Goof	

(31 words. -3.2 for each error)

V. Review of previous lessons. Practice sentences which can be used (words which must be fingerspelled are underlined):

1. I will call you about 8:45 tonight.
2. Please practice your vocabularies of signs.
3. I can't understand a word he says.
4. Last Friday, I went to the store.
5. On Sunday, we didn't go to church because I was sick.
6. Do you understand what you have to do?
7. It cost me $3.69 in tolls.
8. February 22 is Washington's birthday.
9. 1776 was a great year for America.
10. Did you believe his story?
11. He called her four times before she came.
12. Did you know it is already 9:30?
13. We had to do it by ourselves.
14. Many people confuse 6 and 9 in sign language.
15. What do you think about it?
16. How much money do you need? I have $5.00.

VI. Student recitals. Use the above sentences if necessary, but otherwise, utilize sentences students wrote as homework.

VII. Lesson 3 vocabulary of signs.

A. Signs to be taught in this lesson:

162

1. Good	11. Can	21. Afternoon
2. Fine	12. Ability	22. Night (a) & (b)
3. Bad	13. This	23. Evening
4. Lousy	14. This (time concept)	24. All night
5. No good		25. Day and night
6. Thank (you)	15. That (a) & (b)	26. Midnight
7. Excuse (me)	16. Time	27. Yesterday
8. Very	17. Day	28. Tomorrow
9. Sorry	18. All day	29. Do, act, behave
10. Please	19. Morning	30. Can't, cannot
	20. Noon	

(Total signs taught after this lesson: 112)

New signs taught:

Variations of the above signs: New signs (not in the lesson plan):

B. Cloze-Teaching drill sentences:

1. GOOD <u>morning</u>, how are you?
2. Good MORNING, how are you?
3. I am FINE.
4. He <u>has been sick</u>, and <u>felt</u> LOUSY <u>when</u> I called him.
5. He <u>is a thief</u>, and <u>is just</u> NO GOOD <u>at all</u>!
6. Thank you VERY <u>much</u>.
7. EXCUSE me, I am <u>very sorry</u>.
8. Excuse me, I am VERY <u>sorry</u>.
9. Excuse me, I am very SORRY.
10. PLEASE excuse me, I <u>must go</u> now.
11. CAN I <u>help</u> you?
12. <u>It takes</u> ABILITY to <u>get a top job</u>.
13. I CAN'T understand you.
14. THAT <u>is</u> not what I said!
15. THIS <u>book is</u> mine.
16. THAT <u>book is</u> yours.
17. THIS morning, I <u>had a hard</u> TIME <u>waking up</u>.
18. Two DAYS ago, it was _____ (day of the week or day of the month).
19. At NOON, we <u>eat lunch</u>.

20. Children go home from school at 3:00 in the AFTERNOON.
21. This (now) EVENING, we will stay home and watch TV.
22. At NIGHT, most people are asleep.
23. Last night, I stayed awake ALL NIGHT.
24. Most people have to work ALL DAY.
25. At the stroke of MIDNIGHT, Cinderella's coach turned into a pumpkin.
26. YESTERDAY was _____ (day of the week).
27. Tomorrow will be _____ (day of the week).
28. What do you DO for a living?

    C. Practice on Lesson 3 vocabulary of signs, using vary/verify drill.

VIII. Bingo game if not played in last class session.

IX. Homework assignment:

    A. Pass out list of words for which signs will be taught in Lesson 4 (or refer students to Homework Assignment, page 61 of their workbook). Assign one or two words to each student and ask them to write three Cloze drill-type sentences (such as have been provided for Lessons 1 through 3) using the words assigned. Emphasize that the sentences should be such that if the assigned word were left out, the context of the rest of the sentence would suggest the missing word. Request also that they endeavor to include as many words as possible for which they already know the signs.

        Note: Regarding the assignment described above, the instructor should be forewarned that after Lesson 4, no further learning drill-type sentences will be provided in this manual, so, if he wishes to continue this effective type of teaching drill, he will either have to compose his own or utilize those brought to class by students. The latter course of action is recommended.

    B. Remind students that they are still required to bring the usual three sentences for recital purposes as well as the learning-drill-type sentences.

X. Pass out DUP material, if any.

XI. Concluding remarks.

(SM 60)

PRACTICE SENTENCES

TO DO, ACT, BEHAVE

The verbs underlined should be fingerspelled. The verbs capitalized are all
signed DO.

1.   What do you DO on Sundays?
2.   What does your father DO on Saturday?
3.   What was the boy DOING?
4.   What will you DO tomorrow?
5.   What can I DO to help you?
6.   I don't care what you DO. You, yourself, DO what you decide.
7.   Why did you want to DO that?
8.   What must I DO next? or (What do I have to DO next?)
9.   What have you DONE with my book?
10. What time do you have to DO your homework?
11. Mary DID all the work alone. Why didn't you help her DO it?
12. I have DONE all the work you told me to DO.
13. Bob won't DO his work.
14. Mrs. Brown is DOING much good for her church.

The verbs ACT, PERFORM, and BEHAVE are also signed DO.

1.   Many children ACTED nicely. One boy ACTED silly.
2.   Jane's dog ACTS sick. She will take him to the doctor.

BEHAVE and PERFORM are also signed as DO.

1.   The pupils BEHAVED well when the teacher was away.
2.   The deaf actors PERFORMED very well in the "The Cat and the Canary."

(SM 61)

WORDS FOR WHICH SIGNS WILL BE TAUGHT IN LESSON 4

1.	Help	22.	High school
2.	Must	23.	Minute, second
3.	Get	24.	Hour
4.	Have	25.	Later, afterwhile
5.	Work	26.	Week
6.	Job	27.	Next week
7.	Necessary, have to, ought to, should, need	28.	Month
8.	No (none)	29.	Next month
9.	Experience	30.	Year
10.	Expert	31.	Next year
11.	Again	32.	Last week
12.	Slow	33.	Last month
13.	For	34.	Last year
14.	Learn	35.	Last night
15.	--er sign	36.	Today (b)
16.	Student	37.	This morning
17.	Teach	38.	This afternoon
18.	Teacher	39.	This evening
19.	School	40.	One month ago
20.	College	41.	Two years from now
21.	University	42.	___ years from now, etc.

(SM 56)

WORD-DESCRIPTIONS OF SIGNS IN LESSON 3 VOCABULARY

1. GOOD: Right hand in open-hand, fingers-closed position, palm to body. Touch fingertips to lips or chin, then push hand forward and slightly downward. Similar to THANK sign. (For more emphasis, place back of right hand in the palm of left hand at end of sign.)

2. FINE: Right 5-hand, palm to left. Touch thumb to chest, then move hand forward a few inches in a fast, happy gesture.

3. BAD: Right hand in open-hand, fingers-closed position, palm to self and fingertips toward ceiling. Place fingertips on chin, and in a sharp, choppy gesture, rotate hand so palm faces outward (and is alongside face), then slap it sharply downward so that fingertips end up pointing toward floor.

4. LOUSY: Right hand in 3-hand position, palm to left and thumb on nose (with fingertips pointing to ceiling). Arc hand from thumb-on-nose position sideways and upward (to a position alongside and a little bit to the front of the face), then slap sharply downward as in BAD. (Note: Hand remains in 3-hand position throughout.)

5. NO GOOD: Fingerspell NG, moving hand several inches sideways between the N and the G in a snapping motion.

6. THANK (YOU): Sign GOOD, but drop the hand farther and extend it slightly forward.

7. EXCUSE (ME): Left open-hand, fingers-closed, palm to ceiling and fingertips to right front. Right hand in right-angle hand, palm toward floor. Wipe fingertips of right hand across palm of left hand twice, moving from heel of palm toward palm knuckles. (Then sign ME.)

8. VERY: Both hands in V-hand position, fingertips forward and palms facing each other. Touch fingertips of V-hand fingers together, being careful not to touch thumbs or palms together, then separate fingertips a couple of inches.

9. SORRY: Place right A-hand, palm toward body, on center of upper chest and move in a circular motion.

10. PLEASE: (Also means ENJOY, and some deaf use this sign to mean LIKE.) Right hand in open-hand, fingers-closed position, palm flat against the chest, rubbed in a circular motion.

11. CAN: Both A-hands, palms to floor. Drop slightly.

12. ABILITY: Sign CAN, CAN, CAN (also used to denote POSSIBLE or POSSIBLY, and occasionally for OPPORTUNITY and/or CHANCE).

13. THIS: Left hand in open-hand, fingers-closed position, palm facing ceil-
    ing and fingertips toward right front; right hand in Y-hand position,
    palm toward floor. Place right hand in center of left palm. (Also
    used to mean THAT in some contexts.)

14. THIS (time concept): In such usages as "this morning," "this evening,"
    "at this time," THIS is signed exactly like NOW (see Lesson 2).

15. THAT: (a) Sign like THIS (above). Used for emphasis, or as an indefinite
    article.

    (b) Right hand in Y-hand position, palm facing the object being
    identified, push hand toward object a few inches.

16. TIME: Tap index finger of right hand on back of left wrist (natural
    gesture).

17. DAY: Left arm (palm flat and toward floor) straight across waist. Place
    elbow of right arm on left fingertips. Right arm at right angle to
    left arm. Right D-hand and arm describe semicircle in front of face
    and body from right to left, right elbow remaining on left fingertips.
    (This is not as complicated as it looks on paper.)

18. ALL DAY: Both hands in open-hand, fingers-closed position; left hand palm
    down, with arm held across the waist. Placing right elbow on back of
    left hand, and using right elbow as the pivot (or fulcrum), describe
    an arc of almost 180 degrees from right to left with the right forearm
    and hand, beginning the sign with the right hand palm up and to the ex-
    treme right, and ending it with the right hand palm down and almost
    touching the left elbow.

19. MORNING: Left hand open-hand, fingers-closed; right hand cupped-hand.
    Put fingers of left hand midway between wrist and right elbow. Right
    hand extended forward, palm up.

20. NOON: Same right angle arms as DAY, except that right hand is a B-hand,
    not D-hand, and remains stationary to indicate the sun is directly
    overhead.

21. AFTERNOON: Both hands in open-hand, fingers-closed position; left hand
    in same position as described for ALL DAY; right elbow on back of left
    hand, palm toward floor and hand held about eight to twelve inches in
    front of and above left forearm, pat right hand downward a few inches
    twice.

22. NIGHT: (a) With both hands in right-angle position, palms to floor, place
    right wrist on top of back of left hand.

    (b) Both hands in open-hand, fingers-closed position, palms facing
    self, drop both toward each other, crossing and stopping almost paral-
    lel. Signifies darkness, pulling the curtains. (Platform usage only.)

23. <u>EVENING</u>: Similar to NIGHT (above) except that right hand is raised (with right forearm remaining against back of left hand) so that fingertips point <u>forward</u> instead of toward floor.

24. <u>ALL NIGHT</u>: Similar to ALL DAY (described earlier) except that the 180 degree arc described by the right forearm and hand travels <u>downward</u> (below the horizon formed by the left forearm and hand), and the right hand begins the sign palm <u>downward</u> and ends it palm toward ceiling.

25. <u>ALL DAY AND ALL NIGHT</u>: (Can also be used for DAY AND NIGHT.) Sign ALL DAY, then ALL NIGHT, without inserting AND, and keeping the motion continuous.

26. <u>MIDNIGHT</u>: Is signed almost exactly like NOON, except that the right hand and arm are pointed directly at the floor.

27. <u>YESTERDAY</u>: Right <u>A-hand</u>, palm to left. Touch thumb to front part of cheek then to back part of cheek near ear. (Can use <u>Y-hand</u> also.)

28. <u>TOMORROW</u>: Right <u>A-hand</u>, palm to left. Touch ball of thumb to cheek, then move hand forward a few inches pivoting hand so that sign ends with hand, palm to body, thumb pointing to ceiling. (Hand remains in <u>A-hand</u> position throughout.)

29. <u>DO, ACT, BEHAVE</u>: Both hands in <u>C-hand</u> position, palms to floor. Move both hands away from each other a few inches then back toward each other. Repeat.

30. <u>CAN'T, CANNOT</u>: Both hands in <u>index-hand</u> position, palms to floor. Begin sign with right hand about six inches <u>above</u> left hand, then drop right hand to about six inches <u>below</u> left hand, with right index finger <u>striking left index finger</u> as it drops.

LESSON 4

(SM 63-69)

Seventh Class Session

GENERAL INSTRUCTIONS

Lesson 4 introduces 42 additional signs to the ones the students already know. This might appear to be a lot, but most of the signs are new only in the sense that they are different <u>ways</u> in which to use the signs taught previously, rather than completely new signs. Some completely new signs are introduced, to be sure, but many of them are base signs upon which another sign is built by the addition of --er (as in TEACH plus --er, to give TEACHER). The material therefore should be fairly easy for the students to assimilate.

It is anticipated that in this class the instructor will spend considerable time in teaching drill, particularly in sifting through the Cloze sentences his students have brought to class to see just how well they have grasped the concept of constructing Cloze-type sentences, or whether they need additional explanation and illustrations of what the instructor wants.

It would be helpful for the instructor to write on the chalkboard (or over-head projector transparency) a few of the Cloze drill sentences provided (for the last time) in this lesson, leaving a blank where the word for which a new sign is being taught would normally go--and ask the students to guess what the missing word could be. He can further instruct his students that, when composing their sentences, they either <u>underline</u> the word around which the sentence is built, or enclose it in parentheses, so that the <u>instructor himself</u> will know which word the sentence was written for.

Because of the amount of time the instructor is likely to have to devote to teaching his students how to construct Cloze sentences from the lists of words he will be providing them from this time on, no test is scheduled for this class session. Tests, at least during the first few weeks in which they are administered, tend to consume a considerable portion of the scheduled class time--anywhere from thirty to forty-five minutes at first--so, for the first few weeks, tests are kept short so that more time can be devoted to drills and practice.

In addition, when it was anticipated that a particularly important unit of learning would consume class time in excess of normal, either the usual test or one of the routine drills was omitted from the lesson plan.

Periodically, there will appear lessons in which the whole class session is devoted to drilling on previous vocabulary, remediation, and recitals--with no new signs introduced. These sessions were designed more or less to allow the students a "breather"; an opportunity to rest from the constant inflow of material which must be memorized, mastered, and added to their repertoires, and a chance to "digest" what they have already learned. It also affords the instructor the opportunity to make a more thorough evaluation of the progress of individual students in the class, and to work with individual students in correcting any errors in technique that may have developed. These "breather" sessions will usually appear when the signs taught in the class session immediately preceding were those associated with the emotions, to enable the instructor to work with the students on facial expression, body movements, emphasis, mood, and the like.

However, the instructor should make it a practice to glance through the lesson following the one he is teaching at the moment--and if a test is scheduled, to inform his class of the fact. While this may lead to some "exam fever" among his students, tests are given so often in the course that the students soon become inured to the process and begin to regard the tests as a challenge rather than a threat.

MATERIALS NEEDED FOR LESSON 4

For instructional pruposes:

1. If available, overhead projector transparencies with:

    a. Grades, means, and so on, for test given in Lesson 3.
    b. Cloze sentence examples.
    c. Lesson 4 practice sentences.

2. Lesson plan.
3. Password game.

DUP materials (if necessary: SM Page

1. Lesson 4 vocabulary word-descriptions (4-DUP-V, four pages)   63
2. List of words to be taught in Lesson 5 (4-DUP-M, one page)   68

LESSON PLAN OUTLINE

Seventh Class Session

I. Roll call. (Use one of the variations described in Chapter 2, C, 1.)

II. Announcements, if any.

III. Return graded fingerspelling test papers. Announce class average. Write scores on the chalkboard (or overhead projector transparency can be prepared ahead of time), and comment on any patterns of mistakes which indicate need for further drill. Inform students that their grades on this particular test will not be included when computing their final grades.

IV. Fingerspelling drill. Use letter groups which include those missed by the majority of the students on the test when fingerspelled in a word. Be sure and include discrimination drill. (See Preliminary Lessons 1 and 2 for words which can be used for discrimination drills.) Do not forget vocalization drill during this part of the lesson.

V. Review of signs in Lessons 1 to 3.

   A. Sentences which can be used for review (see also, the Cloze sentences in Lessons 2 and 3):

      1. Good morning, how are you today?
      2. Please say goodbye to her for me.
      3. He helps himself to my things!
      4. I can't understand a word he says.
      5. Please excuse me, I'm very sorry.
      6. They are coming at 11:30 tomorrow morning.
      7. You must take your medicine every 4 hours day and night.
      8. Last month's phone bill was $12.95. That's too high!
      9. What time did they leave yesterday?
      10. Are you sure you practice your signs and fingerspelling enough?
      11. I can't tell you at this (now) time what I will do.
      12. How can you be so stupid?
      13. I think he has a lot of ability.
      14. It is different when you do it yourselves.
      15. That boy is a lousy fingerspeller!
      16. How old is your sister?

   B. Vary and verify drill. At this point, one of the students can be called upon to conduct the drill for a given lesson, after which the instructor can quickly review the signs. (Note: Students who conduct the drills should be excused from recitals.)

VI. Student recitals, using homework sentences.

VII. Introduce Lesson 4 vocabulary of signs.

A. Signs to be taught in this lesson:

1. Help	15. --er sign	29. Next month
2. Must	16. Student	30. Year
3. Get	17. Teach	31. Next year
4. Have (possessive)	18. Teacher	32. Last week
5. Work	19. School	33. Last month
6. Job	20. College	34. Last year
7. Necessary, etc.[1]	21. University	35. Last night
8. No (none)	22. High school	36. Today (b)
9. Experience	23. Minute, second	37. This morning
10. Expert, skill	24. Hour	38. This afternoon
11. Again	25. Afterwhile, later	39. This evening
12. Slow	26. Week	40. One month ago
13. For	27. Next week	41. Two years ago
14. Learn	28. Month	42. 2 (up to 5) years from now, and so forth

(Total signs taught after this lesson: 154)

New signs taught:

Variations of the above signs: New signs (not in the lesson plan):

B. Cloze drill sentences. (It is anticipated that instructor will endeavor to use those brought to class by students, but these can be used instead--or to illustrate the type of sentence they should try to compose in the future.)

1. Can I HELP you?
2. You MUST have experience to GET a job.
3. You must HAVE experience to get a JOB.
4. You must have EXPERIENCE to get a job.

---

[1]Teach "unnecessary" or "no need" (NEED plus AWAY version of the sign).

5. I have NO work experience.
6. I need money and have to get a job.
7. A man who has a lot of ability is an EXPERT.
8. Say that AGAIN, slowly please.
9. Say that again SLOWLY, please.
10. His mother does everything FOR him. He doesn't do anything FOR himself.
11. You are LEARNING sign language.
12. You are STUDENTS in my class.
13. I TEACH you sign language. I am your TEACHER.
14. Children learn things in SCHOOL.
15. When they finish school, they can go to COLLEGE if they study hard.
16. After they finish grammar school, kids go to HIGH SCHOOL.
17. Our classes last ____ (no. of hours) HOURS.
18. An hour has 60 MINUTES.
19. Goodbye, I will see you LATER this afternoon.
20. A WEEK has seven days.
21. A MONTH has four weeks, and a YEAR has 52 weeks.
22. NEXT WEEK, we will have a test.
23. NEXT MONTH will be ____ (name of month).
24. How many of you will be here NEXT YEAR?
25. Up to LAST WEEK, you had learned 92 signs, plus numbers.
26. It was very _____ (adjective; cold, hot, etc.) LAST NIGHT.
27. LAST MONTH was _____ (name of month).
28. LAST YEAR, 19__, was a very good (bad) year for all of us.
29. TODAY, you are learning the signs for week, month and year.

C. Vary and verify drill on Lesson 4 vocabulary of signs.

VIII. Password game, if there is time (at least 30 minutes of class time remaining).

IX. Distribute DUP list of words for Lesson 5 vocabulary if necessary, and remind students of Cloze sentence homework, assigning words to each student while you are reminding them.

X. Concluding remarks. (There will be a comprehension test in the language of signs in the next class session.)

PRACTICE SENTENCES

1. I will call you about it.

2. Please practice your vocabulary words.

3. Will you be OK now?

4. Different people practice in different ways.

5. Hello! How are you tonight?

6. What are you going to do now?

7. Do you understand me?

8. I don't know what he thinks about it.

9. I know I'm dumb. Don't confuse me.

10. I do not understand how people can be so dumb!

11. Did you tell him about the phone call?

12. I will phone you around 8:30.

13. It cost me about $3.50.

14. There were 45 people at her party.

15. My son is 18 years old now.

(SM 63)

WORD-DESCRIPTIONS OF SIGNS IN LESSON 4 VOCABULARY

1. <u>HELP</u>: Right hand, palm flat and toward ceiling. Left <u>A-hand</u> placed on center of right palm and both hands raised slightly.

2. <u>MUST</u>: <u>X-hand</u>, palm to floor, drop a few inches.

3. <u>GET</u>: Relaxed <u>C-hands</u>, palms facing each other but right hand above left hand (reverse if southpaw), separated by a few inches. Close hands to <u>S-hands</u> rapidly, bringing hands together so that right <u>S-hand</u> is on top of and touching left <u>S-hand</u>, right little finger to left thumb.

4. <u>HAVE</u> (possessive): Both <u>right-angle</u> hands, palms to body. Bring finger-tips to chest, separated by about six inches.

5. <u>WORK</u>: Both <u>A-hands</u>, palms to floor. Cross wrists with right hand on top. Brush right upper wrist forward a couple of times across back of left wrist.

6. <u>JOB</u>: Same as WORK.

7. <u>NECESSARY, HAVE TO, NEED, SHOULD, OUGHT TO</u>: All signed MUST.

8. <u>NO</u> (as in "I have no job."): Both hands in <u>O-hand</u> position, palms facing each other and separated by about six inches. Push hands toward audience a few inches, separating them by about twelve inches. (Just one hand can also be used.)

9. <u>EXPERIENCE</u>: <u>Open-and-hand</u> (fingers straight instead of curved). Place thumb and fingertips at temple. Draw hand outward an inch or so, closing fingers and thumb meanwhile, ending up with <u>and-hand</u> a few inches from head.

10. <u>EXPERT, SKILL</u>: Left hand, palm flat, fingers closed, palm to right. Cup right hand along outer (little finger) edge of left palm, closing hand around it. Then move right hand downward, closing hand to <u>A-hand</u>, palm forward. (Left hand does <u>not</u> move.)

11. <u>AGAIN</u>: Left hand, palm flat and facing ceiling. Right <u>right-angle</u> hand, palm to ceiling, is turned over, palm to floor and fingertips in center of left palm.

12. <u>SLOW</u>: Left hand, palm flat and facing floor. Right hand, palm flat but relaxed. Fingertips of right hand are drawn slowly along back of left hand and wrist from fingertips back to wrist and arm. (<u>Note</u>: Hands should be almost parallel.)

13. FOR: Sign THINK, then move hand a few inches from the forehead, turn-
    ing it so that it is palm forward, fingertip to ceiling. (You will
    often see a deaf person saying--"for for." This is deaf "idiom"
    for WHAT FOR.)

14. LEARN: Left hand in open-hand, fingers-closed position, palm to ceiling
    and fingertips to right front. Right hand in open-and-hand, fingers-
    closed position. Place right fingertips against left palm, then lift
    it upward and backward until the back of the right hand is at the
    forehead, meanwhile closing hand to and-hand position. (Some deaf
    people do this twice, but do not bring the hand all the way to the
    forehead. They also use this for STUDENT.)

15. -ER SIGN (agent sign): With both hands in open-hand, fingers-closed
    position, about twelve inches apart, palms toward each other and
    fingertips forward, place the heels of both palms against the sides
    of the chest and move them down to the waistline. (This is the "per-
    son" sign. For example, WORKER would be signed WORK, then ER. BAKER
    would be signed COOK, then ER, and so on.)

16. STUDENT: Sign LEARN, then -ER.

17. TEACH: Both hands in and-hand position, palms and fingertips forward.
    Both hands begin the sign in a position about level with your eyes
    and about a foot apart. Push both hands forward at the same time.
    Do this twice, rapidly.

18. TEACHER: Sign TEACH, then sign -ER.

19. SCHOOL: Clap both hands twice. (Denotes teacher clapping her hands
    for attention.)

20. COLLEGE: Start sign in same position as for SCHOOL, then sweep the right
    hand up in a circular motion to a position about six inches above left
    palm, keeping palms parallel to each other.

21. UNIVERSITY: Sign COLLEGE, and while right hand is circling above left
    hand, change the hand position to U-hand, palm forward and fingertips
    to ceiling.

22. HIGH SCHOOL: Fingerspell HS fast (mouthing the words "high school"),
    moving the hand quickly sideways about four inches while the hand is
    changing from H to S.

23. MINUTE, SECOND: Left hand in open-hand, fingers-closed position, palm to
    right and fingertips to ceiling. Right hand in index-hand position,
    palm to left. Place heel of right hand against palm of left hand, with
    fingertip pointing to ceiling. Move index finger of right hand about
    a half-inch clockwise (toward left little finger).

24. HOUR: Position hands as for MINUTE, but have right index hand describe
    full clockwise circle around left palm, keeping index fingertip toward
    ceiling.

25. AFTERWHILE, LATER: Position hands as for MINUTE, then turn right index
    hand clockwise to the right (right fingertips point first to ceiling,
    then end up pointing forward). Left hand remains stationary. Do this
    rapidly twice. (You can place thumb of right hand against center of
    left palm while doing this.)

26. WEEK: Left hand in open-hand, fingers-closed position, palm to right and
    fingertips pointing to right front. Right hand in index-hand position,
    fingertip pointing to ceiling, palms facing each other. Place heel of
    right hand against heel of left palm and slide right hand across left
    palm from heel of hand toward fingertips.

27. NEXT WEEK: Sign WEEK, then slide right index hand off end of left hand
    and move it forward a few inches. Do this in a circular motion so
    that right index hand ends up a few inches above and directly over
    left hand.

28. MONTH: Both hands in index-hand position. Left hand palm to right, fin-
    gertip to ceiling. Right hand palm to self, fingertip to left. Place
    back of right index finger against side of left fingertip and draw it
    downward toward wrist.

29. NEXT MONTH: Sign WILL, then MONTH.

30. YEAR: Both hands in S-hand position, palms to self and knuckles facing
    each other. Place right hand above left hand, then circle it forward,
    downward, back, and place it again in position on top of left hand.
    Right fist, in other words, circles around left fist.

31. NEXT YEAR: Can be signed FUTURE, then YEAR, or you can use the more com-
    mon one that follows: Both hands in S-hand position, palms to self
    and knuckles facing each other as in YEAR. Place right hand on top of
    left, then while left hand remains stationary, right hand changes to
    index-hand position and moves forward, fingertip pointing forward.

32. LAST WEEK: Sign WEEK PAST.

33. LAST MONTH: Sign PAST MONTH.

34. LAST YEAR: Both hands in S-hand position. Place right fist on top of
    left fist, then with right hand in index-hand position, palm to self
    and fingertip to ceiling, "throw" your index finger back over your
    shoulder, or point it back over your shoulder. Left S-hand remains
    stationary.

35. LAST NIGHT: Sign YESTERDAY NIGHT.

36. TODAY: (Often signed just NOW, NOW.) Sign NOW DAY.

37. THIS MORNING: Sign NOW MORNING.

38. THIS AFTERNOON: Sign NOW AFTERNOON.

39. THIS EVENING: Sign NOW EVENING.

40. ONE MONTH AGO: Sign MONTH, then follow directions for last part of LAST YEAR, with index finger "thrown" back over shoulder.

41. TWO YEARS AGO: (up to five years ago) Follow directions for LAST YEAR, but "throw" the number of fingers over your shoulder as there are years you want to indicate.

42. TWO (UP TO FIVE) YEARS FROM NOW: Follow directions for "S" type of NEXT YEAR, but right hand, after hitting left fist, changes into 2-hand or 3-hand according to number of years you want to indicate. Then move right hand forward.

(SM 68)

WORDS FOR WHICH SIGNS WILL BE TAUGHT IN LESSON 5

1.	Male	19.	Wife
2.	Female	20.	Which
3.	Man	21.	When (specific)
4.	Woman	22.	When (during, while)
5.	Baby	23.	Book
6.	Baby	24.	Read
7.	Boy	25.	Study
8.	Girl	26.	Write
9.	Gentleman	27.	Pencil, pen
10.	Lady	28.	Type, typewriter
11.	Father	29.	Secretary
12.	Mother	30.	Lesson
13.	Son	31.	Paper
14.	Daughter	32.	Print
15.	Sister	33.	Often
16.	Brother	34.	Once
17.	Marry, wed	35.	Sometimes
18.	Husband	36.	Always
		37.	Never

LESSON 5

(SM 70-75)

Eighth Class Session

GENERAL INSTRUCTIONS

It is suggested that, beginning with Lesson 5, no more new students be admitted to the course unless the prospective students already have some facility in fingerspelling and know at least a few signs. It would take a disproportionate amount of instructor time to bring raw beginning students up to the level of ability the rest of the class should have achieved by this time, for it must be remembered that the class, at this point, will have learned 134 signs plus any additional ones the instructor has introduced during classroom work. A student who does not know these particular signs will, therefore, have his work cut out for him trying to catch up with the rest of the students, while at the same time, keeping up with the current lesson material being introduced.

Lesson 5 marks the introduction of group practice. The purpose of group practice is to free the instructor for giving individual help to students in a more relaxed situation than one in which the student recites in front of the whole class.

By the scores on the initial test of fingerspelling comprehension, and from classroom observation of student performances and responses during drills, the instructor will have by this time a pretty good idea of whom among his students are progressing rapidly, and which ones are falling behind the rest. It is suggested, therefore, that the instructor group the students according to their levels of achievement, without its being obvious that he is grouping the slow ones together and putting the faster ones in another group.

He should try to see that the groups are kept small--about five or six to a group, depending upon the size of the class--and that they seat themselves in circles where everyone has a clear view of everyone else's hands. He should then instruct them to practice their homework "recital" sentences (not the Cloze sentences) on each other, and explain that he will be circulating and lending help where it is needed.

He should then make the rounds, keeping one eye on the slower student group, and moving in to help as soon as the need becomes obvious. Once he has "touched base" with the faster groups, he can casually draw up a chair and join in the slow group.

During this time, he should make every effort to analyze the problems being encountered by individual students (something he may not have had time to do previously) which are holding the students back, and try to come up with remediation treatment which will help them overcome the difficulties. It may be that remediation can be initiated on the spot, or it may be that the treatment is such that it would benefit the whole class to observe. In the latter case, the instructor should make note of what is needed, and incorporate it as part of his lesson plan for the next class session. Suggestions for remediation for specific performance errors are incorporated in the sections on Teaching Fingerspelling; Use of Videotaping Equipment in Remediation; and General Teaching Techniques.

The instructor is reminded to teach variations of the signs provided in this manual. For example, MOTHER and FATHER have colloquial signs which can be roughly interpreted as MOMMIE and DADDY, and are made simply by touching the thumb of the 5-hand to the chin or forehead twice. Also, HUSBAND and WIFE are frequently signed with the back of the C-hand touching the forehead (instead of the male or female sign) at the beginning of the sign. When MARRY, WED is taught, the sign for WEDDING should also be taught, etc. This is an important part of the students' learning, and should not be overlooked by the instructor who may be overly conscientious about following the lesson plans exactly as presented. Flexibility should be the keynote of all his teaching.

MATERIALS NEEDED FOR LESSON 5

For instructional purposes: Lesson plan.

DUP materials (if necessary):   SM Page

1. Vocabulary word-descriptions of signs in Lesson 5 (5-DUP-V,
   three pages)   70
2. List of words to be taught in Lesson 6 (5-DUP-M, one page)   74
3. Practice sentences for MUST, NEED, NECESSARY, HAVE TO, etc.
   (5-DUP-P, one page)   73

LESSON PLAN OUTLINE

Eighth Class Session

I.   Roll call. (It is suggested that no more beginners be admitted to the course at this point. They will be too far behind the others to catch up, and this would tend to discourage them, leading to later dropping out of the class, and may delay the progress of the others in the class.)

II.   Announcements.

III.   Fingerspelling drill. Use the same format as in previous lessons. Be sure to include vocalization drills.

IV.   Vocabulary drill on lessons to date. Use previously furnished Cloze sentences, and so on.

V.   Comprehension test. Follow same procedure as in previous test, signing and fingerspelling each sentence twice, then waiting for students to write answers.

Comprehension Test

1. Hello! <u>It</u> <u>is</u> <u>a</u> <u>beautiful</u> morning.
2. He <u>is</u> <u>really</u> <u>an</u> expert <u>at</u> this.
3. Please <u>see</u> me about your lesson.
4. <u>It</u> <u>is</u> confusing <u>when</u> you don't know their names.
5. We would <u>like</u> to thank you for your help.
6. I can't understand how <u>he</u> can say that.
7. We have ___ (number) students <u>in</u> our <u>class</u>.
8. <u>She</u> can't practice with us tonight.
9. <u>It</u> <u>is</u> different <u>when</u> you <u>try</u> to do <u>it</u> yourself.
10. They are not coming this morning. They'll be here tomorrow night.

(79 words. -1.2 for each error.)

VI.   Collect papers, then go over test item by item.

VII.   Give Lesson 5 vocabulary, utilizing student-provided Cloze sentences, then vary/verify drill on Lesson 5 signs.

Signs to be taught in Lesson 5:

1. Male	13. Son	25. Study
2. Female	14. Daughter	26. Write
3. Man	15. Sister	27. Pencil
4. Woman	16. Brother	28. Typewriter
5. Child	17. Marry, wed	29. Secretary
6. Baby	18. Husband	30. Lesson
7. Boy	19. Wife	31. Paper
8. Girl	20. Which	32. Print
9. Gentleman	21. When (specific	33. Often
10. Lady	22. When (during)	34. Once
11. Father	23. Book	35. Sometimes
12. Mother	24. Read	36. Always
		37. Never

(Total signs taught after this lesson: 191)

New signs taught:

Variations of the above signs: New signs (not in the lesson plan):

VIII. Break class into groups for recital practice, putting students who appear to be progressing more slowly than the others in a group by themselves. (Instructor should work with these students himself during group practice.)

IX. Homework assignment: Same as Lesson 4. (If outside assignments have been given students, completion of the first assignment should fall due around the tenth class session. In this event, students should be reminded at this time of the approaching due date.)

X. Pass out DUP materials if any.

XI. Concluding remarks.

(SM 73)

PRACTICE SENTENCES

Must, Need, Have to, Should, Ought to, Necessary

Note: All words underlined in each sentence are indicated by the single sign for MUST. (Do not add the sign for TO.)

1. The children have to return to school on Sunday afternoon.
2. I must have more money before I can buy a new car.
3. The boy must learn to do better work.
4. I should learn to speak more carefully.
5. You ought to walk faster, as it is getting late.
6. I must be home before 9.
7. It will be necessary for you to come back tomorrow.
8. My friend's husband had to work late last night.
9. You have to take your medicine now.
10. He has to get up early tomorrow morning.
11. We had to run to catch the bus.
12. It is necessary to get permission from the office before you can visit the classroom.
13. It isn't necessary to make an appointment.
14. He ought to be here before too long.
15. You should be ashamed of yourself!
16. I need some new clothes.
17. Will it be necessary for me to go to the doctor's office with you?
18. It wasn't necessary for you to wait for me.
19. That was an unnecessary expense. (Sign NOT for un-.)
20. Did you have to do that?
21. You must work harder or you'll fail the course.
22. Do you need any more help?
23. I don't need any help from you.
24. At what time should we meet you?

(SM 70)

WORD-DESCRIPTIONS OF SIGNS IN LESSON 5 VOCABULARY

1. <u>MALE</u>: (The basic position for all signs denoting male gender. Derived from the hand holding the brim of a hat.) Right hand in <u>open-and</u> hand, closing to <u>and-hand</u> as the hand "takes hold of a hat brim."

2. <u>FEMALE</u>: The basic position for all female signs. <u>A-hand</u>. Move the ball of your thumb across your cheek from each toward mouth. (Derived from the days of the bonnet ribbons women used to have crossing their cheeks.)

3. <u>MAN</u>: Sign MALE, then measure a height taller than yourself with a <u>right-angle</u> hand. (The sign described for MALE is often used with <u>and-hand</u> pushed forward about four inches to indicate MAN. Shortcut method.)

4. <u>WOMAN</u>: Sign FEMALE, then measure height taller than yourself with <u>right-angle</u> hand.

5. <u>CHILD</u>: <u>Right-angle</u> hand. Measure a height considerably smaller than yourself. For CHILDREN, do this twice more, moving hand to the right as you measure out each child.

6. <u>BABY</u>: Natural sign--cradle a baby in your arms.

7. <u>BOY</u>: Same as MAN, only measure a height smaller than yourself or make MALE sign twice, quickly.

8. <u>GIRL</u>: Sign FEMALE twice, rapidly, or sign FEMALE then measure height considerably shorter than yourself with <u>right-angle</u> hand.

9. <u>GENTLEMAN</u>: Sign MALE, then FINE.

10. <u>LADY</u>: Sign FEMALE, then FINE (often used for WOMAN, too).

11. <u>FATHER</u>: Right hand in <u>A-hand</u> position, palm to left. Place thumb on forehead, then open hand quickly to <u>5-hand</u>.

12. <u>MOTHER</u>: Same as for FATHER except that thumb is placed on <u>chin</u> instead of forehead.

13. <u>SON</u>: Sign MALE, then BABY.

14. <u>DAUGHTER</u>: Sign FEMALE, then BABY.

15. <u>SISTER</u>: Sign FEMALE, then ALIKE.

16. <u>BROTHER</u>: Sign MALE, then ALIKE.

17. <u>MARRY, WED</u>: Clasp hands, right hand on top of left, palm to palm.

18. <u>HUSBAND</u>: Sign MALE, then MARRY.

19. <u>WIFE</u>: Sign FEMALE, then MARRY.

20. <u>WHICH</u>: Both hands in <u>A-hand</u> position, palms facing each other but separated by a couple of inches. Move each hand up and down alternately.

21. <u>WHEN</u> (specific): Both hands in <u>index-hand</u> position. Left hand palm upward, or facing the body, remains stationary. Right hand describes a circle with its fingertip, palm away from the body, around the left finger then back until the right fingertip touches the left fingertip.

22. <u>WHEN</u> (during): Both hands in <u>index-hand</u> position, parallel, palms down. Move both forward a few inches, describing a slight, downward arc.

23. <u>BOOK</u>: Place both hands (in <u>open-hand, fingers-closed</u> position) in a "prayer" attitude, then, keeping the outside edges of the palms together, open the hands like a book.

24. <u>READ</u>: Left hand in <u>open-hand, fingers-closed</u> position, palm to self. Right hand in <u>2-hand</u> position, palm to floor and fingertips to left palm. (This denotes the two eyes.) With fingertips pointing to left palm, move them back and forth as if reading a page of print printed on your left palm.

25. <u>STUDY</u>: Point the fingertips of right bent <u>4-hand</u> at left palm and sign FINGERSPELL at the palm of your left hand.

26. <u>WRITE</u>: Natural sign. Using left palm as a piece of paper, "hold a pencil" in your right hand and "write" on your left palm.

27. <u>PENCIL</u>: Pretend to hold a pencil in your right hand. Bring it to your mouth as if moistening the tip, then sign WRITE.

28. <u>TYPEWRITE</u>: Natural sign. Pantomime typing on a typewriter.

29. <u>SECRETARY</u>: Pretend to remove a pencil from your ear, then sign WRITE. You may follow this with the -ER sign if you wish, but it is not necessary. This sign is sometimes made with <u>U-hand</u> instead of "pencil-gripping" hand. The <u>U-hand</u> touches the ear, then comes down and traces a line across the left palm.

30. <u>LESSON</u>: Left hand in <u>open-hand, fingers-closed</u> position, palm to self, fingertips to ceiling. Right hand in <u>right-angle hand</u> position, palm to left, and knuckles to ceiling. Place outside edge of right hand against left palm fingertips, then lift it away a little bit and place it against left palm center.

31. PAPER: Both hands in <u>open-hand, fingers-closed</u> position. Left hand
     palm upward, fingertips to right front. Right hand palm to floor,
     fingertips to left front. Brush right palm <u>backward</u> a couple of
     times against left palm, moving from fingertips to palm of left hand.

32. PRINT: Left hand <u>open-hand, fingers-closed</u>, palm to ceiling, fingertips
     forward. Right hand in <u>20-hand</u> position. Place thumb of right hand
     against left palm and make 20 two or three times.

33. OFTEN: Left hand in <u>open-hand, fingers-closed</u> position, palm to ceiling.
     Right hand in <u>right-angle</u> hand, palm to floor. Touch fingertips of
     right hand to left palm three times, moving fingertips from the base
     of the left palm to the fingertips.

34. ONCE: Left hand in <u>open-hand, fingers-closed</u> position, palm to ceiling.
     Right hand in <u>index-hand</u> position. Touch right fingertips to left
     palm, then hold up one finger, palm to body. For twice, use <u>V-hand</u>
     position and do the same. For thrice, use <u>3-hand</u> position and do the
     same.

35. SOMETIMES: Sign ONCE twice, quickly. (When SOMETIMES is signed very
     slowly, it means OCCASIONALLY or ONCE IN A WHILE.)

36. ALWAYS: Right <u>index-hand</u> position, palm to ceiling, describes a couple
     of largish circles in the air.

37. NEVER: Right <u>B-hand</u>, palm to left. Starting at about eye level, finger-
     tips pointing forward, hand describes a large question mark in air.
     (The tail of the ? should go off to your <u>right</u> in a chopping motion.)

(SM 74)

WORDS FOR WHICH SIGNS WILL BE TAUGHT IN LESSON 6

1. Remember	19. Big, large
2. Forget	20. Small, little
3. Why	21. Keep
4. Most	22. Borrow
5. Because	23. Lend
6. On	24. Careful, be careful
7. In	25. Law
8. Out	26. Rule
9. With	27. Mother-in-law
10. Together	28. Father-in-law
11. Going together, steady dating	29. Sister-(etc.) in-law
12. Far	30. Aunt
13. Near	31. Uncle
14. Around	32. Cousin
15. Ask	33. Niece, nephew
16. Before	34. Grandmother
17. Better	35. Grandfather
18. Best	

LESSON 6

(SM 76-82)

Ninth Class Session

GENERAL INSTRUCTIONS

Since Lesson 7 will include the first written performance test, the instructor should endeavor to drill students rather thoroughly on signs taught up to and including Lesson 6. In addition, when students are responding in signs during drills, the instructor should frequently call the student's attention to the beginning hand-position he is using in executing the sign by asking "What hand-position are you using?"

At this time, also, the instructor should endeavor to focus his students' attention on the beginning hand-position only--hammering it into them until he is certain they all understand that only the beginning hand-position will be required on the test, and not (repeat, not) full word-descriptions of the signs in the test. If the instructor does not make this unmistakably clear, he will regret it when he attempts to correct the test papers, for while some students will follow directions and limit themselves to giving the hand-positions at the beginning of the sign, others will attempt to gain points with the instructor by writing out complete word-descriptions of the sign, and some of the student-composed word-descriptions would baffle a cryptologist. (The author, after many years of sad experience with students who attempted to give full word-descriptions of the signs despite instructions to the contrary, has developed a tactic which the instructor may want to use. When she is giving her classes the instructions prior to administering the performance test, she informs the class that any student will automatically lose 10 points from whatever score he makes, if he does not follow directions and limit himself to the beginning hand-position only.)

Cloze sentences (and recital sentences) will not be needed for Lesson 7, since most of the class time will be consumed by the administration of the performance test and the teaching of "Comin' thru the Rye." (However, if the instructor prefers not to teach the song, he should require Cloze sentences as usual, and treat the vocabulary of signs in Lesson 7 as if the signs were simply a regular lesson instead of those used in a song. He should follow the same format for drilling on the signs as he has been provided for the first six lessons. However, there will not be sufficient time for the usual drill on fingerspelling.)

Note: There are several songs in the Appendix which the instructor may wish to use instead of or in addition to those provided in the lesson plans. These songs may be added to the usual lesson format; if they are used in place of the songs provided in the lesson plans, the vocabularies of signs (for the songs originally provided) should be taught on schedule regardless of whether or not they are taught as songs. This is important, for subsequent lessons presume the signs used in the songs have been learned.

The instructor will note that the "classic" sign for BECAUSE has been given in the word-descriptions. Briefly, this is the version of BECAUSE which is signed KNOW, MOST, and has been provided regardless of the fact that most deaf people use a shorter version which involves the use of only one hand. The reason for this is a simple one: most students taught the shorter version (using only one hand) will go through a period of learning the sign in which they fail to make the essential downward arc of the hand after they sign KNOW--and the result is a sign which is almost impossible to distinguish from the sign for FORGET. Some students, in fact, never quite master this downward arcing of the hand, and go through life signing BECAUSE and FORGET exactly alike. By introducing them initially to the KNOW, MOST version of BECAUSE, the instructor forestalls the development of this habit, and as the KNOW, MOST version becomes fixed in the student's repertoire, so does the essential downward arcing of the hand. In time, the students will learn the shorter version using only one hand, but the downward arc will be fixated to the point where the student will be able to perform the one-handed version of BECAUSE accurately, since he will unconsciously be adding an imaginary MOST to the last part of the sign.

MATERIALS NEEDED FOR LESSON 6

For instructional purposes:

1. Lesson plan.
2. If OH projector and screen available, transparency of practice sentences on Must, Need, Have to, Should, etc. (Uncover sentences one at a time and ask individual students to recite.) (5-DUP-TRM; one page.)

DUP materials (if necessary):   SM Page

1. Word-descriptions of signs in Lesson 6 (6-DUP-V; four pages) ...   76
2. Words to the song, "Comin' thru the Rye" (6-DUP-M, b; one page)   83
3. List of words to be taught in Lesson 7 (6-DUP-M, a; one page)   81

LESSON PLAN OUTLINE

Ninth Class Session

I. Roll call.

II. Announcements, if any.

III. Return test papers and discuss them. Comment on patterns of errors if any such patterns were discernible. Write scores and means on chalkboard (or project on overhead projector screen).

IV. Fingerspelling drill. Concentrate on letter groups students missed on test. Include vocalization and discrimination drills.

V. Fingerspelling test. Fingerspell each item twice, then wait for students to write answers. When test is over, collect papers and review test.

1. Read your books.
2. I forgot him.
3. They are not here.
4. You are right.
5. Please excuse me.

6. I like ham.
7. The leak was large.
8. Drills build skill.
9. Make a cake.
10. Am I wrong?

(32 words. -3.1 for each error.)

VI. Review of vocabulary of signs from previous lessons.

A. Use Lesson 5 test sentences, as well as Cloze sentences.

Note: Those Cloze sentences brought by students which were not used in the teaching/learning drills previously conducted are excellent for use in future drills.

B. Assign one student to each of the five previous lessons, and have each conduct a vary/verify drill on the lesson he was assigned.

Note: About this time, instructor should stiffen his requirements for correct execution of the signs, and be stricter about sloppiness.

VII. Student recitals. Use practice sentences (Must, etc.) from Lesson 5.

VIII. Give vocabulary of signs for Lesson 6.

A. Signs to be taught in Lesson 6:

192

1. Remember	13. Near	25. Law
2. Forget	14. Around	26. Rule
3. Why	15. Ask	27. Mother-in-law
4. Most	16. Before	28. Father-in-law
5. Because	17. Better	29. Sister-(etc.)
6. On	18. Best	in-law
7. In	19. Big, large	30. Aunt
8. Out	20. Small, little	31. Uncle
9. With, without[1]	21. Keep	32. Cousin
10. Together	22. Borrow	33. Niece, nephew
11. Going together, steady dating	23. Lend	34. Grandmother
12. Far	24. Careful, be careful	35. Grandfather

(Total signs taught after this lesson: 226)

New signs taught:

Variations of the above signs: New signs (not in the lesson plan):

B. Utilize student-provided Cloze sentences for learning drill.

C. When all signs have been taught, conduct vary/verify drill.

IX. Announcements about Lesson 7:

A. There will be a performance test, in which students will be expected to know the beginning hand-position for each of the signs taught to date. They should, therefore, review all the word-descriptions, practice the signs, and pay particular attention to the position their hands are in when they begin each sign.

B. Lesson 7 will also begin their education in "singing" in sign language with the introduction of "Comin' thru the Rye," which the instructor will teach them after the test.

X. Homework assignment:

---

[1]"Without" is not included in word-descriptions. Instructor should teach it anyway.

A. Cloze sentences and recital sentences will <u>not</u> be needed for next lesson!

B. Outside Assignment I will be due at the next class session (if assigned).

C. If instructor knows the words to "Drinking Cider thru a Straw," the song can be employed to afford practice in the signs for relatives. He can therefore require as homework that his students find the song and practice it for the next class session <u>in addition</u> to other homework.

XI. Pass out DUP materials. Ask that students try to memorize the words to "Comin' thru the Rye" before next class session.

XII. Concluding remarks.

(SM 76)

WORD-DESCRIPTIONS OF SIGNS IN LESSON 6 VOCABULARY

1. REMEMBER: Sign KNOW or THINK, then with both hands in A-hand position, palms almost facing each other, press ball of right thumb to thumbnail of left thumb. (The first part of the sign can also be made with the thumb against the temple instead of fingertips.)

2. FORGET: Right hand in open-hand, fingers-closed position, palm to face and fingertips to left. Pass fingertips across forehead and off to one side an inch or two, closing hand to A-hand position, palm to self, as you do so.

3. WHY: Sign KNOW, then draw hand away and down, ending in Y-hand position, palm toward body.

4. MOST: Both hands in A-hand position, palms facing each other. Left hand remains stationary. Right hand moves up from below, brushing knuckles of left hand in passing, and continues upward for a few inches.

5. BECAUSE: Sign KNOW, then quickly follow with MOST.

6. ON: Both hands in open-hand, fingers-closed position, palms to floor. Tap back of left hand with fingers of right hand.

7. IN: Both hands in and-hand position. Left hand palm to right, fingertips to right, knuckles to front. Place fingertips of right and-hand inside circle formed by left and-hand fingers and thumb.

8. OUT: Left hand in C-hand position and curled around right hand which is in open-and position, palm to floor, fingertips extending down below left hand. Draw right hand up through left hand above and to the right, BOTH hands closing to and-hands as the right hand passes through and out.

9. WITH: Both hands in A-hand position. Palms facing each other, knuckles forward. Bring them together from a few inches apart.

10. TOGETHER: Sign WITH, but after bringing hands together, move them forward a few inches.

11. GOING TOGETHER OR STEADY DATING: Sign TOGETHER two or more times.

12. FAR: Both hands in A-hand position, palms facing each other, hands touching. Left hand remains stationary, but right hand moves forward several inches toward right front.

13. NEAR: Both hands in right-angle hand-position, left hand near the body, right hand a few inches farther away. Bring right hand inward until the inside of the right hand's fingers rest on the backs of the left hand's fingers. (When object referred to is other than that represented by the self, sign moves in the opposite direction.)

14. AROUND: Left hand in <u>and-hand</u> position, palm and fingertips toward ceil-
     ing. Right hand in <u>index-hand</u> position. Circle right index finger
     around fingertips of left hand.

15. ASK: (a) Both hands in <u>open-hand, fingers-closed</u> position. Bring palms
     together in a "praying" gesture, lowering them slightly after they are
     together.

       (b) (Slang version) Left hand in <u>index-hand</u> position, fingertip
     toward ceiling and palm to right. Right hand in <u>V-hand</u> position, but
     with fingers crooked. Straddle left index finger between crooked V
     fingers of right hand.

       (c) Right <u>index-hand</u>. Crook index finger (making hand into an
     <u>X-hand</u>) pushing hand forward very slightly as you crook the finger.

16. BEFORE: Both hands in <u>B-hand</u> position. Left hand palm forward, finger-
     tips to ceiling. Right hand placed back to back with left hand (right
     palm toward body). Bring right hand back toward body a few inches.

17. BETTER: Right hand in <u>open-hand, fingers-closed</u> position, palm to body,
     fingertips to left. Pass fingertips across mouth, from left to right
     and close hand to <u>A-hand</u> position, palm to shoulder and thumb toward
     ceiling.

18. BEST: Sign GOOD, then MOST. Or sign BETTER, and when hand is in <u>A-hand</u>
     position, raise it several inches quickly until it is level with top
     of head.

19. BIG, LARGE: Both hands in <u>L-hand</u> position, palms to floor and fingertips
     to front. Start with hands close together but not touching, then
     separate hands widely.

20. SMALL, LITTLE: (a) Both hands in <u>open-hand, fingers-closed</u> position or
     slightly cupped palms facing each other, fingertips to front. Bring
     hands together without quite touching each other. Can be repeated once,
     separating hands an inch or two, then bring together again, still with-
     out touching.

       (b) With hand in "coin-flipping" position, move thumb upward in tiny
     strokes against ball of index finger.

       (c) Measure off a tiny space between thumb and index finger.

21. KEEP: Both hands in <u>K-hand</u> position, palms facing each other and finger-
     tips to front. Place right hand on top of left hand (little finger side
     of right hand against thumb side of left hand).

22. BORROW: Sign KEEP, but position hands farther away from body, then bring
     close to body.

23. LEND: Exactly the opposite of BORROW. Position hands close to body, then
     push out several inches. (Signed in the direction of the intended transfer.)

24. <u>CAREFUL, BE CAREFUL</u>: Sign KEEP, raising hands slightly after they are in KEEP position. (BE CAREFUL is frequently signed KEEP, KEEP.)

25. <u>LAW</u>: Left hand in <u>open-hand, fingers-closed</u> position, palm to right. Right hand in <u>L-hand</u> position. Place palm of right L on palm of left hand in a firm, definite gesture.

26. <u>RULE</u>: Similar to the sign for LAW except <u>R-hand</u> is used. Place right hand on palm of left hand twice, the <u>R-hand</u> moving slightly back toward wrist the second time.

27. <u>MOTHER-IN-LAW</u>: Sign MOTHER, then LAW (most common). Or MOTHER, IN, LAW.

28. <u>FATHER-IN-LAW</u>: Sign FATHER, then LAW. (Same comments apply as for MOTHER-IN-LAW.)

29. <u>SISTER-IN-LAW, BROTHER-IN-LAW, SON-IN-LAW, DAUGHTER-IN-LAW</u>: Same as above. Sign each--SISTER, BROTHER, SON, DAUGHTER--then follow the sign with the sign for LAW.

30. <u>AUNT</u>: Right hand in <u>A-hand</u> position, palm to front, knuckles to ceiling. Trace a short, vertical line from cheekbone to angle of jaw with thumb. Do this twice, rapidly.

31. <u>UNCLE</u>: Right hand in <u>U-hand</u> position, palm to front, fingertips to ceiling. Trace a line from hairline to temple with side of index finger. Do this twice rapidly.

32. <u>COUSIN</u>: Right hand in <u>C-hand</u> position, palm to left and fingertips to side of the face. Move fingertips back and forth from palm to body position to palm forward position. Repeat once.

33. <u>NIECE, NEPHEW</u>: Right hand in <u>N-hand</u> position, palm to front (or can face the cheek) knuckles to ceiling. For NIECE, circle N fingertips near cheek or jawbone. For NEPHEW, circle N fingertips near forehead. (Small circles, please, or they will think you are signing CRAZY.)

34. <u>GRANDMOTHER</u>: Sign MOTHER, then when hand is open, describe a small circle with right <u>open-hand, fingers-closed</u>; with left hand in <u>A-hand</u> position, palm up, held waist high, opening to <u>5-hand</u> at the same time the right hand opens.

35. <u>GRANDFATHER</u>: Sign like GRANDMOTHER, except that sign begins with FATHER instead of MOTHER.

(SM 81)

WORDS FOR WHICH SIGNS WILL BE TAUGHT IN LESSON 7

1. If
2. Somebody
3. Meet
4. Come, coming
5. Go, going
6. Away, gone (away)
7. Through
8. River
9. River (Rye)
10. Kiss
11. Every
12. Lassie
13. Laddie
14. Yet, still
15. All
16. Smile
17. At
18. From
19. Town, village, city

20. Greet
21. Frown, scowl, cross
22. Among
23. Crowd, group, class
24. There (poetic)
25. Sweetheart, boyfriend
26. Dearly
27. Love
28. Home
29. Choose, pick
30. Where
31. Pretty
32. Beautiful
33. Ugly, homely
34. Sing, song, music
35. Singer, musician
36. Any
37. Anywhere
38. Anything

(SM 83)

COMIN' THRU THE RYE

Note: "Comin' thru the Rye" is a song, lyrics written by Robert Burns, which had its basis in an old fiesta custom in a hamlet on the River Rye in northern England. On a certain festival day, damsels from outlying farms had to pick their way across stepping stones in the shallow river in order to get to the fair. If any lassie was caught by any of the local laddies while crossing the river, the lads had the right to claim a kiss from the lass.

> If a body meet a body
> Comin' thru the Rye,
> If a body kiss a body
> Need a body cry?

Chorus:

> Every Lassie has her laddie
> Nane they say ha'e I,
> Yet all the lads they smile at me
> When comin' thru the Rye.

> If a body meet a body
> Comin' frae the town,
> If a body greet a body
> Need a body frown?

Chorus:

> Every Lassie has her laddie
> Nane they say ha'e I
> Yet all the lads they smile at me
> When comin' thru the Rye.

> Amang the train there is a swain
> I dearly love mysel',
> But what's his name or where' his hame
> I dinna choose to tell.

Chorus:

> Every Lassie has her laddie
> Nane they say ha'e I,
> Yet all the lads they smile at me
> When comin' thru the Rye.

LESSON 7

(SM 83-90)

Tenth Class Session

GENERAL INSTRUCTIONS

Lesson 7 is characterized by the introduction of two new learning experiences for the students: a written performance test and learning to sing in
the language of signs.

While the written performance test will not tell the instructor how well individual students can use the signs they have learned, nor how fast they can recall those signs, it will provide valuable information on whether or not the individual student can remember the signs at all, for if he knows what position
his hands are in when the sign is begun, it stands to reason he will remember the
rest of the motions which go into the making of a given sign.

In addition, the performance test helps to identify those students who are not
quite precise about the execution of a given sign--the ones who have developed
slight imperfections or fuzziness in their signing which the instructor may not
have noticed during classroom performance. A student, for instance, who responds
on the test that KNOW is made with an open-hand, fingers-closed hand-position
(when a right-angle or cupped-hand is actually required), can be identified as
one who either executes the sign with his hand blocking half of his face, or bends
his wrist at an awkward angle while making the sign for KNOW. In either case, the
execution of the sign is sloppy and imprecise, but it may easily have escaped the
instructor's notice during rapid classroom drills.

The instructor would, of course, catch the more gross errors in technique, but
the slight deviations which are not quite wrong, yet not quite right either, often
generate only a slight dissonance in the instructor's eye, too slight to trigger
his impulses to correct, or they may escape his notice entirely. Unfortunately,
these minor deviations often summate to give an overall impression of awkwardness
in the student's use of signs--and quite frequently are rooted in faulty hand-
positions.

The performance test, therefore, can provide the instructor with clues as to why
a certain student is not coming across as well as he should, even though he may appear to know all the signs, recall and use them with ease during recitals --yet
give the impression of being "out of kilter" somehow.

While it is always possible that the student giving an out-of-true response on
a test actually does know and execute the sign correctly and precisely, and his
slightly deviant response on the test is due only to a foggy grasp of what the
various hand-positions are called, the instructor can use the test as an indicator

for a personal check on exactly how such students execute a sign. If it turns out that the student was only confused about the name of the hand-position, the instructor can correct his impression--and thereby insure that the student will understand the word-descriptions better in the future. If it happens that the deviant response was due to the student's not using the correct hand-position for the sign, then the instructor can immediately set about correcting the flawed technique and be alert to any regression on the part of that student thereafter.

To repeat an earlier warning, the instructor is again reminded of the importance of making sure that his students understand and follow the directions for giving answers on the test. If he does not, he can count upon having to spend anywhere from 30 minutes to an hour per paper in correcting the papers--an experience he is not likely to enjoy, nor want to repeat.

When the test has been administered, and the papers collected, the instructor should employ the test as a drill, using the varying/verifying method. He should encourage the students to examine their hand-positions as they give their responses, for part of the purpose of the test is to alert the students to the necessity of being precise in their execution of given signs. When the students learn that they may be called upon to give the hand-positions for the signs on tests, they will thereafter pay more attention to exactly how a sign is made, rather than content themselves with learning an "approximation" of the sign.

After the test and review are completed, the instructor can then introduce the class to "Comin' thru the Rye." This particular song is an old one, easily learned, and adaptable to various styles of signing without making students unduly uncomfortable during their first attempt at emoting in the language of signs. It can be sung to a jumpy, peppy beat, or slowly and fluidly. It can also be jazzed up and transformed into a comedy routine, or acted out. It can be used to illustrate the changes which occur when a conversational sign must be replaced by a platform sign, and when words which are normally fingerspelled must be signed even though no sign exists for the word. This introduces the students to the concept of interpreting--which involves paraphrasing, defining, and explaining a concept--as opposed to verbatim translation of spoken or written English into the language of signs. Since students will frequently have to resort to interpretation of their own messages when they are conversing with a deaf person of limited language ability, training in substitution of more easily understood synonyms for abstract terms is a vital part of the process of learning to communicate meaningfully in the language of signs.

In addition, learning to sing in sign language helps the students to develop expressiveness in their signing and fingerspelling of messages. It also teaches them the use of phrasing, pauses, and emphasis, if the instructor insists that the signing of a song be synchronized with the words of the song as they are sung vocally. This means that the signs for a word must be held--or drawn out--if the word itself is drawn out when sung vocally; delivered quickly if the word is sung quickly; emphasized with force if the word in the song is emphasized; muted when the sung word is muted; and so forth.

For this reason, it is suggested that the instructor try to obtain records or tapes of the songs he teaches--or recruit a good singer from among his students (or sing, himself, if he can) who can sing for the class a few times while they practice synchronizing their signing with the beat or rhythm of the song. However, the instructor should try to prevent overuse of any student-singer if he finds one among his students who knows or can learn the words to the songs. (To avoid burdening one student with all the vocalizing, it is suggested that the instructor endeavor to tape-record the singer's rendition of the song, and use the tape thereafter.)

Unfortunately, the songs provided in this manual, while more or less classics in the sense that they are familiar to most people who have any interest in music, are also old. This means that they are hard to obtain in record form or on tapes--and the sheet music is extremely difficult to find except in large metropolitan music shops which specialize in back issues of once-popular songs. The instructor's best bet would be to search among collections of old-time favorites for the music he needs. (An alternative, of course, is to teach some of the currently popular songs. If this is done the signs provided herein for the songs in this manual still should be taught on schedule. This is necessary because subsequent lessons presuppose the signs provided by the songs have been taught.)

MATERIALS NEEDED FOR LESSON 7

For instructional purposes:

1. Copies of performance test, Lesson 7 (7-DUP-TEST, three pages).
2. Overhead transparency with words of the song printed thereupon.
3. Record or tape of "Comin' thru the Rye" (or sheet music).
4. Tape recorder or record player.

DUP materials (if necessary):

1. Vocabulary word-descriptions for Lesson 7 (7-DUP-V; four pages).
2. List of words for which signs will be taught in Lesson 8 (7-DUP-M; (one page).

LESSON PLAN OUTLINE

Tenth Class Session

Note: Assignment I due at this time.

I. Roll call.

II. Vocabulary drill on all previous lessons. Continue this until all students are present, but not longer than 20 minutes. Latecomers after this may begin the test immediately upon their arrival. (Regardless of the time of their arrival, make sure all students have 30 minutes in which to complete the test.)

III. Performance test: Pass out mimeographed performance test.

Instructions for giving performance test and grading same:[1] Make sure students read the directions carefully. Emphasize that they are not to attempt to give full word-descriptions of each sign, but to limit themselves to the beginning hand-position only. Give students an example, choosing one of the words on the test, HOW. Show students how the hands, both of them, are put into the A-hand position at the beginning of the sign. Explain that this is all that is wanted--just the beginning position of each hand. If only one hand is needed, the space in the column for the other hand is to be left blank.

IV. Drill: When 30 minutes are up, collect test papers, then use the test as a drill. While drilling, ask each student who is responding which hand-position he is using to make the sign.

V. Lecture on purpose of learning to sing in the language of signs. Points to make:

A. Teaches students to sign smoothly and gracefully.

B. Begins their training in "substitutions," where synonyms must be substituted for words that do not have signs.

C. Introduces them to the beauty which can be expressed in sign language.

D. Prepares them for possible future interpreting in that signs used in songs are "platform" signs--larger, smoother, and more flowing than conversational signs--as are the signs used in platform interpreting for deaf people.

E. Helps them to remember the signs, for students rarely forget a sign

---

[1]See Appendix for a master copy of the correct (or acceptable) responses to test items, and grading instructions.

learned in a song.

    F.   Last, but not least, helps train them to be expressive in their use of the language of signs, and the use of pauses, emphasis, and so forth in expressing moods.

VI.   Teach "Comin' thru the Rye," using the words of the song as the teaching drill. (<u>Note</u>: There are additional signs to be taught, which are indicated by <u>asterisk</u>* in the list below.)

Signs to be taught in this lesson:

1.	If	20.	Greet
2.	Somebody	21.	Frown, scowl, cross
3.	Meet	22.	Among
4.	Come, coming*	23.	Crowd, group,* class*
5.	Go, going	24.	There (poetic)
6.	Away, gone (away)	25.	Sweetheart, boyfriend
7.	Through	26.	Dearly
8.	River*	27.	Love
9.	River (Rye)	28.	Home
10.	Kiss	29.	Pick, choose
11.	Every	30.	Where (a) & (b)
12.	Lassie	31.	Pretty
13.	Laddie	32.	Beautiful*
14.	Yet, still	33.	Ugly, homely*
15.	All	34.	Sing, song, music*
16.	Smile	35.	Singer, musician*
17.	At	36.	Any*
18.	From	37.	Anywhere*
19.	Town, village, city	38.	Anything*

(Total signs taught to date: 264)

New signs taught:

Variations of the above signs: New signs (not in the lesson plan):

VII. Student recitals of the song (which should occupy the remaining class time). (Ask for volunteers to sign "Drinking Cider thru a Straw" if it was assigned.)

VIII. Homework assignment:

    A. Practice "Comin' thru the Rye" in front of mirrors.

    B. Cloze sentences for Lesson 8.

IX. Pass out DUP materials if any.

    A. Lesson 7 vocabulary word-descriptions

    B. List of words to be taught in Lesson 8.

X. Collect Outside Assignment I if required of students.

XI. Concluding remarks.

LESSON 7

PERFORMANCE TEST

Name _____
LH or RH

1. Index hand (IH)
2. Open hand, fingers closed (OH, FC)
3. Open hand, fingers spread (5H)
4. Cupped hand (CH)
5. Right angle hand (RAH)
6. Right angle index hand (RAIH)
7. And hand (AH)
8. Open and hand (OAH)
9. Clawed hand (CLH)
10. A, B, Y (etc.), hand (A), (B), (Y), etc.

RH = Right hand   LH = Left hand

Which of the above hand-positions do you use for the following signs? Give the BEGINNING hand-position for each hand (if both hands are used--or the appropriate (left or right) hand if only one is used). If left-handed, please indicate on the upper right corner of your paper. (Please limit yourself to beginning hand-position only. For the instructors' sake, do not attempt to give full-word description of the sign.) The above abbreviations may be used, but try not to use the numbers--it complicates the chore of correcting the papers.

	LH	RH			LH	RH
1. I				7. What (a)		
2. Me				8. What (b)		
3. Mine				9. How		
4. Myself				10. Know		
5. Yourself				11. Think		
6. Practice				12. Hello		

206

No.	Word	LH	RH
13.	Different		
14.	Same (a)		
15.	Same (b)		
16.	Sorry		
17.	Please		
18.	Fine		
19.	Excuse		
20.	Your		
21.	Can		
22.	Ability		
23.	Can't		
24.	Introduce		
25.	Call (summon)		
26.	Call (by name)		
27.	Call (phone)		
28.	Morning		
29.	Good		
30.	Night		
31.	Work, job		
32.	Help		
33.	Experience		
34.	Get		
35.	This, that		
36.	Tell		

No.	Word	LH	RH
37.	Must, necessary, etc.		
38.	Again		
39.	Slow		
40.	No (none)		
41.	Remember		
42.	Man		
43.	Woman		
44.	Far		
45.	Near		
46.	Never		
47.	Always		
48.	For		
49.	Which		
50.	When		
51.	When (during)		
52.	Why		
53.	Because		
54.	Most		
55.	Themselves		
56.	On		
57.	Sunday		
58.	Have		
59.	Meet		
60.	But		

(SM 84)

WORD-DESCRIPTIONS OF SIGNS IN LESSON 7 VOCABULARY

1. IF: Two F-hands, palms facing each other, fingertips pointing forward.
        Move up and down alternately.

2. SOMEBODY: Right index-hand, fingers to ceiling and palms facing each other.
        Describe small circle with hand, using elbow as fulcrum (or pivot).

3. MEET: Both index-hands, fingers to ceiling and palms facing each other.
        Bring hands together until thumbs touch along their length. (Please
        note index-hands. Important!)

4. COME, COMING: (a) Both hands in index-hand position, palms toward body,
        fingers pointing to each other. Circle each index finger around the
        other, each circle bringing hands closer to body, circles moving counter-
        clockwise in relation to right hand. (Platform version.)

        (b) (Conversational version.) Right index-hand makes a largish,
        beckoning gesture, ending sign with fingertip pointing to the floor in
        front of signer. (Both hands can be used in this sign, and, depending
        on the emphasis given it, the number of times it is repeated, can be
        used to indicate: a chronic dropper--a pest. Or a good friend who drops
        by frequently--or someone who keeps trying to catch you at home, in vain.)

        (c) Usually used as in invitation--or command. Same as COMING (b)
        except that open-hand, fingers-closed position is used.

5. GO, GOING: (a) (Not in poem, but handy to know at this point.) Exactly as
        COMING, but reverse direction of circles and move hands away from body.
        (Platform version.)

        (b) (Conversational version.) Right index-hand points to floor then
        moves away and up until finger is pointing to right front. (Same com-
        ments apply as in COMING (b) regarding use of both hands, emphasis or
        lack of it, and repetition of this sign.)

        (c) Same as in GOING (b) except that right-angle hand is used, and
        hand straightens out to open-hand, fingers-closed at the end of sign.
        (Most often used as a command: "Go away!")

6. AWAY, GONE (AWAY): Same as GOING (c).

7. THROUGH: Both hands in open-hand, fingers-closed position. Left hand faces
        body. Push outer edge of right hand through left hand, passing between
        second and third fingers of left hand.

8. RIVER: With both hands in 4-hand position, palms down, put the right hand
        behind the left hand, then, wiggling the fingers, push both hands off to
        left-front to indicate rippling waves flowing down a river.

9. RIVER (RYE): Generally spelled out, but for poems, it is signed like this: Make the letter R, then sign RIVER.

10. KISS: Right open-hand, fingers-closed, palm to body. Touch fingertips to mouth, then to cheek.

11. EVERY: Both A-hands. Left hand remains stationary. Palms facing each other. Brush knuckles of right hand downward twice against heel of left hand.

12. LASSIE: Sign FEMALE twice (GIRL).

13. LADDIE: Sign MALE twice (BOY).

14. YET, STILL: Y-hands, palms toward floor, both hands parallel and about six inches apart. Move hands forward in a down-and-up semicircle.

15. ALL: Both hands in open-hand, fingers-closed position. Left hand palm to self and fingertips to right. Right hand palm forward, fingertips to ceiling, alongside left hand. Pivot right hand at wrist and place back of right fingers against palm of left fingers. (This is the conversational version. In the platform version, the right hand exaggerates the pivoting movement to a large, sweeping circle.)

16. SMILE: Right index-hand. Trace an upward line from the corner of the mouth to describe a broad smile.

17. AT: Usually spelled out, but in poetic usage only, sign TO.

18. FROM (Used as "frae" in song): Left hand in index-hand position, palm to right, finger to ceiling. Right hand in X-hand position, palm to left. Put knuckle of right index (X) finger against knuckle of left index finger and pull right hand back a couple of inches. (Almost like pulling a bowstring back from a bow.)

19. TOWN, VILLAGE, CITY: Both hands open-hand, fingers-closed position. Palms almost facing each other. Touch fingertips to each other to make an inverted V, like a house roof. Move hands sideways, touching fingertips several times.

20. GREET: Sign HELLO. (Or pantomime lifting your hat and bowing.)

21. FROWN, SCOWL, CROSS: 5-hand, palm to face. Crook fingers to make a clawed-hand (and grimmace). Or push your nose up (head, too) with index fingertip, looking snooty. (This last for the song only.)

22. AMONG (Used as "amang" in song): Left hand in open-and hand-position, palm toward ceiling. Right hand in right-angle, index-hand position, palm to floor. Circle right fingertip in and out and around left fingertips.

23. CROWD, GROUP, CLASS (used for "twain" in song): Both slightly bent,
    curved 5-hands, fingers slightly spread, palms forward and separated
    by several inches. Move both hands outward in a circular movement,
    right hand circling to the right and left hand circling to the left,
    turning both hands so that palms face body and little fingers are al-
    most, but not quite touching.

24. THERE: Right open-hand, fingers-closed position, palm to ceiling. Move
    slightly forward. (Or in a different poem, sweep it sideways from
    center front to right.)

25. SWEETHEART, BOYFRIEND (used for "swain" in song): Sign MALE, then both
    hands in A-hand position, thumbs upward and palms to body. Bring hands
    together so knuckles are against knuckles--then wiggle thumbs up and
    down simultaneously.

26. DEARLY: Both hands, palms flat and facing body. Cross wrists and place
    palms against chest.

27. LOVE: Same as above, but use A-hands. (Actually DEAR and LOVE are inter-
    changeable. But when they come together as in this poem, use one for
    LOVE and the other for DEARLY.)

28. HOME: Right and-hand. Bring fingertips to mouth to show putting some-
    thing in the mouth, then open hand to open-hand, fingers-closed posi-
    tion and place palm on cheek to show BED. (Denotes bed and board.)

29. CHOOSE, PICK: F-hand, palm forward. Bring back several inches.

30. WHERE: (a) Right hand in index-hand position, palm forward and fingertip
    to ceiling. Wiggle fingertip from side to side.

       (b) Sign like HERE, but make circles much larger. (Platform usage,
    generally, but also used in some localities to indicate conversational
    WHERE.)

31. PRETTY: Right hand in 5-hand position, palm to left and thumb pointing
    to shoulder or ear. Move fingertips across the face (but not touching
    it) and downward in a circular motion, closing hand to and-hand posi-
    tion, palm to body, with hand to right of and alongside chin.

32. BEAUTIFUL: Sign PRETTY, then open hand quickly to open-and position,
    raising it a few inches as it opens.

33. UGLY, HOMELY: Right hand in X-hand position, palm to floor and knuckles
    to left. Place hand close to left side of nose and draw straight across
    the face without touching face. (This denotes the crooked nose some
    ugly people have.)

34. <u>SING, SONG, MUSIC</u>: Both hands in <u>open-hand, fingers-closed</u> position. Hold left arm out in a circle, palm facing self. Wave right hand back and forth (almost like a harp-playing gesture) in the circle of the left arm.

35. <u>SINGER, MUSICIAN</u>: Sign MUSIC, then -ER.

36. <u>ANY</u>: Right hand in <u>A-hand</u> position, palm to self, but slightly toward ceiling. Turn hand quickly to palm forward (but with palm facing slightly toward floor too).

37. <u>ANYWHERE</u>: Sign ANY, and then WHERE. (A variation of this is ANY, WHAT, using the natural gesture WHAT, and using only the right hand.)

38. <u>ANYTHING</u>: Sign ANY, and then WHAT, WHAT, WHAT, using the one-handed natural gesture for WHAT, and moving the hand sideways between each WHAT.

(SM 89)

WORDS FOR WHICH SIGNS WILL BE TAUGHT IN LESSON 8

1.	Neighbor	19.	Fun
2.	Friend	20.	Make fun of
3.	Enemy	21.	Here
4.	Like	22.	Happy
5.	Dislike	23.	Sad
6.	Family	24.	See
7.	After	25.	Look
8.	People	26.	Watch
9.	Play	27.	Who
10.	Thing, things	28.	Face, looks (like)
11.	Bring	29.	Want
12.	Make	30.	Fly
13.	Coffee	31.	Airplane
14.	Clean, nice, pure	32.	Ride (car)
15.	Dirty	33.	Ride (horse)
16.	Find, found	34.	Right (left)
17.	Funny (ha ha)	35.	Left (right)
18.	Funny (peculiar), queer	36.	Believe

LESSON 8

(SM 91-97)

Eleventh Class Session

GENERAL INSTRUCTIONS

Note: By the time the instructor has reached this point, he should be thoroughly conversant with the procedures and techniques of teaching manual communication. From this point onward, therefore, it is assumed that he will need little in the way of general instructions on how to conduct a class session, so, after Lesson 8, the general instructions section in each lesson will be discontinued. Any specific instructions the author feels will be helpful to the instructor will be included instead in the lesson plans. The materials needed for each particular session will be listed at the beginning of each lesson plan, for it is felt that after teaching eleven class sessions with the help of this manual the instructor will need little help in conducting the remaining class sessions of the course.

At this point, if he has not begun doing so before this, the instructor should discuss with his students some of the language problems of deaf people which are reflected in the language of signs. The introduction of the need for substitution, paraphrasing, defining, and explaining concepts--which was brought to the students' attention when the song "Comin' thru the Rye" was taught--calls for some elaboration on this facet of deafness. A good way of introducing the topic is to project on a screen the sample letter from a deaf person (provided with DUP materials) which vividly illustrates the type of grammatical peculiarities so often noted in the language of deaf people.

Since this will be relevant to the students' future ability to converse easily and meaningfully with a wide variety of deaf people, this part of their instruction should not be overlooked or skimmed over. Therefore, part of every class session from this point on should include discussions of the many different factors which influence the language of signs: from the language limitations which are reflected in the idiomatic language of signs; through the psychological impact of deafness on the person, his parents and relatives, and his co-workers; to the socioeconomic and educational implications all of this has for the deafened person's ability to make his way in the world.

The instructor should welcome and encourage questions from his students which trigger such discussions, and should be willing to temporarily abandon whatever he may be doing at the moment, drilling or teaching, to discuss any topic suggested by questions from his students, or which occurs to him as he teaches a particular way of using signs. When the topic is exhausted (or is such that he can request his students to do some outside research on it), he can then return to whatever he was doing prior to the interruption.

In addition, the instructor will often find that current events he reads or hears about in the field of deafness are things which would be of interest to his students, who may not have the instructor's sources of information. He should, if possible, arrange to schedule some class time for discussion of current topics as they arise, and should encourage his students to ask questions or volunteer opinions.

Sometimes, however, the students will be the ones to read or hear about a new development about which the instructor himself has not yet learned. This is a situation in which caution is indicated. Unless the student has brought factual information to class, and can explain it clearly, the instructor would be wise to withhold his opinion until he has had a chance to find out what it is all about. He must remember that students in manual communication classes will tend to view him as an authority on all things pertaining to deafness (the "halo" effect), and a casual opinion carelessly expressed without full knowledge of the facts can (and probably will) be taken as a statement of the instructor's opinions about the way things should be, a conviction the students may adopt as their own.

Other than the introduction of more or less regular discussion periods into the classroom procedures, the teaching format from Lesson 8 to the end of the manual does not vary much from that described up to Lesson 8. The instructor will probably find it helpful to refer back occasionally to an earlier lesson where specific instructions were given for conducting a particular type of class, but, on the whole, the instructor will have no trouble in maintaining consistency and continuity in his teaching methods by use of the lesson plans alone.

MATERIALS NEEDED FOR LESSON 8

For instructional purposes:

1. OH transparency of sample letter (or duplicated copies of it).
2. OH transparency (or copy) of "Comin' thru the Rye" (and/or "Drinking Cider through a Straw").
3. Tapes of the songs, and tape player (or record and record player).
4. Lesson plan.

DUP materials (if necessary):

1. Word-descriptions of Lesson 8 vocabulary (8-DUP-V; four pages).
2. List of words for which signs will be taught in Lesson 9 (8-DUP-M, one page).

LESSON PLAN OUTLINE

Eleventh Class Session

I. Roll call.

II. Discuss performance test (and Assignment I if given): Before returning
test papers, pick out a few at random, go through them for specific types
of errors, and call upon these students to give the signs. If many in
the class missed a particular sign, drill on the sign is indicated. (It
is assumed that the instructor will have made it a practice to either
write on the chalkboard or on an OH projector transparency, the scores
obtained, the number of students making a particular score, and the class
average.)

If Assignment I was given and collected during the preceding class session, this should also be discussed in terms of what the students had
discovered was going on in the local community of deaf people, and where
they could go to have the best chance of meeting deaf people and completing Assignment II.

III. Vocabulary drill on all preceding lessons. Sentences which can be used
during vary/verifying drill:

1. Good night, I will see you in the morning.
2. What do you think of him?
3. My mother said I can go with you tonight.
4. My sister-in-law came to see us and brought her beautiful children.
5. Say that again slowly, please.
6. Can you help me find a job?
7. How many of you will be here next year?
8. That is no excuse for doing a bad job!
9. Several of my friends came over last evening.
10. Sixty-nine is how much more than 42?

IV. Comprehension test: Sign each sentence twice (underlined words must be
fingerspelled).

1. What an ugly girl she is!
2. My daughter is confused as to which boy she likes more.
3. Do you remember what he said to us last Sunday?
4. I want to get a different opinion on it.
5. Her plane leaves at 11:45 tomorrow night.
6. Please excuse me, I forgot my lesson.
7. How are you going to get experience unless you work?
8. This afternoon we will all work together.
9. I can't understand why you did that!
10. She never lends her typewriter to anyone.

(Total words in test: 81. -1.2 for each error.)

V. Drill, using test sentences after papers are collected.

VI. Teach Lesson 8 vocabulary. Utilize Cloze sentences provided by students.

Signs to be taught in this lesson:

1.	Neighbor	19.	Fun
2.	Friend	20.	Make fun of
3.	Enemy	21.	Here
4.	Like	22.	Happy
5.	Dislike	23.	Sad
6.	Family	24.	See
7.	After	25.	Look
8.	People	26.	Watch
9.	Play	27.	Who
10.	Thing, things	28.	Face, looks (like)
11.	Bring	29.	Want, don't want[1]
12.	Make	30.	Fly
13.	Coffee	31.	Airplane
14.	Clean, nice, pure	32.	Ride (car)
15.	Dirty	33.	Ride (horse)
16.	Find, found	34.	Right (left)
17.	Funny (ha ha)	35.	Left (right)
18.	Funny (peculiar), queer	36.	Believe

(Total of signs taught to date: 300)

New signs taught:

Variations of the above signs: New signs (not in the lesson plan):

---

[1]"Don't want" is not included in word-description. Instructor should teach it anyway.

VII. Discussion of language problems of deaf people as reflected in the form of sign language they use, and its implications for the student learning manual communication.

VIII. Student recitals of "Comin' thru the Rye" (and "Drinking Cider through a Straw" if assigned and taught). Try and choose students who did not get the chance to recite in preceding class session.

IX. Homework assignment, same as for previous lessons.

Note: At this point, it would be a good idea for the instructor to pause and "take stock" of his teaching and his course. A good way to do this is to request that the students write a brief evaluation of the course (and his teaching) to date, and suggest ways it could be improved. (A sample evaluation form which can be used for this purpose will be found in the Appendix.) This can either be done in the classroom, or assigned as homework. To permit students to express themselves freely, they should not put their names on their papers. (The comments students make can form the topic of an informal discussion in the class session following that in which the instructor gets back the evaluation papers. Don't be defensive--you can learn much from this.)

X. Pass out DUP materials:

A. Vocabulary word-descriptions of signs in Lesson 8 (8-DUP-V, four pages).

B. Practice sentences on DO, ACT, BEHAVE (8-DUP-P, one page).

C. List of words for which signs will be taught in Lesson 9.

XI. Concluding remarks.

EXAMPLE OF LOW-VERBAL DEAF ADULT GRAMMAR[1]

DEAR _____

LETTER SENT YOUR GOT ME HELLO ME. ME HELLO LETTER SENT YOU FOR FAIR.
YOU TAKE DINNER ME, SATURDAY OK? ME TIME 8 P.M. GO HOUSE YOUR YOU PICKUP
OK? QUICK SENT LETTER ME TELL NO, OTHER TIME ME GET SATURDAY MORNING, OK?
IF NO GET, PICK UP YOUR HOUSE TIME 8. ADDRESS MY:

615 GREENWOOD DRIVE.

ZIPPER FOR FLY FAST: 91403

PHONE NO. MY AUNT: 784-1904

UP THUMB

_____

_____

[1]Copy of an actual letter.

(SM 91)

WORD-DESCRIPTIONS OF SIGNS IN LESSON 8 VOCABULARY

1. NEIGHBOR: Sign NEAR, then -ER.

2. FRIEND: Both hands in X-hand position. Place right index finger on top
    of left index finger and hook them together firmly. (You will quite
    often see this sign done twice, with fingers changing position until
    the left hand is on top of the right.)

3. ENEMY: Both hands in right-angle index position. Palms to body, finger-
    tips touching each other. Separate hands quickly, then sign -ER.

4. LIKE (as opposed to dislike): Place thumb and second finger of right
    hand, fingers spread and palms to body, against chest. Move hand out-
    ward, closing fingers to an 8-hand position.

5. DISLIKE: Sign LIKE then turn hand to palm forward position vigorously,
    snapping it. Or sign LIKE, then AWAY.

6. FAMILY: Both hands in F-hand position, palms facing forward. Put the
    tips of both index-thumb fingers together, then separate several
    inches, move them forward, simultaneously turning both hands together,
    keeping both hands in F-hand position throughout sign.

7. AFTER: Both hands in B-hand position. Left hand palm to body, finger-
    tips to right front. Right hand, palm to left. Touch little finger
    side of right hand to upper edge of left hand, then raise it and push
    it forward across the left hand a few inches. This also means ACROSS
    and OVER when that word is used to mean something like "over the river."

8. PEOPLE: Both hands in P-hand position (actually K-hands), palms and
    fingertips forward. Hold both hands up near the face or neck and de-
    scribe small, alternating circles forward and backward.

9. PLAY: Both hands in Y-hand position, palms facing body and thumbs to
    ceiling and little fingers to floor. Shake both hands up and down.

10. THING, THINGS: Right hand in open-hand, fingers-closed position, palm
    to ceiling. Lift and lower the hand an inch or two, moving it sideways
    each time you lift.

11. BRING: Both hands in open-hand, fingers-closed position, palms to ceiling.
    Place both hands to your right and several inches forward, then bring
    both hands back to a position directly in front of the body and close
    to it.

12. MAKE: Both hands in S-hand position. First part of sign, the right hand
    is placed on top of left hand, both palms facing body. Separate hands
    slightly, then second part of sign, the right hand is again placed on
    top of left, but the palms now face each other (or would, if hands were
    not one on top of the other). (Do NOT confuse this sign with COFFEE.
    Very common error.)

13. COFFEE: Both hands in S-hand position, palms to body. Left hand re-
    mains stationary. Right hand is placed on top of left, then moved in
    a coffee-grinding type circle.

14. CLEAN, NICE, PURE: Both hands in open-hand, fingers-closed position.
    Left palm faces ceiling, fingertips toward right front. Right palm
    faces floor, then slide it across left palm to left fingertips. (Can
    use P-hand for PURE.)

15. DIRTY: Place back of right 5-hand, fingertips to left front against
    underside of chin and wiggle fingers alternately.

16. FIND, FOUND: Almost like CHOOSE. Difference is in CHOOSE, the palm
    faces forward. In FOUND, you use an F-hand, palm to floor, finger-
    tips forward. Bring hand back toward body, raising palm to palm for-
    ward position. Both the sign for CHOOSE and the sign for FIND end up
    the same way. The difference is in the beginning hand-position.

17. FUNNY (Ha-ha-type): H-hand. Place fingertips on bridge of nose, then
    draw downward down nose, ending with hand in N-hand position, in front
    of face, repeating once, quickly.

18. FUNNY (PECULIAR) OR QUEER: Right hand in C-hand position, palm to left.
    Place hand in front of face (usually the nose), then rotate until palm
    is down toward floor. Hand remains in place, it just rotates.

19. FUN: Sign FUNNY, then, with both hands in H-hand position, palms to
    floor, strike the palms of right H-hand fingers across backs of left
    H-hand fingers.

20. MAKE FUN OF: Sign FUN, then bring right H-hand back up (striking left
    H-hand fingers as it comes up), then down again, again striking left
    H-hand fingers as it passes downward.

21. HERE: Both hands, palms flat and facing ceiling. Describe small, flat
    horizontal circles with each hand, each hand moving in opposite
    directions.

22. HAPPY: Right hand open-hand, fingers-closed position. Place palm against
    chest and brush upward. Repeat once or twice.

23. SAD: Open hand, fingers spread slightly. Place in front of face and
    lower a few inches, with appropriately mournful expression on face.

24. SEE: Right hand in V-hand position. Palm toward body, fingertips to
    ceiling. Place fingertips on upper right cheek, then push forward a
    few inches.

25. LOOK: Sign SEE, but turn hand so fingertips point forward and palm is
    facing floor and move hand forward a few inches. (Used when you say
    something like, "Look at that gal's wacky hair-do.") This is NOT used
    to say, "It looks like rain," or "She looks like her mother." These
    have their own signs which follow in this lesson.)

26. WATCH: Sign LOOK, but push the hand forward more vigorously, and place heel of right hand on back of left hand.

27. WHO: Right hand in right-angle index position, palm to self and finger-tip pointing to chin. Move finger in little circles around chin.

28. FACE, LOOKS (LIKE): Similar to WHO, but fingertip circles whole face. This is used when you wish to say, "She looks like her mother." When you use it in this way, follow LOOKS with the sign for SAME or ALIKE.

29. WANT: Both hands in 5-hand position, palms to ceiling. (One hand can be used.) Crook fingers, while moving hand back toward self an inch or two.

30. FLY: Right hand in Y-hand or ILY position. Raise it over your head (palm to floor and knuckles facing forward), and push it forward several inches.

31. AIRPLANE: Sign FLY twice.

32. RIDE (in a car): Left hand in C-hand position, palm to right and thumb-index edge of hand on top. Sit fingers of right curved N-hand on thumb of left hand and move both hands forward a few inches.

33. RIDE (a horse): Left hand in open-hand, fingers-closed position, palm to right, fingertips pointing forward. Right hand in V-hand position, palm to floor and fingertips of V to floor. Straddle edge of left palm with two fingers of the V-hand and gallop hands forward in little hops.

34. RIGHT (opposite of left); Right hand in R-hand position. Move hand to the right in a short, straight, abrupt movement.

35. LEFT: Like RIGHT above, except that L-hand is used, and the hand moves to the left.

36. BELIEVE: Sign THINK, then MARRY.

(SM 96)

WORDS FOR WHICH SIGNS WILL BE TAUGHT IN LESSON 9

1.	Fast	19.	Dinner
2.	Money	20.	Won't, refuse
3.	Buy	21.	Win
4.	Shopping	22.	Lose (a game)
5.	Both	23.	Lose (something)
6.	Quit	24.	Color
7.	Late	25.	Red
8.	Early	26.	Yellow
9.	Finish	27.	Blue
10.	Grow, spring	28.	Green
11.	Summer	29.	Purple
12.	Autumn, fall	30.	Black
13.	Winter, cold	31.	Pink
14.	Other	32.	White
15.	Eat, ate, food	33.	Brown
16.	Drink	34.	Gray
17.	Breakfast	35.	Silver
18.	Lunch	36.	Gold

LESSON 9

(SM 98-102)

LESSON PLAN OUTLINE

Twelfth Class Session

MATERIALS NEEDED FOR LESSON 9

<u>For instructional purposes</u>:

1. Password and/or Bingo game.
2. Lesson plan.

<u>DUP materials</u> (if necessary):

1. Word-descriptions of signs in Lesson 9 (9-DUP-V, four pages).
2. Words to song, "You'll Never Know" (9-DUP-M,a, one page).
3. Words for which signs will be taught in Lesson 10 (9-DUP-M,b, one page).

   I.   Roll call.

  II.   Warm-up drill in fingerspelling. (<u>Combine with review of signs</u> by fingerspelling words for which signs have been taught, requiring students to repeat the fingerspelled word(s), then to give the correct sign(s). Verify as usual by calling on other students to tell whether first student was right or wrong. This is rather important, for the comprehension test which will be given in this session is a new type.)

 III.   Comprehension test. <u>Fingerspell</u> each sentence once, then <u>sign</u> it once, then fingerspell it a second time, slightly faster than the first time it was fingerspelled. (Underlined words must be fingerspelled when the sentences are signed.)

   1. How many years have you <u>been</u> in school now?
   2. My daughter <u>is</u> <u>a</u> very pretty 21-year old girl.
   3. <u>Are</u> your neighbors friendly people?
   4. How <u>are</u> you doing with your sweetheart now?
   5. Every girl should have <u>a</u> boyfriend, don't you think?
   6. I don't <u>live</u> very far from the big city.
   7. They have <u>been</u> going together for <u>a</u> <u>long</u> time now.
   8. Don't make fun of people. <u>It</u> often <u>turns</u> them <u>into</u> enemies.
   9. I love music, if <u>it</u> <u>is</u> played well, and if <u>the</u> singer <u>is</u> a good one.

10. My cousin and I went through school together.
11. Don't scowl. It makes your pretty face ugly.
12. If you will stay a little longer, I will make some coffee.

(Total words: 124. -0.8 for each error.)

IV. Collect papers and use test sentences as a drill.

V. Give vocabulary of signs for Lesson 9, using Cloze sentences as usual.

Signs which will be taught in this lesson:

1. Fast	19. Dinner
2. Money	20. Won't, refuse
3. Buy	21. Win
4. Shopping	22. Lose (a game)
5. Both	23. Lose (something)
6. Quit	24. Color
7. Late	25. Red
8. Early	26. Yellow
9. Finish	27. Blue
10. Grow, spring	28. Green
11. Summer	29. Purple
12. Autumn, fall	30. Black
13. Winter, cold	31. Pink
14. Other	32. White
15. Eat, ate, food	33. Brown
16. Drink	34. Gray
17. Breakfast	35. Silver
18. Lunch	36. Gold

(Total signs taught to date: 336)

New signs taught:

Variations of the above signs: New signs (not in the lesson plan):

VI. Vary/Verify drill on Lesson 9 vocabulary of signs.

VII. Pasword and/or Bingo game.

VIII. Announcement: The next class session will be a "Breather" session, in which intensive practice will be conducted on all signs learned to date, so remind students to up-date their recital sentences, and practice them at home, as well as practice "Comin' thru the Rye" (and/or any songs taught instead of or in addition to "Comin' thru the Rye"). No new signs will be introduced in the next class session. The one immediately following will involve learning a new song--"You'll Never Know" --and students should try to learn the song before coming to class.

IX. Homework assignment. Covered in VIII above.

X. Pass out DUP materials:

A. Word-descriptions of signs in Lesson 9 (9-DUP-V, four pages).
B. Words to "You'll Never Know" (9-DUP-M,a, one page).
C. Words for which signs will be taught in Lesson 19 (9-DUP-M,b, one page).

XI. Concluding remarks.

(SM 98)

WORD-DESCRIPTIONS OF SIGNS IN LESSON 9 VOCABULARY

1. FAST: Both hands in L-hand position, palms facing each other, fingertips
   to front, and one hand slightly closer to chest than the other. Crook
   index fingers as if pulling the trigger of a gun. Or right hand in
   T-hand position, palm to left, knuckles to front. Snap thumb up into
   air as if flipping a coin.

2. MONEY: Left hand in open-hand, fingers-closed position, palm facing ceiling. Right hand in and-hand position, palm to left. Pat backs of
   fingers against palm of left hand.

3. BUY: Sign MONEY, then bring right and-hand forward as if handing money
   to someone. (Palm facing ceiling.)

4. SHOPPING: Sign BUY, BUY rapidly.

5. BOTH: Left hand in C-hand position, palm to body, fingertips to right.
   Right hand in V-hand position, palm to body, fingertips to ceiling.
   Place backs of V-hand fingers against palm of left hand. Close left
   hand around the V-hand fingers and draw right hand down and out of
   left fist. (V-hand fingers closing to H-hand position as it passes
   through left hand.)

6. QUIT: Left hand in loose S-hand position, palm to right with knuckles
   forward. Right H-hand, palm to left. Close left hand around the two
   right H-hand fingers then draw fingers of right hand quickly up and out
   and back toward body.

7. LATE: Right open-hand, fingers-closed hand, palm to rear, fingertips to
   floor. Hold palm about waist level alongside the body. Wave fingertips forward and backward a couple of times. (Also used for HAVEN'T
   and NOT YET.)

8. EARLY: (a) (Gallaudet version.) Left hand in open-hand, fingers-closed
   position, palm to floor. Right hand in touch position. Touch tip of
   middle finger (other fingers remain extended) of right hand to back of
   left wrist, then bring heel of right hand against back of left wrist
   quickly, the right hand's fingers relaxing to a loose C-hand or sloppy
   A-hand configuration.

   (b) (Illinois version.) Touch tip of right index finger to nose
   (palm to self), then, with palm still facing self, lower hand quickly,
   ending with hand in Y-hand position (or NOW sign, made with one hand),
   palm to self.

9. FINISH: (a) FINISHED, ALREADY: 5-hand position, palm to body. Twist wrist quickly so palm faces forward.

   (b) END: Left hand in B-hand position, palm to body, fingertips to right. Right hand in open-hand, fingers-closed position, palm to floor. Run palm of right hand along index finger edge of left hand to fingertips, then turn right hand to palm left and run palm across fingertips of left hand. (Denotes a "chopping off" of something.) Also means ALREADY HAVE or HAVE in some contexts. Often abbreviated to just the last, "chopping o-f" part of the sign when used as HAVE.

10. GROW, SPRING: Both hands in and-hand position. Left hand palm to right, fingertips to right. Push right hand through left hand from bottom (little finger side) upward, fingers of right hand opening as they come out at the top. (For SPRING, repeat this once, quickly.)

11. SUMMER: Right hand in X-hand position, palm to floor, knuckles to left. Draw across forehead from left to right (denotes wiping sweat off brow).

12. AUTUMN, FALL: Left hand and arm in NOON position. Right hand in B-hand position, palm to floor, fingertips to left. Bring index edge of right hand against elbow of left arm in two short, chopping "blows." (Denotes the slashing of trees in the fall for the maple sap.)

13. WINTER, COLD: Both hands in S-hand position, palms toward each other. Shake hands a couple of times to denote shivers from the cold.

14. OTHER: Exactly the reverse of ANY. Palm to floor, then to self.

15. EAT, ATE, FOOD: Right hand in and-hand position, palm to self. Bring fingertips to lips.

16. DRINK: Right hand in C-hand position, palm to left and knuckles pointing forward (as if holding a glass). Bring thumb to mouth and tilt hand as if tilting glass of water when drinking.

17. BREAKFAST: Sign EAT, then MORNING.

18. LUNCH: Sign EAT, then NOON.

19. DINNER: Sign EAT, then NIGHT.

20. WON'T, REFUSE: Right hand in A-hand

21. WIN: Sign GET, then raise hand as if to wave a flag with right hand-- pretend you are holding a small pennant and whirling it.

22. LOSE (a game): Sign STAND (V fingertips of right hand "standing" on palm of left open-hand, fingers-closed), then "fall" (bring heel of right V-hand down to palm of left hand).

23. LOSE (something): Both hands in right-angle hand position, palms to
    self and fingertips to self. Touch backs of both sets of fingernails
    together, then move fingers downward, separating hands and opening
    fingers to spread position, fingertips to floor and palms facing each
    other.

24. COLOR: Right hand in index-hand position, palm to self and fingertip
    pointing to ceiling. Touch fingertip to chin, then open hand to
    5-hand position and wave fingers in front of chin (wiggle them), palm
    to self.

25. RED: Right hand in index-hand position, palm to self and fingertip to
    ceiling. Draw fingertip down chin a couple of times. (Derived from
    pointing to women's red lips.)

26. YELLOW: Right hand in Y-hand position. Turn hand from palm inward to
    palm outward several times, with a slight downward "dip" each time.

27. BLUE: Right hand in B-hand position. Turn hand palm inward then palm
    outward a couple of times, with fingertips "dipping" slightly each time.

28. GREEN: Right hand in G-hand position. Shake hand from palm inward to
    palm outward a couple of times.

29. PURPLE: Right hand in P-hand position. Follow above directions for
    shaking hand.

30. BLACK: Right hand in right-angle index-hand, palm to left. Draw thumb
    edge of index finger across forehead.

31. PINK: Right hand in P-hand position, palm to self. Touch second finger
    of P to chin and draw downward an inch or so on the chin.

32. WHITE: Right hand in 5-hand position. Place hand against center of
    chest, then draw it forward, closing hand to and-hand position a few
    inches in front of chest.

33. BROWN: Right hand in B-hand position, palm forward and fingertips to
    ceiling. Place thumb edge of index finger against cheekbone and draw
    whole hand downward to jaw line.

34. GRAY: Both hands in 5-hand position, palms to self and fingertips point-
    ing to each other. Brush fingertips of each hand back and forth
    against fingertips of other hand.

35. SILVER: Sign WHITE, then MONEY.

36. GOLD: Touch index finger of right hand to ear lobe, then sign YELLOW.
    (Denotes the gold of earrings.)

(SM 105)

YOU'LL NEVER KNOW

You'll never know
Just how much I love you
You'll never know
Just how much I care

And if I tried
I still couldn't hide
My love for you

You ought to know
For haven't I told you so
A million or more times

You went away
And my heart went with you
I say your name
In my every prayer

If there is some other way
To prove that I love you
I swear I don't know how

You'll never know
If you don't know now.

(SM 103)

WORDS FOR WHICH SIGNS WILL BE TAUGHT IN LESSON 10

1. Just (exactly)	20. Swear (vow)
2. Much (b)	21. Let
3. Care (love)	22. Happen
4. Try	23. Feel
5. Hide	24. Feel hurt (emotionally)
6. Ought	25. Depressed, discouraged
7. Haven't	26. Excited
8. So	27. Touch
9. Or	28. Hate
10. Heart	29. Eager, zealous
11. Prayer	30. Stubborn
12. Church	31. Between
13. Temple	32. Bother
14. Some (indefinite)	33. Interrupt
15. Some (part of)	34. Silly
16. Way	35. Misunderstand
17. Show (demonstrate)	36. Complain
18. Show (movie)	37. Seek, look for
19. Show (play or drama)	38. Sensitive, sensitivity

"BREATHER" SESSION

(SM 104)

LESSON PLAN OUTLINE

Thirteenth Class Session

Note to Instructor: This class should be devoted primarily to student recital and practice in delivering sentences/messages/songs in the language of
signs. Encourage students to offer constructive criticism to their fellow
students. At the same time, keep the classroom atmosphere relaxed so that
occasions for side-excursions into discussions of the many aspects of deafness
and deaf people will occur. Instructor should focus his attention on, and encourage students to comment upon:

1. Facial expression of reciting students.
2. Speed, fluency, and clarity of fingerspelling.
3. Speed, fluency, and clarity of signing.
4. Precision in execution of signs.
5. Rhythm, expression, and emphasis in singing in sign language.

He may also want to take the opportunity to ask for student feedback on how
they are reacting to the course as conducted, what has proved to be helpful,
and any suggestions they might have on how it might be improved.

MATERIALS NEEDED FOR THIS SESSION

1. List of all signs taught to date (or use master vocabulary list).
2. All sentences used: Cloze, practice, and test sentences.
3. Fingerspelling letter groups list.
4. Words to "Comin' thru the Rye" (and/or substitute).
5. Paper and pencils (if instructor decides to have students write their
   reactions/feedback on the course).

  I. Roll call.

 II. Return test papers and discuss grades, class average, and so on.

III. Student recitals.

   A. Have students sign and/or fingerspell sentences--and have other
      students respond to the content of the signed/fingerspelled sen-
      tences. (Example: First student signs, heatedly: DID YOU HAVE

230

TO DO THAT? Second student responds: WELL, IT SEEMED LIKE A GOOD IDEA.) This trains them in <u>conversation</u>.

B. Have students fingerspell test sentences, other students sign same sentence back after repeating fingerspelled sentence.

C. Reverse of B, above.

D. Use student-composed recital sentences.

E. Assigning one student to each of the lessons taught to date, have selected student drill his fellows on that particular lesson, using very/verify technique. (<u>Note</u>: Student can sign those signs he remembers and fingerspell those he does not.)

IV. Be sure and allow time for side-excursion discussions, and <u>provoke</u> them if students do not ask questions leading to such discussions.

V. Homework assignment:

A. Memorize "You'll Never Know."
B. Cloze sentences for Lesson 10.
C. New recital sentences.
D. (If instructor chooses.) Brief composition giving reactions to the course thus far, unless assigned as homework in previous session. In the latter case, collect papers.

VI. Concluding remarks.

LESSON 10

(SM 105-111)

LESSON PLAN OUTLINE

Fourteenth Class Session

MATERIALS NEEDED FOR LESSON 10

<u>For instructional purposes</u>:

1. OH projector transparency of "You'll Never Know," or copy of the words/music to the song.
2. If available, record or tape (and player) of the song.
3. Lesson plan.

<u>DUP materials</u> (if necessary):

1. Word-descriptions of signs in Lesson 19 (10-DUP-V, four pages).
2. List of words to be taught in Lesson 11 (11-DUP-M, one page).
3. Extra copies of "You'll Never Know" (9-DUP-M,a; one page).

   I. Roll call.

  II. Fingerspelling drill. Use letter groups indicated by words missed on test given in Lesson 9. Be sure and include discrimination drills as well as vocalization drill. Toward the end of the drill, ask students to respond by not only fingerspelling, but by giving the <u>sign</u> for the word as well.

 III. Comprehension test: As in Lesson 9, fingerspell, then sign, then finger-spell each sentence.

    1. <u>The</u> dumb secretary typed <u>the</u> lesson all wrong!
    2. I know I'm dumb. Don't confuse me more than I already am!
    3. Sometimes I <u>am</u> happy. Other times <u>I</u> <u>am</u> sad.
    4. She has red hair and green eyes and <u>lives</u> around <u>the</u> lake.
    5. I have to go home now, because <u>it</u> <u>is</u> getting late.
    6. Early last summer, my family and I went to <u>the</u> Golden State, California.
    7. We will have dinner about 7:30 if you would <u>be</u> here by that time.
    8. Can I get you anything while I'm in <u>the</u> city?

9. My husband <u>yells</u> <u>at</u> me when I go shopping for <u>new</u> <u>dresses</u>.
10. That's the <u>way</u> <u>it</u> goes. You win <u>a</u> few and lose <u>a</u> few.

(Total words: 113. -0.9 for each error.)

IV. Collect papers, then use test sentences as a drill.

V. A. Teach song, "You'll Never Know." (Remainder of the class should be occupied by teaching the song and by student recitals of the song.)

    B. Signs which will be taught in this lesson:

1. Just (exactly)	20. Swear (vow)
2. Much (b)	21. Let
3. Care (love)	22. Happen
4. Try	23. Feel
5. Hide	24. Feel hurt (emotionally)
6. Ought	25. Depressed, discouraged
7. Haven't	26. Excited
8. So	27. Touch
9. Or	28. Hate
10. Heart	29. Eager, zealous
11. Prayer	30. Stubborn
12. Church	31. Between
13. Temple	32. Bother
14. Some (indefinite)	33. Interrupt
15. Some (part of)	34. Silly
16. Way	35. Misunderstand
17. Show (demonstrate)	36. Complain
18. Show (movie)	37. Seek, look for
19. Show (play or drama)	38. Sensitive, sensitivity

(Total signs taught to date: 374)

New signs taught:

Variations of the above signs: New signs (not in the lesson plan):

VI. Discuss student evaluation papers. Encourage free discussion. (Again, don't be defensive if students are critical.)

VII. Homework assignment: Practice "You'll Never Know," and write usual Cloze sentences. Remind students to up-date recital sentences.

VIII. Pass out DUP materials (listed at beginning of lesson plan).

IX. Concluding remarks.

(SM 106)

WORD-DESCRIPTIONS OF SIGNS IN LESSON 10 VOCABULARY

1. JUST (exactly): Both hands in 20-hand position. Left hand palm to ceiling, knuckles forward. Right hand palm to floor, knuckles forward. Place fingertips of 20-fingers of right hand precisely on fingertips of left 20-hand.

2. MUCH: In poetic usage, this is signed like LARGE or BIG, with hands in cupped-hand position instead of L-hand position.

3. CARE: In poetic usage, this is signed like one variation of SELFISH, the description of which follows: Right hand in C-hand position, palm to self. Place fingertips on chin (knuckles to ceiling), then close hand to S-hand position, keeping hand close to chin.

4. TRY: Both hands in A-hand or T-hand position, palm to self, thumbs to ceiling. Move hands forward in a down and up movement, turning hands to palm forward position.

5. HIDE: Left hand in cupped-hand position, palm to floor, fingertips pointing to right front. Right hand in A-hand position, palm to left, knuckles pointing to left front. Touch right thumbnail to lips then move it forward and under left cupped hand, ending up with right hand "hidden" under left palm--or, in other words, left hand covering right hand, right thumb touching left palm.

6. OUGHT: Sign MUST, NECESSARY, and so on.

7. HAVEN'T: Sign LATE.

8. SO: Sign THAT (poetic license!).

9. OR: Left hand in L-hand position, palm facing body and index fingertip pointing to right front. Right hand in index-hand position, palm to floor. Touch right fingertip (index finger) to left thumb, then to left index fingertip.

10. HEART: Both hands in index-hand position, palms to self. Touch both left and right fingertips to left chest and trace a heart, left fingertip tracing the left side of the heart and the right fingertip tracing the right side of the heart.

11. PRAYER: Natural sign. Place hands palm to palm in a praying gesture.

12. CHURCH: Left hand in open-hand, fingers-closed position, fingertips to right front and palm to floor. Right hand in C-hand position, palm forward. Place thumb joint against back of left palm. Repeat once.

13. TEMPLE: Same as CHURCH, but T-hand position instead of C-hand position
    is used.

14. SOME: In poetic usage, one should use the sign for SOMETHING or in
    other words, the same sign as "A body" in "Comin' thru the Rye."

15. SOME: (As in, "Some people just can't see dirt.") Both hands in open-
    hand, fingers-closed position. Left hand palm to body, fingertips to
    right front. Place heel edge of right hand (little finger edge), palm
    to left and fingertips pointing to left front, against left palm and
    draw it downward until edge of right little finger is in center of
    left palm.

16. WAY: Similar to LET, except that the forward motion of the hands is more
    pronounced and extends farther from the body.

17. SHOW (demonstrate): Left hand in open-hand, fingers-closed position, palm
    forward and fingertips to ceiling. Right hand in index-hand position,
    palm to self. Place right fingertip in center of left palm, then move
    both hands forward a few inches.

18. SHOW (movie): Both hands in 5-hand position. Left hand palm to body,
    fingertips to right. Right hand palm facing left hand palm, fingertips
    to ceiling. Without touching hands, flicker the right hand back and
    forth across the left hand.

19. SHOW (play or drama): Both hands in A-hand position, palms forward and
    knuckles to ceiling. Raising both hands to shoulder level, move them
    alternately in and out in short, circular movements.

20. SWEAR (vow): Place right index-hand fingertip to mouth, then move right
    hand forward and to the right, opening it to open-hand, fingers-closed
    position, with palm facing outward and fingertips to ceiling--sort of
    like natural sign for HALT.

21. LET: Both hands in open-hand, fingers-closed position, palms facing each
    other and separated several inches. Push both hands forward several
    inches in a down and up motion (similar to WHEN (during) sign). You
    can also use L-hands for this sign.

22. HAPPEN: Both hands in index-hand position, palms to ceiling (or to each
    other), fingertips pointing forward. Rotate both hands to palm to the
    floor position, lowering them as you do so and bringing them closer to-
    gether. (You may encounter a situation wherein a deaf person, with a
    challenging expression on his face, will say "HAPPEN, HAPPEN." This
    is a deaf idiom which means "What if . . . ." In other words, what if
    something should go wrong, or just in case. . . .)

23. FEEL: Right hand in 5-hand position, with middle finger bent slightly
    toward palm. Place fingertip of middle finger against upper chest and
    draw upward a few inches.

24. FEEL HURT (emotionally): Sign FEEL, then flick hand outward (keeping hand in FEEL position, fingerwise) as if shaking a drop of water off your middle finger.

25. DEPRESSED, DISCOURAGED: Sign FEEL, but after hand has risen upward on chest, run it lightly back downward nearly to the waistline.

26. EXCITED: With both hands, sign FEEL, but bring both hands upward and off the chest completely. A variation of this is to have the hands alternate while doing this. This usually means EXCITING. Can also be used to mean THRILL.

27. TOUCH: Right hand in FEEL position, but instead of touching chest, middle finger touches back of left palm.

28. HATE: Both hands in 8-hand position, palms forward, fingertips to ceiling. Open hands to 5-hand position quickly, moving them forward abruptly.

29. EAGER, ZEALOUS: Both hands in open-hand, fingers-closed position, fingertips forward. Place palms together and rub them back and forth.

30. STUBBORN: Right hand in B-hand position, palm forward and fingertips to ceiling. Place thumb-edge of hand against forehead, and keeping it there, bend hand to right-angle hand-position. Or you can place your thumb against your temple while doing this.

31. BETWEEN: Left hand in open-hand, fingers-closed position with thumb extended, palm to right self, fingertips pointing to right front. Right hand in B-hand position, palm to left and fingertips to left front. Place little finger edge of right hand between thumb and index finger of left hand and rock hand (right hand) back and forth from left to right and back again.

32. BOTHER: Hands in same position as for BETWEEN, but instead of rocking right hand back and forth, hit left palm against membrane between thumb and index finger of left palm with little finger edge of right hand a couple of times.

33. INTERRUPT: Hands in same position as for above, but hit little finger edge of right hand ONCE against base of left thumb (on membrane of thumb of left hand).

34. SILLY: Right hand in Y-hand position, palm to self. Brush thumb several times against side of nose. Also means FOOLISH.

35. MISUNDERSTAND: Right hand in V-hand position, palm to self and fingertips to ceiling. Touch fingertips of V to forehead (balls of the fingertips), then turn hand to palm outward and touch fingernails of V to the same place on the forehead.

36. COMPLAIN: Right hand in <u>clawed-hand</u> position, palm to self. Touch
    fingertips to chest (thumb, too) a couple of times.

37. SEEK, LOOK FOR: Right hand in <u>C-hand</u> position, palm to left. Describe
    circle in front of eyes. (Denotes the looking for something through
    a telescope.)

38. SENSITIVE, SENSITIVITY: (a) Touch middle fingertip of right <u>touch-hand</u>
    to left chest (above heart) twice.

    (b) Touch middle fingertip of right <u>touch-hand</u> to back of left
    hand (actually, sign TOUCH twice).

(SM 110)

WORDS FOR WHICH SIGNS WILL BE TAUGHT IN LESSON 11

1. First, second, third, etc.

2. 10th, 11th, etc.

3. Last

4. Finally

5. Young

6. New

7. Next

8. Give (a) & (b)

9. Full

10. Enough

11. Empty

12. Bald

13. Mind going blank

14. Hot

15. Cool, pleasant

16. Sunny (personality)

17. Hold

18. Hurt

19. Enter (into)

20. Kind (kindly)

21. Kind (type)

22. Mean (unkind)

23. Mean (intend)

24. Laugh

25. Hard, difficult

26. Warm

PART III

INTERMEDIATE SECTION

The Idiomatic Language of Signs

LESSON 11

(SM 113-136)

LESSON PLAN OUTLINE

Fifteenth Class Session

Note: This session marks the end of the beginning course and the start of the intermediate course. The student should now increasingly be taught how to use signs and fingerspelling in the idiomatic language of signs. For this purpose, an excerpt from Babbini's "Concept Analysis of the Idiomatic Language of Signs" has been included among the DUP materials to be duplicated and distributed to the students. It should be used as a foundation upon which students can be trained to understand the language of signs as deaf people use it. It is recommended that the instructor examine the material in the excerpt and plan to add his own examples to those provided therein. A good method for doing this painlessly is to write a word on the blackboard (one for which the instructor knows several different ways of signing exist) and ask students to compose sentences illustrating as many different concepts as possible.[1]

MATERIALS NEEDED FOR LESSON 11

For instructional purposes:

1. Copy of the excerpts, plus additional examples the instructor should prepare and have on hand.
2. Lesson plan.

DUP materials (if necessary):

1. Excerpts from Concept Analysis booklet (11-DUP-M,b; nineteen pages).
2. Word-descriptions of signs in Lesson 11 (11-DUP-V, four pages).
3. Words for which signs will be taught in Lesson 12 (11-DUP-M,a; one page).

  I. Roll call.

 II. Announcements, if any.

III. Return test papers from Lesson 10 test and discuss grades, and so forth.

---

[1]Also helpful would be the booklet by Madsen (in bibliography), for he expands on many of the concepts described here and offers many examples in addition.

IV. Drills: Fingerspelling, on letter groups indicated by words missed on test given in Lesson 10 as well as signs missed. Include discrimination and vocalization drills, vary/verify drills.

V. Comprehension test: Sign each sentence once, then repeat same sentence in fingerspelling only.

1. Who was that man? He looked very <u>familiar</u>.
2. My grandfather came from <u>Ireland</u>.
3. On <u>the</u> 22nd of <u>May</u>, we are going to <u>Los Angeles</u>.
4. How <u>do</u> you like this wonderful <u>weather</u>?
5. Read it <u>carefully</u> and you won't get confused.
6. Oops, I <u>almost</u> forgot my <u>coat</u>.
7. It is <u>easy</u> once you know how.
8. I <u>graduated</u> from <u>high</u> school in 1941 (whatever the date was).
9. <u>Do</u> you remember the lesson from last Thursday?
10. Life is a funny thing, isn't it?
11. How are you liking this <u>course</u> now?
12. It isn't <u>too</u> <u>hard</u> now is it?
13. You will <u>soon</u> learn to understand sign language <u>easily</u>.
14. Don't you <u>just</u> love <u>these</u> <u>tests</u>?
15. I knew you would--that's why I give <u>them</u> all <u>the</u> <u>time</u>.

(Total words: 113. -0.8 for each error.)

VI. Student recitals of "You'll Never Know."

VII. Explain purpose of concept analysis insofar as the language of signs is concerned. Distribute excerpts DUP material (<u>only</u>) and allow students to examine the different interpretations of the word LIGHT, and explain that LIGHT will be taught in Lesson 12, at which time they will begin to learn many different ways of signing the words for which only one or two word-descriptions are included in their vocabulary word-descriptions --and that, from then on, they will have to <u>remember</u> the extra signs, the different ways of signing a given word, for it will not be possible to provide them with word-descriptions of all the variations.

VIII. Teach signs in Lesson 11 vocabulary.

Signs which will be taught in this lesson:

1. First, second, third, etc.
2. 10th, 11th, etc.
3. Last
4. Finally
5. Young
6. New
7. Next[1]
8. Give (a) & (b)
9. Full
10. Enough
11. Empty
12. Bald
13. Mind going blank
14. Hot
15. Cool, pleasant
16. Sunny (personality)

---

[1]There are several variations of NEXT. Teach all of those you know.

242

17.	Hold$_1$	22.	Mean (unkind)
18.	Hurt[1]	23.	Mean (intend)
19.	Enter (into)	24.	Laugh
20.	Kind (kindly)	25.	Hard, difficult
21.	Kind (type)	26.	Warm

(Total signs taught after this lesson: 400)

New signs taught:

Variations of the above signs: New signs (not in the lesson plan):

IX. Drill on Lesson 11 signs, explaining other ways of signing the words, depending upon the context of the sentence. (That is, full can mean a full glass, a full classroom--or a full stomach.)

X. Homework assignment:

A. Increase recital sentence requirements to at least five connected sentences, or, in other words, short paragraphs.

B. Remind students that Assignment II will be due in the next class (if it was assigned).

C. Using Concept Analysis booklet, go back through previous lessons and find words for which there are several different concepts, and write sentences illustrating these concepts.

XI. Pass out remaining DUP materials.

XII. Concluding remarks.

---

[1]When teaching the sign for HURT, a bit of pantomime that will help students associate the sign with something is: call one of the students up in front of the class and come up behind him. Show the class right-angle index hands, then poke the student in the ribs, hard! He'll usually jump and yelp--and the class will get the idea. If this is done, they'll rarely forget the sign.

(SM 132)

WORD-DESCRIPTIONS OF SIGNS IN LESSON 11 VOCABULARY

1. FIRST, SECOND, THIRD, and so on: Place hand in 1, 2, 3 hand-position,
    palm outward, then turn quickly to palm inward sharply.

2. TENTH, ELEVENTH, etc.: Sign the number, then follow with rapidly finger-
    spelled TH.

3. LAST: Both hands in I-hand position, little fingers pointing forward,
    and palms both facing halfway between self and each other. Left hand
    remains stationary. Right hand moves from slightly above left hand to
    slightly below, right little finger striking left little finger as it
    passes. (Almost like CAN'T, only the little fingers are used instead
    of index fingers as in CAN'T.)

4. FINALLY: Signed similar to LAST. However, the sign begins with the hands
    about a foot apart. Both little fingers describe a circular, downward
    arc, then upward, coming together in LAST. A variation of this is:
    the left hand remains stationary while the right hand describes the
    aforementioned arc then LAST.

5. YOUNG: Both hands in right-angle hand-position. Place fingertips against
    upper chest, palms to body and knuckles facing each other. Brush both
    hands upward a few inches. Repeat once or twice. Be careful not to
    "claw" hands, as this will denote MONKEY, instead of YOUNG.

6. NEW: Both hands in cupped-hand position, palms facing body. Left hand
    with fingertips to the right. Left hand remains stationary. Right
    hand, fingertips to ceiling. Move right hand upward, brushing back of
    right hand against palm of the left hand from little-finger edge of
    left hand toward index-finger edge.

7. NEXT: Both hands in cupped-hand or right-angle hand-position. Both palms
    toward body, left fingertips pointing to right and right fingertips
    pointing to left. Place back of right hand between left hand and body,
    then raise it over left hand and place it against the back of left
    hand, right palm against back of left hand. (There are several varia-
    tions of this.)

8. GIVE: (a) Both hands in and-hand position, palms and fingertips facing
    each other. Move both hands forward as if handing something to some-
    one, hands remaining in and-hand position. For GIVE ME or GAVE ME,
    reverse directions hands move, that is, start the sign with the hands
    away from the body and bring them back toward self.

    (b) With right hand in X-hand position, palm to left, knuckles to
    ceiling, move hand forward, turning knuckle to forward position. Palm
    remains facing left.

9. FULL: Left hand in S-hand position, palm to the right and knuckles facing forward. Right hand in open-hand, fingers-closed position, palm to floor and fingertips to left-front. Draw right palm across left fist (top edge) from right to left.

10. ENOUGH: Exactly as in FULL, except that palm of right hand is drawn across top of left fist from left to right twice.

11. EMPTY: Left hand in open-hand, fingers-closed position, palm to floor and fingertips to right front. Right hand in 5-hand position with middle finger bent slightly toward palm. Right hand palm to floor, fingertips pointing to left-front. Draw middle fingertip of right hand across back of left hand from wrist to knuckles.

12. BALD: Like EMPTY, except middle finger of right hand traces a path from center of forehead to center of back of head.

13. MIND GOING BLANK: Like BALD, above, except that middle finger traces a line across forehead above eyebrows from temple to temple.

14. HOT: Right hand in C-hand position, palm to body. Place fingertips against chin, then snap hand to palm outward (or to floor) position quickly, as if one had burned one's fingers.

15. COOL, PLEASANT: Both hands in open-hand, fingers-closed position, palms toward self and hands positioned on either side of face/jaw (about twelve inches apart). Bending hands at palm, move fingertips up and down in a "fanning" motion (as if fanning yourself with your finger-tips).

16. SUNNY (personality): Like COOL, above, except that fingers are rippled alternately instead of moving up and down as a unit.

17. HOLD: Both hands in C-hand position, palms to floor and knuckles facing forward. Close both hands to S-hand position, bringing them back a few inches toward body. (This sign depends upon what you are holding. Pantomime is important here. A rope? A child's hand, a boat, or what?)

18. HURT: Both hands in right-angle index hand-position, palms facing each other, knuckles facing front, hands separated by several inches. Bring index fingertips a few inches closer to each other in a sharp, abrupt motion.

19. ENTER, INTO: Left hand in open-hand, fingers-closed position, right hand in B-hand position. Both hands palm to floor. Left hand fingertips pointing to right-front, right hand fingertips forward. Left hand remains stationary. Place back of right hand fingers against palm of left hand index-finger edge then move right hand forward and under left palm, keeping back of right hand against left palm. (Not really as complicated as it sounds.)

20. <u>KIND</u> (kindly): Place right index finger (palm to left) against chin,
then follow with the following: both hands in <u>right-angle</u> hand position, palms facing each other, knuckles forward. Circle fingertips of
each hand around fingertips of other hand in a clockwise motion.

21. <u>KIND</u> (as in "What kind of ----?"): Fingerspell!

22. <u>MEAN</u> (unkind): Place right <u>cupped-hand</u> fingertips, palm to body, against
chin then close both hands to <u>A-hand</u> position, palms to each other and
thumbs on top. Brush knuckles or right hand downward against left hand
ONCE. (Second part of this sign is much like EACH or EVERY, but knuckles
are brushed downward just once instead of twice.)

23. <u>MEAN</u> (intend): Left hand palm upward, <u>open-hand, fingers-closed</u> position,
fingertips pointing to right front. Right hand in <u>M-hand</u> position with
fingers extended. Place fingertips of right hand against palm of left
hand, raise them, rotate hand slightly, then place fingertips against
palm of left hand again.

24. <u>LAUGH</u>: Like SMILE, only you repeat it once or twice swiftly. There are
many variations of this.

25. <u>HARD</u> (difficult): Both hands in <u>V-hand</u> position, but with fingers crooked.
Left hand palm downward, knuckles to right-front. Right hand palm to
ceiling, knuckles to left-front. Bring right hand down vigorously on
top of left hand, knuckles meeting back to back. Can also be signed
with both hands in <u>S-hand</u> position, but the "crooked 'V'" is more common.

26. <u>WARM</u>: Right hand in <u>C-hand</u> position, palm to self. Place backs of fingertips against underside of chin, then straighten hand in an upward and
outward motion, ending with <u>open-hand, fingers-closed</u> position a few
inches in front of the mouth.

(SM 135)

WORDS FOR WHICH SIGNS WILL BE TAUGHT IN LESSON 12[1]

1.	Light	11.	Close
2.	Dark	12.	Under
3.	Live	13.	Over
4.	Address	14.	Put
5.	Long	15.	Pull
6.	Short	16.	Run
7.	Maybe	17.	Walk
8.	Only	18.	Stand
9.	Use	19.	Sit
10.	Open	20.	Fall (down)

---

[1]Many of the words above are signed several different ways, depending upon the meaning of the word in context of the sentence. For this reason, it will be unnecessary to construct Cloze sentences for these particular words. You will find many such sentences in the examples given in the section on Concept Analysis you will in the Lesson 11 material.

(SM 115-131)

EXCERPTS FROM: CONCEPT ANALYSIS OF THE IDIOMATIC LANGUAGE OF SIGNS[1]

INTRODUCTION

A student who has completed one or two semesters of training in the language of signs and fingerspelling, and sets out to put his newly acquired skills to use in conversing with deaf people, often finds himself in the position of a foreigner with a limited command of English attempting to follow rapid, dialectical and idiomatic English as spoken by the native American. It is understandable that such a student often feels lost, and begins to doubt his own ability as well as the comprehensiveness of the material his instructor used to train him.

One factor often overlooked by the student in his confusion is that it is not usually his vocabulary of signs which is at fault, for, when one stops to consider, one will usually recognize that many or most of the signs used by deaf people are understood by the student by the time he has had at least two semesters of training. It is the way in which the signs are put together--the way they are used--which baffles the student and prevents his comprehension of what is being said.

Just as the English language has its idioms and local dialectical variations which baffle and confuse a foreigner trying to apply classroom-acquired knowledge of formal English to the rapid conversational exchange of words among ordinary Americans, the language of signs also has its idioms, figures of "speech," local dialects, subtleties of mood and implication, and its "rules." Until the student has mastered this idiomatic sign language, he cannot claim to have mastered the art of communicating with deaf people however adept he may become at the formal language of signs as a pictographical approximation of English. Nor will he be able to fully appreciate the amazing versatility of the language of signs, in which a wide range of emotions, meaning, and information can be conveyed by a few signed and fingerspelled words--which may or may not bear any resemblance to the English language in grammatical structure or syntax.

Complicating the student's attempts to communicate in the language of signs is the well-recognized fact that the majority of deaf people today have had little exposure to, and therefore scant understanding of, the idioms of the English language itself. When the student signs and fingerspells in the formal language of signs a common idiom such as "He is a deadbeat," the deaf person to whom this is said may either not understand at all--or misinterpret the statement to mean "he was beaten dead" or "he should be beaten to death"--or, if he is slightly more sophisticated, "he is dead beat (tired)." Only the highly verbal, well-educated

---

[1]Babbini, Barbara E. Unpublished workbook for intermediate advanced students. Institute for Research on Exceptional Children, University of Illinois, Urbana, Illinois, 1970.

deaf person would understand that the student was telling him that a certain man was a chronic nonpayer of his debts.

By the same token, a deaf person might say to the student in the course of a conversation "Think self." The unwary student might assume that this inexplicable combination of signs meant that he was being asked to think of himself, or asked what he thought, or that the deaf person was saying that he considered the student to be at fault for something, and so forth. Only the student who has become aware of the idiosyncracies of the idiomatic language of signs would (if he had not encountered that particular expression before) be able to figure out that he was being told to use his own judgment, to suit himself, to make up his own mind, or to draw his own conclusions about something.

Another facet of the language of signs is that one sign can be used for many different words depending upon the context of what is being said. If the concept in a word for which no sign exists is similar in meaning to one for which a sign exists, that sign is often used for the word without a sign. Examples of this are the words OUGHT TO, HAVE TO, SHOULD, NECESSARY, MUST--all of which have the common denominator of implied need, need to act, or need to conform to certain standards; and all of which are indicated by the single sign for NEED.

On the other hand, there are also words for which the signs change according to the concept being expressed. One does not use the same sign for TRAIN when one speaks of a railroad train, for example, that one would use when speaking of training one's dog.

Along with the conceptual factors there are shadings or differences in meaning lent by emphasis or lack of it, by nodding or shaking of the head, by the facial expression assumed by the speaker. For instance, the words "You will" can, depending upon the emphasis placed upon the signs, change from the question "You will?" to "YOU will?" or from a simple confirmation-seeking question to scathing sarcasm. Or, it can change from "You will (pass that exam, I'm sure)" to "You WILL (or I'll spank the pants offa you)"--all by varying the facial expression and the amount of emphasis placed upon the individual words separately or as a unit. Or, the positive statement "You understand" can be changed to the negative "You (don't) understand" by the speaker's shaking his head--or to a question by raising the eyebrows with a questioning look.

There are several words, also, which are used by themselves to transmit a complete sentence--the meaning of which changes subtly according to the facial expression and amount of emphasis used. To exemplify this, the word FOR can be used to indicate "What for?" or "Oh heck, what do I have to do that for?," or "Why in the name of Heaven did you do that?" If one notes that "idea," "why," "yes," and "no" can also be varied in this way when used as single sign responses, one begins to appreciate the importance of emphasis and facial expression to the meaning of what is being said.

Directionality--or the direction in which the sign is made--is also important to meaning. A single sign response such as "no," made with the fingertips pointing toward one, means that the speaker himself has been or will be

refused something; whereas if it is made with the fingertips pointing toward
the listener, it means the <u>listener</u> has been or will be refused something.
And, furthermore, when the fingertips point neither at the speaker nor the
listener, but in some generalized direction away from the speaker, it means
that somebody has or is going to say "no" to something.

Since most students in classes in the language of signs are those with normal hearing, of interest also are homonymns (words that sould alike, but are
spelled different) and homorphemes (words that look alike, but sound different).
For the student who aspires to become an interpreter for deaf people, these
words can be a trap into which he, in common with even veteran interpreters,
can oftimes fall. TO, TWO, and TOO all sound alike--but are signed quite differently, as are THERE, THEIR, and THEY'RE. Also commonly missigned are HER
(possessive pronoun, as in "her coat") and HER (object, as in "I told her"),
which both sound alike and are spelled alike, but which have different signs
which are often confused.

Finally, there is the growing emphasis on "new" signs, some of which have
rapidly been accepted and put into use by both the deaf people themselves and
by those who work or associate with them. Among those granted almost immediate acceptance and utilized are the first-letter signs in which the first letter of the word being signed is incorporated into the "old" sign. Examples of
this are TRY, RESPONSIBILITY, PLACE, LIVE, FAMILY, FREE, MEAN (in the sense of
meaning), USE, SITUATION--all of which have "old" signs to which the first letter of each of the words has been added.

Other "new" signs have been less successful in gaining acceptance, probably
because of limited possibilities of their being used in daily conversation among
deaf people not involved in educational programs. In some cases, a "new" sign
fails to gain acceptance because it bears little resemblance to an "old" sign
it may have been designed to replace or supplant, and cannot be used with as
much versatility as the "old" one could.

A few of the "new" signs which have partially succeeded in replacing "old"
signs are some of the conjugations of the verb TO BE. The "old" language of
signs had but one sign for all of the conjugations--AM, ARE, IS, BE, etc., were
all denoted by the same index-finger sign--whereas the "new" language of signs
provides different alphabet letters for each, and combines these with the "old"
movement and direction.

The student, therefore, may find himself encountering both "old" and "new"
signs as well as variations in idiom, dialect, facial expressions, emphasis--
and individual idiosyncracies in style of performing any given sign, as well
as in fingerspelling.

The examples which follow are designed to give the student in manual communication a start toward learning the patterns of grammatical structure in the
idiomatic language of signs. The examples given are by no means exhaustive, nor
are the suggested substitute ways of signing the example sentences the only ways
to express the concepts in the example sentences. In every case, attempts were
made to provide the most common method of translating the concept in the sentence,

but there will be regional variations as well as additional ways of transmitting the concept in idiomatic sign language but space limitations precluded the descriptions of these. The instructor in a class in manual communication or interpreting for deaf people can probably give examples of further ways to paraphrase or interpret the example sentences in this manual.

It is hoped, however, that the students and the instructor will use this material primarily to <u>build</u> upon; to increase their awareness of the complexities of the idiomatic language of signs; and to further the development of ability to identify and interpret other idiosyncracies not illustrated herein.

<u>Note</u>: A limited number of copies of the full booklet on Concept Analysis of the Idiomatic Language of Signs are available upon request from the author. However, the Madsen booklet previously mentioned is recommended.

(SM 119)

EXAMPLES OF TRANSLATIONS OF COMMONLY USED SENTENCES
INTO IDIOMATIC SIGN LANGUAGE

In the examples below, the multiple conceptual meanings of a given word are illustrated in sentences commonly used by people with normal hearing. Immediately beneath each sentence is given the "translation" into idiomatic sign language of the concept of the word as implicit in the context of the sample sentence. In other words, what the word <u>means</u> in the sentence context is translated into idiomatic sign language best understood by the majority of deaf people today. Students should take notes on other ways of translating the given sample sentences into idiomatic sign language which their instructor may be able to show them.

ABOUT

1. I was <u>just about</u> ready to give up.

    ALMOST

2. He <u>abruptly faced about</u> and marched off.

    pantomime turning abruptly, using two <u>index hands</u>

3. He lives <u>about</u> a mile from me.

    ABOUT

4. I lost my earring somewhere <u>about</u> here.

    AROUND or AREA

5. She is finally up and <u>about</u> again after that long illness.

    AROUND or ASSOCIATING

Others:

LIGHT

1. Will you <u>light</u> the fire for me, please?

    pantomime striking a match and putting it to something
    or START

2. <u>Turn out the lights</u>, please.

    pantomime lights going off

3. She was wearing a coat that was too <u>light</u> and almost froze.

    light-<u>weight</u> sign

4. She <u>made light of</u> the situation.

    FUN, or THINK EASY

5. She had on a <u>light</u> blue dress.

    use sign for LIGHT (as opposed to dark)

6. There isn't enough <u>light</u> in here.

    BRIGHT

7. I ate a <u>light</u> lunch.

    LIGHT (weight)

8. I slept very <u>lightly</u> last night.

    LIGHT (weight)

9. The medicine made me very <u>light-headed</u>.

    DIZZY

10. The birds <u>light on</u> trees.

    pantomime birds perching on twigs

11. Teacher seems to feel <u>light-hearted</u> tonight.

    HAPPY or LIGHT (weight) FEEL (touching heart)

12. <u>The light finally dawned upon me.</u> (idiom)

    rephrase to: "It finally think appear to me." (FINALLY is
    signed like LAST)

13. Homer really was <u>lit</u> at the party last night.

      DRUNK

14. The house was all <u>lit up</u> when we got home.

      pantomime, with both hands, many overhead lights going on.

   <u>Note</u>: There are many more ways to sign LIGHT, all having to do with direction in which the light shines, that is, in the face, headlights of a car shining forward, a flashlight wavering around, sunlight, spotlights, all or most of which are signed with the same basic "light going on" sign in which the hands begin the sign in <u>and-hand</u> position and open to <u>open-and</u> hand-position. The direction, position, and use of one or two hands will determine what kind of light is being described, as well as which of the many LIGHT signs you should use. In addition, there are the GLOW signs to further describe kinds of light; sunrise light, sunset light, firelight, twinkling lights of a city or town in the distance, and so on.

Others:

LIKE

1. I <u>like</u> pie, especially cherry pie.

      LIKE (opposite of dislike)

2. It <u>looks like</u> rain.

      SEEMS GOING TO

3. You <u>look like</u> your mother.

      FACE SAME

4. That is a <u>likely</u> story.

      Put an "Oh sure" expression on your face then say
      "That is a true ? story."

5. If you <u>like</u> ----.

    LIKE WANT or simply IF WANT WANT

6. He is <u>like</u> his father in that.

    SAME (using <u>Y-hand</u> sign for SAME)

Others:

APPEAR

1. She <u>appears</u> to be a nice person.

    SEEMS

2. He <u>appeared before</u> the judge to answer the charges.

    CONFRONTED (faced)

3. A hole <u>appeared in the face</u> of the dam.

    APPEARED (popped up) IN FRONT

4. <u>Apparently</u> he was mistaken about that.

    SEEMS

Others:

BEAT

1. She was <u>beating</u> the cake batter when I arrived.

    pantomime holding a bowl and beating batter with a spoon

2. <u>The cop walked his lonely beat.</u>

    rephrase to: THE COP, ALONE, BACK AND FORTH, STREETS EMPTY
    (exaggerate the <u>empty</u> sign)

3. My heart <u>beat</u> in time with the <u>beat</u> of the music.

    rephrase to: MY HEART (pantomime beat of heart by fist on
    chest) SAME MUSIC (pantomime index finger to ear, then "conduct"
    orchestra using index fingers as baton)

4. The Dodgers <u>beat</u> the Cardinals last night.

    DEFEATED

5. He <u>beat up</u> his wife last night.

    pantomime: With index finger upheld, beat it with the other
    fist, using back-and-forth sidewise motion

6. <u>He beat the drums vigorously.</u>

    pantomime beating drum with heavy, exaggerated gestures.

7. He is a <u>deadbeat</u>.

    rephrase to: HE ALWAYS AVOIDS (evades) PAYING.

8. He <u>beat his head against the wall</u>.

    pantomime: Touch your forehead, then smack your fist against
    the other palm repeatedly

9. They <u>beat back the charge of</u> the opposing team.

    DEFEND PUSH BACK

10. Boy, am I <u>beat</u>!

    a. slang sign for DEAD
    b. exaggerated sign for TIRED
    c. pantomime, with index fingers, the legs stretched out in
        front of you in exhaustion

11. The world will <u>beat a path</u> to your door if ----.

      pantomime, with wiggling <u>4-hands</u>, people lining up and
      swarming forward

Others:

CARE

1. He really <u>cares</u> for her.

        a. LOVES
        b. CHERISHES (FEEL, then fist-to-chin sign for SELFISH)
        c. fingerspell CARES

2. I <u>don't care</u> much for that kind of a person.

      rephrase to: That kind of a person I don't like very much
      or use exaggerated sign for COW (using <u>Y-hand</u>, and moving hand
      away from temple)

3. I <u>don't care</u> what you do about it.

      DON'T CARE

4. <u>Take care of</u> yourself.

      CAREFUL or KEEP, KEEP

5. We left our dog <u>in the care of</u> our neighbors.

      SUPERVISE or rephrase to: WE LEFT OUR DOG HOME, NEIGHBORS
      WILL KEEP KEEP

6. Don't let me burden you with my <u>cares</u>.

      TROUBLES or PROBLEMS.

Others:

MAKES GOOD

1. He <u>makes</u> good money.

        EARNS

2. He <u>made good</u> the loss.

        CONTRIBUTED (out of his own pocket) EVEN

3. Rock Hudson <u>made good</u> as an actor.

        SUCCEEDED

4. My mother <u>makes good</u> pies.

        COOKS DELICIOUS

5. We made good <u>time</u> on the road.

        SPEED

Others:

DRAW

1. He <u>drew</u> a sketch of the old man.

    DRAW

2. The horse <u>drew</u> the cart through the streets.

    PULLED

3. Flowers <u>draw</u> bees to themselves.

    ATTRACT

4. <u>Draw your own conclusions</u> about that.

    THINK SELF (idiomatic usage) or DECIDE YOURSELF (more formal)

5. She <u>drew</u> a pail of water from the well.

    pantomime pulling a bucket of water from a well

6. She <u>drew</u> $10 from the bank.

    TOOK OUT (reverse of DEPOSIT)

7. The game ended in a <u>draw</u>.

    TIE EVEN

Others:

PUT ON, TAKE OFF

1. <u>Put on</u> your coat (hat, sweater, pants, shoes, etc.).

    <u>Take off</u> your coat (hat, sweater, pants, shoes, etc.).

    pantomime to suit the thing being put on--or taken off

2. He isn't really hurt, he's just <u>putting on</u>.

    PRETENDING

3. He did a <u>take-off</u> of the President.

    COPIED (do this with impish, waggish expression)

4. The car <u>took off</u> like it was jet-propelled.

    using <u>3-hand</u>, pantomime car shooting off fast

5. He was <u>taken off</u> the list.

    DELETED

6. Leona was <u>taken off</u> to be spanked.

    pantomime grabbing a child by the collar and marching her off

7. I <u>took</u> my case <u>off</u> the agenda.

    use opposite of FILED--UNFILED

8. The airplane <u>took off</u> like a homesick angel.

    pantomime airplane taking off and climbing sharply

9. <u>Put</u> it <u>on</u> the table.

    sign as given

Others:

RUN

1. I wonder who will <u>run</u> for President in the next election.

 VOLUNTEER COMPETE

2. She has a <u>run</u> in her stocking.

 pantomime run spurting up the stocking-clad leg

3. He hit a <u>home-run</u> yesterday.

 fingerspell H-R, with the hand going from center-front at
 the H and out about eighteen inches to the right at the R

4. The train <u>runs</u> between Los Angeles and San Francisco.

 use "back and forth" sign

5. He was <u>run in for drunk driving</u>.

 rephrase to "POLICEMAN CAUGHT PUT JAIL FOR DRUNK DRIVING"

6. He was <u>run over</u> by the car.

 pantomime car (<u>3-hand</u>) bumping over an object in the street

7. Did you <u>run into</u> the wall?

 pantomime, with index-hand, someone banging into the wall and
 bouncing off of it. The wall is indicated with open-hand

8. She <u>ran</u> an ad in the paper, hoping to sell her car.

 FILED

9. Did he <u>run</u> down this street?

 RUN

10. Boy, have I ever had a <u>run of bad luck</u>!

 rephrase to: SINCE (lately) EVERYTHING HAPPENS HAPPENS
 HAPPENS BAD

11. Did you <u>run into</u> Mary at the store?

 HAPPEN BUMP INTO (meet)

12. He <u>runs</u> a turret lathe.

 WORKS ON, or pantomime (with index fingers) spinning of a lathe

13. He __runs__ a machine shop.

     MANAGES

14. Don't __run down__ your friends.

     ALWAYS CRITICIZE CRITICIZE CRITIZE, or ALWAYS PUT DOWN PUT DOWN
     PUT DOWN (using __thumbs-down__ sign)

15. We __ran out of__ gas on the freeway.

     USE UP (all gone)

16. The horse __ran out of__ the money.

     DIDN'T WIN ANY OF

17. My shoes are __run over at__ the heels.

     rephrase to: MY SHOE HEELS (pantomime feet slanting
     sideways and back because of run over heels)

18. The cashier __ran off with__ the money from the play.

     STOLE DISAPPEAR (opposite of popped up) AWAY

19. He left the motor __running__ in his car.

     a. pantomime, with index finger, the fan of the car circling
     b. pantomime, with a similar sign to both hands playing a
         clarinet, the valves of a car lifting and closing (slang
         version)
     c. make sign for MACHINE rapidly several times

20. Children love to watch trains __running__ by on their trips.

     pantomime train driveshaft in operation

21. The trains are not __running__ today.

     rephrase to: NO (none) TRAINS BACK AND FORTH TODAY

22. You left the water __running__ in the sink.

     use __4-hand__ to pantomime water flowing from faucet

23. I caught several fish in that __run__.

     use sign for crowds flocking to a place

24. __Run__ the clothes through the washing machine again.

     PUT

25. I got a royal runaround from him.

    rephrase to: HE EVADED, EVADED, EVADED, WON'T TELL STRAIGHT

26. The ship ran aground in the fog.

    pantomime, with 3-hand, a ship going up on ground, then add STUCK

27. He ran amok and killed fifteen people.

    BECAME CRAZY

28. The warden ran them off the property.

    CHASED

29. Pat ran up a big bill at that store.

    PILED UP

30. Don't run across the street without checking for cars.

    DON'T RUN ACROSS STREET WITHOUT FIRST LOOK, LOOK FOR CARS

31. I happened to run across this article the other day.

    HAPPEN FIND

32. She ran on and on about her troubles.

    TALKED, TALKED, MONOTONOUS

33. He was the runner-up in the 100-yard dash.

    fingerspell or rephrase to: HE CAME IN 2nd . . . or 3rd, and so on

34. Lew is sort of run-down in health at present.

    BREAKDOWN ("roof-collapsing" sign)

35. The ice cream melted and ran all over the table.

    SPREAD

36. The cold made my nose run.

    SNIVEL (4-hand to nose to show dripping from nose)

37. They gave us the run of the house while they were away.

    FREEDOM THEIR HOUSE

38. It was just the common, run of the mill sort of thing.

>   REPEAT REPEAT DAILY or SAME (Y-hands) ALL OVER

39. The heat made her make-up run.

>   SPREAD (smear) ALL OVER HER FACE

40. He runs arms for the rebels in Cuba.

>   SECRET SMUGGLES GUNS

41. We ran short of money on our trip.

>   ALMOST USE UP

42. Can you run off another ten copies for us?

>   pantomime cranking handle of mimeograph machine or use inverted
>   COPY and repeat a couple of times (for example, Xerox copies)

43. His wife ran off with another man.

>   DISAPPEAR (opposite of popped up) AWAY (use emphasis when making
>   the signs)

44. Let's run through Act 3 again.

>   TRY or TRY AGAIN or ALL OVER AGAIN

45. We're running "run" into the ground.

>   rephrase to: WE ARE PICKING ON "RUN" TOO MUCH

46. My daughters run through a couple pairs of shoes each a month.

>   WEAR OUT

47. They have a running battle going.

>   rephrase to: THEY SINCE CONTINUE ALWAYS FIGHT, FIGHT, FIGHT

Others:

LESSON 12

(SM 137-140)

LESSON PLAN OUTLINE

Sixteenth Class Session

<u>Note</u>: Assignment II is due at this time if assigned.

MATERIALS NEEDED FOR LESSON 12

<u>For instructional purposes</u>: Same as for Lesson 11.

<u>DUP materials</u> (if necessary):

1. Vocabulary word-descriptions for Lesson 12 (12-DUP-V, three pages).
2. List of words to be taught in Lesson 13 (12-DUP-M, one page).

  I. Roll call.

 II. Fingerspelling drill. Utilize letter groups which have not been drilled
      upon for some time. Discrimination drill, using words given in Prelim-
      inary Lesson 1 which have not been used previously. Vocalization drill--
      first with fingerspelling alone, then with <u>signs</u>.

III. Fingerspelling comprehension test. Spell each word three times <u>as fast
      as they can be spelled</u>.

1.	Gate	11.	Thread	21.	Bomb
2.	Home	12.	Mean	22.	Quick
3.	Rat	13.	Eaten	23.	Room
4.	The	14.	Goat	24.	Rate
5.	Thick	15.	Jane	25.	Vista
6.	Coat	16.	Sand	26.	Adz
7.	Same	17.	Disturb	27.	Rise
8.	Weak	18.	Food	28.	Stool
9.	Thyme	19.	Heist	29.	Herd
10.	Loam	20.	Woes	30.	Learn

(Total words: 30. -3.3 for each error.)

IV. Review and drill on test as well as on signs learned in previous lessons. Practice sentences which can be used:

1. I never know what to expect from you!
2. Well, I'll be a dirty dog!
3. My mother makes the best pies you ever ate!
4. People are funny.
5. Did you bring your girlfriend with you?
6. That girl is really beautiful, isn't she?
7. May I borrow your phone for a few minutes?
8. There were 12 people in the room when I got there.
9. Bald men are supposed to be good dancers.
10. It started out to be a cool morning, but later it got warm.
11. That darn dog hid my shoes under my bed.
12. Open the window, please, and close the door.
13. My mind went blank at the time. Later on, I remembered.
14. That man hit the boy in the face! How mean of him!
15. I didn't mean to laugh at you, but you looked so funny (odd).
16. Some of the people here gave a lot of money to the fund.
17. I finally found out how you are supposed to do that.
18. How about going to a movie with me tomorrow night?
19. For the last time, clean your room!
20. Hey, that hurt! Be a little more careful.
21. Young lovers find it hard to be separated.
22. I was just standing there, minding my own business.
23. Haven't (late) you heard about Hannah?
24. The car was too full to get anything more into it.
25. I swear I'll never go anywhere with him again.
26. Most of us went because we didn't want to hurt her feelings.
27. I give him to you. You can have him!
28. She is a very nice looking woman, gray-haired and pleasant (sunny).
29. My wife bought herself a new hat today. It set me back $27.95!
30. Be very careful what you say to him. He often misunderstands people.

V. Teach signs in Lesson 12 vocabulary. Illustrate variations of each as they come to mind. Have students help and use the Concepts Analysis booklet. Signs to be taught in this lesson:

1.	Light	8.	Only	15.	Pull
2.	Dark	9.	Use	16.	Run
3.	Live	10.	Open	17.	Walk
4.	Address	11.	Close	18.	Stand
5.	Long	12.	Under	19.	Sit
6.	Short	13.	Over	20.	Fall (down)
7.	Maybe	14.	Put		

(Total signs taught to date: 420)

New signs taught:

Variations of the above signs: New signs (not in the lesson plan):

Note: The number of signs taught in the vocabularies from now on will be smaller than was the case earlier in the course. This is because it is assumed that from this point on, the instructor will be teaching many signs in addition to those for which word-descriptions are provided in this manual. Students should be advised to keep a written record of the extra signs taught in class, and perhaps one will be kind enough to make a copy for the instructor at the end of each class in which extra signs are taught.

VI. Drill on signs in Lesson 12, including some idiomatic sign language usages.

VII. Homework assignment: Same as for Lesson 11 (collect Assignment II papers), but call students' attention to the instructions for writing sentences using the words for which signs will be taught in Lesson 13 (given on the DUP sheet).

VIII. Pass out DUP materials.

IX. Concluding remarks.

(SM 137)

WORD-DESCRIPTIONS OF SIGNS IN LESSON 12 VOCABULARY

1. LIGHT (as opposed to dark): Both hands in and-hand position, palms facing
    each other, fingertips facing each other and touching. Move hands up-
    ward and outward, separating them and opening them to 5-hand position,
    palms facing body.

2. DARK: Both hands in open-hand, fingers-closed position, palms to body.
    Hold hands out in front of yourself, at about face level, fingertips
    to ceiling. Cross hands in front of chest, fingertips of left hand
    facing right and right hand facing left, palms remaining toward body.

3. LIVE (I live in Podunkville): Can use either one or both hands. Hands
    can be in either L-hand or A-hand position. Palm to body, thumb toward
    ceiling. Place hand (or hands) on chest, then brush upward a few inches.

4. ADDRESS: Sign HOME, then LIVE, using A-hand position.

5. LONG: Left hand in open-hand, fingers-closed or B-hand position. Palm
    to floor. Draw right index finger along back of left hand and up the
    arm as far as you care to go. Distance you draw the finger denotes
    length--the shorter, the shorter, and so on.

6. SHORT: Both hands in H-hand position--or rather, sign NAME, then move the
    right H back and forth along the left H. (Note to teacher: Be sure
    students don't confuse this with CUT.)

7. MAYBE: Both hands in open-hand, fingers-closed position, palms to ceiling
    and fingertips forward. Move hands up and down in a "balancing" motion.
    (Also used to indicate MIGHT as in "I might do that.")

8. ONLY: Sign SOMEBODY.

9. USE: Right hand in U-hand position, fingertips to ceiling and palm forward.
    Move hand in a circular motion, keeping fingertips and palms facing the
    same way as described. Also used to mean WEAR, as in "I will wear my
    red dress."

10. OPEN: Both hands in B-hand position, palms forward and fingertips to
    ceiling. Place index-edges of both hands together, then separate them,
    rotating hands, palms facing each other position and separated by a few
    inches. Denotes double doors opening.

11. CLOSE: Reverse of OPEN. Have hands in palm facing each other position,
    then close them to palms forward, index-edge of hands touching each other.

12. UNDER: Left hand in open-hand, fingers-closed position, palm to floor and fingertips to right front. Right hand in A-hand position, palm to left and thumb on top. (Thumb extended, please.) Move right hand under left palm but not touching it.

13. OVER: Both hands in open-hand, fingers-closed position, palms to floor, fingertips facing (left to right-front and right to left-front) forwardish. Move right palm above left hand, moving from right to left. Do not touch left hand with right.

14. PUT: Both hands in and-hand position, palms and fingertips forward. Move both hands forward a few inches--or if you are asking someone to put something on a table, say, push the hands toward the table.

15. PULL: Natural sign. Pretend to grab a rope and pull.

16. RUN: Both hands in L-hand position, palms to floor and index fingers pointing forward, touch thumbs together, then crook index fingers a couple of times. In this case, the index fingers denote the legs. (This is used ONLY for the action verb as in "running to catch a bus." There are forty-seven different ways to sign RUN.)

17. WALK: Both hands in B-hand position, palms to floor and fingertips forward. Since the hands in this sign denote the feet, walk them forward, moving fingertips from forward position to fingertips-to-floor and back alternately.

18. STAND: Left hand in open-hand, fingers-closed position, palm to ceiling and fingertips forward. Stand the fingertips of right V-hand on palm of left hand.

19. SIT: Both hands in H-hand position, with fingers crooked. Both palms to floor, fingertips of H's facing floor also. Sit the right H on left H.

20. FALL (down): Sign STAND, then rotate right hand quickly to palm upward position, bumping back of right hand against left palm. (Many variations of this, though.)

(SM 139)

WORDS FOR WHICH SIGNS WILL BE TAUGHT IN LESSON 13

1. Start

2. Keys

3. Stop

4. Take

5. Wash

6. Sick

7. Well

8. Weak

9. Weak in the head (feebleminded)

10. Strong

11. Powerful

12. Anyway or it doesn't matter

13. Wish, hunger

14. Desire, yearn

15. Thirsty

16. Vegetables

17. Potatoes

18. Onions

19. Tomatoes

20. Pumpkin

21. Water

22. Watermelon

LESSON 13

(SM 141-144)

LESSON PLAN OUTLINE

Seventeenth Class Session

MATERIALS NEEDED FOR LESSON 13

For instructional purposes: Lesson plan.

DUP materials (if necessary):

1. Lesson 13 vocabulary word-descriptions (13-DUP-V; two pages).
2. List of words to be taught in Lesson 14 (13-DUP-M; one page).

   I. Roll call.

  II. Fingerspelling drill. Use letter groups in words missed on Lesson 12 fingerspelling test.

 III. Return test papers, then, selecting words from the test at random, finger-spell each at high speed in a fast drill. Discuss grades and class average.

  IV. Review of previous lessons. Select students to conduct drill on single lessons, using last few lessons (8 through 12).

   V. Comprehension test. Sign each sentence once, then fingerspell it once.

       1. Have you anything to say for yourself?
       2. That is not what I meant!
       3. They finished both chores this afternoon.
       4. Most of us remember our childhood with pleasure.
       5. Stop complaining. There isn't much you can do about it now.
       6. The teacher seemed to be depressed yesterday.
       7. What do you do for a living?
       8. Do you have any experience at this kind of work?
       9. You'll never know what might (maybe) happen in the future.
      10. The other day, I went with my uncle to see my father.
      11. Tomorrow, my parents come to visit us for 3 weeks.
      12. Where were you last Tuesday? I was looking for you.
      13. Did you find the book you lost?
      14. The gentleman is a jerk.
      15. I was so embarrassed--I forgot his name!

(Total words: 123. -0.8 for each error.)

VI. Collect papers, then show students how to sign each test sentence in
idiomatic sign language. Then call upon individual students to recite
the sentences, using idiomatic sign language.

Note: This will be standard procedure for all tests from this point
on. The instructor should sign the sentences as a deaf person of
average language achievement would sign them, and then fingerspell the
exact words of the sentence. The students, therefore, get the gist of
the sentence when it is signed--and the exact wording from the fingerspelled repetition (or, at least they should).

VII. Teach Lesson 13 vocabulary.

Signs to be taught in this lesson:

1. Start	9. Weak in the head	15. Thirsty
2. Keys	(feebleminded)	16. Vegetables
3. Stop	10. Strong	17. Potatoes
4. Take	11. Powerful	18. Onions
5. Wash	12. Anyway or "it doesn't	19. Tomatoes
6. Sick	matter"	20. Pumpkin
7. Well	13. Wish, hunger	21. Water
8. Weak	14. Desire, yearn	22. Watermelon

(Total signs taught to date: 442)

New signs taught:

Variations of the above signs: New signs (not in the lesson plan):

VIII. Drill on Lesson 13 vocabulary of signs. Practice sentences: (Teach
signs for all words students do not yet know.)

1. Don't start anything you can't finish.
2. She lost her keys somewhere around here.
3. We had to stop what we were doing and look for them.
4. Be sure and wash your face and your ears!
5. I got mud all over my jacket and had to wash it.
6. When are you going to wash the car? It's filthy!
7. She has been sick a long time, and is only now up and about again.
8. You make me sick with your constant complaining.

9. That was the most idiotic thing I've ever heard of!
10. It doesn't matter what you do now.
11. She had some strong objections to what he was planning to do.
12. He sure mixes a powerful cocktail (drink).
13. I am famished. Let's stop for something to eat.
14. I wish you would learn to quit when you're ahead.
15. She has long yearned for a trip to Europe.
16. When we finished our walk, we were very thirsty.
17. Do you like vegetables?
18. Potatoes are fattening if you eat enough of them.
19. Peeling onions often makes people cry.
20. We have some tomato plants in our back yard.
21. Do you like pumpkin pie?
22. Water, water everywhere, and not a drop to drink.
23. The watermelon wasn't ripe.

Note: Use, also, some of the sentences students brought to class. The emphasis here should be on training the students to use appropriate facial expression, emphasis, and so on, and to use sign language the way deaf people use it. It might be well for the instructor to study the above list of sentences, and decide in advance of class time just how a deaf person of average language ability would sign it (and, perhaps, make notes of his interpretations so that he can refer to his notes during the class).

IX. Homework assignment: Same as for Lesson 12. Remind students to compose sentences for each of the words for which signs will be taught in Lesson 14 (not Cloze-type sentences, but recital-type sentences) IN ADDITION TO the usual recital sentences.

X. Pass out DUP materials.

XI. Concluding remarks.

(SM 141)

WORD-DESCRIPTIONS OF SIGNS IN LESSON 13 VOCABULARY

1. START: Left hand in <u>open-hand, fingers-closed</u> position, palm to right and
    fingertips half-way between forward and toward ceiling. Right hand in
    <u>index-hand</u> position, palm to floor. Place tip of right index finger
    between first and second fingers on left hand, then turn right hand to
    palm to self position, finger remaining between fingers of left hand.
    Denotes the turning of an ignition key.

2. KEYS: Signed like START, but uses <u>X-hand</u> position and does not go between
    fingers of left hand.

3. STOP: Both hands in <u>open-hand, fingers-closed</u> position. Left hand palm
    to ceiling, fingertips to right front. Right hand, palm to left, fin-
    gertips forward. Bring right hand sharply down until the little finger
    edge of right hand hits the center of left palm.

4. TAKE: Put out hand, palm to floor, grasp an imaginary something, and
    bring it close to body.

5. WASH: Natural signs. If you are washing your face--make a face washing
    gesture. If washing hands, ditto. If washing clothes, pretend you're
    using an old washboard. If washing a car, pretend you're washing the
    roof of the car, and so on.

6. SICK: Right hand in <u>5-hand</u> position. Bend middle finger down toward palm.
    Touch middle fingertip to forehead and look ill.

7. WELL: (Opposite of sick, not the deep ones.) Both hands in <u>open-hand,</u>
    <u>fingers-closed</u> position. Place hands against chest, then bring them
    forward, closing hands to fists--sort of like a little boy does when
    he wants you to feel his muscles. Only use both hands simultaneously.

8. WEAK: Left hand in <u>open-hand, fingers-closed</u> position, palm to ceiling
    and fingertips forward. Right hand in <u>right-angle</u> hand-position, palm
    to floor. Place fingertips of right hand against center of left palm
    then bend and straighten fingers a couple of times.

9. WEAK IN THE HEAD (FEEBLEMINDED): Place fingertips of right <u>right-angle</u>
    hand against forehead and bend and straighten them like in WEAK.

10. STRONG: Natural sign. Both hands in "feel my muscles" position.

11. POWERFUL: Left hand and arm in "feel my muscles" position, fist clenched,
    with right hand in <u>open-hand, fingers-closed</u> position, draw a big
    muscle of left arm.

12. ANYWAY OR "IT DOESN'T MATTER": Left hand in right-angle hand-position, palm and fingertips to ceiling. Right hand in open-hand, fingers-closed position. Brush little finger hand back and forth across fingertips of left hand, letting the fingertips of left hand flap back and forth as you do this.

13. WISH, HUNGER: Right hand in C-hand position, palm to self, thumb on top. Place fingertips and thumb against upper chest and draw hand downward several inches.

14. DESIRE, YEARN: Sign WISH, using both hands (C-hands) one after the other.

15. THIRSTY: Right hand in index-hand position, palm to self and fingertip to ceiling. Place fingertip of right hand against upper part of throat and draw it downward a few inches.

16. VEGETABLES: Spell VEG.

17. POTATOES: Left hand in A-hand position, palm to floor. Right hand in a crooked V-hand position. Place fingertips of right crooked V on back of left palm. (Denotes sticking a fork into a potato.)

18. ONIONS: Right hand in X-hand position. Place knuckle of the X finger against temple and move it (knuckle remaining in place) back and forth from palm down to palm forward position a few times. (Denotes the knuckle rubbing the eye often associated with peeling onions.)

19. TOMATOES: Sign RED, then hold left hand in S-hand position, palm to floor. Bring right hand down and "slice" right index finger against thumb-index side of left fist. (Denotes slicing a tomato.)

20. PUMPKIN: Left hand in S-hand position, palm to floor. Right hand in 8-hand position. Flick middle finger against back of left hand a couple of times (the way one thumps a melon to see if it is ripe).

21. WATER: Right hand in W-hand position, palm to left and fingertips to ceiling. Place index finger against chin.

22. WATERMELON: Sign WATER, then PUMPKIN.

(SM 143)

WORDS FOR WHICH SIGNS WILL BE TAUGHT IN LESSON 14

1.	Apple	19.	Bath
2.	Peach	20.	Bathroom
3.	Cake, cookies, biscuits	21.	Fire
4.	Bread	22.	Table
5.	Butter	23.	Chair
6.	Milk	24.	Plate, place
7.	Tea	25.	Fork
8.	Buttermilk	26.	Cup
9.	Vinegar	27.	Glass
10.	Wine	28.	Napkin
11.	Whiskey	29.	Sweet
12.	Drunk	30.	Sour
13.	Cook	31.	Bitter (disappoint)
14.	Kitchen	32.	Sugar
15.	Room	33.	Pie
16.	Dining room	34.	Meat
17.	Living room	35.	Spoon
18.	Bedroom	36.	Knife

LESSON 14

(SM 145-149)

LESSON PLAN OUTLINE

Nineteenth Class Session

MATERIALS NEEDED FOR LESSON 14

<u>For instructional purposes</u>: Same as for Lesson 13.

<u>DUP materials</u> (if necessary:

1. Vocabulary word-description of signs in Lesson 14 (14-DUP-V; four pages).
2. List of words to be taught in Lesson 15/16 (14-DUP-M,a; one page).
3. Words to the poem, "Eye Opener" (14-DUP-M,b; one page).

  I. Roll call.

 II. Pass out test papers and discuss. Use test sentences again as a review drill.

III. Review drill of last several lessons. Use student-composed sentences too.

 IV. Comprehension test. Sign each sentence once, then fingerspell once.

    1. I couldn't find my keys, so I couldn't start the car and warm it up.
    2. She is always complaining, and I wish she would stop.
    3. It started to rain, but we went anyway.
    4. She was just getting well, then she got sick again.
    5. He is a rather weak man, very easily influenced by a strong person.
    6. He came over and helped me wash the windows in the house.
    7. Ken's car has a very powerful engine.
    8. Jim isn't really feebleminded--just stupid.
    9. Water is good when you are thirsty.
   10. Do you like green tomato pickles?
   11. At the picnic, we finished off three big watermelons.
   12. Fried onions are one of my favorite vegetables.
   13. I wish he would shut up--he's always talking.
   14. People like him make me yearn for a dog muzzle.
   15. The recipe calls for onions, tomatoes, and green peppers.

(Total words: 139. -0.7 for each error.)

V.   Collect papers, and use test sentences as a drill.

VI. Teach signs for Lesson 14. Utilize student-composed sentences, and
     combine teaching the new signs with student recitals--have students
     come to front of class and sign out their sentences (the ones including
     the words which are to be taught), ask others what they think was said,
     and then provide the sign and have the reciter repeat the sentence and
     include the new sign.

     Words to be taught in this lesson:

     1. Apple   13. Cook   25. Fork
     2. Peach   14. Kitchen   26. Cup
     3. Cake, cookies,   15. Room   27. Glass
         biscuits   16. Dining room   28. Napkin
     4. Bread   17. Living room   29. Sweet
     5. Butter   18. Bedroom   30. Sour
     6. Milk   19. Bath   31. Bitter (disappoint)
     7. Tea   20. Bathroom   32. Sugar
     8. Buttermilk   21. Fire   33. Pie
     9. Vinegar   22. Table   34. Meat
     10. Wine   23. Chair   35. Spoon
     11. Whiskey   24. Plate, place   36. Knife
     12. Drunk

     (Total signs taught to date: 478)

                              New signs taught:

     Variations of the above signs: New signs (not in the lesson plan):

VII. Homework assignment: Try and memorize words to "Eye Opener" poem, which
      will be taught in the next two lessons. Although the signs will be
      taught in the form of a poem, students are to construct sentences as
      usual for use in later drills.

VIII. Pass out DUP materials.

IX.   Concluding remarks. It might be well to remind students that Assignment
      III will come due in the session after the next one.

(SM 145)

WORD-DESCRIPTIONS OF SIGNS IN LESSON 14 VOCABULARY

1. APPLE: Right hand in X-hand position, palm to floor. Place knuckle of
the X against the CHEEK, then twist wrist so that hand rotates back
and forth from palm to the floor to palm to the self. Repeat once.

2. PEACH: Right hand in open-and position, palm to self. Place fingertips
against cheek (thumb, too), then draw it down and out, closing hand to
and-hand position. Almost like EXPERIENCE. (Denotes fuzz on the peach.)

3. CAKE, COOKIES, BISCUITS: Left hand in open-hand, fingers-closed position,
palm to ceiling, fingertips to right front. Right hand in C-hand position, with fingers spread. Place fingertips of right hand against left
palm, raise them, turn hand slightly then place them against left palm
again.

4. BREAD: Left hand in cupped-hand position, palm to self and fingertips to
right. Place left hand close to chest. Right hand in right-angle position, palm to self. Draw fingertips or little finger edge of right
fingers down the back of the left hand. (Denotes the slicing of bread
in the way European women do it, holding the bread against the chest
and drawing a knife downward to slice it.)

5. BUTTER: Left hand in open-hand, fingers-closed position, palm to ceiling
and fingertips to right front. Right hand in H-hand position, palm to
floor and fingertips to left front. Place fingertips of H against palm
of left hand and draw backward as if spreading butter with a knife.

6. MILK: Natural sign. Pantomime milking a cow.

7. TEA: Left hand in A-hand position, right hand in F-hand position. Left
palm faces self, right palm faces floor. Place fingertips of F inside
circle made by left thumb and index finger and, keeping them there,
wiggle hand back and forth. (Denotes the tea-bag being dipped in a cup.)

8. BUTTERMILK: Sign BUTTER, then MILK.

9. VINEGAR: Right hand in V-hand position, palm to left and fingertips to
ceiling. Place side of index finger against chin. Repeat once.

10. WINE: Right hand in W-hand position, palm to side of cheek. Without
touching cheek, but keeping hand close to cheek, fingertips to ceiling,
describe small circles.

11. WHISKEY: Both hands in index-hand position BUT with little fingers ex-
tended too. Palms facing each other, fingertips to right and left fronts.
Place little finger of right hand on top of index finger of left hand.
Repeat once. (Denotes measuring fingers of whiskey.)

12. DRUNK: Right hand in 4-hand position, palm to floor and fingertips to
     left. Moving from right to left, wiggle fingers across the forehead,
     without actually touching forehead.

13. COOK: Both hands in open-hand, fingers-closed position, fingertips to
     right and left fronts. Left hand palm to ceiling, right hand palm to
     floor. Place right hand on left hand, then turn right hand and place
     back of right hand against left palm.

14. KITCHEN: Sign COOK, then with both hands in open-hand, fingers-closed
     position, fingertips forward, palms facing each other but about eight
     to ten inches apart, move hands so that left hand is near body, palm
     to body, and right hand is eight to ten inches in front of left hand,
     palm to body. This sign, the last part of it after COOK, means ROOM.

15. ROOM: Both hands in open-hand, fingers-closed (or R-hand) position, palms
     facing each other (separated by about eight to ten inches). Bring left
     hand (unchanged as to hand-position) close to waist, palm to self, while
     simultaneously moving right hand (changes to right-angle hand) forward
     to a position about eight to ten inches directly in front of left hand,
     with right palm facing left. (Forms a square with the hands.)

16. DINING ROOM: Sign EAT, then ROOM.

17. LIVING ROOM: Sign LIVE, then ROOM.

18. BEDROOM: Place right hand, in open-hand, fingers-closed position, fingers
     to ceiling, against cheek, then sign ROOM.

19. BATH: A-hands either side of upper chest. Rub up and down.

20. BATHROOM: Sign BATH, then ROOM.

21. FIRE: Both hands in open-and-hand position, palms and fingertips to ceil-
     ing. Moving hands alternately, wiggle fingers, and raise and lower each
     hand a few inches while wiggling. (Denotes flames rising and falling.)

22. TABLE: Both hands in open-hand, fingers-closed position. Both palms to
     floor. Right hand fingertips face left and left hand fingertips face
     right. Place right hand palm on top of back of left hand and pat it a
     couple of times.

23. CHAIR: Same as SIT.

24. PLATE, PLACE: Both hands in P-hand position, palms to floor, fingertips
     forward. Touch middle fingers of P's together, describe horizontal
     circle, bringing hands back toward body, then touch fingertips together
     again. Same fingertips, I mean.

25. FORK: Left hand in open-hand, fingers-closed position, palm to ceiling,
     right hand in V-hand position. Touch V fingertips to palm, lift them,
     turn hand, then touch palm again. (This sign is made like MEAN, except
     that V fingers are used instead of M fingers.)

26. CUP: Left hand in open-hand, fingers-closed position, palm to ceiling
      and fingertips to right front. Right hand in C-hand position, palm to
      left. Place little finger edge of right hand in center of left palm.

27. GLASS: Sign CUP, then raise right hand an inch or two above left palm.

28. NAPKIN: Right hand in B-hand position, palm to self and fingertips to
      ceiling. Move hand back and forth from right to left and back in front
      of lips in a wiping gesture. Do not touch lips, but keep fingers close
      to lips. (Can also be made with hand in A-hand position.)

29. SWEET: Right hand in B-hand position, palm to self and fingertips to ceil-
      ing. Place fingertips on upper part of chin, then draw them downward,
      ending with right hand in right-angle hand-position. Repeat once.

30. SOUR: Right hand in index-hand position, palm to left. Placing fingertips
      of index finger against chin, rotate hand until palm is to self. (De-
      notes the screwing up of the mouth against sourness.)

31. BITTER: (Also means DISAPPOINT and MISS, as in "I missed you when you were
      away.") Right hand in index-hand position, palm to self. Bounce index
      finger off chin once.

32. SUGAR: Signed like SWEET, but instead of using B-hand position for the
      hand, you use the U-hand position.

33. PIE: Both hands in open-hand, fingers-closed position, left palm to ceil-
      ing, and right hand with palm to left. With little finger edge of right
      hand, cut a "wedge" from left palm.

34. MEAT: Left hand in open-hand, fingers-closed position, but with thumb ex-
      tended (exposing membrane between thumb and palm), and palm to self;
      right hand in F-hand position (but with index finger and thumb separated
      by about an inch), palm to floor. With thumb and index finger of right
      hand, take a good grip on the membrane between thumb and palm of left
      hand, and shake both hands slightly as a unit. (Note: Do not wiggle
      them separately. The hands move simultaneously, and remain together.)

35. SPOON: Left hand in open-hand, fingers-closed position, palm to ceiling
      and fingertips toward right; right hand in H-hand position, palm to
      ceiling and fingertips pointing to left center. With the fingertips of
      right hand, "scoop" imaginary food out of center of left palm (as if you
      were spooning up ice cream).

36. KNIFE: Both hands in index-hand position, palms facing half-way between
      self and each other, and fingertips pointing toward floor (almost). With
      right index finger, "whittle" the left index finger as if you were sharp-
      ening a pencil with a knife. (Almost like the widely used "shame on you"
      gesture--except that fingertips point to floor, and palms of hands face
      each other almost. The inner edge of the right index finger scrapes the
      thumb-side edge of the left index finger.)

(SM 148)

WORDS FOR WHICH SIGNS WILL BE TAUGHT IN LESSONS 15 AND 16

1. Curlers

2. Forehead

3. Cheeks

4. A'gleam (shiny)

5. Lotion

6. Potions, medicine

7. Ocean

8. Cleansing

9. Pore

10. Closing

11. Cream (face)

12. (Un)powder

13. (Un)rouge

14. Lips

15. Eyed (gazed)

16. (Un)tied

17. Bit

18. Wide

19. (Un)girdled

20. Hips

21. Clothes

22. Dresses

23. Old fashioned

24. Slippers

25. Kippers (fish)

26. Frocks

27. Zippers

28. Just (recently)

29. Up (get up)

30. Sniveling

31. Cold (in the head)

32. Hope

33. Nerves

34. Steady, quiet

35. Rock

36. View

37. True (sure)

38. True (honest)

39. Hell

40. Damn

41. Shock

42. Continue, stay

(SM 150)

EYE OPENER

By Richard Armour

Young Man, have you seen her in curlers
With forehead and cheeks all a-gleam
With lotions, and potions, and who knows what oceans
Of cleansing and pore-closing creams?

Young Man, have you seen her unpowdered
Unrouged on the cheeks and the lips
Have you eyed her untied
And a good bit more wide
Ungirdled, I mean, at the hips?

Young Man, have you seen her in work clothes
In dresses outmoded and old
In slippers like kippers
And frocks without zippers
Just up from a sniveling cold?

You haven't? Then young man, here's hoping
Your nerves are as steady as rock
When you do get a view
Of your true love that's true
You're in for a hell of a shock!

LESSONS 15 AND 16

(SM 150-156)

LESSON PLAN OUTLINE

Twentieth Class Session

MATERIALS NEEDED FOR LESSON 15

For instructional purposes:

1. OH projector transparency with words to "Eye Opener" on it, projector and screen and/or extra copies of the poem.

2. Lesson plan.

DUP materials (if necessary):

1. Word-descriptions of signs in Lesson 15/16 (15/16-DUP-V; four pages).
2. List of words to be taught in Lesson 17 (15-DUP-M; one page).

  I. Roll call.

 II. Return test papers and discuss grades, errors, class average, and so forth.

III. Fingerspelling drill. Utilize discrimination word-pairs given in Preliminary Lesson 2. Be sure and include vocalization drill.

 IV. Student recitals (takes the place of review drill). Concentrate upon teaching students to use idiomatic sign language in delivering their recital sentences.

  V. Comprehension test. Sign (in idiomatic sign language) each sentence once, then fingerspell once.

    1. What happened to your coat? It is covered with dirt!
    2. I'm a meat and potatoes man myself.
    3. He likes his whiskey on the rocks, without water.
    4. Excuse me, I dropped my fork.
    5. My mother makes wonderful apple pies. Peach too.
    6. She is a very bitter person. Always depressed.
    7. Do you want sugar in your tea?
    8. Jerry really was drunk at the party.

284

9. I put her in the back bedroom.
10. Will you put the milk and butter on the table, please?
11. Cold buttermilk on a hot day is one of the most refreshing drinks.
12. She knew he was coming, so she made a cake.
13. San Francisco has the best French bread I've ever eaten.
14. She put too much vinegar in the salad. It was very sour.
15. Bring a chair and sit down.

(Total words: 131. -0.8 for each error.)

VI. Collect papers and use test as a drill/recital exercise.

VII. Teach Lesson 15/16 signs. This is an "Eye Opener," a Richard Armour poem, and very useful in teaching students to be humorous, witty, and expressive in their signing.

Signs to be taught in this lesson:

1. Curlers	15. Eyed (gazed)	29. Up (get up)
2. Forehead	16. (Un)tied	30. Sniveling
3. Cheeks	17. Bit	31. Cold (in the head)
4. A'gleam (shiny)	18. Wide	32. Hope
5. Lotion	19. (Un)girdled	33. Nerves
6. Medicine, potions	20. Hips	34. Steady, quiet
7. Ocean	21. Clothes	35. Rock
8. Cleansing	22. Dresses	36. View
9. Pore	23. Old fashioned	37. True (sure)
10. Closing	24. Slippers	38. True (honest)
11. Cream (face)	25. Kippers (fish)	39. Hell
12. (Un)powder	26. Frocks	40. Damn
13. (Un)rouge	27. Zippers	41. Shock
14. Lips	28. Just (recently)	42. Continue, stay

(Total signs taught after this lesson: 520)

New signs taught:

Variations of the above signs: New signs (not in the lesson plan):

VIII. Student recitals of "Eye Opener." Encourage students to "ham it up."

IX. Homework assignment: Practice "Eye Opener." Remind students that Assignment III is due at the next class session (if it was assigned).

X. Pass out DUP materials.

IX. Concluding remarks. No new vocabulary will be introduced in the next class session. It will be a "Breather" session devoted primarily to practice of "Eye Opener" and a review of all previous lessons and songs.

(SM 151)

WORD-DESCRIPTIONS OF SIGNS IN LESSONS 15 AND 16 VOCABULARY

1. CURLERS: Both hands in the R-hand position, palms to head and fingertips
    facing each other. Beginning at the hairline (forehead), rotate both
    hands from palms to head to palms forward position, moving hands toward
    the nape of the neck (over the top of the head) to denote the rollers
    women use in their hair.

2. FOREHEAD: Right hand in open-hand, fingers-closed position, palm to fore-
    head. Pass the fingertips of the hand across the forehead. (Fingertips
    point to left.)

3. CHEEKS: Pinch cheek with right hand (thumb and crooked index finger of
    hand do the pinching).

4. A'GLEAM (SHINY): Left hand in open-hand, fingers-closed position, palm
    to floor and fingertips to right front. Right hand in 5-hand position,
    with middle finger bent slightly toward palm. Touch fingertip of mid-
    dle finger of right hand to back of left palm then raise right hand,
    wiggling the fingers of right hand as you raise it several inches.

5. LOTIONS: Left hand in cupped-hand position, palm to ceiling and finger-
    tips to right front. With right hand in C-hand position, palm to
    left, pantomime pouring lotion out of a bottle into palm of left hand,
    then make a washing motion as if smoothing lotion on the hands.

6. MEDICINE, POTIONS: Left hand in open-hand, fingers-closed position, palm
    to ceiling, with fingertips to right front. Right hand in 5-hand po-
    sition with middle finger bent slightly toward palm (as in SHINY).
    Touch fingertip of middle finger of right hand to center of left palm
    and move it in tiny circles, keeping it against left palm.

7. OCEAN: Sign WATER (right hand in W-hand position, palm to left and fin-
    gertips to ceiling. Touch index finger of "W" to lips) then with both
    hands in open-hand, fingers-closed position, palms to floor and finger-
    tips forward, move both hands up and down, moving them also sideways
    to denote big ocean waves.

8. CLEANSING: Sign CLEAN twice, quickly.

9. PORE: Spell out.

10. CLOSING: Sign CLOSE with both hands in B-hand position, palms toward each
    other and fingertips to ceiling, turn hands to palm forward position,
    index sides of hands touching. (Denotes closing of double doors.)

34. STEADY, QUIET: Place index finger of right hand in a "shhh" gesture
against lips, then both hands in open-hand, fingers-closed position,
palms to floor and fingertips forward. Move both hands smoothly away
from each other, horizontally.

35. ROCK: Sign HARD, using S-hand position, not the crooked X-hand.

36. VIEW: Sign EYED.

37. TRUE: Right hand in index-hand position, palm to left. Place side of
index finger against chin, then move it upward until fingertip is
level with the nose. (Also means SURE.)

38. TRUE: Sign the above TRUE, then follow it with left hand in open-hand,
fingers-closed position, palm to ceiling and fingertips to right front.
Right hand in H-hand position (for HONEST), palm to left and fingertips
forward. Place side of middle finger in left palm near the heel of
the hand, then move it forward to the fingertips of left hand. (This
sign is also used for HONEST.)

39. HELL: Right hand in H-hand position, palm to ceiling, and fingertips forward. Move whole hand abruptly sideways, from center front to the right.

40. DAMN: Similar to HELL above except that D-hand is used, and palm faces
floor, not ceiling.

41. SHOCK: Both hands in A-hand position, palms to floor and knuckles forward.
Begin sign with hands parallel but not touching, then separate them
widely, doing so in an abrupt, vigorous motion, stopping the movement
abruptly when hands are about eighteen inches or two feet apart. Look
stunned!

42. CONTINUE, STAY: Both hands in A-hand position, thumbs extended, and palms
to floor. Place ball of right thumb on top of left thumbnail, and push
both hands downward and forward a few inches (STAY), or forward several
inches (CONTINUE).

(SM 155)

WORDS FOR WHICH SIGNS WILL BE TAUGHT IN LESSON 17

Construct sentences using the following words, and including in the sentences words for which you have already learned the signs.

1.	Busy	14.	Visit
2.	Idle	15.	Enjoy
3.	Lazy	16.	Rather
4.	Doubt	17.	Almost
5.	Cheap	18.	Easy
6.	Expensive	19.	Responsible, responsibility
7.	Dry	20.	Balance
8.	Wet	21.	Obey
9.	False	22.	Disobey
10.	Liar	23.	Dismay
11.	Smart (a), (b), and (c)	24.	Disgust
12.	Arrive	25.	Burden
13.	Leave (depart)		

"BREATHER" SESSION

(SM 157)

LESSON PLAN OUTLINE

Twenty-First Class Session

Note: Assignment III due (if it was assigned).

MATERIALS NEEDED FOR THIS SESSION

For instructional purposes:

1. OH transparency with words of "Eye Opener" on it.
2. Lesson plan.

DUP materials: None. (These were passed out in the last class session.)

I. Roll call.

II. Pass out test papers and discuss as usual. Drill on the sentences in the test.

III. Student recitals of "Eye Opener." Every student should have a chance to recite and perfect his ability to deliver the poem in as humorous a fashion as possible, so the instructor should work hard on building expressiveness into the students' renditions of the poem.

IV. Comprehension test: Sign each sentence once and fingerspell once.

1. Women shouldn't go shopping with their hair in curlers.
2. All the creams and lotions in the world couldn't make her pretty.
3. The bullet got him in the center of the forehead.
4. She was wearing too much rouge and looked like a clown.
5. Men like to eye women on windy street corners.
6. The zipper on my gold dress broke.
7. I need a new pair of slippers. My old ones are worn out.
8. Are you sure you tied the dog up?
9. I was shocked at the way she behaved.
10. He went out and bought himself $200 worth of new clothes.
11. We caught 47 fish on our fishing trip.
12. I was just going to phone you a minute ago.
13. He claimed his story was the absolute truth.

14. We stayed at the Holiday Inn when we were there.
15. Excuse me, I must go powder my nose.

(Total words: 142. -0.7 for each error.)

V. Collect test papers and drill as usual.

VI. Homework assignment: Study vocabulary word-descriptions, and, in addition to beginning hand-position, take note of what direction palm faces. Another performance test coming up in the next lesson. Collect Assignment III.

VII. Concluding remarks.

LESSON 17

(SM 158-161)

LESSON PLAN OUTLINE

Twenty-second Class Session

MATERIALS NEEDED FOR LESSON 17

For instructional purposes: Copies of performance test, Lesson 17 (17-DUP-TEST, five pages).

DUP materials (if necessary):

1. Word-descriptions of signs in Lesson 17 (17-DUP-V, two pages).
2. List of words to be taught in Lesson 18 (17-DUP-M, one page).

I.   Roll call.

II. Return Lesson 16 test papers, discuss, and drill on test sentences as before.

III. Review of signs taught. Should be fairly comprehensive, since test will follow.

IV. Administer Performance Test.[1] Allow thirty minutes to complete.

V.   Collect papers and review as usual.

VI. Teach signs in Lesson 17. Utilize student-composed sentences, and drill/recite as in Lesson 16. Signs to be taught in this lesson:

1. Busy	10. Liar	18. Easy
2. Idle	11. Smart	19. Responsible,
3. Lazy	(a), (b), and (c)	responsibility
4. Doubt	12. Arrive	20. Balance
5. Cheap	13. Leave (depart)	21. Obey
6. Expensive	14. Visit	22. Disobey
7. Dry	15. Enjoy	23. Dismay
8. Wet	16. Rather	24. Disgust
9. False	17. Almost	25. Burden

(Total signs taught to date: 545)

---

[1]See Appendix for master copy of correct or acceptable answers to Performance Test items.

New signs taught:

Variations of the above signs: New signs (not in the lesson plan):

VII.   Drill on signs in Lesson 17. Use fast vary/verify drill, as it is
        unlikely that much time will remain.

VIII.   Homework assignment: Write a short paragraph about any topic student
        desires, and practice same until it can be delivered flawlessly. This
        will be used to evaluate student's achievement--and students and instruc-
        tor will both evaluate each student on a special evaluation form (pro-
        vided in Appendix).

IX.   Pass out DUP materials.

X.   Concluding remarks. Inform students that, except for the "testing" im-
        plicit in the final evaluation process (in which they will use their
        homework paragraphs), the performance test in this class marks the end
        of formal tests in the course.

        Note: Instructor may wish to grade students on the basis of test
        scores; however, if he does this, it is a nice gesture to allow students
        to drop their two worst tests from the score they have amassed. (After
        all, students do have off-days, just as instructors do.) Otherwise,
        grading can be based on completion and quality of work on assignments,
        class participation, actual performance in classroom recitals, test
        scores, and so on. For more detail on grading students, see section on
        Testing and Evaluation, Chapter 2, C, 4. Whatever the instructor decides
        to use as the basis for assigning any grades given, he should explain to
        the students how he plans to grade.

PERFORMANCE TEST

MANUAL COMMUNICATIONS CLASS

Name _____

Date _____

Lefthanded? _____

Hand-Positions:

1. Right-angle hand (RA)
2. Right-angle-index hand (RAI)
3. And-hand (And)
4. Open-and hand (OAH)
5. Index-hand (Index)
6. Open hand-fingers closed (OH)
7. 5-hand (5)
8. Cupped-hand (Cup)
9. Clawed-hand (CLH)
10. A-hand, B-hand, etc. (A, B, etc.)

Palm-Directions (Palm faces):

1. Ceiling (Ceil)
2. Floor (Fl)
3. One's own body (Self)
4. Right (Rt.)
5. Left (Left)
6. Each other (Each)
7. Forward (Front)
8. Right of center front (Right front)
9. Left of center front (Left front)

Which of the above hand-positions and palm-directions do you use for the following words? Give hand-positions for each hand if both hands are used. Give, also, the direction the palm faces for each hand. Use abbreviations given in parentheses, NOT the numbers, please.

Important notice! DO NOT ATTEMPT TO GIVE FULL WORD-DESCRIPTIONS. LIMIT YOUR-SELVES TO BEGINNING HAND-POSITIONS AND DIRECTIONS PALMS FACE AT BEGINNING OF SIGN. STUDENTS NOT FOLLOWING DIRECTIONS WILL BE PENALIZED 10 POINTS ON THEIR GRADE.

1. Myself:	Left hand:	Right hand:
	Left palm:	Right palm:
2. How:	Left hand:	Right hand:
	Left palm:	Right palm:
3. Know:	Left hand:	Right hand:
	Left palm:	Right palm:

4.	Same:	Left hand:	Right hand:
		Left palm:	Right palm:
5.	About:	Left hand:	Right hand:
		Left palm:	Right palm:
6.	Will:	Left hand:	Right hand:
		Left palm:	Right palm:
7.	Morning:	Left hand:	Right hand:
		Left palm:	Right palm:
8.	Fine:	Left hand:	Right hand:
		Left palm:	Right palm:
9.	Again:	Left hand:	Right hand:
		Left palm:	Right palm:
10.	Introduce:	Left hand:	Right hand:
		Left palm:	Right palm:
11.	Both:	Left hand:	Right hand:
		Left palm:	Right palm:
12.	Get:	Left hand:	Right hand:
		Left palm:	Right palm:
13.	Must:	Left hand:	Right hand:
		Left palm:	Right palm:
14.	Most:	Left hand:	Right hand:
		Left palm:	Right palm:
15.	Slow:	Left hand:	Right hand:
		Left palm:	Right palm:

16.	Remember:	Left hand:	Right hand:
		Left palm:	Right palm:
17.	Father:	Left hand:	Right hand:
		Left palm:	Right palm:
18.	Grandfather:	Left hand:	Right hand:
		Left palm:	Right palm:
19.	Far:	Left hand:	Right hand:
		Left palm:	Right palm:
20.	Meet:	Left hand:	Right hand:
		Left palm:	Right palm:
21.	Quit:	Left hand:	Right hand:
		Left palm:	Right palm:
22.	Happy:	Left hand:	Right hand:
		Left palm:	Right palm:
23.	In:	Left hand:	Right hand:
		Left palm:	Right palm:
24.	Late:	Left hand:	Right hand:
		Left palm:	Right palm:
25.	Tomorrow:	Left hand:	Right hand:
		Left palm:	Right palm:
26.	Do:	Left hand:	Right hand:
		Left palm:	Right palm:
27.	Where:	Left hand:	Right hand:
		Left palm:	Right palm:

28. <u>Any</u>:   Left hand: Right hand:

Left palm: Right palm:

29. <u>Borrow</u>:   Left hand: Right hand:

Left palm: Right palm:

30. <u>Law</u>:   Left hand: Right hand:

Left palm: Right palm:

31. <u>Aunt</u>:   Left hand: Right hand:

Left palm: Right palm:

32. <u>Ugly</u>:   Left hand: Right hand:

Left palm: Right palm:

33. <u>People</u>:   Left hand: Right hand:

Left palm: Right palm:

34. <u>Make</u>:   Left hand: Right hand:

Left palm: Right palm:

35. <u>Clean</u>:   Left hand: Right hand:

Left palm: Right palm:

36. <u>Dirty</u>:   Left hand: Right hand:

Left palm: Right palm:

37. <u>Week</u>:   Left hand: Right hand:

Left palm: Right palm:

38. <u>Hurt</u>:   Left hand: Right hand:

Left palm: Right palm:

39. <u>After</u>:   Left hand: Right hand:

Left palm: Right palm:

40. Find: Left hand: Right hand:

                   Left palm: Right palm:

41. Funny: Left hand: Right hand:

                   Left palm: Right palm:

42. Hot: Left hand: Right hand:

                   Left palm: Right palm:

43. New: Left hand: Right hand:

                   Left palm: Right palm:

44. Summer: Left hand: Right hand:

                   Left palm: Right palm:

45. Enemy: Left hand: Right hand:

                   Left palm: Right palm:

46. Family: Left hand: Right hand:

                   Left palm: Right palm:

47. See: Left hand: Right hand:

                   Left palm: Right palm:

48. Never: Left hand: Right hand:

                   Left palm: Right palm:

49. Stubborn: Left hand: Right hand:

                   Left palm: Right palm:

50. Finally: Left hand: Right hand:

                   Left palm: Right palm:

(SM 158)

WORD-DESCRIPTIONS FOR SIGNS IN LESSON 17 VOCABULARY

1. BUSY: Sign WORK several times, using brief, short movements and moving
    hands back and forth from left to right.

2. IDLE: Hook thumbs of 5-hands into imaginary suspenders and wiggle
    fingers.

3. LAZY: Right hand in L-hand position, palm to self and index-finger to
    ceiling. Pound your palm a couple of times against your left upper
    chest.

4. DOUBT: Both hands in A-hand position, palms to floor. Move each hand
    up and down alternately.

5. CHEAP: Both hands in open-hand, fingers-closed position. Left palm
    faces right, fingertips forward. Right hand palm faces floor, finger-
    tips to left palm. With left hand remaining stationary, brush right
    fingertips downward across left palm.

6. EXPENSIVE: Sign MONEY, then raise right hand and flick it into open-hand,
    fingers-closed position as if you had hit its thumb with a hammer.

7. DRY: Like SUMMER and UGLY, but the X-hand finger is drawn in front of
    the chin.

8. WET: Sign WATER, then with both hands in and-hand position, palms to
    ceiling, open and close hands from and-hand position to open-and posi-
    tion and back to and-hand position. Sort of like squeezing a soppy
    cotton ball between the fingertips.

9. FALSE: Right hand in right-angle index position, palm to left and index
    fingertip pointing to left. Move index finger across chin from right
    to left. (Also means LIE.) You can also use right-angle hand-position
    instead of right-angle index hand-position.

10. LIAR: Sign FALSE, then PERSON.

11. SMART: (a) Right hand in index-hand position, palm forward and index
    finger pointing to ceiling. Touch index finger to temple then oscil-
    late it upward.

    (b) With right hand in 5-hand position, middle finger bent toward
    palm, touch tip of middle finger to forehead at temple, then turn it
    from palm to self to palm forward in a brisk motion.

(c) (Slang version) With right hand in C-hand position, palm to left, place the length of the thumb against the forehead--thus measuring a "thickness" of "brains" bigger than ordinary. This is sometimes elaborated upon by piling "C" upon "C," moving the hands in steps away from the head. Your teacher can demonstrate this version.

12. ARRIVE: Both hands in right-angle hand-position, palms toward each other and knuckles forward. With left hand several inches in front of right hand (and remaining stationary), bring right hand forward and place backs of right fingers against palms of left fingers. Also is used for GET in sentences like "When I get home, I'm going to go right to bed."

13. LEAVE (depart): Both hands in open-hand, fingers-closed (or cupped-hand) position. Palms to floor. Bring both hands backward toward body, closing them to A-hand position, palms forward and knuckles to ceiling.

14. VISIT: Both hands in V-hand position, palms to self, fingertips to ceiling. Move each hand in circles alternately. Signed somewhat like PEOPLE.

15. ENJOY: Sign PLEASE.

16. RATHER: Sign PLEASE, then -EST, like the ending gesture of BEST.

17. ALMOST: Exactly the opposite of THAN. Both palms face ceiling, and right hand comes from below the left hand, striking left fingertips as it rises.

18. EASY: Sign ALMOST twice, with hands relaxed.

19. RESPONSIBLE, RESPONSIBILITY: Right hand in R-hand position, palm to self and fingertips on shoulder and lower shoulder slightly.

20. BALANCE: Almost exactly like MAYBE, except that palms face floor.

21. OBEY: Right hand in A-hand position, palm to self. Touch thumb to temple, then lower hand, opening it to open-hand, fingers-closed position, palm to ceiling and fingertips forward.

22. DISOBEY: Sign THINK, then right hand in A-hand position, palm to self turn hand to palm outward vigorously.

23. DISMAY: Right hand in clawed-hand position, palm to self and fingertips to chest. Place fingertips against chest and move them in a circle, keeping fingertips against chest.

24. DISGUST: Sign DISMAY.

25. BURDEN: Sign RESPONSIBLE, but use right-angle hand instead of R-hand. Can also be made with both hands (both on one shoulder) for emphasis.

(SM 160)

WORDS FOR WHICH SIGNS WILL BE TAUGHT IN LESSON 18

Construct sentences using the following words and including in the sentences words for which you have already learned the signs.

1.	Agree	13.	Imagination
2.	Disagree	14.	Memorize
3.	Angry	15.	Reason
4.	Accept, receive	16.	Inform
5.	Reject, decline	17.	Information
6.	Honor	18.	Wait
7.	Respect	19.	California
8.	Humble, simple, plain	20.	New York
9.	Proud	21.	Chicago
10.	Pass	22.	Detroit
11.	Race	23.	San Francisco
12.	Idea	24.	St. Louis

LESSON 18

(SM 162-166)

LESSON PLAN OUTLINE

Twenty-third Class Session

MATERIALS NEEDED FOR LESSON 18

<u>For instructional purposes</u>:

1. Bingo and Password games.
2. Lesson plan.
3. Evaluation sheets (see Appendix).

<u>DUP materials</u> (if necessary):

1. Vocabulary word-descriptions for Lesson 18 signs (18-DUP-V, two pages).
2. List of words for which signs will be taught in Lesson 19 (18-DUP-M,a; one page).
3. Words to "Believe Me if All Those Adhering Strange Charms . . ." (18-DUP-M,b; one page).
4. Practice Sentences in Idiomatic Sign Language (18-DUP-M,c; one page).

I. Roll call.

II. Return Performance Test papers and discuss/drill as usual.

III. Give Lesson 18 vocabulary of signs. Signs to be taught in this lesson:

1.	Agree	13.	Imagination
2.	Disagree	14.	Memorize
3.	Angry	15.	Reason
4.	Accept, receive	16.	Inform
5.	Reject, decline	17.	Information
6.	Honor	18.	Wait
7.	Respect	19.	California
8.	Humble, simple, plain	20.	New York
9.	Proud	21.	Chicago
10.	Pass	22.	Detroit
11.	Race	23.	San Francisco
12.	Idea	24.	St. Louis

<u>Note</u>: Teach signs for other cities as well.

(Total signs taught to date: 567)

New signs taught:

Variations of the above signs: New signs (not in the lesson plan):

IV.   Drill on signs in Lesson 18. Use student-composed sentences.

V.   Student recitals. Begin with student-composed sentences, then, if some
      of the students feel prepared to recite their evaluation paragraphs,
      begin evaluating students at this time. Continue until end of session.

VI.   Pass out DUP materials.

VII. Homework assignment: Keep practicing paragraphs. Memorize words to
      "Believe Me if All Those Adhering Strange Charms" if possible.

VIII. Concluding remarks.

(SM 162)

WORD-DESCRIPTIONS OF SIGNS IN LESSON 18 VOCABULARY

1. AGREE: Sign THINK, then ALIKE, keeping hands separated by a few inches instead of touching index fingers together.

2. DISAGREE: Sign THINK, then ENEMY, omitting the -ER part of the ENEMY sign.

3. ANGRY: Right hand in clawed-hand position, palm to self and knuckles facing left. Place fingertips and thumb-tip against chest, then drag the hand upward and off the chest, keeping palm toward body.

4. ACCEPT, RECEIVE: Both hands in open-and position, palms facing each other. Place both thumbs against chest, then close hands to and-hand position.

5. REJECT, DECLINE: Left hand in open-hand, fingers-closed position, palm to ceiling and fingertips to right front. Right hand in cupped-hand or right-angle hand-position, palm to self and fingertips to ceiling. Place right fingertips against chin, then place them against left palm near heel of hand, then brush them across left hand palm and fingers and off the ends of the fingers. (Denotes wiping something off a slate.) (Similar to EXCUSE.)

6. HONOR: Right hand in H-hand position, palm to left and fintertips to ceiling. Place index finger against forehead, then lower hand out and away from face, keeping fingers in H-hand position.

7. RESPECT: Exactly like HONOR, but use R-hand position instead of H-hand position.

8. HUMBLE, SIMPLE, PLAIN: Right hand in index-hand position. Place right finger against lips (in a "Shh" gesture), then sign SOME. (Part-type SOME, not somebody-type.)

9. PROUD: Right hand in A-hand position, palm to floor and knuckles pointing to left. Place thumb-nail against chest near waist and draw hand upward. (This is derived from the buttons popping off a shirt when the thumb is drawn up.)

10. PASS: Both hands in A-hand position, palms facing each other and knuckles forward. With left hand in advance of right hand, bring right hand forward and pass left hand.

11. RACE: Sign like PASS, but alternate left and right hands "passing" each other.

12. IDEA: Right hand in I-hand position, palm to self and fingertip to ceiling. Place little fingertip against temple, then move it straight forward a few inches away from temple.

13. IMAGINATION: Almost like IDEA. Instead of moving hand straight forward, draw it out further, describing a small circle with hand. (Often made with both hands alternating in IDEA sign.)

14. MEMORIZE: Right hand in C-hand position, palm to self and knuckles to ceiling. Place thumbnail against forehead or temple, and keeping it there, close-hand to S-hand position.

15. REASON: Right hand in R-hand position, palm to self and fingertips pointing to temple. Describe small circle around temple.

16. INFORM: Right hand in and-hand position, palm to self and fingertips to temple. Place thumbnail against forehead, then move hand forward, opening it as you do so to 5-hand position, palm to ceiling and fingertips forward.

17. INFORMATION: Same as above, but left hand joins in on this one in this way. Left hand in and-hand position, and after right hand has touched temple, BOTH hands go forward and open up to 5-hand position, palms to ceiling and fingertips forward. Move both hands outward to the sides when they are open.

18. WAIT: Sign HOPE, but omit the THINK part of the HOPE sign.

19. CALIFORNIA: Touch right ear lobe with right index finger, then sign YELLOW. (California is called the "golden" state. This is also the sign for GOLD.)

20. NEW YORK: (For this sign, think YORK and it will be easy to remember.) Left hand in open-hand, fingers-closed position, palm to ceiling and fingertips forward. Right hand in Y-hand position, palm to floor. Place right hand on left palm and brush it across left palm from heel of hand to (and beyond) fingertips.

21. CHICAGO: Right hand in C-hand position. Make inverted "S" in air (like for NEVER).

22. DETROIT: Same as CHICAGO, but use D-hand position.

23. SAN FRANCISCO: Spell S and F quickly.

24. ST. LOUIS: Spell St. L quickly.

(SM 164)

WORDS FOR WHICH SIGNS WILL BE TAUGHT IN LESSON 19

Construct sentences using the following words and including in the sentences words for which you have already learned the signs.

1.	Adhering, sticky	10.	Gay
2.	Charms	11.	Indeed
3.	Admiring (slang)	12.	Confess
4.	Wonderful	13.	Bloom
5.	Admiring (formal)	14.	Meeting
6.	Come off	15.	Tight
7.	Suppress	16.	Rolls off of
8.	Emotions	17.	Platonic
9.	Unaccustomedly		

(SM 167)

BELIEVE ME IF ALL THOSE ADHERING STRANGE CHARMS . . .
(Parody of "Believe Me if All Those Endearing Young Charms . . .")

Believe me if all those adhering strange charms
Which I gaze on with admiring dismay
Are going to come off on the shoulders and arms
Of this suit I had cleaned just today.

Thou will still be adored, as this moment thou art,
My sweetheart, my loved one, my own.
But I will strongly suppress the emotions I feel
And love you but leave you alone.

'Tis not that thy beauty is any the less,
Nor thy cheeks unaccustomedly gay.
They are lovely, indeed, I will gladly confess,
But I think I should leave them that way.

For the bloom of thy youth isn't on very tight,
And the powder rolls off of thy nose.
So my love is platonic, my dear, for tonight--
For these are my very best clothes.

(SM 166)

PRACTICE EXERCISE

How would you translate the following sentences into idiomatic sign language?

1. He is about forty years old.

2. His salary is above $10,000 per year.

3. The soprano was accompanied by a full orchestra.

4. Please advise us of any change in your plans.

5. The army effected a very successful withdrawal from the field of battle.

6. The affects of deafness on an individual have profound implications.

7. She has a very affected manner of speaking.

8. His words had tremendous effect upon those present when he spoke.

9. This will afford an opportunity for you to practice analyzing the concepts of words.

10. He is an all-round good athlete.

11. We had no alternative but to punish him.

12. We anticipate no problem in obtaining the money.

13. He is apt to misunderstand what people say to him.

14. We could not ascertain whether or not what he said was true.

15. Attached hereto you will find a copy of the summons.

LESSON 19

(SM 167-170)

LESSON PLAN OUTLINE

Twenty-fourth Class Session

Note: This is the next to last class session.

MATERIALS NEEDED FOR LESSON 19

For instructional purposes: Evaluation sheets.

DUP materials: Vocabulary word-descriptions of signs in Lesson 19 (19-DUP-
V, two pages).

I. Roll call.

II. Return Assignment III (if assigned. If not, go on to step III), and
comment upon the ideas for projects the students presented. (It is hoped
that the instructor will have written his reactions and comments to each
proposal on the papers before returning them.)

III. Teach signs in Lesson 19, and have students practice the song, and drill
as usual, but drill should be kept fairly short as the bulk of the session should be devoted to student practice and recitals, which will help
them prepare for their final evaluation performance.

Signs to be taught in this lesson:

1. Adhering, sticky
2. Charms
3. Admiring (slang)
4. Wonderful
5. Admiring (formal)
6. Come off
7. Suppress
8. Emotions
9. Unaccustomedly
10. Gay
11. Indeed
12. Confess
13. Bloom
14. Meeting
15. Tight
16. Rolls off of
17. Platonic

(Total signs provided in course: 586)

IV. Continue student-evaluation recitals for rest of class session.

V. Homework assignment: Continue practice. If student has done poorly on first evaluation performance, he can have another chance when everyone in the class has been evaluated, if there is time.

VI. Pass out DUP materials.

VII. Concluding remarks.

(SM 168)

WORD-DESCRIPTIONS OF SIGNS IN LESSON 19 VOCABULARY

1. ADHERING, STICKY: Both hands sign this alternately. First, the left
    hand is in a 5-hand position. When the left hand is in the 8-hand
    position, the right hand is in the 5-hand position. Keep opening and
    closing the hands in 5-hand to 8-hand positions, drawing the hands
    backward from directly in front of you until they are near your shoul-
    ders. (Denotes the tackiness of a sticky substance.)

2. CHARMS: Spell out, usually, but in poems and songs, sign BEAUTIFUL or
    ATTRACT.

3. ADMIRING: First, touch your nose with your right index finger, then:
    left hand in open-hand, fingers-closed position, palm to ceiling and
    fingertips to front. Right hand in 20-hand position, palm to floor,
    fingertips forward. Place thumb of right hand near base of left palm,
    then slide it forward, opening and closing index-finger and thumb as
    you slide it. (Slang sign. Denotes the nose hitting the floor and
    bouncing when someone falls hard for someone else.)

4. WONDERFUL: Sign like SUNDAY, but have the hands near the shoulders and
    be more emphatic about the sign.

5. ADMIRING: (Formal) Sign THINK, then WONDERFUL.

6. COME OFF: With right hand in open-and hand-position, palm and fingertips
    to left, place back of thumb against lower left arm then close hand to
    and-hand position. Then raise the hand and place it a few inches closer
    to the elbow and repeat the closing of the hand. Repeat twice more,
    ending near the shoulder. (For this poem only.)

7. SUPPRESS: Left hand in S-hand position, palm to right self and thumb on
    top. Right hand in open-hand, fingers-closed position, palm to floor
    and fingertips to left front. Place right palm on top of left fist and
    lower both hands abruptly. (Push left hand down with right palm in
    other words.)

8. EMOTIONS: Both hands in A-hand position, palms to self. Place fingers
    against chest, then move both hands upward, opening hands to 5-hand
    position, palms still to self and fingertips to ceiling.

9. UNACCUSTOMEDLY: Sign NOT LIKE ALWAYS.

10. GAY: Both hands in 5-hand position, middle fingers slightly bent toward
    palms, palms forward and fingertips to ceiling. Start sign with hands
    in front of face (but several inches in front, please), then oscillate
    hands backward and upward several inches.

11. INDEED: Sign SURE.

12. CONFESS: Sign MY, then brush hand upward slightly and bring it forward
      a couple of inches, ending with hand in open-hand, fingers-closed po-
      sition, palm to ceiling and fingertips to left front, a few inches in
      front of chest. (Be careful with this sign--you can butcher it up
      and make it into VOMIT very easily.)

13. BLOOM: Both hands in and-hand position, palms and fingertips to each
      other and knuckles to ceiling. Place both thumbs together, finger-
      tips touching them keeping thumbs together, open hands and spread fin-
      gers to open-and position.

14. MEETING: Opposite of BLOOM. Have hands in open-and position, thumbs
      touching, then close hands to and-hand position, fingertips touching.
      Repeat once.

15. TIGHT: Both hands in A-hand position, left hand palm to floor, right
      hand palm to left front. Cross wrists and place front of right wrist
      on back of left wrist and wiggle right fist back and forth. (Like a
      person trying to get free when his wrists are tied together.)

16. ROLLS OFF OF: Both hands in V-hand position. Alternately touch index
      fingers of each hand to the side of the nose then drop hand, ending
      sign with hands palm up, fingertips forward. Please note the alter-
      nately.

17. PLATONIC: Sign FRIENDS twice, alternating the fingers on top--first right
      hand finger on top, then left hand finger on top.

LAST CLASS SESSION

LESSON PLAN OUTLINE

Twenty-fifth Class Session

MATERIALS NEEDED FOR LAST CLASS SESSION

1. All papers, assignments, and so forth, which instructor has not yet returned to students.
2. Evaluation of the course forms (see Appendix; SM page 179).

   I. Roll call.

  II. Return any test papers, assignments, and so on, the instructor was de-
layed in correcting and returning.

 III. Evaluation of the course. Instructor should pass out evaluation forms
to students for their reactions, comments, and suggestions pertaining to
the course, and the techniques of teaching the instructor employed. (As
an alternate, the instructor can pass this out as homework in the next-
to-last session.)

  IV. Summary of the course and discussion of individual performances, strengths
and weaknesses as shown by evaluation scores. (Note: If some students
still remain to be evaluated, this should be done right after roll call.)

   V. Discussion of how students might best increase their manual communication
ability from that point onward—associating with deaf people; enrolling
in more advanced courses in manual communication (if such classes are
available, where they are located); and so forth.

  VI. Whether the instructor has enjoyed teaching the course or not, it is a
nice touch to say that he has and to wish the students luck in whatever
endeavor they are about to engage in which will call upon their newly
acquired skill in manual communication.

 VII. Farewell address. Instructor should compose his own.

APPENDIX

(SM 171-178)

MASTER VOCABULARY LIST

Lesson 1 (page 118):
  (39 signs)

1. And
2. Confused
3. Don't know
4. Goodbye
5. He, him, she, her
    (a), (b), and (c)
6. Hello
7. Himself, herself
8. His, hers
9. How
10. I
11. It (a) and (b)
12. Its
13. Know
14. Me
15. Mine
16. My
17. Myself
18. No
19. Not (a) and (b)
20. Our, ours
21. Ourselves
22. Practice
23. Question mark sign
24. Right (correct)
25. Their
26. They, them
27. Themselves
28. Think
29. Understand
30. We, us
31. What (a) and (b)
32. Wrong
33. Yes
34. You (pl.)
35. You (sing.)
36. Your (pl.)
37. Your (sing.)
38. Yourself
39. Yourselves (a) and (b)

Lesson 2 (page 140):
  (32 signs)

40. About
41. Am, are, is, be (a) and (b)
42. But
43. Call (named)
44. Call (phone)
45. Call (summon)
46. Did you, do you, etc.
47. Different
48. Dumb, stupid, ignorant
    (a) and (b)
49. Fingerspelling
50. Friday
51. Introduce
52. Language
53. Long time ago, a
54. Monday
55. Name
56. Now
57. Same, alike (a), (b),
    and (c)
58. Saturday
59. Sign
60. Story, sentence
61. Sunday
62. Tell, say, said
63. Thursday
64. To
65. Today
66. Tuesday
67. Was, were (new signs)
68. Was, past, back, ago, before
    (a) and (b)
69. Wednesday
70. Will, would, future, next
71. Word

Master Vocabulary List, cont'd.

Numbers Lesson (page 149):
    (11 signs)

72. Few
73. How many, how much
74. How old
75. Less
76. Many
77. More
78. Much, above (a)
79. Number
80. Old
81. Several
82. Than

Lesson 3 (page 157):
    (30 signs)

83. Ability
84. Afternoon
85. All day
86. All night
87. Bad
88. Can
89. Can't, cannot
90. Day
91. Day and night
92. Do, act, behave
93. Evening
94. Excuse (me)
95. Fine
96. Good
97. Lousy
98. Midnight
99. Morning
100. Night (a) and (b)
101. No good
102. Noon
103. Please
104. Sorry
105. Thank (you)
106. That (a) and (b)
107. This
108. This (time concept)
109. Time
110. Tomorrow
111. Very
112. Yesterday

Lesson 4 (page 169):
    (42 signs)

113. Afterwhile, later
114. Again
115. College
116. --er sign
117. Experience
118. Expert, skill
119. For
120. Get
121. Have (possessive)
122. Help
123. High school
124. Hour
125. Job
126. Last month
127. Last night
128. Last week
129. Last year
130. Learn
131. Minute, second
132. Month
133. Must
134. Necessary, etc.
135. Next month
136. Next week
137. Next year
138. No (none)
139. One month ago
140. School
141. Slow
142. Student
143. Teach
144. Teacher
145. This afternoon
146. This evening
147. This morning
148. Today (b)
149. Two years ago
     (up to 5)
150. Two (up to 5) years
     from now
151. University
152. Week
153. Work
154. Year

Master Vocabulary List, cont'd.

Lesson 5 (page 180):
    (37 signs)

155. Always
156. Baby
157. Book
158. Boy
159. Brother
160. Child, children
161. Daughter
162. Father
163. Female
164. Gentleman
165. Girl
166. Husband
167. Lady
168. Lesson
169. Male
170. Man
171. Marry, wed
172. Mother
173. Never
174. Often
175. Once
176. Paper
177. Pencil
178. Print
179. Read
180. Secretary
181. Sister
182. Sometimes
183. Son
184. Study
185. Type, typewriter
186. When (during)
187. When (specific)
188. Which
189. Wife
190. Woman
191. Write

Lesson 6 (page 189):
    (35 signs)

192. Around
193. Ask (a), (b), and (c)
194. Aunt
195. Because

Lesson 6, cont'd.

196. Before
197. Best
198. Better
199. Big, large
200. Borrow
201. Careful, be careful
202. Cousin
203. Far
204. Father-in-law
205. Forget
206. Going together, or
     steady dating
207. Grandfather
208. Grandmother
209. In
210. Keep
211. Law
212. Lend
213. Most
214. Mother-in-law
215. Near
216. Niece, nephew
217. On
218. Out
219. Remember
220. Rule
221. Sister-, son-, brother-,
     daughter-in-law, etc.
222. Small, little (a), (b),
     and (c)
223. Together
224. Uncle
225. Why
226. With

Lesson 7 (page 199):
    (38 signs)

227. All
228. Among
229. Any
230. Anything
231. Anywhere
232. At
233. Away, gone (away)
234. Beautiful

Master Vocabulary List, cont'd.

Lesson 7, cont'd.

235. Choose, pick
236. Come, coming (a), (b),
    and (c)
237. Crowd, group, class
238. Dearly
239. Every
240. From
241. Frown, scowl, cross
242. Go, going (a), (b),
    and (c)
243. Greet
244. Home
245. If
246. Kiss
247. Laddie
248. Lassie
249. Love
250. Meet
251. Pretty
252. River
253. River (Rye)
254. Sing, song, music
255. Singer, musician
256. Smile
257. Somebody
258. Sweetheart, boyfriend
259. There
260. Through
261. Town, village, city
262. Ugly, homely
263. Where
264. Yet, still

Lesson 8 (page 212):
    (36 signs)

265. After
266. Airplane
267. Believe
268. Bring
269. Clean, nice, pure
270. Coffee
271. Dirty
272. Dislike
273. Enemy
274. Face, looks (like)
275. Family
276. Find, found

Lesson 8, cont'd.

277. Fly
278. Friend
279. Fun
280. Funny (amusing)
281. Funny (peculiar) or queer
282. Happy
283. Here
284. Left (right)
285. Like
286. Look
287. Make
288. Make fun of
289. Neighbor
290. People
291. Play
292. Ride (car)
293. Ride (horse)
294. Right (left)
295. Sad
296. See
297. Thing, things
298. Want
299. Watch
300. Who

Lesson 9 (page 222):
    (36 signs)

301. Autumn, Fall
302. Black
303. Blue
304. Both
305. Breakfast
306. Brown
307. Buy
308. Color
309. Dinner
310. Drink
311. Early (a) and (b)
312. Eat, ate, food
313. Fast
314. Finish (a) and (b)
315. Gold
316. Gray
317. Green
318. Grow, Spring
319. Late

Master Vocabulary List, cont'd.

Lesson 9, cont'd.

320. Lose (a game)
321. Lose (something)
322. Lunch
323. Money
324. Other
325. Pink
326. Purple
327. Quit
328. Red
329. Shopping
330. Silver
331. Summer
332. White
333. Win
334. Winter, cold
335. Won't, refuse
336. Yellow

Lesson 10 (page 232):
   (38 signs)

337. Between
338. Bother
339. Care
340. Church
341. Complain
342. Depressed, discouraged
343. Eager, zealous
344. Excited
345. Feel
346. Feel hurt (emotionally)
347. Happen
348. Hate
349. Haven't
350. Heart
351. Hide
352. Interrupt
353. Just (exactly)
354. Let
355. Misunderstand
356. Much (b)
357. Or
358. Ought
359. Prayer
360. Seek, look for
361. Sensitive, sensitivity
      (a) and (b)

Lesson 10, cont'd.

362. Show (demonstrate)
363. Show (movie)
364. Show (play or drama)
365. Silly
366. So
367. Some (indefinite)
368. Some (certain, or part)
369. Stubborn
370. Swear (vow)
371. Temple (religious)
372. Touch
373. Try
374. Way

Lesson 11 (page 240):
   (26 signs)

375. Bald
376. Blank (mind)
377. Cool, pleasant
378. Empty
379. Enough
380. Enter, into
381. Finally
382. First, second, etc.
383. Full
384. Give (a) and (b)
385. Hard (difficult)
386. Hold
387. Hot
388. Hurt
389. Kind (kindly)
390. Kind (type of)
391. Last
392. Laugh
393. Mean (unkind)
394. Mean (intend)
395. New
396. Next
397. Sunny (personality)
398. Tenth, eleventh, etc.
399. Warm
400. Young

Master Vocabulary List, cont'd.

Lesson 12 (page 264):
    (20 signs)

401. Address (home)
402. Close (shut)
403. Dark
404. Fall (down)
405. Light
406. Live (reside)
407. Long (length)
408. Maybe
409. Only
410. Open
411. Over
412. Pull
413. Put
414. Short
415. Sit
416. Stand
417. Run
418. Under
419. Use
420. Walk

Lesson 13 (page 270):
    (22 signs)

421. Anyway (doesn't matter)
422. Desire, yearn
423. Feebleminded
424. Keys
425. Onions
426. Potatoes
427. Powerful
428. Pumpkin
429. Sick
430. Start
431. Stop
432. Strong
433. Take
434. Thirsty
435. Tomatoes
436. Vegetables
437. Wash
438. Water
439. Watermelon
440. Weak
441. Well (healthy)
442. Wish, hunger

Lesson 14 (page 276):
    (36 signs)

443. Apple
444. Bath
445. Bathroom
446. Bedroom
447. Bitter, disappoint
448. Bread
449. Butter
450. Buttermilk
451. Cake, cookies, biscuits
452. Chair
453. Cook
454. Cup
455. Dining room
456. Drunk
457. Fire
458. Fork
459. Glass
460. Kitchen
461. Knife
462. Living room
463. Meat
464. Milk
465. Napkin
466. Peach
467. Pie
468. Plate, place
469. Room
470. Sour
471. Spoon
472. Sweet
473. Sugar
474. Table
475. Tea
476. Vinegar
477. Whiskey
478. Wine

Lessons 15 and 16 (page 283):
    (42 signs)

479. Bit (little bit)
480. Cheeks
481. Cleansing
482. Closing
483. Clothes
484. Cold

Master Vocabulary List, Cont'd.

Lessons 15 and 16, cont'd.

485. Cream (face)
486. Curlers
487. Damn
488. Dress
489. Eyed
490. Fish (kippers)
491. Forehead
492. Frocks
493. Girdle
494. Gleam, shine
495. Hell
496. Hips
497. Hope, hoping
498. Just (recently)
499. Lips
500. Lotion
501. Medicine, potion
502. Nerves
503. Ocean
504. Old-fashioned, outmoded
505. Pore
506. Powder (face)
507. Quiet, steady
508. Rock
509. Rouge
510. Shock
511. Slippers
512. Sniveling
513. Stay, continue
514. Tied
515. True, honest
516. True, sure
517. Up (from)
518. View
519. Wide
520. Zippers

Lesson 17 (page 293):
(25 signs)

521. Almost
522. Arrive
523. Balance
524. Burden
525. Busy
526. Cheap
527. Disgust

Lesson 17, cont'd.

528. Dismay
529. Disobey
530. Doubt
531. Dry
532. Easy
533. Enjoy
534. Expensive
535. False, untrue
536. Idle
537. Lazy
538. Leave (depart)
539. Liar
540. Obey
541. Rather
542. Responsible, responsibility
543. Smart (a), (b), and (c)
544. Visit
545. Wet

Lesson 18 (page 303):
(24 signs)

546. Accept, receive
547. Agree
548. Angry
549. California
550. Chicago
551. Detroit
552. Disagree
553. Honor
554. Humble, simple, plain
555. Idea
556. Imagination
557. Inform
558. Information
559. Memorize
560. New York
561. Pass
562. Proud
563. Race
564. Reason
565. Reject, decline
566. Respect
567. San Francisco
568. St. Louis
569. Wait

Master Vocabulary List, cont'd.

Lesson 19 (page 310):
     (17 signs)

570.   Adhering, sticky
571.   Admiring (formal)
572.   Admiring (slang)
573.   Bloom
574.   Charms
575.   Come off (on)
576.   Confess
577.   Emotions
578.   Gay (bright)
579.   Indeed
580.   Meeting
581.   Platonic
582.   Rolls off (of nose)
583.   Suppress
584.   Tight
585.   Unaccustomedly
586.   Wonderful

SONGS WHICH CAN BE TAUGHT IN THE LANGUAGE OF SIGNS

<u>Note</u>: The songs which follow are those which can be readily adapted into the language of signs. Some are simply love songs and others are seasonal in that they can be taught at specific times of the year when they are appropriate to the season. Still others have been selected because they afford practice and training in expressing different concepts, moods and emotions, or changes in pacing, rhythm, or speed/force of delivery. Still others are included simply because they are beautiful songs to <u>hear</u>, and students like learning them even if the signs required are not as beautiful as those required by other songs less pleasing to the <u>ear</u>. (Edelweiss is an example of the latter type, a song beautiful to hear but not particularly beautiful in signs. However, the beauty of the music and the vocalization tends to color the students' perception of the beauty of the signs, and the song is often one of the favorites they learn.)

CLIMB EV'RY MOUNTAIN

Climb ev'ry mountain, search high and low
Follow ev'ry byway, ev'ry path you know
Climb ev'ry mountain, ford ev'ry stream
Follow ev'ry rainbow, until you find your dream

A dream that will need all the love you can give
Ev'ry day of your life for as long as you live.

Climb ev'ry mountain, ford ev'ry stream
Follow ev'ry rainbow until you find your dream.

SOUND OF MUSIC

My day in the hills has come to an end I know
A star has come out to tell me it's time to go
But deep in the dark green shadows
Are voices that urge me to stay
So I pause, and I wait, and I listen
For one more sound
For one more lovely thing that the hills may say

The hills are alive with the sound of music
With songs they have sung for a thousand years
The hills fill my heart with the sound of music
My heart wants to sing every song it hears

My heart wants to beat like the wings of the birds
That rise from the lake to the trees
My heart wants to sigh like a chime that flies
From a church on the breeze

To laugh like a brook as it trips and falls
Over stones on its way
To sing through the night like a lark
Who is learning to pray

I go to the hills when my heart is lonely
I know I will hear what I've heard before
My heart will be blessed with the sound of music
And I'll sing once more.

EDELWEISS

Edelweiss, Edelweiss, every morning you greet me
Small and white, clean and bright
You look happy to greet me

Blossoms of snow may you bloom and grow
Bloom and grow forever
Edelweiss, Edelweiss
Bless my homeland forever.

MY FAVORITE THINGS

Raindrops on roses and whiskers on kittens
Bright copper kettles and warm woolen mittens
Brown paper packages tied up with strings
These are a few of my favorite things

Cream colored ponies and crisp apple strudels
Doorbells and sleighbells and schnitzel with noodles
Wild geese that fly with the moon on their wings
These are a few of my favorite things

Girls in white dresses with blue satin sashes
Snowflakes that stay on my nose and eyelashes
Silver white winters that melt into Springs
These are a few of my favorite things

When the dog bites, when the bee stings
When I'm feeling sad
I simply remember my favorite things
And then I don't feel so bad.

GOD BLESS AMERICA

While the storm clouds gather
Far across the sea
Let us pledge allegiance
To a land that's free
Let us all be grateful
For a land so fair
As we raise our voices
In a solemn prayer

God bless America, land that I love
Stand beside her and guide her
Through the night with a light from above
From the mountains to the prairie
To the oceans bright with foam
God bless America, my home sweet home
God bless America, my home sweet home.

AUTUMN LEAVES

The autumn leaves drift by my window
Those autumn leaves of red and gold
I see your lips, those summer kisses
Those sunburned hands I used to hold

Since you went away, the days grow long
And soon I'll hear old winter's song
But I miss you most of all, my darling
When autumn leaves start to fall.

WHITE CHRISTMAS

I'm dreaming of a white Christmas
Just like the ones we used to know
Where the treetops glisten, and children listen
To hear sleighbells in the snow

I'm dreaming of a white Christmas
With every Christmas card I write
May your days be merry and bright
And may all your Christmases be white.

SILENT NIGHT

Silent night, holy night
All is calm, all is bright
Round yon virgin mother and child
Holy infant so tender and mild

Sleep in heavenly peace
Sleep in heavenly peace

Silent night, holy night
Son of God, love's pure light
Radiant beams from thy holy face
With the dawn of redeeming grace

Jesus, Lord, at thy birth
Jesus, Lord, at thy birth.

ON THE STREET WHERE YOU LIVE

I have often walked down this street before
But the pavement always stayed beneath my feet before
All at once am I
Several stories high
Knowing I'm on the street where you live

Are there lilac trees in the heart of town?
Can you hear a lark in any other part of town?
Does enchantment pour out of every door?
No, it's just on the street where you live

And, oh, that towering feeling
Just to know somehow you are near
That overpowering feeling
That any moment you may suddenly appear
People stop and stare
They don't bother me
For there's nowhere else on earth
That I would rather be

Let time go by, I don't care if I
Can be here, on the street where you live.

TO EACH HIS OWN

A rose must remain with the sun and the rain
Or its lovely promise won't come true
To each his own, to each his own
And my own is you

What good is a song if the words don't belong
A dream must be a dream for two
No good alone, to each his own
And my own is you

If a flame is to grow, there must be a glow
To open each door there's a key
I need you I know, I can't let you go
Your touch means too much to me

Two lips must insist on two more to be kissed
Or they'll never know what love can do
To each his own, I've found my own
One and only you.

EXAMPLES OF ANALYSES OF TEST MISTAKES

The following examples show how the instructor can analyze student mistakes on comprehension tests so that he can institute appropriate remediation treatment. By tallying particular types of errors, he is enabled to see where the areas of weakness are, and identify the offending letters, groups of letters, or signs on which more drilling is needed, and by jotting down what the fingerspelled words were mistaken for, identify areas in which discrimination drilling should be provided. In the first example (taken from the words in the fingerspelling test given in Lesson 3), individual words are analyzed for particular types of errors. In the second example (in which words were fingerspelled in the test are underlined), comprehension test sentences are analyzed for numbers of students missing given words/signs. A brief explanatory analysis follows each example.

I. Fingerspelling test analysis (with words selected from test in Lesson 3):

Word in test:	Missed completely (did not write anything):	Letter or letter groups missed:
Call:	0	C A LL Ca ALL
		Mistaken for:
		Mall Cell Ball
Me:	_____	M E
		Ma
Mean:	_____	M E A N MA EA AN
		Man Men Met Meat

Analysis: A lot of students are confusing C with B and M. Also, either the E or the A in mean is seen, but many students are not seeing both. N is confused a bit with T. Many students missed mean altogether.

Remediation: 1. Drill with letter groups EA
2. Discrimination drills on M-C; N-T; B-C; A-EA; and E-A

II. Comprehension test analysis (with sentence from test in Lesson 5):

1. Hello   it   is   a   beautiful   morning. _____
                                                    (Missed completely)

___ ___ ___ ___ ___ ___

                                        (afternoon   night   )

<u>Analysis</u>: (with words analyzed for type of mistake as in the F/S analysis) Most students mistook morning for afternoon. A few are having trouble separating several short words (<u>it is a</u>) and ran them together. Beautiful probably suffered from their confusion about "it is a."

<u>Remediation</u>: Drill on fingerspelled short sentences. Drill on discrimination between one and two short words. (And drill on EA if errors indicate this group was missed in "beautiful.") Drill on morning, afternoon, and beautiful.

MASTER COPIES OF PERFORMANCE TEST ANSWERS

Instructions for use: The answers given in the master copies of the two performance tests which follow are those the students should make to the test items. There are, however, some acceptable variations of hand-positions which, while not as precise as those indicated by the master copy descriptions, will show that the student does know how to execute a sign. (Some of the more acceptable variations are given in parentheses.) A student giving one of the alternate responses—or even an acceptable variation not listed on the master copies—may either be somewhat vague as to what to call a certain hand-position which does not fit cleanly into one or another of two specific hand-positions, or he may not really know how to execute the sign with precision. The instructor, therefore, should make a notation on the student's paper which calls his attention to the better description (or hand-position), but give the student credit for a correct answer. He should also keep a record of these "sloppy" or imprecise answers and make it a point to check the way the students in question execute those particular signs. If the student really is sloppy in execution of the sign, he can then correct his performance, but it may be that the student executes the sign correctly but became confused when it came to describing the sign by using the hand-positions (or palm-directions) provided in the test.

Grading Performance Test I: Total possible score on Performance Test I is 120 (100%). For each completely missed sign, deduct two points. For responses which are partly correct, but show rather bad technique (for example, "again" is described as requiring two OH (open hands) instead of the correct OH and RA (right-angle) or cupped hands, which would make the sign very sloppy), deduct one point (and write "Sloppy" on the student's paper to explain why the point was deducted). Deduct total points missed from the total possible (120), then multiply the result by .833 to get the student's percent grade.

Grading Performance Test II: Total possible score on Performance Test II is 200 points (100%). Deduct 4 points for each completely missed sign. Deduct 2 points for sloppiness (as described above for Performance Test I) in any sign, and one point for any sign in which the palm-direction is wrong for either hand (but not both) if the hand-positions are correct. If palm-direction is wrong for both hands (if both are used in making the sign), the instructor should sign the word to himself, the way it was described, according to palm-direction, and if the sign is still recognizable as such, deduct only two points. If the erroneous palm-direction makes the sign unrecognizable or unexecutable, he should treat it as a complete error regardless of the fact that the hand-positions are correctly given. Deduct the total points missed from the total possible (200), and multiply the result by .50 to get the student's percent grade.

LESSON 7

PERFORMANCE TEST

Name Master Copy
LH or RH _____ *

*If student is left-
handed, reverse LH and
RH; when grading paper.

1. Index hand (IH)
2. Open hand, fingers closed (OH, FC)
3. Open hand, fingers spread (5H)
4. Cupped hand (CH)
5. Right angle hand (RAH)
6. Right angle index hand (RAIH)
7. And hand (AH)
8. Open and hand (OAH)
9. Clawed hand (CLH)
10. A, B, Y, (etc.) hand (A), (B), (Y), etc.

RH = Right hand   LH = Left hand

Which of the above hand-positions do you use for the following signs? Give the BEGINNING hand-position for each hand (if both hands are used—or the appropriate (left or right) hand if only one is used). If left-handed, please so indicate in the upper right corner of your paper. (PLEASE LIMIT YOURSELF TO BEGINNING HAND-POSITION ONLY. FOR THE INSTRUCTOR'S SAKE, DO NOT ATTEMPT TO GIVE FULL WORD-DESCRIPTION OF THE SIGN.) The above abbreviations may be used, but do not try to use the numbers—it complicates the chore of correcting the papers.

	LH	RH
1. I		IH
2. Me	IH or RAIH	
3. Mine	OH, FC	
4. Myself	A	
5. Yourself	A	
6. Practice	IH	A
7. What (a)	5H	5H or IH

	LH	RH
8. What (b)	5H	IH or 5H
9. How	RAH or A	RAH or A
10. Know		RAH
11. Think		IH or RAI
12. Hello		OH, FC
13. Different	IH	IH
14. Same (a)	IH or nothing	IH or Y

No.	Word	LH	RH
15.	Same (b)	Reverse of 14	(IH or Y on right)
16.	Sorry		A
17.	Please	OH, FC	OH, FC
18.	Fine		OH, FS or 5H
19.	Excuse	OH, FC	A (or S)
20.	Your		OH, FC
21.	Can	A	A
22.	Ability	A	A
23.	Can't	IH	IH
24.	Introduce	N (or U or H)	N (or U, H)
25.	Call (summon)	CH or OH, FC	Same as LH
26.	Call (by name)	N, U or H	N, U or H
27.	Call (phone)		Y
28.	Morning	OH, FC (or cupped)	OH, FC (or cup)
29.	Good		OH, FC
30.	Night	RA	OH, FC or CH
31.	Work, job	A or S	A or S
32.	Help	OHA or S	OH, FC
33.	Experience		OAH
34.	Get	C	C
35.	This, that	OH, FC	Y (or IH)
36.	Tell		IH
37.	Must, necessary, etc.		X
38.	Again	OH, FC	RAH
39.	Slow	OH, FC (or FS)	5H (or 4H)
40.	No (none)	0	0
41.	Remember	A	A, RAH or RAIE
42.	Man		OAH
43.	Woman	A	A
44.	Far	A	A
45.	Near	OH, FC	OH, FC or RAH
46.	Never		B
47.	Always		IH
48.	For		IH
49.	Which	A	A
50.	When	IH	IH
51.	When (during)	IH	IH
52.	Why		RAH
53.	Because	A	RAH
54.	Most	A	A
55.	Themselves		A
56.	On	OH, FC	OH, FC
57.	Sunday	OH, FC	OH, FC
58.	Have	RAH	RAH
59.	Meet	IH	IH
60.	But	IH	IH

Lesson 17

MASTER COPY

MANUAL COMMUNICATIONS CLASS

PERFORMANCE TEST II

Name _____

Date _____

Left-handed? _____

Hand-Positions:

1. Right-angle hand (RA)
2. Right-angle-index hand (RAI)
3. And-hand (And)
4. Open-and hand (OAH)
5. Index-hand (Index)
6. Open hand-fingers closed (OH)
7. 5-hand (5)
8. Cupped-hand (Cup)
9. Clawed-hand (CLH)
10. A-hand, B-hand, etc. (A, B, etc.)

Palm-Directions (Palm faces):

1. Ceiling (Ceil)
2. Floor (Fl)
3. One's own body (Self)
4. Right (Rt.)
5. Left (Left)
6. Each other (Each)
7. Forward (front)
8. Right of center front (Right front)
9. Left of center front (Left front)

Which of the above hand-positions and palm-directions do you use for the following words? Give hand-positions for each hand if both hands are used. Give, also, the direction the palm faces for each hand. Use abbreviations given in parentheses, NOT the numbers, please.

Important notice! DO NOT ATTEMPT TO GIVE FULL WORD-DESCRIPTIONS. LIMIT YOURSELVES TO BEGINNING HAND-POSITIONS AND DIRECTIONS PALMS FACE AT BEGINNING OF SIGN. STUDENTS NOT FOLLOWING DIRECTIONS WILL BE PENALIZED 10 POINTS ON THEIR GRADE.

1. Myself:	Left hand:	Right hand:	A
	Left palm:	Right palm:	Left
2. How:	Left hand: A	Right hand:	A
	Left palm: Each (or Rt.)	Right palm:	Each (or Left)
3. Know:	Left hand:	Right hand:	RA (or OH?)
	Left palm:	Right palm:	Self (or Face)

4. Same:	Left hand:	Index (or blank)	Right palm:	Index (or Y)
	Left palm:	Floor (or blank)	Right palm:	Floor (Fl)
5. About	Left hand:	And	Right hand:	RAI (or Index)
	Left palm:	Right	Right palm:	Left (or Self)
6. Will:	Left hand:		Right hand:	5 (or OH)
	Left palm:		Right palm:	Left
7. Morning:	Left hand:	OH (or cupped)	Right hand:	Cup (or OH)
	Left palm:	Self	Right palm:	Ceil
8. Fine:	Left hand:		Right hand:	5
	Left palm:		Right palm:	Left
9. Again:	Left hand:	OH (or Cup)	Right hand:	RA (or Cup)
	Left palm:	Ceil	Right palm:	Ceil
10. Introduce:	Left hand:	H (or U)	Right hand:	H (or U)
	Left palm:	Each (or Rt)	Right palm:	Each (or Left)
11. Both:	Left hand:	C	Right hand:	V (or 2)
	Left palm:	Self (or Rt)	Right palm:	Self
12. Get:	Left hand:	Claw (or C)	Right hand:	Claw (or C)
	Left palm:	Each (or Rt)	Right palm:	Each (or Left)
13. Must:	Left hand:		Right hand:	X
	Left palm:		Right palm:	Floor (or down)
14. Most:	Left hand:	A	Right hand:	A
	Left palm:	Each (or Rt.)	Right palm:	Each (or Left)
15. Slow:	Left hand:	OH	Right hand:	OH (or 4, or B)
	Left palm:	Fl (or down)	Right palm:	Fl (or down)

16.	Remember:	Left hand:	A (blank is OK)	Right hand:	A, RA, or RAI
		Left palm:	Rt (or blank)	Right palm:	Self
17.	Father:	Left hand:		Right hand:	A (or 5)
		Left palm:		Right palm:	Left
18.	Grandfather:	Left hand:	A (or 5)	Right hand:	A (or 5)
		Left palm:	Rt (or Self)	Right palm:	Left
19.	Far:	Left hand:	A	Right hand:	A
		Left palm:	Each (or Rt)	Right palm:	Each (or Rt)
20.	Meet:	Left hand:	Index	Right hand:	Index
		Left palm:	Each (or Rt)	Right palm:	Each (or Left)
21.	Quit:	Left hand:	O (or Open S)	Right hand:	H or U
		Left palm:	Rt	Right palm:	Left
22.	Happy:	Left hand:		Right hand:	OH (or 5)
		Left palm:		Right palm:	Self
23.	In	Left hand:	And	Right hand:	And
		Left palm:	Rt	Right palm:	Floor (Fl)
24.	Late:	Left hand:		Right hand:	OH
		Left palm:		Right palm:	Fl, Self, or "Back"
25.	Tomorrow:	Left hand:		Right hand:	A
		Left palm:		Right palm:	Self (or Left, face)
26.	Do:	Left hand:	C	Right hand:	C
		Left palm:	Floor (Fl)	Right palm:	Floor (Fl)
27.	Where:	Left hand:		Right hand:	Index
		Left palm:		Right palm:	Front

28. Any:	Left hand:		Right hand:	A
	Left palm:		Right palm:	Self
29. Borrow:	Left hand:	K	Right hand:	K
	Left palm:	Rt	Right palm:	Left
30. Law:	Left hand:	OH	Right hand:	L
	Left palm:	Rt (or Each)	Right palm:	Left (or Each)
31. Aunt:	Left hand:		Right hand:	A
	Left palm:		Right palm:	Front
32. Ugly:	Left hand:		Right hand:	X (or? Index?)
	Left palm:		Right palm:	Floor (Fl)
33. People:	Left hand:	K or P	Right hand:	K or P
	Left palm:	Front	Right palm:	Front
34. Make:	Left hand:	S	Right hand:	S
	Left palm:	Self	Right palm:	Self
35. Clean:	Left hand:	OH	Right hand:	OH
	Left palm:	Each (or Ceil)	Right palm:	Each (or Floor)
36. Dirty:	Left hand:		Right hand:	5 or OAH
	Left palm:		Right palm:	Floor (Fl)
37. Week:	Left hand:	OH	Right hand:	Index
	Left palm:	Self	Right palm:	Front
38. Hurt:	Left hand:	RAI	Right hand:	RAI
	Left palm:	Each (or Rt)	Right palm:	Each (or Left)
39. After:	Left hand:	B (or OH)	Right hand:	B (or OH)
	Left palm:	Self	Right palm:	Left

40. Find:	Left hand:		Right hand: F	
	Left palm:		Right palm: Front	
41. Funny:	Left hand:		Right hand: N (or U)	
	Left palm:		Right palm: Self (or Face)	
42. Hot:	Left hand:		Right hand: C (or Claw)	
	Left palm:		Right palm: Self (or Face)	
43. New:	Left hand: Cup (or RA)		Right hand: Cup (or RA)	
	Left palm: Self		Right palm: Self	
44. Summer:	Left hand:		Right hand: X	
	Left palm:		Right palm: Floor	
45. Enemy:	Left hand: RAI (or Index?)		Right hand: RAI (or Index?)	
	Left palm: Each (or Rt)		Right palm: Each (or Left)	
46. Family:	Left hand: F		Right hand: F	
	Left palm: Front		Right palm: Front	
47. See:	Left hand:		Right hand: V (or 2)	
	Left palm:		Right palm: Self (or Face)	
48. Never:	Left hand:		Right hand: B (or OH)	
	Left palm:		Right palm: Left front	
49. Stubborn:	Left hand:		Right hand: OH	
	Left palm:		Right palm: Front	
50. Finally:	Left hand: I		Right hand: I	
	Left palm: Each (or Rt)		Right palm: Each (or Left)	

(SM 179)

EVALUATION OF MANUAL COMMUNICATION CLASS

As you know, a good teacher constantly strives to improve both his/her teaching methods and the materials he/she uses in conducting the course. One way of doing this is to study the end performance of the students and compare it with the goals it was hoped would be achieved at the beginning of the course. However, this alone is not sufficient for the instructor to determine how successful the methods are, nor how they might be improved. Often, feedback from the students can help pinpoint areas of strength and weakness in the conduct of the course, both with respect to teaching performance and to the overall course content and organization. It would be appreciated if you would take a few minutes to complete the following questionnaire on a separate sheet of paper. So that you may feel free to express your opinions freely, no names should be written on the evaluation sheets.

Date_____

1. What aspects of the course do you feel were most beneficial to you in learning manual communication skills?

2. What aspects were least beneficial?

3. Please comment on teaching performance with regard to: review, student participation, lesson presentation, lesson organization, questioning techniques, use of instructional aids, or anything else you might wish to comment upon.

4. What is your opinion of the overall organization of the course?

5. Suggestions or recommendations for improving the course.

A SELECTED ANNOTATED BIBLIOGRAPHY OF BOOKS, FILMS,
AND TEACHING MEDIA ON THE LANGUAGE OF SIGNS,
FINGERSPELLING, AND DEAFNESS

(Revised 1970 by the NAD and 1971 by the author)

The following bibliography was prepared by the Communicative Skills Program
of the National Association of the Deaf (NAD), and is reproduced herein by
permission of Mr. Terrence J. O'Rourke, Program Director. The author has made
some changes and additions to the original bibliography to further update the
material therein. (Such additions are indicated by an asterisk.* The author's
recommendations, if any, are italicized at the end of each summary. Prices
quoted are subject to applicable state and local taxes as well as postage
charges.)

*1. Babbini, Barbara E. An Introductory Course in Manual Communication:
       Fingerspelling and the Language of Signs. Northridge, Calif: San
       Fernando Valley State College, 1965. No longer available. The pres-
       ent manual is a revision of this book. (Some copies may still be in
       libraries of training programs.)

*2. Babbini, Barbara E. Manual Communication: Fingerspelling and the
       Language of Signs. A Course of Study Outline for Students. Urbana,
       Ill.: University of Illinois Press, 1974.

This manual is a student's workbook designed to be used in classes taught by
instructors using the present manual, and the material therein is coordinated
with the lesson plans given in the present manual. Included are a brief history of the language of signs; Do's and Don'ts in the Language of Signs and
Fingerspelling; word-descriptions of the signs given in each lesson; practice
words, numbers and sentences for each lesson; homework assignments, and an
Appendix which includes a bibliography of books and articles on the language
of signs, fingerspelling, and deafness in general. Also included in the Appendix are charts upon which students can record grades received on tests and
assignments.

Illustrations include drawings of the handshapes of the manual alphabet; the
numbers from 1 to 10; and the fundamental hand-positions upon which the word-
descriptions of the signs are based.

Recommended as a workbook for students in classes taught by the user of this
manual.

3. Benson, Elizabeth. Sign Language. St. Paul, Minnesota: St. Paul Area
       Technical Vocational Institute, 1964. (Available without cost while
       supply lasts.)

St. Paul Area Technical Vocational Institute has published Sign Language, a manual of Dr. Elizabeth Benson's materials for the teaching of the language of signs. Previously unpublished, these materials were collated and used by Dr. Bronson in classes at Gallaudet College under the title, "Suggestions Relative to the Mastery of Signs."

The 590 signs described in verbal notations constitute a basic sign language vocabulary, the unique factor being Dr. Benson's original arrangement of the vocabulary into nineteen discrete categories under such headings as "Animals," "Opposites," "Recreation," "Time," and "Verbs."

Because verbal descriptions are not accurate, students must be shown the proper signs by a competent teacher. Then this manual becomes appropriate for re-view. Thirty-one pages are devoted to descriptions of signs that are presented in the illustrated format of David O. Watson's book, Talk with Your Hands.

The index is in two parts: first comes an alphabetically arranged basic word index of 340 entries; second is a sign language index alphabetically listing the 590 signs described in the manual.

Because this is not per se a lesson plan or course of study outline, the success of the manual would depend on the teacher and the practice materials he might devise to teach his classes.

4.   Bornstein, Harry, Lillian B. Hamilton, and Barbara M. Kannapell. Signs
        for Instructional Purposes. Washington, D.C.: Gallaudet College
        Press, 1969. (Available without cost while supply lasts.)

As the title indicates, this book contains signs developed specifically for instructional purposes. Development of these signs was undertaken by the Office of Institutional Research and members of the faculty at Gallaudet Col-lege in an attempt to represent, with individual signs, those usually lengthy words and phrases which, because they are important to a subject matter, are frequently used in class.

This book, Signs for Instructional Purposes, the outcome of their efforts, is a dictionary of 465 signs which have been classified according to four educa-tional divisions: (1) science and mathematics, (2) humanities, (3) social studies, (4) professional studies. Each division has a section devoted to words pertaining to subjects in that division, as well as sections for terms in specific subject areas.

Those already proficient with the language of signs can most readily appreci-ate the five basic rationales used for sign invention: (1) an existing sign with a letter cue, (2) a compound of two existing signs, (3) a compound of a letter and an existing sign, (4) a completely new sign, and (5) a new sign with a letter cue. In addition, consultants created a small number of signs "spontaneously," that is, without any construction guide. The supplementary notations printed with the illustrations indicate both placement, movement and configuration of the hands, as well as the existing sign, if any, used in making the new sign.

The illustrations by Betty Miller are sufficiently descriptive and clear that those familiar with sign language should be able to reproduce the signs without further help. The only difficulty with Miss Miller's illustrations is this: "reading" illustrated signs and reproducing them accurately becomes more difficult when there is no body orientation to rely on. The work done by Stokoe underscored the fact that there are three necessary elements in any sign: the dez (configuration of the hands), the sig (the movement), and the tab (the part of the body in which the sign is made). While eliminating the body outline makes the illustrations crisp and uncluttered (there is no "noise"), it also eliminates the background locus that is the basis for tab elements in signing.

Reproduced in black on a white background, with red lines and arrows to indicate the appropriate motions, five to six illustrations appear on each page. The text is small (5 1/2 x 9"); but the balance and variety of the page layouts and the inherent attractiveness of the illustrations themselves enhance the text and make study of the dictionary a pleasant experience.

One other notable feature is the use of both the English and French languages in printing the text. So that a larger audience might find the text useful, each sign is labeled with its French equivalent. All prose discussions are printed in both languages, and a bilingual index is also included.

Recommended especially for those involved in instruction of deaf persons on the secondary and college levels, this book should be studied by all proficient with the language of signs.

One note of caution to readers: because these signs were developed specifically for classroom use, they at this time are known to and fill the needs of a numerically small segment of the deaf population.

Useful for those training interpreters for educational situations at the high school or college level.

5. Casterline, Dorothy C., Carl C. Croneberg, and William C. Stokoe, Jr. Dictionary: American Sign Language. Washington, D.C.: Gallaudet College Press, 1965 ($6.95).

The dictionary lists approximately 3,000 signs (morphemes) of the American Sign Language in symbolic notation and is as complete an inventory of the lexicon of the language as the state of linguistic analysis will allow. An entry for each sign gives information about its formation, its grammatical and syntactical features--illustrated by brief sign language phrases--an indication of its usage, whether standard, dialectical, formal, or other, and some of its approximate English equivalents. Introductory material explains, with photographic illustrations, the basic structure of signs and the system of symbols used for writing them in an essay on the language and its grammar.

A valuable addition to the instructor's library. Excellent reference book for students.

6. Davis, Anne. The Language of Signs: A Handbook for Manual Communication with the Deaf. New York: Executive Council of the Episcopal Church, 1966 ($4.75).

This handbook contains approximately 650 signs which are considered a basic vocabulary for manual communication with deaf persons. The book presents the signs in photograph form, very few with superimposed arrows to indicate the motion of the sign. Generally, the verbal descriptions accompanying each photograph are considered sufficient for duplication. Starting with the manual alphabet and the basic hand-positions, the handbook progresses through sixteen discrete categories including "Family Relationships," "People and Professions," "Pronouns," "Time Words," "Verbs," and "Mental Actions." The Supplementary Sections, A through E, contain church signs and words commonly used in religious services. Some of these signs are peculiar to the Episcopal deaf community. A standard bibliography and an alphabetic index are included.

The book is complete in itself and the clarity of the photographs will permit its use as an independent study tool for teacher and student. To facilitate its use with the 8mm training films, "The Sign Language of the Deaf," the words are listed as they appear on the films. The sections of the handbook are also numbered to correspond with the reels of film in the series.

7. Falberg, Roger M. The Language of Silence. Wichita, Kansas: Wichita Social Services for the Deaf, 1963 ($2.75).

This book, neither an illustrated textbook nor a technical treatise, explores the subtleties of manual communication and is intended to supplement a good dictionary of signs. Attention is called to the nuances of the language of signs of which only the fluent user is aware. Maximum benefits will accrue to the student who is willing to practice with the deaf themselves after learning the manual alphabet and acquiring a basic vocabulary of signs.

The author emphasizes the relation of signs to their referents (picture concepts) and cautions that the language of signs stands somewhere in between picture-language and written language on the development scale. From his point of view, the language of the deaf is more directly traceable to referents than is oral language.

A distinct feature of this book is a lesson plan which provides explanations and practice within troublesome areas, such as the formation of the tenses; the use of function words, the negatives, the possessives, the compulsion words (must, demand-require, need, furnish-possess-must), the comparatives, and time indicators; the refinements to have, has, and had; words with multiple referents; and the highly developed use of flowing signs in poetry and songs.

Falberg also attempts a broad classification of the more commonly used signs: (1) signs that show structure, (2) signs that show function, and (3) the spatial indicators, that is, pointing or showing the position of referents in real space.

An appendix contains pointers in the use of the manual alphabet, an exercise in the formation of numbers, and a vocabulary checklist which refers one to descriptions of signs and their nuances as discussed in the text.

Spiral binding makes it possible for the reader to open the book flat, leaving both hands free for practice. There are, however, only a few illustrations and descriptions of signs, used to clarify certain applications.

Interesting background information.

8. Fant, Louie J. Say It with Hands. Washington, D.C.: American Annals of the Deaf, Gallaudet College Press, 1964 ($3.50).

This book offers a good lesson plan to be used by any teacher of the language of signs. It is also a good reference book for those who have already had a course in the language of signs and for students to use providing they have an opportunity to practice with someone who is proficient in receptive and expressive languages of signs. It should be emphasized that the author intended this book as a lesson plan rather than a dictionary.

There is some well-written introductory material on the nature of the language of signs, hints on learning fingerspelling, the importance of facial expression and body movements, and an explanation of the lesson plan. This introduction gives the beginning student an explanation and understanding of the basic aspects of the language of signs.

The forty-six lessons and the grouping of signs are built around handshapes, because the author believes that one will learn the signs more readily and remember them more easily by this method. All signs made while the hands are in the A shape constitute one lesson, those made with closed fists another, and so on. This book contains valuable tips on shortcuts, abbreviations, and sign language etiquette. At the end of each lesson are practice sentences which not only contain material learned in that lesson, but also many signs learned in previous lessons. These sentences also provide fingerspelling practice. The drawings showing the execution of signs are adequate for the intended use of the book.

Recommended as a supplementary reference book.

9. Greenberg, Joanne. In this Sign. New York: Holt, Rinehart, and Winston, 1971 ($5.95).

While not a book on the language of signs per se, this novel by Joanne Greenberg deals with sign language in that it portrays the lives of a fictional deaf couple, Janice and Abel Ryder, in the years between the two World Wars and thereafter. It portrays their attempts to communicate with the world about them with and without the use of Sign (the term Mrs. Greenberg uses to mean the language of signs), and offers a compassionate but realistic account of their struggle against all but insurmountable odds to achieve security for themselves

and their two normal children despite the dual handicaps of limited education
and limited communication skills.

As an honest and accurate portrayal of the life-styles of countless deaf
people of the Ryders' achievement level in communication and language skills,
In this Sign cannot be surpassed. Mrs. Greenberg shows remarkable insight
in her writing of the story, for one gains the impression she has been "inside"
of a deaf person and looked out upon the world through his eyes, seeing all the
distortions of reality he sees, making all of the assumptions a deaf person
would make based upon these distortions, and reacting the same way a deaf person would react given the limited and distorted information he has. At the
same time, Mrs. Greenberg allows one to understand the reactions of the hearing people in the Ryders' environment and to analyze the resulting conflicts
into the basic units of mutual misunderstanding attributable to the communication barrier.

Where most other writers-about-deaf-people are content to end their stories,
Mrs. Greenberg begins hers. A deaf person's problems do not end when he has
mastered the pronunciation of the word "ball," for instance, although other
writers would have one think they do; that the deaf person is instantly transformed from a nonspeaking, noncomprehending, rejected-by-his-parent(s) emotional
misfit, into a fluently speaking, skillful-lipreading, loved-and-accepted-by-
proud-parents, emotionally stable person simply through his mastery of the difficult task of speaking one word intelligibly. Unfortunately such writers, in
their attempts to leave the reader happy and optimistic, often mislead people
into thinking that the average deaf person should be able to do everything a
normal person can do, and that those who cannot must have been those who were
not sufficiently motivated during childhood to master that initial word, "ball."
Or that they are stupid in addition to being deaf. Mrs. Greenberg takes the
reader through the lives of an average deaf couple, beginning her story at the
point where their formal education ends, and their real education begins, an
education which costs them far more in terms of time, money, and emotional
damage than their formal education cost their state, and a struggle for which
their formal education left them ill-prepared.

The absence of sentimentality in the book may depress those who are accustomed
to the practice most writers about deaf people employ: that of presenting
deaf people in the best and most optimistic light possible, or as objects to
inspire sympathy or pity. However, the experience of being deaf, even for the
few hours it takes to read the book and experience the Ryders' experiences, is
far more conducive to the understanding of deaf people than any sugar-coating
of reality would be. Unpalatable as it may be, deaf people do get gulled into
buying expensive luxuries they cannot afford; deaf people are sometimes so un-
sophisticated they do not realize that items they buy on credit must be paid
for eventually or they will be sued; deaf people do wind up in courts of law
on charges they do not, or only dimly understand; deaf people are at the mercy
of interpreters who may or may not have their best interests at heart; deaf
people do lack the sophistication which would enable them to understand the
motives of hearing people about them; deaf people do misperceive events, misunderstand, and are misunderstood by hearing people they encounter in their
daily lives; deaf people do develop near-paranoid suspicions of hearing persons

as a result of repeated misunderstandings, and these suspicions do cause them to react in ways which, while perfectly logical and justifiable from their own points of view, are incomprehensible to hearing people; deaf persons often are conditioned from childhood to regard sign language as a vulgar form of communication not to be used in public, until experience teaches them otherwise; and, finally, despite all this, deaf people do manage to carve out their own little niches in life which, while perhaps appalling to a person with normal hearing, suits the deaf persons and affords them a measure of security and happiness—and often it is the language of signs which helps them across the gulf separating them from their fellow man, deaf or hearing.

Highly recommended for every person in training to work with deaf people in any capacity whatsoever. It should be required extra reading for every student in manual communication.

10. Guillory, LaVera M. Expressive and Receptive Fingerspelling for Hearing Adults. Baton Rouge, Louisiana: Claitor's Book Store, 1966 ($1.00).

This manual is an attempt to present a pedagogically consistent method for teaching fingerspelling to adult hearing persons with fully developed reading and writing skills.

The author points out that a resurgence of interest in fingerspelling was caused by the introduction of the Rochester Method of Instruction to the School for the Deaf in Baton Rouge, Louisiana. Recognizing that fingerspelling requires receptive as well as expressive skills, and that the speed of the practitioner precludes the reading of individual letters, the author hypothesized that fingerspelling might be taught through application of the phonetic method of teaching reading and writing. (Readers should note that phonetic symbols cannot be duplicated manually, and thus, the designation "phonetic method of fingerspelling" is a misnomer. However, since no apt alternative designation has suggested itself, the term "phonetic method" will be used throughout this review.) This manual is a plan for learning to fingerspell the basic phonetic elements found in the English language instead of learning the individual letters of the manual alphabet.

In the introductory material the author stresses that the student must see whole words in receiving the fingerspelled message and he must spell and speak whole words simultaneously when expressing the fingerspelled messages.

Common faults in fingerspelling and hints for expressive and receptive fingerspelling are included in this section along with "The First Lesson and Introduction to Phonetic Fingerspelling," which is a demonstration of the syllabication recommended for clear fingerspelling with simultaneous speech.

There are twenty-three pages of drill material in this manual. Beginning with two-letter configurations, the author drills each phonetic element by adding initial letters to make an English word until the whole family of words has been mastered. For example, the basic phonetic element ab is drilled as cab, dab, fab, gab and so on.

Forty-seven basic phonetic units are drilled in this manner, the accompanying illustrations in black line drawings introducing the proper hand configurations. Beginning with the phonetic units starting with the letter "a," the drills proceed through the e-, i-, o-, and u- phonetic units. The letters of the manual alphabet are not taught individually and the illustrations of the alphabet are appended solely for purposes of reference and clarity.

Variety is introduced with the nonsense sentences composed of three-letter rhyme words, followed by four-letter word drills and practice sentences using both the three- and four-letter words.

Commonly used words, conversational sentences, selected long words, digraphs (two-letter combinations representing one sound) and digraph words, prefixes and suffixes are drilled in separate lessons. The syllabication drill focuses on compounds and words formed with prefixes and suffixes.

This manual is best-suited for classroom situations where a teacher can observe the drill practice of groups of students and recommend individual practice "therapy" where necessary.

Highly recommended as a supplementary test to be used with this manual.

11. Hoemann, Harry W., ed. Improved Techniques of Communication: A Training Manual for Use with Severely Handicapped Deaf Clients. Bowling Green, Ohio: Bowling Green State University, 1970 (price, if any, unknown).

The difficulties faced by rehabilitation workers with the language handicapped deaf adult in Lapeer and Lansing, Michigan, in teaching the basic English skills necessary for a prelingually deaf adult to function in the world of work are familiar to all involved with deaf education. For those particular workers in Michigan, however, concern with the problem took concrete form in a workshop of deaf professionals sponsored by Catholic University in Knoxville, Tennessee in August, 1967. The Michigan rehabilitation workers had found that manual communication is a valid instructional medium; however, because the manual communication system and the system of written English are different, conventional sign language could not be used to reinforce the patterns of English. By developing signs that would bring the manual communication system into a visible English form for classroom use, and extracurricular conversation, perhaps reinforcement of basic English language patterns would ensue.

This manual, the outcome of the workshop, has as its outstanding feature "A Prescriptive Dictionary for Improved Manual Communication," which aims to reduce the discrepancies between the conventional sign language of the deaf and the English language. This illustrated dictionary, appearing on pages 6-52, does not aim at standardization of signs; it is an approach to the problem, rather than a fixed symbol system.

Individual signs for prefixes (for example, re-, pre-), suffixes (for example, -tion, -ment), inflected forms of auxiliary verbs (have, has, had), forms of the verb to be (am, are, was, were), indicators for past and participial forms

(-ed, -ing), pronouns, selected prepositions and conjunctions, were developed
to reduce syntactical discrepancies. Reduction of lexical discrepancies was
encouraged by the development of signs for such categories as measurements,
work-oriented words, money matters, vehicles, wearing apparel. Signs defying
such classification are grouped as: selected adjectives and adverbs, initial-
ized verbs and nouns (i.e., signs whose forms resemble the referrent).

Developed for rehabilitation workers with the adult deaf who are proficient
in sign language and who are attempting to improve the English language skills
of deaf clients, the manual contains 261 numbered entries. Not all of these
entries are illustrated, the editor presupposing that proficiency with manual
communication would enable the user to reproduce the sign from the verbal notations that sometimes appear in lieu of illustrations.

The task remains for the rehabilitation worker to devise lessons to teach the
basic English language concepts and to teach the signs which make visible and
reinforce those concepts, thus encouraging simultaneous development of the
sign language vocabulary and English language vocabulary in the language of
the handicapped deaf adult.

Those concerned with the teaching of language to the deaf may profit from a
study of this dictionary and the accompanying discussions, "Increasing Com-
patibility between Sign Language and English," and "Techniques for Using Improved Manual Communication as a Language Training Tool."

Useful to those in programs for training rehabilitation personnel working with
retarded deaf people and perhaps teachers of deaf children, since it emphasizes language structure in signs. The form of sign language used, however,
would not be understood by the majority of deaf adults today.

12. Kosche, Martin. Hymns for Signing and Singing. 116 Walnut Street,
         Delavan, Wisconsin 53115 (date and price, if any, unknown).

Reverend Kosche has developed a book of hymns suitable for rendering in the
language of signs by copying many of the songs in the Lutheran Humnal and sug-
gesting suitable signs for difficult words. The full line of a hymn as it
appears in the original is reproduced, and suggested sign substitutions appear over the original words. In this manner, the same book can be used by
normal hearing people during Lutheran church services. The author acknowledges
that the book is still in rough form, and invites suggestions for improvement.
There are occasional footnotes containing descriptions of how to make signs
that are not too well known, such as "veins" and "throne."

While the book is best suited for use by someone already familiar with the
language of signs, beginning interpreters might obtain some clues from the
substitutions suggested for words often used during religious services.

Useful for training interpreters for religious interpreting.

13. Landes, Robert M. Approaches: A Digest of Methods in Learning the Language of Signs. Virginia Baptist General Board, P.O. Box 8568, Richmond, Virginia 23226, 1968 ($2.95).

This manual, Approaches, purports to be a "Digest of Methods in Learning the Language of Signs." However, because this manual never considers extant methods for learning this language, it cannot present a condensation of those methods, nor a considered discussion of them. One wishes that the primary difficulty here were generated solely by the misleading character of the title.

The essential problem is in pedagogy. The author's approach is eclectic. Be assured that eclecticism does not necessarily generate disorder; and, in many teaching situations, an eclectic approach is commendable! The criticism is this: because the manual has no inherently unified program for developing graded skills, it fails to offer a coherent pedagogical basis for teaching or learning.

This course, designed to teach a basic sign language, requires three additional texts: a dictionary of signs, a publication of the Department of Health, Education and Welfare, called "Orientation of Social Workers to the Problems of Deaf Persons," and George B. Joslin's manual for the Southern Baptist Convention, "Manual for Work with the Deaf."

In Chapter 2, "Fingerspelling and the Manual Alphabet," the author presents some mnemonic aids that are of note and which will be useful to students who have difficulty remembering the configuration of individual letters of the manual alphabet. Chapters 3 through 5 introduce specific factors for consideration by students of sign language and interpretation, but the discussions are marred by imprecise definition and categorization.

One of the cardinal rules of sign language is "sign what you mean, not what you say." Landes exemplifies this concisely and well in Chapter 3 when he lists thirty-one sentences using the word run and indicates the different concept conveyed in each sentence.

Practice materials are introduced with the explanation of the number system in Chapter 7. This is a thorough description of the counting procedure and also describes the method for denoting scriptural chapter and verse numbers in sign language.

The remaining Chapters 8 to 26 constitute the bulk of the text and are consistent in format, the vocabulary study followed by practical sentences and a lesson from The Story of Jesus by Frank C. Laubach. The author asserts that the aim of the textbook is "to teach a basic sign language, and to that end the materials should be followed as closely as possible in order to assure continuity and progression of thought." The text format itself presents numerous problems: the stories from the Life of Christ are included for the purpose of developing interpreting insights and two per class should be read. A class of students learning sign language will neither have the vocabulary nor the skill to interpret these stories. Further, the basic vocabulary study for each chapter is not consistently reinforced by the practical sentences nor the stories.

By collating the stories in an appendix with appropriate vocabulary practice (the names of biblical persons and places), students will be saved the necessity of thumbing through material for which they are not yet ready.

Only if the teacher presents a carefully prepared basic introduction to the language of signs, using a good dictionary, will this text be of any use. The teacher will remain the informant for the class and will produce the drill materials in fingerspelling and the language of signs necessary to establish basic competency.

The manual might in fact be more successful if it were aimed at persons who have completed a basic course in the language of signs and are now able to undertake a new course with a specialized focus, the text being specifically designed for use by religious groups who have ministries to the deaf.

The second edition of Approaches, published in 1969, is, according to the preface, "revised only slightly and then only in order to clarify meaning." In fact, the revision excises only a few sentences and does not focus on the essential difficulties in the text. The criticisms for the first text remain applicable to the second edition.

The now-printed text, compiled in a 7" x 10" three-ring loose-leaf binder, permits the pages of the text to lie flat. The pagination has been changed to simple numerical order, and this is a decided improvement over the chapter-page system of the original. Some of the illustrations have been changed. These simple improvements make the text visually more pleasing.

Chapter 27, "Resources," is unchanged in the second edition.

14. Long, J. Schuyler. The Sign Language: A Manual of Signs. Reprint of second ed., Washington, D.C.: Gallaudet College Press, 1962 (price unknown, if any).

Dr. Long stated that the purpose of his book was to provide a standard reference for those desiring to learn the language of signs, for those desiring to refresh their memories, and for those desiring to learn unfamiliar signs. Further, he stated that he wished to fulfill what he felt was a need of deaf persons for a standard by which the usage of the original, pure, and accurate signs would be perpetuated.

The book contains over 1,400 signs, all of which have written descriptions and photographs showing the positions for making the signs. Arrows are used to illustrate the movements involved in executing each of the manual symbols. The signs are grouped under chapter headings such as numbers and counting, animals, auxiliary verbs, occupations, and so on. There is an alphabetical index of all terms.

There is a chapter on the history, development, and usage of both the language of signs and fingerspelling. Also included is a brief but clear explanation of the role of manual communication in the social and educational life of deaf people. The book concludes with pictorial representations of sample sentences, the Lord's Prayer, and an appendix of Catholic signs.

"The Sign Language" is primarily a dictionary of signs, not a manual of the language of signs. Study of the book without the assistance of a competent instructor will not make for facility in manual communication. It is one of the early references on the language of signs. The original photographs have been retained in the 1963 reprint and are consequently outdated and detract from the appeal of the book.

15. Madsen, Willard J. Conversational Sign Language: An Intermediate Manual. Washington, D.C.: Gallaudet College Press, 1967 ($2.50).

This book is a valuable contribution to the library of printed material available to teachers and students of the language of signs. Unique in its emphasis on continued instruction for those who have completed a basic course in manual communication, the manual encourages the development of skills in conversing in the "idiom" of the deaf adult.

The manual is divided into three parts: (1) a general review of basic signs and fingerspelling practice, (2) English idioms in sign language, and (3) sign language idioms.

The basic sign language vocabulary of 500 words, presented in review lists, is adapted from Louie J. Fant's book, Say It with Hands. An illustrated review of numbers and counting and a review of time words and phrases follows.

Inclusion of the four lessons in fingerspelling practice is warranted because of the nature of that skill. Clarity and rhythm are the objectives, and, to that end, the author includes practice in fingerspelling nonsense words, limericks and tongue-twisters, and well-known quotations in these lessons.

The final section of Part I, "Helpful Hints and Aids for Better Manual Communication," extends from page 23 to page 38. According to the author, this Addendum is simply a compilation of "problem signs" and explanatory notes that he has found helpful in teaching both intermediate and advanced courses in the language of signs. This section includes an explanation of the use of the infinitive to, the need for indicators of space relations in conversation, signs for major American cities and foreign countries, and guides for singing "The Star-Spangled Banner," "God Bless America," and "America, the Beautiful."

In his introduction to Part II, the author discusses the difficulties of translating English idioms into sign language and stresses the fact that Parts II and III are concerned primarily with developing proficiency in communicating with the deaf adult who may have poor English language skills.

In Part II, 229 idioms found in English are presented in eleven lessons. The idioms are listed in the left-hand columns. In the right-hand column, "sign to use or sign hint," the corresponding signs or appropriate pantomimic gestures are listed. Each of the lessons is followed by an Application, that is, a series of sentence-drills incorporating the idioms introduced in the lesson.

The sign language idioms presented in Part III are expressions peculiar to the language of signs and are common in the informal everyday conversations of deaf people. Rarely found in formal conversations, these idioms are used occasionally in interpreting when they are effective in communicating the speaker's ideas.

Following the format established in Part II, the sign language idioms are listed in the left-hand column. (Where it is impossible to construct the idiom in any pattern of "broken English," an explanation of the handshape and movement necessary to make the idiom or to convey the idea or expression is given.) The right hand column lists the corresponding English rendition for the idiom. Sign language idioms (146) are introduced in the eleven lessons, each lesson followed by an Application, as in Part II. Once the text appears in print, the visual distractions of the mimeograph format and the awkward typing alignment will be corrected.

Note that the index is presented in two sections: an alphabetical index for Parts I and II of the manual appears on pages 105-114; the index to the sign language idioms (pages 115-116) simply lists the idioms found on each page of Part III.

It is advisable for students to remember that although descriptions for making the idioms are given in the text, this is not a self-teaching manual. Because it is impossible to "capture" the idiom in a verbal description or even in an illustration, a skilled "informant" who can reproduce the sign is mandatory. Only under the tutelage of a skilled teacher and through social interchange with deaf adults can a student hope to develop skill in expressing the nuances of conversational sign language idioms.

Highly recommended as a supplementary text at the intermediate level, or as a text for an intermediate/advanced course.

16. Myers, Lowell L. The Law and the Deaf. Dept. of Health, Education, and Welfare, Washington, D.C. 20201, 1969 (no listed price).

The Law and the Deaf is a book that has a wealth of legal information concerning deafness and the problems that deafness creates. The book will prove interesting to all persons involved with the deaf. Modestly, the author has stated that it "was written to be used in training persons who plan to become (or are) professional counselors of the deaf . . . and for use by . . . members of the legal profession." In like manner, educators, interpreters, the deaf themselves, and many others who have no legal background could profit from the book also.

The interpreter will find the book valuable in defining his legal responsibilities when interpreting. Topics include working with attorneys; methods of testifying, including leading questions; proof of the interpreter's oath; methods of interpreting, including how errors in translating are handled; the significance of statements in conversations made through the interpreter; and the requirements for interpreters in criminal cases.

Recommended as required reading for intermediate/advanced and interpreting students.

*17.   O'Rourke, T. J., Dir. A Basic Course in Manual Communication. NAD Communication Skills Program, 814 Thayer Ave., Silver Springs, Md. 20910, 1971 ($4.50, transparency masters available without cost).

The latest addition to the family of illustrated textbooks on the language of signs, the NAD's ABC handbook is a handy-sized paperback very similar in content and organization to the popular Say It with Hands by Louie J. Fant, and, by the writers' own admission, was based on that book. In one respect, namely the quality of the illustrations of the signs, ABC is an improvement over the Fant book, but in other respects, the improvements are a bit harder to discern. In fact, one might conclude that certain changes in format from that used by Fant were changes which it would have been better not to make, for it makes the book somewhat inconvenient for a student to use. Whereas Fant presented practice sentences at the end of each "lesson" of illustrated signs, and often added special notes pertaining to alternate meanings or usages of particular signs, the writers of ABC grouped all practice sentences together at the back of the book, with the first part of the book devoted exclusively to illustrations of the signs to be learned in consecutive lessons. This means that a student must refer back and forth between the "lessons" in the first part of the book and the practice sentences for those lessons in the back, an inconvenience which reduces the book's effectiveness. In addition, except for an occasional extra word or two giving alternate meanings of illustrated signs, no attempts have been made to provide extra information on usage of signs, which places the full burden of providing this extra information on the shoulders of the instructor.

In common with the Fant book, the writers of ABC have made efforts to group the signs according to three basic parts: the handshape used; the direction of movement relative to the body; and the type of movement made. While this is a convenience for the writer of a book on the language of signs, it can hardly be said to be a convenience for a student, who normally has trouble enough mastering a new form of communication without the added complication of being required to learn at the same time--and keep separate--several signs of high-similarity in handshape used, in directionality, or in type of movement. In this writer's opinion, this was the chief drawback of the Fant book, and one she is sorry to see repeated in ABC.

The writers of ABC claim that the book is admirably suited for use as both an instructor's manual and a student's text, and have prepared a set of 8 1/2" by 11 1/4" transparency masters from which overhead projector transparencies can be made and projected on a screen during classroom instruction. These transparency masters are simply enlarged reproductions of the same 565 illustrations of signs which appear in the handbook, and since only one sign appears on a master, the 565 pages of the set, even without the transparencies to be made from the master set, makes a rather bulky, heavy package to carry around unless a permanent storage place can be found which is convenient to the classroom.

The writers' rationale in preparing the transparency masters apparently was that a projected picture of a sign would make it unnecessary for a student to divide his attention between the illustration of a given sign in his textbook and the instructor's simultaneous demonstration of the same sign. Unfortunately, the writers did not explain how the instructor is supposed to hold his students' attention any better against the competition of a projected picture of a sign than he would against the competition of the same picture in a textbook, nor how a picture of a sign, projected or not, can add to the effectiveness of the instructor's demonstration of the same sign in the classroom. One is left to assume that the student will come to associate the picture with the living demonstration, and therefore be better able to recall the demonstration later when he reviews the picture of the sign in his handbook when studying at home.

As an instructor's manual, ABC has certain advantages and certain disadvantages. Among the former are the excellent collection of practice sentences grouped together at the back of the book, which grouping makes it easy for the instructor to review previous lessons simply by turning back a page or two and selecting random practice sentences. In addition, there are the transparency masters if the instructor wishes to illustrate each sign as he teaches it. On the other hand, there is little in the way of information for the instructor on how to present the material in a given lesson, for no lesson plans have been provided since it is assumed that the instructor will develop his own. And, since both the instructor and the student will have access to all of the practice sentences in the book, the instructor himself will have to compose test sentences based on the material covered previously, or run the risk of having his students recognize test sentences the instructor selected from those practice sentence lists. An instructor using ABC as a teaching manual will, therefore, find it a compact, handy little book, but one around which he will have to build his own course of study outline and daily lesson plans. As the writers of ABC state, he will not be a slave to the book, but he will have to have considerable teaching experience if the book is to be a servant to him. A novice instructor would have to do considerable ad-libbing to develop a full course of study from the basic guidelines offered by the book.

As a student's reference text, except for the aforementioned inconvenient location of the practice material, the book has much to offer. The illustrations are, for the most part, clear and accurate approximations of the signs. The practice sentences are excellent and numerous, and the index makes it easy to locate the sign for a given word or words. The vocabulary of signs is a basic one and should provide the student with a good foundation upon which he can build his manual communication skills. About the only negative factor is the cost, for most students would prefer to spend a few cents more and get a hard cover book on signs than to pay $4.50 for a paperback.

Highly recommended as a supplementary reference text for students. (Unless the instructor wishes to make a considerable investment in overhead projector transparencies of limited usefulness, the transparency masters are not recommended.)

*18. Quigley, S. P., ed. <u>Interpreting for Deaf People</u>. Workshop report.
      U.S. Dept. of Health, Education, and Welfare, Washington, D.C., 20201,
      1965 (available without cost while the supply lasts).

This book was the result of a three-week workshop in which ten recognized experts on the language of signs and interpreting for deaf people worked together
to develop a handbook for interpreters and for agency personnel who utilize the
services of such interpreters.

It contains sections dealing with the formation of the Registry of Interpreters
for the Deaf (RID); the RID code of ethics; reviews of books and films on sign
language and interpreting; and a list of the workshop participants and consultants.

Also included are chapters dealing with general aspects of interpreting:
physical factors; platform interpreting; fingerspelling as an interpretive
medium; oral interpreting; interpreting of idiomatic expressions; and interpreting for deaf people of severely restricted language skills.

There are also chapters on interpreting in specific situations: legal; medi-
cal; religious; job placement; and counseling or psychotherapeutic settings.
The final chapter of the book deals with the development of a program for
training interpreters.

<u>Highly recommended as a text, or supplementary text, for students in advanced
manual communication classes or classes in interpreting for deaf people.</u>

19. Riekehof, Lottie L. <u>Talk to the Deaf</u>. Springfield, Mo.: Gospel Pub-
     lishing House, 1445 Boonville Avenue, Springfield, Mo. 65802, 1963
     ($4.95).

<u>Talk to the Deaf</u>, subtitled "A practical visual guide useful to anyone wishing
to master the sign language and the manual alphabet," by Lottie Riekehof of
the Central Bible Institute of Springfield, Missouri, is a glossary of about
1,000 basic signs.

The book is divided into three major sections: a brief history of the sign
language, learning to use the sign language and the manual alphabet, and the
main portion, sign language. In this book, signs are classified into twenty-
five categories. The format for presenting the various signs consists of
simple word-descriptions accompanied with synonyms and illustrations. Movements are indicated by broken line drawings and arrows. The author stresses
the importance of studying the word-descriptions in conjunction with the
synonyms. Drawings depict the various signs and are supplemented by descriptions.

<u>May be used as a supplementary reference book, particularly if students are
active in churches having deaf congregations.</u>

20. Sanders, Josef I., ed. <u>The ABC's of Sign Language</u>. Tulsa, Okla.:
    Manca Press, Inc., 1968 ($8.75).

According to the preface, this book was designed "to provide a pre-primer, an
easy palatable introduction to the language of signs for the uninitiated."
And it is precisely this pre-primer approach of <u>The ABC's of Sign Language</u>
that produces the indelible impression in the reader that the "uninitiated"
of the preface are children.

Following the pattern of numerous abecedarian books for children, the editor
and illustrator have produced a sturdy, hardbound picture book dictionary of
126 signs. The format is attractive and consistent; James Harrell's illustrations are realistic and easy to "read."

Each of the 126 signs presented in the book is given fwo full 8 1/2" x 11"
pages. The individual letters of the manual alphabet and the numbers one
through twenty, the numbers 100, 500, and 1,000 are each given one page in
the text. The format for the signs is as follows: the word is centered on
the left-hand page in large upper-case letters with verbal directions for
making the signs printed immediately below. On the right-hand page are the
illustrations for the signs (with arrows indicating the appropriate movements),
an illustration of the referrent itself, and immediately below, the word <u>re</u>-
printed in lower case letters.

The 126 nouns thus illustrated are accurately termed a basic recognition vocabulary (both in the English language and the language of signs) for children.
Such entries as "jump rope," "oil well," "wagon," and "zoo" are further indications of this. One difficulty that a young audience might encounter, however, would be reading the verbal descriptions of the signs.

Adults would need neither the referents pictured, nor the reinforcement provided by the repetition of the printed word. In fact, the "uninitiated"
adult would be more inclined to make a present of this book to a child. However, the price, which is itself prohibitive, would foster "browsing" instead
of buying.

21. Siger, Leonard C. "Gestures, the Language of Signs, and Human Communica-
    tion," <u>American Annals of the Deaf</u>, vol. 113: 1, pp. 11-28, January,
    1968 (no listed price for reprints).

In this article, originally delivered as a paper at the Warburg Institute of
the University of London on June 19, 1967, Dr. Siger cites various historical
instances of the use of gesture systems and manual communication. Having always been a part of human behavior, gesture systems were not specifically devised for purposes of educating deaf persons.

Venerable Bede, an ecclesiastical historian, calls attention to the use of
manual counting systems as early as the eighth century. For purposes of illustration, Dr. Siger has included photographic copies of two tenth century manu-
scripts that depict manual counting systems. Not until 1600, with the publica-

tion of Bonet's <u>Reducción de las latras</u> in Spain (from which our one-handed manual alphabet is derived), do we get the first full-length work on deaf education.

Previous to this, consistent gesture systems were developed as counting systems, mnemonic aids, or as part of an orator's training and practice. Ancient rhetoricians, taking Quintilian as a favored guide, were practiced in the art of gesture. During the Renaissance, the art of gesture in rhetoric was revived, such orators as John Donne being noted for matching the elegance of delivery to the elegance of words.

Gestures are also captured in the Renaissance paintings of the late fifteenth century through seventeenth century. As examples, Dr. Siger presents five figures depicting the use of rhetorical gestures in painting. Chosen from the works of Luini, Pinturicchio, Campi, and Durer, each painting is a representation of the New Testament theme of the "Dispute in the Temple."

A discussion, with accompanying photographs, of the symbolic gestures of the Japanese Buddhists is also included.

Then, Dr. Siger undertakes a discussion of the history of the language of signs of the American deaf, from its beginnings at the French institute of Abbe de l'Epee, to its introduction into the United States by Thomas Hopkins Gallaudet, to its use today. Special note is made of its existence in the National Theater of the Deaf, where, beyond stating the facts of a case or telling the news as in ordinary conversation, it carries, as Dr. Siger says, "the challenging burden of poetic statement."

Dr. Siger's paper is of value to all who are interested in the historical foundations and vestiges of gesture systems in human communication. The paper is itself a fine example of a brief, scholarly, carefully documented research work.

<u>Interesting background information.</u>

22. Smith, Jess M. <u>Workshop on Interpreting for the Deaf.</u> Muncie, Ind.: Dept. of Health, Education, and Welfare, Washington, D.C., 1964 (available without cost).

This particular VRA workshop proved to be very fruitful. There have already been two follow-up workshops and a brand-new national professional organization has sprung up as a result of the endeavors of the participants, consultants, and planners at Muncie. This fact alone should suggest to interested persons that a brief review of the contents of the book can only begin to describe the valuable material to be found there.

Not content to rely entirely upon the experience of American interpreters, the planners of the workshop included two background papers by English writers and one by a Russian. While not all of their comments and suggestions are pertinent to interpreting in this country, the majority are and the inclusion of these three papers adds much to the value of the book. It is probable that they provided many helpful insights which assisted the workshop participants in their discussions. Other background material concerns interpreters in legal situations and a film test for interpreters. There is a list of films available for training in the language of signs, plus a very complete bibliography of books on the same subject.

Four keynote papers are also reprinted in full and, like the English and Russian papers, provide interesting personal glimpses at what it is like to be an interpreter. How the deaf themselves see interpreting and interpreters and the recruitment of interpreters are other good topics in this section.

Reports of the discussions themselves are, for the most part, presented in outline form with enough narrative so that the reader can easily follow the discussions. One topic (training materials) is reported almost entirely in narrative form with important points numbered for easy reference.

Other helpful materials include general guidelines for interpreters and an outline of the structure of a badly needed new organization that was born at the meeting--the Registry of Interpreters for the Deaf (RID).

Recommended as background reading for students in advanced or interpreting classes.

23. Springer, C. J. Talking with the Deaf. Baton Rouge, La.: Redemptorist Fathers, 5354 Plank Road, Baton Rouge, La. 70805, 1961 ($2.50).

This is an illustrated dictionary of the language of signs containing approximately 1,000 terms. Each sign is briefly described verbally and clearly presented pictorially by one or two photographs, some of which have arrows indicating the movements involved in the execution of the sign.

The terminology presented in this text covers basic vocabulary with some emphasis on religious signs. The manual alphabet is presented, but discussion of numbers and counting is limited to digits one through twelve. The signs are presented in alphabetical order, in contrast to most books of this type, which group them by subject or by parts of speech. However, a valuable cross-index of signs that have more than one meaning in English is included.

It is felt that this book would be a suitable text in a course on the language of signs, though it is less complete in the number and scope of its terms than are some other available books. The text would be of particular value for a person interested in religious interpreting for Catholic church work and even work with other denominations, as the religious signs given can be used "regardless of religious affiliation" according to the author.

It is noted that this book is often confused with Father Higgens's text, "How to Talk to the Deaf." Actually, it is an updating of this earlier work and much more appropriate book for today's student of the language of signs.

Useful for those training religious personnel in working with deaf people.

24. Stokoe, William C., Jr. Sign Language Structure: An Outline of the
     Visual Communication Systems of the American Deaf. (Studies in
     Linguistics, Occasional Paper 8) Buffalo, N.Y.: University of Buf-
     falo, 1960 ($2.00).

The monograph by Stokoe represents a different approach to the study and
teaching of the language of signs. Stokoe has applied the principles of
structural linguistics to the visual communication system of the language of
signs. He has attempted to identify the minimal distinctive units of this
language which correspond to the phonemes of spoken language.

For the purpose of this review, only the application of Stokoe's system to
the teaching of the language of signs will be discussed. Stokoe has identified the minimal distinctive features of this language and classified them
into three groups. These groups are: "tab," "dez," and "sig." A knowledge
of the symbols within these groups will enable the beginning student of the
language of signs to produce any sign.

The symbols grouped under the title of "tab" refer to the part of the body
in which the sign is made, for example, at the forehead or the chest. Those
symbols under "dez" refer to the configuration of the hands in making the
sign. The symbols under the "sig" classification indicate the movement which
should be made to produce the correct sign. A knowledge of the symbols in
these three classifications--"tab," "dez," and "sig"--will enable the student
of the language of signs to understand the area of the body in which the sign
should be made, the configuration of the hands in making the signs, and the
motion of the hands necessary to produce the sign.

Recommended as important background reading.

25. Taylor, Lucile N., ed. Proceedings of the Registry of Interpreters for
     the Deaf: Workshop II. Mimeographed. Write to editor, Wisconsin
     School for the Deaf, Delavan, Wisconsin, 53115 (a few copies, avail-
     able without cost).

This book is an edited report of the second workshop held on interpreting for
the deaf in Washington, D.C., in January, 1965. It contains chapters on the
training of interpreters, the implementation of a national Registry for Interpreters, the examination and certification of interpreters, a code of ethics
for interpreters, a constitution for the Registry of Interpreters, and plans
for future action of the registry. Included also is a list of participants
and a statement of action that has resulted from the workshop and the registry.

Most of the chapters, the one on training interpreters in particular, provide
rather generalized guidelines and/or suggestions on the subject areas involved
rather than a complete and detailed coverage of subject. The book provides
valuable data on the registry. However, it was not intended to be used directly
in teaching beginning or advanced students of the language of signs and it
would not be helpful for this purpose.

Recommended as background reading for students in advanced or interpreting
classes.

26. Watson, David O. Talk with Your Hands. Menasha, Wis.: George Banta
        Co., 1963 (write to author, Route 1, Winneconne, Wis., 54986, or to
        NAD for copies, $5.00).

A lively, conversational style of approach is used by David O. Watson, author
and illustrator of Talk with Your Hands, a book on the American language of
signs. The attractiveness of the format and the uniqueness of approach brought
instant popularity to the book when it first appeared in 1964. Words, phrases,
expressions, and sentences are cleverly executed in the language of signs with
lifelike illustrations of hand positionings that are supplemented by engaging
comic-page figures that lend a realistic touch to the total presentation.

The dynamic appeal of Mr. Watson's illustrations is further heightened by the
use of red lines and arrows to indicate the direction the hands are to take
in forming a sign. The flash of red over black on an otherwise all-white
background relieves the tediousness that often goes with deciphering directions. The many body positions that are used throughout the book also relieve
tedium and give a warm human quality to the language of signs.

Mr. Watson offers sign symbols for approximately 1,700 words and terms. He
has grouped them mainly under subject headings. All those parts of speech
that are ordinarily needed for satisfactory presentation of a subject are included. These words are not identified as parts of speech. This is in keeping with the disregard the language of signs has for the grammatical rules
that govern the use of spoken and written language. Mr. Watson does, however,
show how the language of signs can be used syntactically. He does this by
inserting fingerspelled words where they are needed to form grammatically correct sentences.

In a number of instances, the index refers the reader to more than one page
number. This is because of the multiple meanings of many words which are
carried over into the language of signs in the form of multiple sign symbols.
This particular feature of the book should be a great help to readers who are
unaware of the opportunity and need for being selective in use of signs.

Popular with students, this may also be used as a supplementary reference
book, and is recommended as such.

Films and Teaching Media

1. Abelson, Bambii Rae. <u>Alpha-Hands Flash Cards</u>. Buffalo, N.Y.: Kenworthy Educational Service, Inc., 1969.

This teaching aid contains fifty-two 5 1/2" x 8 1/2" illustrated flash cards with letters of the manual alphabet, days of the week, numbers one through ten, names of colors (5), close family relative classifications (uncle, aunt, cousin), and parent-teacher manual.

Mrs. Abelson states in her manual that the "ALPHA-HANDS FLASH CARDS have been created for the purpose of providing a realistic method in <u>communication between</u> the HEARING and the DEAF. A primary function of this teaching device is to aid parents in INTRODUCING LANGUAGE to a deaf child years BEFORE he may enter school." She goes on to discuss such topics as "language," "how the hearing can use the alpha-hands flash cards," "how to teach language to the deaf child," "how does a deaf child learn to differentiate his feelings." No topic is discussed with the necessary depth, and the brevity and superficiality of each discussion precludes the development of a philosophy and method of language teaching. Without this, the flash cards will remain useless for concerned parents of young deaf children. The section "how to shape a letter" will be sufficient to demonstrate the basic problem. The directions appear as follows: "View an Alpha-Hand Flash Card and with your RIGHT HAND about 6" in front of your body imitate the hand position. Try forming two or three letters in this manner. Often it is helpful to do this in front of a mirror. Repeat this procedure daily using 2 or 3 different letters. Practice until you don't have to think letters but they automatically fall from your hand. Within two weeks you will know the entire Manual Alphabet. . . ."

A cursory inspection of the flash cards indicates discrepancies in the author's understanding of and familiarity with the manual alphabet and the basic signs included in the set. The manual alphabet is perceived differently by the signer and by the receiver. However, this fact is ignored in both the flash cards and the accompanying manual. The cards for the letters "a," "q," and "r," the numbers one through ten, "Sunday" and "Thursday" appear as they would to the person reproducing them.

The remaining letters and signs appear as they would to the person receiving the fingerspelled or signed message. The author has either forgotten to specify this, or she is unaware of the fact.

The cards for "red" and "orange" do not take into account the necessity for body orientation. The same difficulty occurs with "uncle," "aunt," and "cousin," and further, the movements indicated for these signs are also incorrect. Persons familiar with the language of signs would be unable to "read" these signs.

Also included is the "v," recognized by a majority of Americans as symbolic of the peace movement. However, it is <u>not</u> the sign for peace of the American Sign Language of the Deaf.

The flash cards are illustrated on both sides. One side pictures the hand configuration with the letter or word printed above it. On the reverse side, only the hand configuration is shown. Since no explanation is included, one would assume that the parent or teacher, after becoming proficient with fingerspelling, might use the cards to quiz the child's recognition of letters and numbers.

2. Babbini, Barbara E. (writer and technical advisor), American Manual
      Alphabet. (8mm cartridge) Training Films Series (Graphic Film Corp.
      Series), Captioned Films and Media Services for the Deaf.

The "American Manual Alphabet" is a training film series produced by Graphic Film Corporation for the U.S. Office of Education, Captioned Films for the Deaf. The series comprise twenty-five lessons and five tests and is available on cartridges for use with the silent standard 8mm. Technicolor Projector, Models 200, 200Z, 200WA, 500, 500Z, 500WA, 500WS, 600, 600AD, 700A, 800, 800WA, and 800WS.

The first grouping of four units introduces the manual alphabet and encourages fluency development. The fifth unit in this grouping is a test.

The second grouping, the largest (six units) grouping of unit materials, focuses on speedbuilding and progresses through combinations of letters, double vowels, and consonants. "Accuracy: Do's and Don'ts" is one unit in the group. Numbers are introduced in the last two units.

The remaining fifteen practice units have been arbitrarily separated into four groups, each followed by a test. Each unit presents a rapid drill of letter groups. For example: Unit 18 drills the combinations BO-BR-BL-CA; Unit 20 drills TH-QU-EX.

Such a film series will be invaluable to teachers of beginning courses in sign language.

Highly recommended for use with this manual.

3. Episcopal Church Training Films (8mm. cartridge) Audio-Visual Library,
      The Episcopal Church Center, 815 Second Avenue, New York, N.Y. 10017.

The Conference of Church Workers among the Deaf, working in cooperation with the National Council of the Episcopal Church, has produced forty black and white Magi-Cartridge reels demonstrating the manual alphabet and the signs for 700 words. Each 8mm. reel has a running time of four minutes. A word is shown once and followed by two depictions of the sign at a pace slow enough to be followed by the student.

Thirty-four of the reels are devoted to basic vocabulary, and six show signs used in church services, as well as signs for denominational names and such words as God, faith, and redemption. One reel illustrates the Lord's Prayer.

The projector used with these cartridges--which requires no threading or re-winding--has a "stop-motion" button on top, which when pressed, will hold the frame steady for purposes of study. The cartridges will automatically repeat themselves unless stopped.

A handbook for students, "The Language of Signs," by Anne Davis, an instructor at the Maryland School for the Deaf, has been prepared for use with these films. The signs are presented in the same order in both the reels and the handbook.

Signs used in these films are, for the most part, clear. They have good back-ground and good basic positions. Different people are used to deliver the signs. A wide variety of subject matter is covered. Some of the signs, how-ever, are incorrect and amateurish and do not always flow smoothly. The most distracting feature, one which could have been edited, is the return of both hands to an "at rest" or clasping position approximately "marriage" after most signs.

4. Fingerspelling Films (8mm. cartridge) (The International Communications Foundation Series), Captioned Films for the Deaf.

Fingerspelling Films is an instructional film series intended for the begin-ning student in fingerspelling. The series is presented in two sets: Set A: Fingerspelling for Dormitory Counselors, and Set B: Fingerspelling for Re-habilitation Counselors. Each set consists of six cartridges that contain 4 1/2 minutes of silent, color films.

The series are presented on 8mm. cartridge, a type of film that is readily usable with a Technicolor 800 Instant Movie Projector. The ease with which the films can be shown and the general excellence of the film presentation itself combine to make Fingerspelling Films an important contribution to the training material that is available for instruction in basic skills in finger-spelling.

The instructional pattern that is used in both sets is a step-by-step procedure that leads the student through a sequence of experiences of increasing complex-ity. Instruction in the manual alphabet is offered first, followed by basic words and conversational type of sentences.

Outstanding features of the film are: (1) excellent photography, (2) clarity and naturalness of fingerspelling, (3) two exposures of certain fingerspelled single letters with the second exposure being different from the first (this tends to reinforce learning), (4) skillful use of facial expression to show how it can add meaning to fingerspelled sentences, and (5) gradual increase of speed of delivery.

Useful addition to fingerspelling practice sessions. Memorization of limited material is a problem, however. Uses same projector as Graphic Films Corp. series (see No. 2, above).

5. <u>Pre-Cana Counseling Film</u> (16mm.), Captioned Films for the Deaf.

This film deals with premarriage counseling for Catholic persons. It is in
the language of signs and fingerspelling and explains the concepts of the
Catholic church about marriage and its religious significance. This is done
at a level that could be understood by most deaf young people.

The main use of this film would be to prepare Catholic couples for marriage
and to train seminarians in the signs and modes of expression needed for pre-
cana counseling. The performers are priests who have a fair competency in
the language of signs, but are not fluent.

6. <u>Say It with Hands</u>, Mr. Louie Fant, Gallaudet College, Washington, D.C.,
    20002 (not available).

This is a series of forty-six reels based on the lesson plan in Mr. Fant's
book, <u>Say It with Hands</u>. Color film is used throughout. It is an experimental series and is not for sale. No copies are available.

The use of color in training films seems to be preferable to black-and-white.
At times, both side and front views of a fingerspelled letter were used, but
this technique does not seem to have been used for the signs, and it might
have been helpful. More than one signer was used, and the utilization of deaf
persons as signers was especially noted.

Both literal translations and idiomatic sign language expressions were used.
Perhaps the transition from one to the other could be made more gradual, however. The question mark was omitted at the end of interrogative forms. The
sign made with both hands forming zeros was used alone for "no-one." Usually
a second sign is used in this case, as the double-zero sign alone is most often
interpreted as "none."

Technical flaws were evident; however, this is understandable in a low-budget
experimental film.

<u>Would be recommended if available (see 7, below).</u>

*7. <u>Say It with Hands</u>, KERA-TV 13, 3000 Harry Hines Boulevard, Dallas, Texas,
    75201. Also, Captioned Films for the Deaf.

Since the time of the first review, a "Say It with Hands" series of twenty-
six half-hour programs providing instruction in manual communication has been
completed. Adapted from Fant's book, the series was originally conceived by
Mrs. Elizabeth Carlton of the Callier Hearing and Speech Center in Dallas,
Texas. That agency developed the series through a cooperative effort involving the NAD Communicative Skills Program, Media Services and Captioned Films
and KERA-TV 13 of Dallas.

Tapes may be obtained on a rental basis ($10.00 per half-hour program which covers shipping) by writing Mr. Barry Wells, Program Director, at the above address.

16mm. kinescopes are available through regular Media Services and Captioned Films distribution libraries. Should you wish to request these films, but do not now have an account with Media Services and Captioned Films, you should write to Dr. Howard Quigley, Director, Educational Materials Distribution Center, 5034 Wisconsin Avenue, N.W., Washington, D.C. 20016.

A three-program, one-and-a-half-hour tape is available from the Communicative Skills Program Office of the NAD to those wishing to preview this program. However, 7 1/2 IPS, two-inch commercial equipment is needed for this purpose.

An excellent but time-consuming teaching aid which requires special equipment and expertise to use. Expensive if it is rented from the Dallas TV program, and costly to purchase. The demonstration reels mentioned in the above review require studio-type equipment, or portable equipment which can take full-size TV tape. Very limited for classroom use--but worth considering if an educational TV channel can be persuaded to offer lessons in the language of signs on local television channels.

8. Sign Language, The. Captioned Films for the Deaf.

A story about Thomas H. Gallaudet and a basic vocabulary drill are presented in this experimental film. The language of signs and fingerspelling are used throughout. The section on Gallaudet's life would be usable as a test or practice lesson for advanced students in manual communication. The vocabulary part gives some basic signs and their English equivalents. This film is clearly experimental and introduces some interesting techniques, but is not a technically polished production.

Of historical interest only.

9. Teaching the Manual Alphabet. (8mm.) Dr. Harry Bornstein, Office of Institutional Research, Gallaudet College, Washington, D.C. 20002.

This is a series of seventeen filmed lessons in fingerspelling, including two tests. The films are in color and require a variable-speed 8mm. projector and a knowledge of how to operate it. The first two lessons introduce the manual alphabet, with individual letters presented in random order. The hand is moved from side to side to show the alignment of the fingers. In these and all subsequent lessons, a pause follows presentation of each fingerspelled letter, word, or sentence during which students viewing the films may write down or recite what was shown. A printed slide giving the meaning then appears.

The next fifteen lessons provide practice in reading fingerspelled words and sentences at gradually increasing speeds. Several techniques were employed to give the student practice in adapting what he learns to real situations. The research staff who made the films used a variety of hands in them: students, deaf children's, staff members' hand with long fingers, short fingers, slender fingers, stubby fingers—and good fingerspellers as well as mediocre. Because, in actuality, one views a person from different positions, the staff filmed the lessons from several different angles.

This would be recommended if it were packaged in 8mm. cartridges so that the same projector could be used as required for use with the Graphic Films Corp. series (2 above). However, it requires a standard 8mm. reel-type projector, and unless both types of projectors are readily available, the Graphic Films series (2 above) would be the better choice.

For general information about captioned films program (which distributes most films described herein), write to:

Media Services and Captioned Films
Division of Educational Services
U.S. Office of Education
Washington, D.C. 20202

For information regarding registration and obtain account numbers (which will permit borrowing films and projectors), write to:

Captioned Films Distribution Services
Conference of Executives of American Schools for the Deaf
5034 Wisconsin Ave., N.W.
Washington, D.C. 20016

INDEX OF MASTER VOCABULARY LIST